A Kerala St

A KERALA

by Christophe

to Su and Phil,

"the neighbours from heaven".

Thanks for all you have done for us & your friendship over many years. Hope you like the book!

Love from Manju and Chris.

Christopher Banner was born in Cleethorpes on the Lincolnshire coast. He was educated at King Edward VII School Sheffield and Mansfield College Oxford, where he read PPE. As a youth he was an adventurous traveller, hitch-hiking around Europe and North Africa, and when he applied to VSO after graduation, it was not a major surprise. His posting to India was the beginning of a life-long love of the country. It was also the reason for his meeting his wife Manga, the start of an even more enduring love affair, and thus the writing of this book. He now lives in retirement in Whitstable, after being employed in the education service for most of his working life.

First published in Great Britain in 2019 by Maya Books, Whitstable, Kent, CT5 1NU

ISBN 978-1-527-24442-9

CONTENTS

MAP OF INDIA

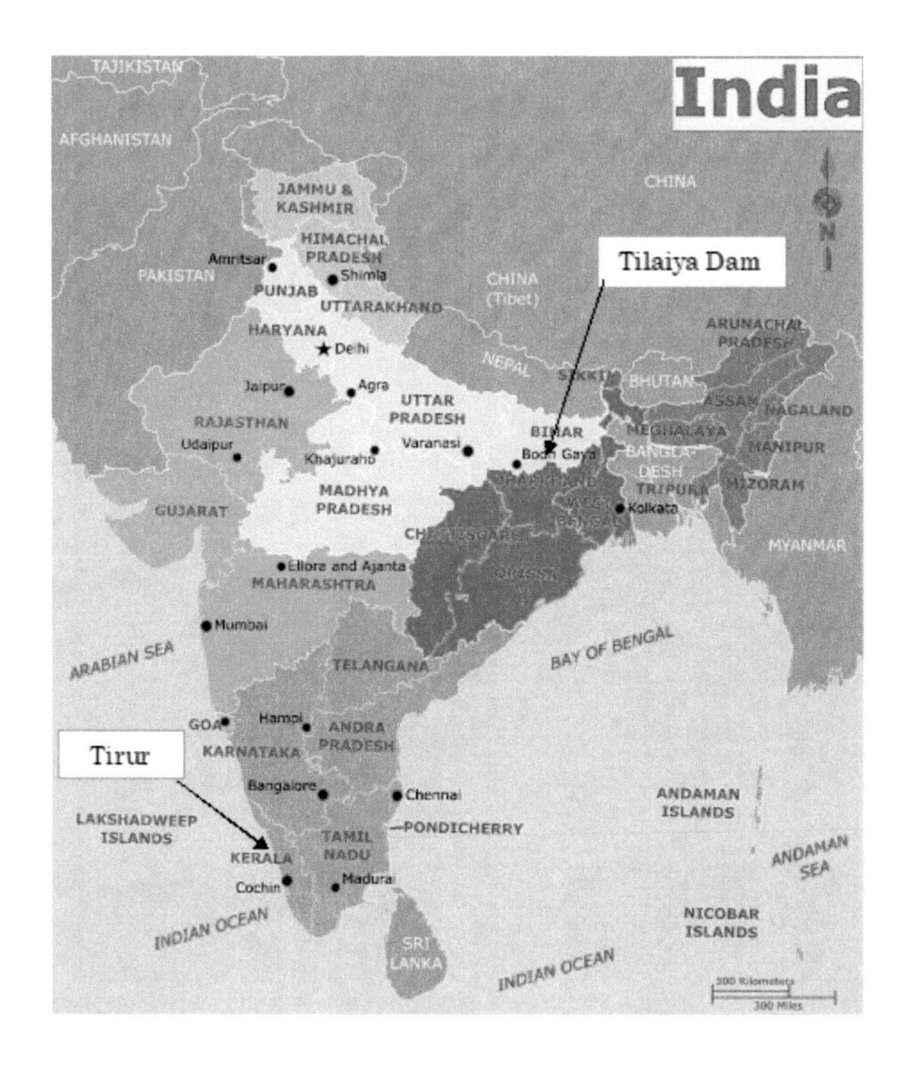
India
TAJIKISTAN
AFGHANISTAN
CHINA
JAMMU & KASHMIR
HIMACHAL PRADESH
Tilaiya Dam
Amritsar
Shimla
PAKISTAN
PUNJAB
CHINA (Tibet)
UTTARAKHAND
HARYANA
Delhi
ARUNACHAL PRADESH
NEPAL
SIKKIM
BHUTAN
Jaipur
Agra
UTTAR PRADESH
ASSAM
NAGALAND
RAJASTHAN
BIHAR
MEGHALAYA
Udaipur
Varanasi
MANIPUR
Khajuraho
Bodh Gaya
BANGLA-DESH
TRIPURA
MIZORAM
MADHYA PRADESH
GUJARAT
Kolkata
MYANMAR
Ellora and Ajanta
MAHARASHTRA
Mumbai
ARABIAN SEA
TELANGANA
BAY OF BENGAL
GOA
Hampi
ANDRA PRADESH
Tirur
KARNATAKA
Bangalore
Chennai
ANDAMAN ISLANDS
LAKSHADWEEP ISLANDS
TAMIL NADU
PONDICHERRY
KERALA
ANDAMAN SEA
Cochin
Madurai
NICOBAR ISLANDS
INDIAN OCEAN
SRI LANKA
INDIAN OCEAN

DRAMATIS PERSONAE

The Kerala family. Mum & Dad in the middle, Manga back row far right.

IN KERALA

Lakshmiammal+...Manga's mother, from Ponnani

Parameswaran+ ... father

Lakshmi and Parameswaran had 7 surviving children, 22 grandchildren and 33 great grandchildren

Viswanathan+...Manga's elder brother

Parameswaran or Rasu+...second brother

Seethalakshmi+...second sister

Rukmani or Manikka [aka Mini-sister / Manikutty]... third sister
Parvathi or Rajam+ ... fourth sister

Balan ... Rajam's husband

Krishnamani [Atimbear*] +... Manikka's husband

Parakutty+...brother Parameswaran's common-law wife

Ravi... Manikka's elder son

Shanta... Ravi's wife, from Sholapur

Aparna [aka Ammu]...their daughter (now in the USA)

Akhilesh [aka Apu]...their son

Raju... Manikka's second son

Geetha... Raju's wife, from Aluva

Keerthana [aka Kitty]...their daughter

IN COIMBATORE

Radhikar... Manikka's daughter

Gopal... Radhikar's husband, from Coimbatore

Vignesh [aka Sonu]...their elder son

Vishnu [aka Manu]...their second son

IN MUMBAI

Lakshmi[+] [known as Rashakka]...Manga's eldest sister Ramaswamy[+]...her husband

Raju[+], Chandran[+], Hari, Ramani and Mangalam... their children. Rajam[+]... 'Bombay' Raju's wife

Nimmy, Vijaya, Renuka, Rajesh... Raju's children

Pushpa...Ramani's wife

Ritesh, Pooja (now in Canada)...Ramani's children Ramanan... Mangalam's husband

Swapna, Rashmi...Mangalam's daughters

EUROPE

Christopher...Manga's husband

Indira and Lakshmi...twin daughters

Grandma[+] & Grandad[+]..parents to Robin, Rosemary & Christopher Rosemary [Rosema]...Christopher's elder sister

Tony[+]... Rosemary's husband

Antonia and Sebastian, their children

Robin[+]... Christopher's elder brother

Julie [Juliema]...Robin's wife

Rika[+]...from Luxembourg

Ashok and Nelphy (also in India)... friends originally from Kerala

Deepak, Riya and Diya, their children

Pete Reffell... Lakshmi's partner

IN AMERICA

Victoria...Manga's eldest daughter David...her husband

Thomas, Zoe, Rebecca and Ronan... their children

NOTES

* Atimbear means brother-in-law in Tamil, the family's native tongue; to be precise, it means elder sister's husband. The Tamil words for mother and father are easy - amma and appa; and grandma and grandpa are pattiamma and pattappa. One's elder sister is akka, hence Mani- akka [Manga's elder sister], and a younger sister would be thungai. An elder brother is anna [so, Raju calls Ravi, Ravi-anna]. An elder brother's wife is manni. Father's elder sister is athai [so Victoria, Lakshmi and Indira would say Rosemary-athai], and one's mother's elder sister is periyamma. The male equivalents are mama and periyappa. One must always use the appropriate title, especially if addressing someone older.

+ Deceased

PREFACE

'Do not benight yourself with work that cannot be completed in one day' - Malayalam Proverb.

I started writing this book to give our daughters Victoria, Indira and Lakshmi an idea of their Kerala heritage, but as the story developed I felt it might interest a wider audience. I certainly hope those parts of the book that include tales of my wife Manga's childhood and the events that took place in a Keralan village a couple of generations ago will both be enjoyable, especially perhaps to the growing number of people who are visiting this beautiful part of India, and act as an important record of the old ways, practices and customs, many of which are disappearing.

History and Geography are integral parts of the story. Then there are the tales about places that we have visited, as well as references to Kerala's arts, customs, festivals, language, religions and food. The book is intended to bring together the flavours, characters and mood of the place that I have come to know and love, rather than stand as a rigorous academic study, but I have done everything within my power to make this story of Kerala historically accurate as well as easy to read and follow.

A great many changes have occurred in India and Kerala since I first visited the country. The pace of change has not abated with the new milennium, but it is beyond the scope of this story to discuss the monumental and complex developments that have occurred in recent years.

Learning more about my favourite part of India has been a fascinating journey for me and if others read this book with pleasure I shall be delighted.

ACKNOWLEDGEMENTS

The books from which I have gleaned information are mentioned where appropriate in the text or in footnotes. But I must acknowledge my debt in particular to John Keay's *India - a History*, William Logan's *Malabar*, Gangadharan's *A History of Kerala*, and to the writers of the various volumes of the *The Kerala Gazette*. I've greatly enjoyed various books and articles by William Dalrymple, including *White Mughals,* and *The Last Mughal*; and *The Smile of Murugan* by Michael Wood, as well as *The Story of India,* the book of his TV series. How these two authors, and John Keay too, manage to write such eminently readable yet scholarly works, and so many of them, is beyond my comprehension. Prof Robert L. Hardgrave Jr, Emeritus Professor in the Humanities, Government and Asian Studies at the University of Texas very kindly sent me his amazing article entitled *Peasant Mobilisation in Malabar: the Mappila Rebellion 1921,* which was published in *Aspects of Political Mobilisation in South Asia,* edited by Robert I. Crane.

Of all the Indian fiction I've read, the most relevant to this book have been *The God of Small Things,* by Arundhati Roy and *The Moor's Last Sigh* by Salman Rushdie: great novels - please read them if you haven't already.

I've tried to acknowledge any direct quotations from these and other works, but it is possible that phrases or sentences first produced by other authors have slipped into my narrative accidentally; if so, I apologise.

I want to say thanks too to all my relations in India for all they do for us on our visits. Manga's sisters have been the source of some of the tales of old times in the village, and others have also searched their memories for us. Raju has recommended, unearthed, and sent me several books and he and his brother Ravi and our nephew Ramani have told me stories about their lives and those of their families, and about Kerala lore. Our friends Ashok and Nelphy have also made contributions. My sister-in-law Julie, and my daughters Victoria, Indira and Lakshmi have been very encouraging and given much good advice and help about content and presentation, and Lakshmi has done all the (very considerable) work involved in publishing the book. My sister Rosemary has spent many hours editing and correcting the draft as well as contributing memories of India and of the family, and has more than anyone made me feel that the book might in the end actually be worth publishing. I have been fortunate in having two editors. Pete Reffell has exhaustively examined the book for signs of bias and uncorroborated statements, and done his best to root out any 'clunky' phraseology. I haven't accepted all his suggestions but there is no question that this book has been greatly improved by his advice. Any mistakes that remain are of course my responsibility.

Nearly all the photos were taken by me and members of our family, particularly Indi. Few date back to the 1960s because for most of the time that I was in India then I didn't possess a camera. Vijay Menon kindly gave me permission to use the photographs on pages xv, 59, 211, 212, 225, and 226.

I am very fortunate that Alison Reffell agreed to design the jacket, and rather hope that potential purchasers will indeed judge this book by its cover!

Finally and most importantly, without my wife Manga there would assuredly have been no book at all, and she has, as you will gather as you read on, contributed most of the more entertaining parts of it. My thanks and profoundest love to you, sweetheart, and I hope you enjoy the finished product.

INTRODUCTION

In his guide book entitled *Hidden Kerala,* Phil Frampton wrote 'Enter India and one enters another world. Entering Kerala is like entering paradise'. His words describe precisely how I felt when I first saw Kerala in December 1967, after having lived in India for nearly 18 months, and I wish I'd thought of them first! Manga and I had been married for just six weeks when we travelled south from the state of Bihar where we were both working, me in the Sainik School in Tilaiya, and Manga in the nearby Holy Family Hospital. Our destination, fifteen hundred miles away, was Manga's home in the village of Trikkandiyur in Malabar, the northern part of the state of Kerala. Malabar! Sounds romantic, mysterious, exotic, and I guess it is - especially if you're in love.

A temple tank

The nearest railway station to the school and the hospital was Kodarma, and there we caught our train - the Tuffan Mail, which was to be our home for the first leg of our journey south. An ancient and rather awe-inspiring steam engine would be pulling us for 1000 miles to the gates of Mumbai [then of course known as

Bombay], a distance that the timetable told us would take 40 hours: a stately average speed of 25 miles an hour! We had third class tickets - all we could afford, since I was a volunteer teacher being paid 'local rates' and that amounted to only 200 rupees a month, the equivalent of £10 in those days: teachers may be highly respected in India, but this is certainly not reflected in their pay. But third class travel is certainly more fun anyway. The other passengers would always want to chat, and share their food and point out the interesting sights.

Tony and friends, 1991. The steam engine is similar to those in service in the 1960s.

The downside was the sleeping arrangements - in the luggage rack if we were lucky. On this occasion though we had found two empty berths in a sleeper and enjoyed a relatively comfortable first night. Third class sleepers have 8 seats per compartment, which convert into 8 berths when there is a mutual agreement that it is time for bed. Then, those who are going to sleep on the bottom tier unroll their rug or, if they are very well prepared, thin mattress and lay it over what were formerly the seats, just bare wood, and lie down, covering themselves with a sheet or blanket depending on the night-time temperature. Those who have middle-tier berths pull down a shelf from the compartment wall, to which it is attached by a hinge and supported by two substantial chains. The top tier is permanently in position and used during the day for luggage. So that's six passengers accounted for.

The other two sit and sleep on the other side of the open corridor that runs the whole length of the carriage. They sit opposite each other by the window during the day, and at night their seats, with the addition of a central portion, become bed number 7, and the shelf above, number 8. We normally favoured the top berths because it was more private up there, and you could even climb up for a lie-down during the day without disturbing other passengers. On the other hand it was rather claustrophobic, there being little headroom; and not an easy climb for the less agile. Also if the fans were working, they were a bit too near one's hands and feet for comfort; one could imagine putting one's fingers or toes through the wire guards as one slept and doing oneself a nasty injury! But generally we would sleep reasonably enough, lulled by the song of the wheels on the rails. Sleep was certainly fitful - a passing train might wake one, or the cries of vendors - I still even now hear in my half-wakeful dreams the call '*Chai... chai... garam chai*' [tea, hot tea] echoing through the night, as the tea sellers bustled through the carriages with their metal urns and unglazed mud cups, baked in the sun. And the wheezing of engines shunting in the sidings, and the snores of our fellow travellers added to the Thesaurus of night-sounds on the railway.

Less romantic were the toilet facilities. They consisted of a hole in the floor, a place to put your feet when you squatted above it and a tin cup to wash your rear. I can't say I've ever been expert at this operation, but on a train that rocked and rolled it became doubly difficult. And the rolling of the train didn't help when one tried to wash and brush one's teeth. The toilets were rarely very dirty or very smelly, but you certainly would not want any of your things to fall on the floor. That apart we almost always really enjoyed our train journeys, and this one in particular was magical. How evocative were the names of the stations we passed! First was Bodh Gaya, about 65 miles north-west from Kodarma. We reached the town when it was still just light enough to pick out the 50 metre tower of the Mahabodhi Temple, built in the fifth or sixth century AD to commemorate Buddha's attainment of enlightenment. A further 80 miles and we were at Mughalsarai, once the site of the busiest railway shunting yards in India and before that, as the name implies, a resting place for the caravans of the Mughals as they made their way east. Then, after we had been travelling for about 8 hours, our train arrived in the middle of the night at Allahabad, another city named by the Mughals. It is a Hindu holy place, formerly known as Prayaga, mentioned in the Vedas and Puranas,[i] and now an important railway junction, as well as at that time having connections to half of the Prime Ministers of India.[ii]

In the morning we found that the train had turned south and was heading towards Mumbai. We would no longer need to wrap ourselves up in the flimsy railway blankets at night, for even in midwinter, the temperature in southern and western India is comfortably warm. Manga and I sat close together peering through the bars of the window at the plains and the sudden bare hills often topped with a temple or palace. Again we were excited by the names of the stations. Fatehpur! But Manga pointed out that it wasn't the famous city built by Akbar the Great; I'd been thinking of Fatehpur Sikri. I did rightly identify Kanpur, the next big station - though only for what some might say was the trivial reason that it was at the local stadium that the Indian off-spinner Jasubhai Patel had taken 9 wickets in an innings in a Test Match against Australia and bowled India to one of their very rare victories in those days! Manga could tell me while we stopped at Jhansi junction about the Rani of that district who had been a heroine of the Indian rebellion of 1857-8, fighting bravely against British forces and earning her enemy's respect: as well as being a dangerous enemy, the Rani was also 'personable, clever and beautiful'[1] according to one British officer.

We ate tasty snacks sold by small boys pushing handcarts at Jhansi - each station seemed to have its own speciality: poori with potato curry was my favourite. Bananas were our staple, as they are filling and of course safe to eat too. There seemed to be a different banana variety in each district. Every now and then a small figure would shuffle through the carriage sweeping up the mess we all made and we'd find a few paisa for him or her. Once a little girl presented me with a 10 rupee note I'd dropped; I was staggered by the honesty

---

[i] Ancient holy texts

[ii] Seven Prime Ministers were either born in Allahabad, were alumni of Allahabad University, or were elected to Parliament from the Allahabad constituency

of someone so desperately poor. And we were entertained at intervals by a ragged singer and flute player. We chatted and exchanged addresses with our new friends in the compartment before night once more suddenly slipped and fell around us - I never could get used to the absence of twilight in the lower latitudes - as we entered Bhopal Junction. But in those days we had no cause to give the place a second thought, other than as the capital city of the state of Madhya Pradesh. The notorious Union Carbide pesticide factory had not even been built.

Rosemary 'on the other side of the open corridor', though in 1991, not 1967.

There was no sleeping berth for us on the second night so we found a place in a 'ladies only' carriage for Manga and as I wandered down the train looking for a comfortable spot, I came across a white face, most unusual in 3rd class. The chap was about my age and turned out to be a Peace Corps Volunteer from the U.S.A. I must say that PCVs were not my favourite people at that time, but this was a little unfair. My only contact had been one day in Patna when I was on a training course, and had come across a large group of them behaving noisily and disrespectfully to their hosts. Maybe I was just being over-protective of the country, or perhaps just jealous of the motor-bikes that they were issued with, but it did feel just a little as if they were re-enacting the colonial experience. But my new friend and I got on very well, chatting through the night about our experiences, motives and achievements, such that they were. Jim said that the fact I'd married an Indian woman told him a lot about me; his comment that he was learning at least as much as he was teaching told me a lot about him. We agreed that it would be good for both sides if some Indian volunteers could come to the West.

A long train, typical of Indian Railways.

Next morning we crossed the dramatic Western Ghats, the chain of mountains that stretch along the west coast of India from Gujarat in the north right down to Kanniya Kumari at its southern tip, and which are sculpted into eccentric shapes by thousands of years of monsoon rains. Now we were nearing Mumbai. The railway line into the city had to cross Thane Creek by a series of low bridges because Mumbai proper is an island. If you take that route, you can see piles of salt drying in the sun, for the shallow creeks and hot weather in these parts make it ideal for producing sea salt. You'd be excused for thinking they were heaps of snow were it not for the fact that the sweat was pouring off your face! But our route took us south rather than into the city, and our next stop was Pune [formerly Poona] where we stayed with my former boss, the Lieutenant-Colonel who had been the Principal of the Sainik School when I arrived there in August 1966.

Colonel Smith and his family had already met Manga briefly, when she first arrived in Mumbai on the same ship as the Colonel's wife's mother the previous March. We enjoyed a happy couple of days at their home before moving on to Dhond, another railway town and the home of Manga's sister Manikka. We spent our first Christmas together there. A year before, I'd stayed with a friend in a mineworkers' dormitory on the Bihar-West Bengal border and hardly noticed the passing of the festival, so it was good this year to be surrounded by my family, albeit the branch that did not celebrate Christmas. But Manga set her alarm-clock for midnight and woke me with a present: a small silver beaker that she had been given when a child. I gave her some gold bordering [zari] for a sari.

A cow on the platform, 1979

We had decided to make one more stopover before reaching Kerala. Normally we would have taken the Madras Mail across the country to Arakkonam in the east and thence to Tirur in a south-westerly direction. This might seem eccentric but in those days that was the only way - it was not until the Konkan Line was completed in 1998 that one could travel due south by train from Mumbai to Kerala. But we were making for Mysore and our route was via Sholapur, my future niece Shanta's home town, and famous for its wonderful bed covers, of which we have several. Here we changed trains and crossed Karnataka state to Bangalore, a journey lasting 24 hours. We were now clearly in the south - at a time when the

North-South Language Wars were attaining serious levels of anger. As we were crossing Madhya Pradesh en route for Mumbai a day or so earlier, we had seen the stations' English names torn down or painted out. Here the trains were daubed with slogans like 'Down with Hindi' and 'English ever, Hindi never'. I suppose I should have felt more at home! However all rail traffic out of Chennai had been cancelled because 'language terrorists' had burnt out two trains that had come from the north. We, however, at no time felt threatened, either in the north or the south. We stayed in the Railway Rest Room in Mysore and enjoyed a day's sight-seeing. We've always had a good time in that lovely city.

And so to Kerala. You can't get there by train from Mysore, so we needed road transport next and a bus took us on the spectacular journey through the Nilgiri Hills, up to 7000 feet among teak forests and tea plantations, to Ootacamund. Beside the bus stop there stood a lighted brazier and an old lady bent over it roasting cashew nuts. The aroma was irresistible and we bought two large portions contained in twists of newspaper for a very few paisa. We took a brief stroll to stretch our legs and came across a jamun tree. The fruit turns your tongue purple.[iii] Manga explained that Rama survived his exile in the forest by eating jamun. It has an interesting taste - acidic but sweet. Manga sprinkled some salt on it from the packet of cashews and it tasted even better.

We boarded the bus again, somewhat refreshed and now very keen to complete our journey, and in a few hours time, just as the sun was setting, we arrived in Manga's home state. Kerala - the most beautiful place in the world - its coconut and areca palms silhouetted against a pale blue sky; its lakes and rivers reflecting the thatched or brown-tiled homesteads which appeared in clearings between the mango, cashew nut and tamarind trees at regular intervals; the startlingly bright green paddy fields supporting hundreds of fishing egrets and storks; telephone wires acting as look-out posts for the ubiquitous kingfishers.

We listened to the train sing out its rhythmical chant translated by the local children as '*kutti - pattaru - chathappina - chutta -*

[iii] The fruit of *Syzygium cumini* is also said to lower blood glucose levels and to be a good source of vitamins A and B, and the leaves and bark are used to control blood pressure.

pappadam -thinnittilla' [which means: the Brahmin chap - since he died - we haven't eaten roasted pappad] - and Manga became more and more excited as we passed the stations that announced our ever-growing proximity to her home - Pattambi, Pallippuram, Kuttipuram, and then the mighty Bharathapuzha River and finally Tirunavaya. We pushed our noses through the iron bars of the windows trying to absorb more of this intoxicating place. Manga pointed out a somewhat forlorn old elephant tied to a tree in a compound just next to the line - it always seemed to be there whenever we passed in future times. The train pulled to a halt to allow an express to pass us, and in the brief period of quiet until the train arrived, we heard the sharp call of a jungle fowl and saw its purple tail disappear into the undergrowth. And then Tudhakal Bridge came into view, 750 feet in length, with its twelve iron girders resting on piers of laterite stones seven feet thick. The bridge was so narrow that when we looked out of the window, we could see nothing but the river below, and it felt as if we were flying.

Ooty station. The Nilgiri Mountain Railway is still powered by steam locomotives.

The next station would be Tirur. Who would be there to meet us? Would the engine stop long enough for us to unload all our cases and jump onto the platform before it hastened impatiently on its journey [I had a recurring nightmare about this!] No need to worry. Tirur Station was eerily quiet at four o'clock in the morning but we disembarked safely into the arms of family and friends. And so, after 84 hours sitting in trains and buses, we had at last arrived at our destination. Now, escorted by the resourceful and ever popular Balan, our brother-in-law, and a posse of his friends, we made our way on foot to Manga's home: a small, neat, whitewashed bungalow with a tiled roof - just two small rooms and 'a long veranda where most of the living is done'[iv] - in a large compound full of tall and graceful coconut palms; dark, dense mango trees, in which monkeys were just stirring; and trees with red, white, pink and yellow blossoms upon which nectar-seeking birds were already feeding in the early morning sunlight. We had indeed entered Paradise.

Shop with brightly coloured fruit

So that is how I became captivated by Kerala. Of course it is not really Paradise, and it certainly was not then. There were beggars on the road in Tirur when we first visited with the children, much to their distress, and a lot of unemployment and under-employment. Brightly dressed women, men very smart in their folded up Persil-white lungis, spectacularly neat and clean children in blue, brown or red school uniforms - and so many of them! - disguised underlying poverty.

Anita Nair makes reference in her introduction to a collection of writings about Kerala to 'the total lack of industry, high unemployment, a competitive and conspicuous consumerism,

---

[iv] This phrase is taken from one of my letters to my parents.

bureaucracy, corruption of which the world knows not.' [2] But the Kerala of the tourist brochures does of course exist too, and there is much about its wonderful colours, sights, smells and tastes in this book.

However, my arrival in the state of Kerala was not the beginning of this story.

CHAPTER ONE

MARRYING INTO KERALA

I met a lady in the meads / Full beautiful, a faery's child.' John Keats, *La Belle Dame Sans Merci*

'The women of the immoral Hindus and the Moslems they have corrupted, of their own accord and desire enter into the bonds of wedlock with the English.' Abdul Lateef Shushtari, *Tuhfat al'Alam*[3]

I met Manga in Sheffield in 1966, about the same time as England were winning their one-and-only football World Cup. It all started when in my final year of university I was thinking about what I might do next. Embarking on a career didn't at the time seem like a very attractive option, and a friend was thinking about doing Voluntary Services Overseas (VSO), so we looked into it a bit further and decided to go ahead. I went up for interview in London and in spite of showing a woeful ignorance of Asian and African culture, especially for a student of Development Economics (well, that was one of my nine Finals' papers), was accepted. Maybe my (very proper in the circumstances) humility stood me in good stead; VSO were not looking for people who thought they were going to be God's gift to the developing world. In due course I received details of my posting - I was to teach English and anything else necessary, at the Sainik School, Tilaiya Dam, in the state of Bihar, north eastern India.

There was to be a training course at Aston University Birmingham, where we would learn a little about teaching English to students for whom it was a foreign language, get to practice on classes of recent immigrants of primary school age, and listen to some lectures from returned volunteers and old India hands. The course was of mixed value. I picked up some helpful tips from the volunteers, and experienced what it was like to engage with a class of children, and learned what I think I knew already - that it was important to become part of your community before thinking of trying to introduce much in the way of change. On the other hand, one of the experts on Asia gave a rather outdated and misleading account of the dangers of polluting high-caste Indians by touching them; there were no language courses, and the education input was haphazard. I gather all that has now improved. What could not be improved, however, were the lodging arrangements, at least for me and a colleague. We were billeted with the head of the Cadbury family, Sir Egbert I think, at the family home. I was driving a 1934 Riley Adelphi at the time, which, although it had only cost me £10 to buy, was a hand-built vehicle of impeccable vintage and great class, and it looked and no doubt felt, rather at home parked in the drive of the imposing Victorian mansion. We strolled round its vast grounds, enhanced with cannons from ships at Trafalgar, bronze statues and the occasional folly. Pictures of the knight's college eight hung in the hall, and oars decorated the staircase. We came down in the mornings a little nervously, to find breakfast laid out in silver lidded dishes - eggs, bacon and the traditional devilled kidneys - but no people, and returned in the evening to dine in a rather gloomy room, only once, if my memory serves me rightly, with the elderly and rather taciturn Sir Egbert present.

I returned from Birmingham feeling that I needed to know more about India if I were to make any useful preparations for the next two years of my life. But how? My mother's younger sister Peggy Weetman, had been in India in the fifties, as a nurse with the Christian Mission in Chanda, Maharashtra, but that seemed to me to be a long time ago; surely her experience would not be relevant, especially as Chanda was down in the Deccan over 600 miles away by road.[i] Anyway, I argued, Auntie Peg's role and mine were very different, and she was of a different generation. So I feverishly worked my way through VSO's reading list without becoming especially enlightened and went to an India party at the Sheffield Commonwealth Club, with the same effect. Bihar was a foreign country to most of the people with whom I spoke. But I did have one stroke of luck: I met a Bengali student, Shyam K. Das, who was a Mining Engineer with a job awaiting in the Bihar coal field! Unfortunately, his final examination was on the next day and he was then flying straight home. We exchanged addresses though, and agreed that I'd spend my first Christmas in India with him. It

---

[i] Peggy Weetman is mentioned in 'India-Past Glimpses of Country Life' by Charles Copland, Melrose Books 2006. First edition pub by Lewis Recordings, 1988. Pages 38-9; photo on p 39

was my mother who suggested I might like to meet an Indian nurse with whom she was working in the neo-natal department of Sheffield's Nether Edge Hospital. This of course was Manga and she was duly invited to tea. It turned out that Manga too had never been to Bihar and that she came from the far south, twice as far from Tilaiya Dam as Chanda. But I was hardly aware of that. Manga was so pretty, with long, silky black hair and big brown eyes, and very slim. In fact we discovered later that I could enclose her waist with my hands. I can't now I'm afraid. It's surprising how one's hands get smaller as one gets older!

Manga was funny too and could tell lots of stories about India. I loved being with her, and we spent as much time as possible together before I had to board my BOAC flight to Calcutta via Karachi. In the meantime, I had learned a few words of Hindi, and how to eat with my hand, so was obviously much better equipped than before! It had been fun, and even though I had a lot to think about, it was firmly in my mind that I must see Manga again, even though it looked as though we were going to be far apart for at least two years.

My first taste of India was the car-ride from Dum Dum airport to the Calcutta YMCA (I'd read about Dum Dum in *Biggles Flies East* and knew that a soft-nosed bullet had been named after it. One up for me). I wish I could remember what I was thinking as we passed miles of roadside shacks and queues of ragged women and children waiting to fill their pots and pans at the occasional standpipe, but although this was my first visit to what was then called a 'Third World' country, I really don't think I was particularly shocked. Perhaps I had read too much about India's poverty, or Manga had warned me too well. I was probably better prepared in fact for the Indian countryside than for that evening's very posh reception at the British Council HQ in the street that was then called Theatre Rd.[ii] The following day, a British Council official was due to embark on a lecture tour - subject: 'Rudyard Kipling: a Re-appraisal' - and he was to drop me and two other volunteers off en route. One of my colleagues was a very learned, personable and mature individual who made a great success of his posting, writing and publishing for example a much-acclaimed English textbook;

[ii] It is now Shakespeare Sarani. I'm rather glad that the English connection has been retained.

the other fled India after a few months. I fell somewhere in between, though I will say that my British Council mentor, Mr. Jacob, did describe me towards the end of my spell as a 'model volunteer'. (He hailed from Kerala and I think might have been biased!). I was the last of the three to be deposited and was therefore treated to a rehearsal of our driver's lecture. From this I gathered that Kipling was now in fashion, and that few Englishmen had written so perceptively about the country, whatever one might feel about his political views.

Cartoon of me by R.B. Jha (Art Teacher)

I remember very clearly my first few days at the Sainik School. There was an English public-speaking competition on the first evening and I was hugely impressed by the boys' speeches, which of course were in their second or third language. I thought at the time that their performance was at least as good as anything that their English counterparts would have been able to achieve. Never mind that I later came to realise the speeches were no doubt learned by heart from a crib sheet of some description: the confidence of their delivery was still admirable. I met some members of the Kodarma Lions Club at the competition and they invited me to speak at their next dinner. I sought the advice of the Principal of the School and he suggested that I wait awhile before accepting such an invitation as none of the other teachers had ever been asked and they might be resentful. So I dutifully declined - and was never invited again! I spent the next evening playing Scrabble with Colonel Smith and his wife together with the young man who was apparently to be my mentor at the school, S.K.Chandra, a teacher of English from West Bengal. On the way back to my lodgings on a warm and balmy night I looked up at the awesomely black sky and muttered 'What a beautiful evening!' Chandra replied that yes it had been lovely but he was worried that I might not find many evenings so good - there was really not much going on in Tilaiya Dam.

In practice I found plenty to do in my evenings. The boys would come round to chat, or to get help with their lessons. I had lots of invitations to dinner, and I needed any time that was left for marking the boys' books, or preparation of lessons. I started studying Hindi under the tutelage of the senior Hindi master, Mr. Kandpal, and also got to play his sitar. I didn't make much progress in either discipline I fear. As far as Hindi was concerned, my excuse was that I was there to promote the use of English. And I've had loved to have played the sitar properly but I'm sorry to say, I was a most inept pupil. Meanwhile, Chandra and I directed a production of 'Julius Caesar', featuring the school's Gurkha gatekeeper and bugler as 'flourish of trumpets'. We rehearsed for night after night, and until recently I remembered almost every speech, word for word. And it was a very entertaining show, lacking subtlety perhaps - what did I know about Shakespeare? - but energetic and good fun.I enjoyed coaching cricket, at which I *was* successful. The pitches were very uneven, and each match was preceded by a ceremony involving a long line of boys walking across the field picking up pebbles. Even this did not help much, so I got the boys together to lay a concrete strip, at first in the nets and then another one on the cricket field proper. The standard of cricket definitely improved and some fine players emerged: Satish, leg-spinner and batsman; Arup, fast bowler; Pradeep, off-spinner; Priyaranjan, wicket-keeper, to name but four.

The cricket team

I wrote home on 20th February 1967:

> Dear Mum and Dad...It's 9.30 am and I'm sitting in my room in nothing but a pair of shorts, and sweating. From which you will gather that it's hot...but I'm told that the temperature will increase by another 30 degrees F during the next few months... We had our first inter-school cricket match yesterday, against the local Roman Catholic fee-paying boarding school, which is 40 miles away. It was a very exciting game - we started at about ten, our field gaily flagged, with the temple in the North West corner, concrete and matting pitch in perfect order [the Catholic Fathers were full of praise for my efforts] and my star fast bowler took three wickets for none in his first two overs. Arup then tired and they progressed to 65 all out, my other star player, Satish, taking three good catches...After lunch we lost a wicket from the first ball, then Satish hit a rapid 30. A mixture of over-confidence and a distressing tendency to play back to everything reduced us to 55 for 8, before a partnership between a lad who fancies himself as the new Sobers, and a twelve year old, saw us through. My heart was in my mouth - I'm always much more nervous than the boys are. And they seem to do better in the real thing than in practice - it was the same with the drama. The Principal was very pleased - we didn't often beat the Catholics in any field - and gave the team a good tea, and invited me for dinner...love from Kiff

We also played a game against the town team - the first time the school had played against adults - and beat them by one wicket. I later wrote home

> Dear Mum and Dad...I gave the team a party and we finished the biscuits and ate the cake you sent - both very good - many thanks...it's really getting too hot for cricket and the dust storms are terrible: two whirlwinds swept across the pitch on Sunday obliterating all vision and stinging the flesh like hail... Otherwise all is well, and I'm really fit and very busy. Lots of love from Kiff.

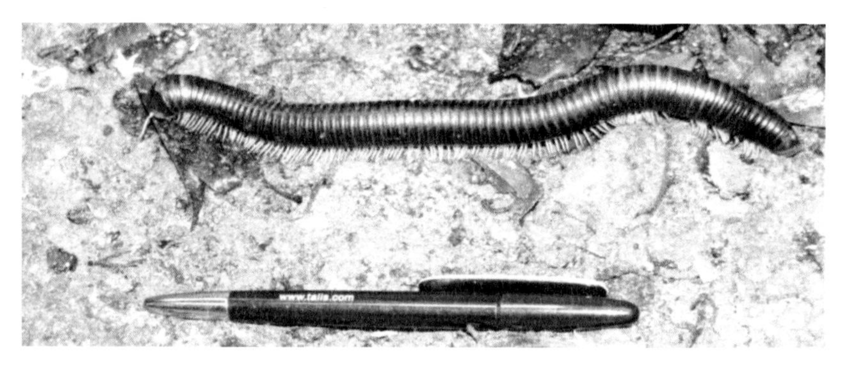

A centipede: nine inches long

And speaking of discomfort, my sister-in-law Julie remembers another of my letters in which I apparently described a solitary meal holding up an umbrella to ward off beetles falling from the ceiling. Insects were indeed something of a problem: termites ate through the pages of my precious *Wisden* that I had brought from England, and mosquitoes were a nuisance, but I only ever saw one scorpion, and in the school at least there were no cockroaches. The sheer size of the centipedes was a bit of a worry though!

Beyond the school boundaries, first, there was Tilaiya Dam itself. This was the first dam constructed by independent India, and the school in fact was using some of the builders' houses and dormitories for its pupils and staff. The dam was a popular place to stroll to: it had a Circuit House [a place for Government officials to stay on their inspection 'circuit'] where one could buy tea and coffee; some very pleasant gardens; and the reservoir itself. The dam was long - a quarter of a mile I'd guess, and must have been 100 feet high, and enclosed what would in normal climatic times have been a big lake across the Damodar River. The dam was part of the Damodar Valley Corporation scheme for irrigation, and was designed to prevent flooding but it had little to do in that direction while I was in Tilaiya. Neither, because there had been so little rain and the water level was consequently low, did it generate much in the way of electricity a visiting engineer told me one day. On the way to the lake one walked through the tiny village that had grown up to service the construction workers and then the school. We did our day-to-day shopping in the market there and joined in the festivals. I still have some photos somewhere of the fearsome image of the goddess that the villagers built for Durga Puja, one of the most important of many Hindu festivals. There was a Dak Bungalow [a travellers' rest house] in the village, though there weren't many travellers in Tilaiya in those days. Manga and I stayed there a couple of times, and the accommodation was simple but clean. I wish we could have afforded the Circuit House, but a volunteer's salary didn't go that far. Not that it would have been very expensive: a volunteer's salary did not in fact go anywhere!

There were occasional trips into the local town. Jhumri Tilaiya lay on the main rail line between Delhi and Calcutta and was the centre of the mica mining industry, but could not be said to be famous for either of these distinctions because the railway station was called Kodarma, and Kodarma was also 'The Mica Capital of the World', although it was a much smaller town and away from major roads and railways. Jhumri Tilaiya does however have fame of a sort; it is apparently the Indian equivalent of Timbuktu - no one really believes it exists![4] Sheet mica by the way is a naturally occurring insulator that was of great value before artificial replacements became available, and is still used, though little is now mined in Kodarma. Mica deposits were discovered there by the British when excavating for a railway cutting in the nineteenth century.[5] A small number of landowners and businessmen became extremely rich by exploiting mica, and their big houses contrasted shamefully with the general squalor of the town. Their labourers, mainly women, meanwhile squatted in groups splitting the sheets of mica and inhaling the toxic dust that this produced. The word 'mica' comes from the Latin micare 'to glow', and as one drove around Kodarma district at night, the headlights of one's car would reflect off the mica dust as if there had been an implausible frost.

We used to go into the town for supplies. From time to time I'd accompany the Quartermaster in the school jeep on his purchasing forays or go by bus with one of the teachers on a domestic shopping trip. And we also visited Jhumri Tilaiya for entertainment. Not that there was much of that on offer. There were however two cinemas, one of which, Jawahar Talkies, specialised in what were known as 'social' films, and the other, Purnima Talkies, showed mainly adventures and comedies. I used to take a group of sixth form boys there for a treat from time to time. We always ended up at the Purnima. Getting to and from the town was a bit of a problem. It was straightforward enough if one could borrow the jeep, but one could only do that on school business [like the cinema trips]. Otherwise it was cycle rickshaw from the school to the main road, where there was a tiny village called Urmamur, with a roadside café where Manga and I later enjoyed many a tasty snack - usually black gram curry and pooris if I remember rightly. A scruffy little spot but the food was delicious; very hot and fresh of course, straight from the pan onto the tin plate. And very spicy: better than ice-cream on a hot day, I was advised, as it would get you sweating. Then I would wait in the shade of a huge spreading peepal tree for a bus, usually crowded, rarely on time and always rickety. Occasionally I took a cycle rickshaw all the way, and that, although I felt it was very unfair on the poor cyclist, was sometimes the only way one could get there - or back. The rickshaw wallahs always charged me more than anyone else on the false assumption that I had more money, and when I was once stuck in town after the last bus left, I refused to agree to the enhanced fare. It was dark but I started walking, expecting them to relent. They didn't and I kept on walking. Eventually I covered the whole distance back to school on foot, seven miles through the Hazaribagh jungle - allegedly tiger-infested, and certainly plagued by bandits. I took comfort from the fact that I was armed with my sturdy, steel-tipped umbrella!

My other pastime was writing a lot of letters: to Mum and Dad of course and also to Manga. Manga kept these and I'm rather embarrassed to read now that I wasn't at first very sympathetic to the local villagers who were already suffering from the failure of one monsoon. I think I took my cue from some of the teachers especially those from Uttar Pradesh, the neighbouring state to Bihar, who were inclined to blame the locals' 'laziness' for their troubles. The only excuse I can offer is that I had a lot to learn in those first few weeks in India, and in this case I listened to the wrong people. I'm glad to say that when I had settled down I was able to see that even the most energetic farmer could not grow crops without water.

Time passed, and back in England, Manga was spending more of her days off with Mum and Dad in Sheffield. She remembers drives in the Peak District and listening to Dad's records. Dad remembered them watching cricket together, Manga cross-legged in front of the TV. And Mum remembered Manga cooking Kerala curries for them, the spices especially mild for Dad's portion. Mum used to buy the ingredients for her from a Health Food shop in Hunter's Bar, on the way into the city. They were lucky it was there, because exotic foodstuffs were hard to come by in those days.

Meanwhile in India, the effects of the drought were becoming more and more obvious as crops dried up in the fields, skeletal cows, unable to find even a blade of grass, tottered and fell to the ground, and malnutrition spread through the people. We were not immune from these problems in the school - living on strict rations, I lost 35 lbs in weight - but of course there was no danger of starvation, and we put our heads down and got on with our work. We had a schoolful of young people to look after, and most of my colleagues had their families to provide for too. But I began to tell Manga she was needed in India. By now I realised how much I was missing her; and at the same time I did genuinely believe that there was much she could offer to the people. I told her of the Holy Family Hospital, which I had visited when accompanying the Principal and his family to its attached church one Sunday. The hospital was just outside Jhumri Tilaiya, and run by nuns of course; it had a good reputation and there were some nurses from Kerala there. Manga thought about it, and eventually put in an application, which was accepted with alacrity. She tells me now that her motivation was quite simply that she was in love.

So in March 1967 I could be found boarding a train at Kodarma station en route for Mumbai, there to meet the S.S.Orsova. Manga had been seen off from Tilbury Docks by my Mum and sister, Rosemary. Rosemary recently wrote to me recalling her memories of that day:

> I vividly remember the farewell - many people were emigrating to Australia on the Orsova and their families on the quayside had very little chance of ever seeing them again; we

> were feeling similarly bereft as there was no thought at all that Manga would ever come back to England. Dad was particularly sad that she was leaving. He gave her one of his most precious possessions - his medal for being a member of the Thanet cricket team that had once won the league, before the Second World War. The Port authorities were obviously sensitive to the awesomeness of the occasion and had rigged up a tiered gallery, like a football stand and we were told on what level our families would be, so we were directly opposite one another - almost able to touch. We threw the streamers we were given and a military band played popular songs - finally: 'We'll meet again, don't know where, don't know when...' as the ship slowly moved away and the paper chains broke. Tears are welling up as I write this so poignant was the moment, although it was so long ago now I recall every detail.

A letter from Mum was waiting for Manga in Aden:

> How I would have loved to have been travelling with you. The Orsova looked so grand sailing down the Thames with the little tugs fussing round her and of course the sun improved the whole scene...Rosemary and I got to the very end of the quay and wondered if you could see us - we caught a glimpse of you. Then we met your friends and got back to the Strand just as Tony [Rosemary's husband] was finishing his shift in the hospital. Rosemary was so pleased he had met you. I caught the 5.05 back to Sheffield and was home by 8.30 pm. Dad and Shelt [our dog] were pleased to see me*. I went to work on Sunday...lots and lots of people enquired after you - your little ears ought to have burnt - so many nice things have been said about you. Manga you must feel very proud to have left this country with so many people thinking so much of you - grand, so <u>grand</u> to have such a wonderful reputation...

Manga really enjoyed the voyage. There was a lot to do, the social life was great and she made plenty of friends. We still have two or three very happy on-board photographs showing a radiant Manga amongst a cheerful group of fellow passengers, one of whom, a Sri Lankan lad, unsurprisingly fell in love with her.

Manga on the Orsova, 1966

Manga later described the journey to me: '*We were woken every morning by a steward with a glass of orange. I shared a cabin with a Parsi girl, who couldn't understand why I didn't let my Sri Lankan friend kiss and cuddle. 'He's a nice boy', she would say. But I was only thinking of you. I used to go and listen to music in the library - especially Beethoven's Fifth Symphony - it reminded me of you because we listened to it in your home. There was another Parsi girl on board. She was bit shy but she got friendly with an Englishman and after fifteen days she came to us and said they were engaged. Another chap, an Indian, always carried Mao's Little Red Book with him. Somebody played a trick on him and said he'd be arrested if he tried to take the book into India so he threw it overboard. We used to play quoits, and swim in the pool. There was a cabaret every evening and you could dance - all sorts of things. I enjoyed our trip round Gibraltar, especially the caves - almost like a cathedral - with lovely stalactites and stalagmites and the monkeys of course. Mrs. Bush, Connie Smith's mother, was a fellow-passenger and she came with us.*[iii] *We couldn't go on shore at Port Said because of the war,*[iv] *but we sailed through the Canal. It was so narrow you felt you could put your arms out and touch both banks.'*

My somewhat shorter trip to Mumbai, on the other side of India, was rather less happy. I left the carriage, at Allahabad I think, to get something to eat, stayed around chatting, and when I went back, it wasn't there. The carriage that is. The back end of the train had been shunted off into a siding and when I tracked it down, there was no sign of my luggage. Everything was in my bag including my camera and toilet things, and of course while I had been searching, the train to Mumbai had gone without me. I managed to catch the next train, but was hours late. So instead of me looking spic and span waiting at the quayside to welcome Manga back to India, it was Manga, looking tired and worried, meeting me at the Railway Station - and it was an unwashed, unkempt and thoroughly disreputable-looking me at that. By a stroke of extreme good fortune, Colonel Smith [the Principal of the Sainik School] had been meeting the Orsova too - as Manga said, his mother-in-law was on board - and he and his family had kindly come with Manga to the station to make sure all was well, so matters could have been worse. But for Manga and me it was a rather inauspicious beginning to our life together in India. We tried to find a hotel for the night, but our taxi driver took us, not surprisingly I suppose, only to the most sleazy dives in the backstreets of the city, designed for sailors and their temporary consorts. So we returned to the station and spent a restless night in the waiting room.

Next day, we headed for Dhond, now Daund, the Crewe of Indian Railways, where the main lines from Mumbai eastwards, Delhi southwards, Chennai northwards and Kolkata westwards all met. And as well as being an important junction, Dhond had loco repair sheds and all the other paraphernalia of a railway town. We went there of course to stay with Manikutti, who became known as Mini-sister - even Manga towered over her! Mini-sister's husband, Krishnamani or 'Atimbear' (brother-in-law) worked on the railways. He had started work as a cook, like many Brahmins, but then joined the railways and reached the rank of driver of Express trains. Sadly,

---

[iii] Connie was the wife of the Principal of the Sainik School.

[iv] The Arab-Israeli War of 1967

Atimbear then started to become deaf - the result, he told Rosemary and Tony, of treatment with large doses of streptomycin for tuberculosis, and could no longer drive engines. The job as a fireman was much less well-paid and money became very tight.

Manga in Dhond, 1967

Manikutti and Atimbear had three children: Ravi, the eldest, Raju and Radhikar. Dhond was a rather dusty old town and not an ideal place to bring up young children. The accommodation for railway families was far from palatial, but worse was that the railway tracks lay between the family's home and the local school, so four times a day, the children had to make their way between grumbling wagons being shunted into and out of sidings, and appearing, says Raju, from nowhere and with no warning. Accidents, sometimes fatal, were not unusual. Raju continues '*so Balamama [Raju's uncle] decided, and I still remember his exact words, "we don't have children for testing their luck between tracks; we'll take them all to Trikkandiyur.*" ' Raju moved to Kerala first, and was followed by the others in due course. .

Many members of the family had gathered to see Manga on her return from England, and to meet me as well. Rajam [Manga's sister, Balan's wife] had arrived with Raju, and a third sister Seethalakshmi too: she was frightened to touch my white skin! Ten of us slept on the floor, squashed like sardines into the little home, which I somewhat uncharitably described in a letter home at the time as a hovel. Care was taken that Manga and I were on opposite sides of the room! There was just enough space for all of as long as no one turned over. The somewhat chaotic situation was exacerbated by the fact that poor Atimbear was suffering from jaundice.

There was no running water and I had bathed in the back yard using a bucket filled at the communal well. The mosquitoes had been particularly bad and I think I must have looked a pretty sorry sight - thin, pockmarked with insect bites, sleep- deprived and unshaven. To quote again from one of my letters home - *'Manga is the one ray of sunshine here...the whole village has been crowding in to see her and she is wonderful with all of them...'* Manga listened gravely to the elders, who were seizing the opportunity of showing off their knowledge of English - trying hard to understand them for it would have never done to call into question their linguistic abilities - hugged loads of babies, commented on new saris, praised shy newly-weds on their golden ornaments, teased youngsters, and answered endless questions about England; all the while dispensing advice about how to treat a badly cut arm or a sore eye, and switching apparently easily between Malayalam, Tamil and Marathi.[v]

After that initiation, things were bound to look up - and indeed they did - although Manga was apprehensive. She wrote to Mum and Dad shortly after disembarking *'This place is so dry and I wonder how Kodarma is going to be. Mrs. Smith didn't give me a very good impression of the place...everything seems fine but I am still not sure how I am going to get on at the hospital.'*

---

[v] Marathi is the language of the state of Maharashtra, in which Dhond lay. It is similar to Hindi in its spoken form, but uses a different script.

After a couple of days in Dhond it was time for me to return to work and we caught the westbound train. My next letter home said,

> Manga spent a couple of nights in Tilaiya [at the Circuit House] and I introduced her to some of the masters and wives, who liked her very much, and on Saturday morning she went to the hospital in the school jeep. She isn't thrilled with the place... Yesterday I went over to see her and was lucky because I got to Urmamur by our milk van and the first car I thumbed took me all the way to the hospital. It only took 45 minutes altogether...The countryside around the hospital isn't very inspiring but we enjoyed ourselves and amused and interested a large crowd of locals when we sat down for a cup of tea and a picnic...all the masters' wives are now wanting to see Manga to have their medical problems solved - I think they're scared of going to hospital - and all the children on site want her to teach them now that Auntie Smith and Auntie Penny have gone...[vi]

The Muslim women and the lower caste women in particular lined up for Manga's attention - the former because they didn't want to visit the [male] doctor on the site, and the latter because they felt that the doctor didn't have much time for them.

We continued to see each other at weekends if I didn't have school duties and enjoyed our picnics. Sometimes Manga came to Tilaiya and sometimes I went to the hospital. Eventually, VSO provided me with a push bike - a ramshackle affair but it got me to the Holy Family. Not that true love always ran smooth. The nuns would sometimes express disapproval of my visits, although they were careful not to upset Manga - she was too important to them: someone told me they had been on a train where the main topic of conversation had been the wonderful new nurse from England who had joined the Holy Family Hospital.

I wrote to Mum and Dad:

> I don't mind cycling the 16 miles to the Holy Family but the difficulties arise when I arrive there - we have now covered every inch of ground within 5 miles of the hospital. Sometimes it strikes me as very funny to be cycling on a dilapidated sit-up-and-beg with a water flask over my shoulder and Manga perched on the

---

[vi] There was a kindergarten at the school which had been run by the Principal's wife and, when she was home from her boarding school, their daughter.

> luggage rack clutching a picnic basket, but when it's hot and sweaty and Manga falls off, and hundreds of villagers give up whatever they're doing to stand and stare, it does test our patience a bit...It would be nice to get further away from here to a new place...

We don't seem to have stinted on our picnics, famine or not. 9th April 1967:

> ...today, a tin of beef from Rob,[vii] 3 eggs (saved by Manga from her last three breakfasts), some sweet bread and biscuits from the hospital - one of the nurses is sympathetic and is always cooking stuff for me - a nice new loaf, ghee, jam and lots of fruit - oranges, bananas, lemons [to make drinks], sour mangoes, which are tasty with salt, and a whole big papaya. Do you get them there? They're a bit like melons but sweeter. These occasions are the only times I eat well...

Sometimes, I stayed overnight at the hospital - once in the hospital grounds in the open air. I slept on a table and woke up with a jolt to see a praying mantis peering intently into my eyes from a distance of about three inches. Another time I stayed with the priest, a Belgian, and enjoyed reading his extensive collection of books by P.G.Wodehouse.

The summer drew on, getting hotter and hotter. The land became drier and drier. Then the monsoon season arrived. Every day our hopes rose as storm clouds appeared on the horizon. Lightning flashed, thunder rumbled but of rain there was not a drop. Soon it became clear that the monsoon had failed for the second successive year. It really was bad news. Now the rivers began to dry up and very little could grow at all in the fields. At the Sainik School, water was available only for a few hours a day, and then only a muddy trickle came out of the tap. It had to be stored in a mudka, an earthenware pot, for the sediment to settle, and by evening, but not before, the water would be cool and clear. [One of the greatest pleasures of returning to England was to have unlimited supplies of clean water at any time we wanted it.] At the hospital things became desperate at times. Nursing had been hard enough

[vii] Rob was my big brother who worked at Heathrow and would occasionally be able to persuade an employee of one of the airlines to lend him their entitlement to cheap air freighting.

when there were just shortages of drugs and equipment; having to economise on water too was close to being the last straw.

Manga in the hills beyond Kodarma

The human cost of the drought was made all too clear to me one evening when I was escorting Manga back to the hospital after a day out. By the time we arrived at the gates, it was getting late. There was no light and the dense silence was suddenly broken by a low groan, or was it a growl? If I'd been alone I think I might have beat a rapid retreat, but being together emboldened us and we crept towards the source of the sound. Before we had gone very far we were assailed by the most appalling smell; it was emanating from the shelter by the gate, and inside lay the body of an old woman with an open wound in her side crawling with a thousand maggots. Manga called the porter to carry the poor woman into the hospital, and nursed her for four days before she died. She had been left in the shelter because her relations had been afraid that they would have been asked to pay for her treatment, and having no money, feared being turned away.

I began to feel that I needed to justify my presence in India in a more practical way than by just teaching English, so I applied to do some famine relief work in the summer vacation. Manga told Mum: *'I love him very much but I am helpless in this desert. I wanted him to cancel his offer to distribute food in the villages because of the heat but he won't listen,'* and she asked Mum to send me a tin of sausages and some bacon; I asked Mum to send Manga some thick vegetable soup powder. At the end of term I duly joined a charitable organisation.

After two months relief work I decided I deserved a holiday and Manga finally agreed to come with me to Kashmir. We could scarcely have chosen a more romantic destination anywhere in the world nor one that stood in such stark contrast to Bihar - pleasantly cool while our home was blisteringly hot, green fields instead of brown, pine forests in place of the scrub land near the school, and distant snow-capped mountains instead of...well, there are certainly no such views in the Ganges plain! A houseboat on the Dal Lake... Manga joking with the cook about the spiciness of Kashmiri dishes... Our boatman sculling us across the lake in his shikar to the Shalimar Gardens... Manga looking winsome in a peasant dress she had bought during a holiday in Austria... Walks up to the temple on the hill above the town in the evenings, the moon reflected in the still waters of the lake and oil lamps twinkling in the valley below us... Watching craftsmen making and painting papier- mâché boxes... Counting our paisa to see if we could afford a small souvenir... Pony-trekking in the mountains, just below the snowline... Manga composed and confident on horseback; my steed bolted!

Manga in Kashmir, 1967

It's hardly surprising that shortly after this dream vacation, we decided we wanted to stay together. Some years after we returned to England, our local paper ran a story about us in their occasional feature 'Man of the Times'. We rather liked the headline: *'Romance flourished in famine-struck country'.* It certainly had, and we were married in Kolkata in November.

CHAPTER TWO

THE FAMILY, THE HOUSE AND THE KERALA IYERS

'I was ever of the opinion, that the honest man who married and brought up a large family, did more service than he who continued single and only talked of population' - Oliver Goldsmith, *The Vicar of Wakefield*

'The Brahman who sees Ceylon will never see his home again' - Malayalam proverb.

Trikkandiyur 1987

In the Preface, I described the journey Manga and I took from the school to her home in Kerala. At the time, in 1967, there was only one house on the family's land, named Variyathmadam. It was a single-storey lime-washed building made of locally quarried laterite blocks and mortar. Originally the roof was thatched with palm leaves but by 1967 they had been replaced by the characteristic red tiles of Malabar, manufactured from local clay in a factory just outside Tirur. Inside, there were two rooms plus the kitchen, and a veranda along the whole width of the building at the front. The rooms were furnished rather barely - as far as I remember there were benches in the veranda which Manga said were put together to make a bed for her father when he grew old, but the rest of the family slept on the floor, each member unrolling every night their thin mattress and brightly coloured cotton sheet which were stored during the day on top of what Manga calls a 'godrej' - a metal wardrobe named after its manufacturer. Otherwise, there were just metal trunks for storing precious saris, one trunk for each sister, and it was a routine for the boxes to be opened and saris admired from time to time. There was no grand prayer room as one might have expected in a Brahmin home - just an alcove in the wall with the images of gods, together with a photo of Manga's Mum and Dad, where agarbathis (incense) burned. Someone painted a portrait of Manga's parents using the photograph as a model and we have a photograph of the painting on our mantelpiece in Whitstable. There was however that essential of nearly every house I've visited in India, and indeed Indians' houses abroad, a Showcase. This contains one's precious possessions: framed formal photographs of family members, usually staring stiffly into the lens, artificial flowers maybe, pottery figures, perhaps a book or two. And after our presents from England had been opened and admired, they frequently found their way straight into the case too, including, rather sadly, toys for the children. On the walls were calendars, or pictures taken from them, advertising local stores. The pictures were sometimes as expected, of gods and goddesses, but more frequently of snow-capped mountains, or even more bizarrely, of fat pink north European children.

Immediately behind the house stood the small bathroom, open to the skies, and containing only a bucket and a metal cup. One filled the bucket from the well in the garden. It was quite a deep well and took a fair amount of effort to raise a bucketful of water. Back in the bathroom one then poured water over oneself using the cup - very cool and refreshing. This is a very water-efficient way of washing, for one wasted not a drop unless one wanted to go back to the well for a second bucket! About 20 yards away from the house stood the earth lavatory in a little corrugated iron hut, not much fun to use especially if taken short in the middle of the night. One rarely saw snakes or threatening creatures of any sort in the garden, but they were always there in one's imagination - particularly in the dark. And although the lavatory was odourless, it was best not to look down into it. The kitchen and garden had changed little since Manga's childhood. The house was by no means typical of a Kerala

Iyer dwelling; characteristically the members of this caste lived in rows of two storey buildings all joined together along long straight streets. Malayalees often had houses in their own compounds like Manga's family, but several storeys high and with sloping roofs constructed with the local tiles

The ancestral home is very important to the Iyer sub-caste of the Brahmins, of which Manga's family are members. So now we've reached the point where we need to say something about India's caste system. One could write a book about caste, but I'm only going to attempt a very quick summary. Divisions in Indian society according to occupation were described in some of the earliest religious writings in the second millennium BC. At first there were just four: rulers, priests, soldiers and merchants. As time went on many more castes came into being, so that for example, the priestly caste, the Brahmins, were divided into those who washed the idols and those who decorated them; those who prepared the holy food and those who placed it before the god, and so on. One stayed in the caste into which one was born - if one's father emptied toilets, then that would be one's job for life, and one's children would follow the same occupation too. Theoretically all castes were of equal importance, all inter-dependent, so that society could no more do without a sweeper than a doctor, but in practice the lower castes were little more than slaves. The Brahmins are at the top of the tree, and the Iyers are a branch of that caste.

The significance of the family home to the Iyers is reflected in the fact that the names of everyone in the family include the house name. Manga's ancestral home is Variyathmadam[i] so Manga's name before she married was 'Variyathmadam Parameswaraniyer [her father's given name, with the cast name appended] Mangalam [her given name]'. V.P.Mangalam for short. And her father's name was 'Variyathmadam Ramaniyer [his father's given name] Parameswaran'. This is fine while you are living in the local community but causes a few problems if you move away and everyone is assumed to have an immutable surname preceded by a given name. Filling in forms for example then becomes a problem. What normally happens these days is that the caste name is used

---

[i] Actually the family is not now living in the ancestral home: but their present house, to which they moved about 80 years ago, retains the old name. The old house was on the other side of the village near the temple.

as a surname, so on official forms now, Manga's maiden name is 'Mangalam Iyer'. It saves a lot of complicated explanations. I once wrote a three-page letter to the Health Authority who couldn't understand how V.P.Mangalam, the name on Manga's nursing registration certificates, had become Mangalam Banner.

In the early 1960s, only Seethalakshmi, Manga's second-eldest sister, was living in the family house with Mum and Dad. Seethalakshmi [called Amakutty in the family] had had a rather sad life, and it showed in her facial expression and manner. She was very dark skinned which in Kerala as elsewhere in India was not regarded with favour and, because her father could not afford much of a dowry, it had been difficult to find a husband for her.

And since she, like other girls of her caste, was not expected to work, and received a rather basic education, marriage was always going to be the most important thing in her life. When a man who had the right background and horoscope and who was prepared to marry a dark wife was found, it was thought her troubles were over. But at the wedding ceremony, the groom refused to tie the knot until more money was found for her dowry. Manga's father had already gone cap in hand to his neighbours to raise the money in the first place so did not know which way to turn. It would have been a terrible disgrace for the wedding to be stopped. Fortunately a cousin knew a moneylender who loaned some extra cash with the family's last pieces of gold as surety; this included even Manga's thin little bangle. She cried when her only valuable possession was taken from her. Had she done something wrong? It was hard to explain to a little girl. The marriage did not last long. The husband went away after a few months - we don't know why of course, and he may have felt he had good reason - and was never heard of again; in any event, it was not he who was disgraced by his behaviour, but Seethalakshmi.

Parvathi [known as Rajam], the sister closest to Manga, and her husband Balan, were living in the accommodation behind Balan's shop. Rajam had been a bright child and had stayed on at school and then attended college where she trained as a teacher. She was able to do this only because the new [Communist] Kerala government was keen to recruit the teachers needed to expand its primary education programme from amongst poorer people, and so helped with the cost of her fees. Even so, Rajam had no money for living expenses and had to pay her way by working in the college. So she got up very early every morning to help in the kitchens, and after studying in the evening, would return to the classrooms to sweep and clean the floors.

The five sisters

Rajam was at the time of my first visit teaching at a school for Muslims [a secular one - the children learned the Koran in the evenings]. She was greatly respected in the village for her work. And her husband Balan was also a valued member of the community. Balan had been lodging with the family whilst working for the 'Radio Electric Emporium of Palghat', the contractors hired to bring the newly installed mains electricity supply to households in Trikkandiyur. This was sometime towards the end of the fifties and Balan seems not to have completed the job around 5 years later, for my nephew Raju remembers Balan explaining to him how he was using a battery to power lights to decorate the outside of the house for the Diwali celebration. By that time Balan and Rajam were married. It was a love marriage and doubly unusual because Balan was a Chettiyar by caste. The Chettiyars are historically traders, lower in the social hierarchy than Brahmins. Rajam and Manga's parents, although orthodox and in theory opposed to inter-caste marriages, were very good and would not, says Manga, stand in the way of true love. Balan was a jack-of-all-trades, a 'fixer', and a small-scale entrepreneur. At the time of our first visit he was looking after the shop and doing so with real energy, dashing off to Kochi, Trivandrum and even Mumbai to buy his stock. Balan continued to work as an electrical wireman, and added another string to his bow by qualifying as a plumber when piped water first came to the village. That was 1983, and co-incidentally, we were in the village at the time. There was great excitement - showering under running water! Everyone needed fittings - taps, basins, shower heads, 'health faucets' used for cleaning one's nether regions after a visit to the lavatory and so on and Balan provided them. Later he also traded in betel nuts and anything else where a profit was possible. He knew everyone in the village, and most of them seemed to owe him a favour.

Manga's Mum and Dad had thirteen children altogether, of whom seven lived beyond childhood. Her eldest surviving brothers were born in 1911 and 1913; one child, also a boy, the firstborn, died before this, when he was just one year old. Nobody talked about him, but Manga remembers that her Mum always felt a burning pain in her stomach on each anniversary of his death... She says '*Anyway after three boys, Mum wanted a daughter. She was told she would have to plant a henna tree in the garden and she did...and then she had ten girls in a row, five surviving!*' First came Rashika (known as Lakshmi), the eldest daughter, in 1915. There seems to have been a nine-year gap between Rashika and the next child, Amakutty, but the family thinks that three babies were lost in this period. Two more babies died before Manikutty who was born in 1930, and then Rajam and Manga arrived at three-year intervals. Mind you, some of these dates are a bit speculative. No one had birth certificates in those days.

Rajam and Balan were looking after Manikutty's second son Raju. The other members of the family had all moved away - Lakshmi, the eldest sister, also widowed, was living in Vasai, just outside Mumbai and close to her five children; Parameswaran was a cook in Coimbatore, working for a Chettiyar who was a cotton mill owner, and the eldest son Viswanathan was in Sholapur working in a railway office. Manikutty and her husband, as we have seen lived and worked in Dhond at that time with their other two children, Ravi and Radhikar. It was not unusual for Kerala families to move out of the state to find work.

I wrote earlier that Iyers are a sub-caste of Brahmins, but they are not the dominant Brahmins in Kerala. They are not Temple priests and for the most part their role in religious life is healing, and the preparation of holy food. In number and importance they are exceeded by the native Malayalee Brahmins, the Namboodiris. (Though I have been told that some Iyers privately look down on the Namboodiris, and don't count them as proper Brahmins, saying that they used to be fishermen before Parasurama promoted them!) The Iyers are relatively recent immigrants to Kerala, and are known as Tamil, Palakkad or East Coast Brahmins; also Pattars. From that, one can gather that they came from Tamilnad via the Palakkad Gap, and, amazingly after some 500 years, they still speak Tamil at home and amongst themselves, and Malayalam, the official language of the state of Kerala only when they need to. Malayalees say that their accent is strange; and at the same time, natives of Tamilnad are amused by the way they speak Tamil! The Kerala Iyer website says that the Tamil of the Palakkad Iyers 'is corrupted [by Malayalam influences] to the extent of 20%', and that people from Tamilnad 'can instantly point out a Palakkad Iyer the moment he starts speaking' partly because 'a Palakkad Iyer prefixes most sentences with an 'Oh". Manga confirms this and says that her niece Mangalam in Mumbai is the greatest offender! Iyers also have their own particular cuisine - more about that later - and certain differences in dress: for example, Namboodiri women cannot wear rings in their noses, but Iyers think that a nose-ring or stud is very important, and the size and value of the stone is a good indication of the wealth of the wearer.

In spite of these peculiarities, Iyers do not appear to be regarded as outsiders in Kerala, and like other visitors over the ages - Jews, Christians and Muslims for example - seem to have been accepted and perhaps even welcomed. I don't imagine for a moment that they have been universally popular and this Malayalee proverb might be significant, although it is usually used in jest: '*Eli, panni, peruchazhy, Patta vanarum tatha evaraivarum illengil Malayalam mahotsavam*' ['If only the rat, monkey, bandicoot and Iyers were not there, Kerala would indeed be a beautiful place']. On the other hand, the Malayalees also say: '*Pattaril pottanilla*' ['there are no fools among the Iyers'] and '*Onnum kanatha Pattar kinattil chadilla*' ['the Kerala Iyer will not jump into the well without first taking aim'] - look before you leap I suppose.

But it is the Namboodiris who are central to the Kerala creation story.

CHAPTER THREE

PARASURAMA: KERALA'S STORY BEGINS

'If you practice, you can carry an elephant' - Malayalam proverb

'The religion of Hinduism teaches that whenever humanity is threatened by extreme disorder and wickedness, Vishnu will descend into the world as an avatar to restore righteousness' - New World Encyclopedia

According to legend it was the god Parasurama who created the land of Kerala. And it was he too who decided that the Namboodiri Brahmins should rule over it.

This is what is written in the *Keralolpatti*, the book that tells all about the origins of the land and people of Kerala. The book is written in modern Malayalam and did not exist before the seventeenth century A.D., according to T.K.Gangadharan[6]. It is not therefore some ancient tome handed down through the centuries but a relatively recent piece of work that brings together many myths and fables about the creation story and subsequent events in this part of India. And it is rather choosy about which myths it repeats and how they are interpreted. In his 1887 manual of the Malabar district, William Logan says that the book is 'full of Brahmanical legends'[7], and Gangadharan agrees, maintaining that the only legends included in the work are those favourable to the 'upper sections of the society'[8]. It is not of course unusual for folk legends to be hijacked by ruling classes and twisted for their own ends - normally to legitimise their dominant position - and this certainly seems to be the case here. But even though we will not expect to learn much about the history of Kerala from the Parasurama legend, it is a good tale and deserves to be repeated here. This is one of several similar versions.

Parasurama is the sixth avatar [incarnation] of the Lord Vishnu. He was born to Renuka, wife of a devout Brahmin, whose destiny was to have a son who, although a Brahmin, would become a warrior[i]

---

[i] The dharma of the Brahmin caste is of course to be a priest or holy man.

and so it proved. Rama, as the boy was named, was really the great God Vishnu, come down to earth to fulfil a promise to rid the world of the murderous Kshatriya[ii] king, Kartavirya Arjuna. As a child, Rama showed much interest in weapons and physical exercise; but on reaching manhood, he felt the need of a more spiritual aspect to his life, and retreated to the mountains to meditate and gain the favour of Lord Shiva. Impressed by his asceticism, Shiva gave Rama a mighty axe named Parasu, with which he would be able to defeat any warrior on earth. And from that day, our hero became known as Parasu-rama. Returning to his family ashram, the young man was met with a strange order. '*You must kill your mother - she has sinned*', cried his father.

What happened next reads rather oddly to anyone from the western tradition: Parasurama obeyed his father without hesitation. This imperative always to trust and respect one's father runs deeply in India. So to many Indians it will not be surprising that Parasurama acted as he did. But even though he had done his duty by obeying his father, according to some interpretations, Parasurama still had to pay a penance, since everyone knows it is wrong to kill one's mother. And his penance was to make war on the Kshatriyas. I think I prefer the version where his father granted Parasurama a boon as a reward for filial obedience and that Parasurama successfully pleaded for his mother to be brought back from the dead, and for he himself to be given everlasting life. In any event, Parasurama now began a war against Arjuna, during which his father was killed by the sons of the evil king. As Parasurama cremated the body, he swore that he would not rest until the entire race of Kshatriyas was exterminated.

He first killed Arjuna's sons and continued till all that generation of Kshatriyas was obliterated.[iii] At length he was persuaded to stop, and he gave all his lands and wealth to the Brahmins and went into the mountains to offer penance for the blood he had shed. Then Varuna, god of the seas, took pity on the penitent and decided to grant him some land on which he could make his home. The extent of this land was to be determined by the distance

---

[ii] The kshatriyas are the warrior caste

[iii] Interestingly, the Kshatriya caste, though common in the rest of India, has not existed in Kerala in modern times

Parasurama was able to throw the holy axe. The great warrior threw his weapon from Kanniya Kumari, past the Cardamom Hills and Periyar Lake, and over the Nilgiri Mountains, all the way to Gokarnam, 250 kilometres north of Mangalore. All the land beneath the flight of the axe rose out of the sea and became a flat coastal plain.

And the land of Kerala rose out of the ocean

Geologists provide a somewhat more prosaic explanation. Kerala, they say, was probably created by submarine geological movements which caused the sea-bed off the south-west coast to rise and this, together with the silt brought down by the rivers of the Western Ghats, formed the new coastal plain. But the story in the *Keralolpatti* does sound like a picturesque way of saying what happened.

The *Keralolpatti* goes on to say that under Parasurama, Brahmins played a dominant role in the regulation of the new country. Parasurama brought a poor Brahmin and his family to live in the new land, and named it 'Kerala' after the god Indra's grandson. Some say that these first Brahmins fled from the country for fear of the many serpents that were there and that when they were replaced by a new, presumably less fearful group, the serpents were made their household gods in order that this should not happen again. These Brahmins were Namboodiris and were located in 64 villages, most of which can still be identified.

Parasurama's country

According to the *Keralolpatti*, the goddess Durga became the guardian of the seashore, and the god Sastha guarded the foothills. Sastha, who is also called Ayyappan, and Durga are still very important Gods in Kerala. In the person of Lord Ayyappan are combined the powers of Lord Vishnu, the protector, who maintains the universe, and those of Lord Shiva, the creator and destroyer. The story of Ayyappan is included in ancient texts called the Puranas, and is designed to symbolise these characteristics. Durga is the universal mother goddess [Devi] in her fearsome form - the multi-armed killer of demons and destroyer of evil.

The most famous shrine to Ayyappan is Sabarimala, high up in the mountains of Kerala. Not only Vaishnavites and Shaivites[iv] are welcome, but also members of other religions, so Sabarimala is very special as a symbol of unity in a state where inter-communal troubles have been mercifully rare. All pilgrims dress in

---

[iv] Worshippers of Vishnu and Shiva, the two most important members of the Hindu Trinity.

black and travel in huge numbers towards the temple especially during the month of March. Manga went there twice with her father. She could only make this pilgrimage when she was very young because women of childbearing age are not allowed to visit the shrine. There is some uncertainty as to why this is. One possibility is that the true devotees have taken a vow of chastity and would be tested too greatly if they were to be exposed to temptation. But other suggestions are that it would be difficult for menstruating women to keep 'purity of body' on the pilgrimage; also that the restrictions on women were imposed for 'security reasons' given the dangerous nature of the trek.

The pilgrimage at the time of Manga's adventures did indeed involve a perilous journey. From Arumeli where the pilgrimage proper began to the temple was a distance of 64 miles to be covered on foot. Much of the way was through virgin jungle with nowhere to take shelter or buy provisions. On most nights, the pilgrims had to make do with a primitive tent made of bamboos and palm fronds, and cook and eat what they had brought with them. Worse than that, the jungle was full of wild animals in those days, and Manga remembers trying hard to be brave as she lay and listened to the sounds of the forest. The night was full of rustlings, and squeakings, and growlings and slitherings - and once Manga heard the roar of a tiger hunting in the distance. Often there were signs of elephants nearby: broken branches, flattened grass and damaged bark on trees chosen as scratching posts, and above all a strong rank odour. Wild elephants may be benign creatures, but they are nonetheless capable of trampling down your camp at night-time and are best avoided if you are on foot. Then there were monkeys - quite threatening in a pack - snakes [though Manga's family does not fear them: they have a pact with the snake kingdom stretching back for several generations] and all manner of creeping and crawling creatures. Manga remembers the leeches as the greatest menace. There were hundreds of them especially in marshy places and they clung to your skin, sucked your blood and then dropped off. If there were enough of them they could seriously weaken you and anyway made you scratch which could lead to sores.

The pilgrims carried their possessions in a palikettu - something like a long pillowcase, carried on the head. There were three compartments - one for food [rice, lentils and salt], another for a few small pots and pans, and a third for a towel, soap and a spare lungi. The pilgrims could only walk for about seven or eight miles a day because they were travelling over tough terrain and at times there were steep slopes to negotiate. Manga remembers particularly the section up Kali Mala, climbing over slippery roots in pouring rain, where she slipped back one step for every two forward. Once she had a fever and was urged on by a friend of her father, who used to eat at the house. '*Ayyappan saranam wa*!' he called out, '*Come on, Ayyappan will help you*!' Manga was given a new lease of life and struggled on.

Before you get to Ayyappan's shrine, you come to a peepal tree into which new pilgrims must stick an arrow. This is because there was once a beautiful woman called Malikappurat who wanted to marry Ayyappan. Ayyappan of course had taken a vow of celibacy, but he did not want to be so impolite as to refuse the lady. He therefore said that he would marry her in the year that no new pilgrims visited his shrine. So every year, Malikappurat [or her image at least] is carried in procession to examine the peepal tree. And every year she finds more arrows stuck into it and therefore she cannot marry, and is taken back into her own temple for another year of unrequited love.

Next, pilgrims come to a shrine to Vava, a Muslim who was a friend to Ayyappan; together they defended Kerala against its enemies. And visitors of all castes and religions will pay homage to Vava. Other religions are involved too: some believe that Ayyappan is an incarnation of Buddha; and the Christian church of St Andrew in Alleppey[v] welcomes the Sabarimala pilgrims as they return from their journey.

Sabarimala is now one of the most-visited religious centres in the world. Estimates vary, but all state that the number of Pilgrims who visit each year is in excess of 100,000,000. It is of course much easier to get to than it was sixty years ago.

There's a metalled road all the way to the town of Pamba, and a 'dolly service'[vi] from there to the temple itself for anyone who can't

---

[v] The modern name of this port is Alappuzha. It is from here that we take a boat to sail on the backwaters.

[vi] A sort of sedan chair

manage to climb the last hill. Nonetheless, the guide refers to two cardiology centres in the vicinity in case of need!

Parasurama also introduced into his new domain schools for martial arts[vii] and brought in Sudras [the caste of manual labourers] to act as bodyguards for the Brahmins. He ordered that these people adopt succession through the mother and asked the Brahmins to do the same, though few did. Parasurama finally designed a system of government for the new lands, but after his departure, peace and justice could not be maintained, so the Brahmins called a meeting and decided that they needed a king. He would be chosen by the Brahmins and rule for twelve years only, before a successor was elected. This ruler or Perumal would have to agree to do only what it was beyond the power of the Brahmins themselves to do, in terms of the settlement of arguments or the protection of the country. So one can see how the story maintains the primacy of the Brahmins in society - the kings are in a sense merely their servants. The first of these kings of Kerala was the Chera Perumal and at the same time, the *Keralolpatti* says there were two other Perumals in neighbouring areas, and they were the Chola Perumal and the Pandya Perumal.

Whilst the *Keralolpatti* may have some basis in history - there were indeed three great kingdoms in the south, and the Cheras, the Pandyas of Madurai and the Cholas of Kanchipuram fought one another over many centuries - the chronology of events is extremely dubious. An example is given by Gangadharan of one Perumal who was supposed to have arrived in Kerala in 428 AD.[9]

Elsewhere he is said to have visited Mecca over 70 years earlier. And to confuse the issue still further, the *Keralolpatti* talks of his meeting the prophet Mohammed while he was there [in 355]. Mohammed however lived in the 7th century! For what it is worth, however, the book gives 216 AD as the date for the beginning of Chera Perumal's reign[viii] In all, the Namboodiris are said to have chosen twenty-five Perumals [including Keralan, another candidate for patronymity of the state], the last of whom, Cheraman,

---

[vii] This would be kalaripayattu, said to be the original martial art, from which judo etc originated

[viii] The first and second Chera Empires are referred to by some historians as the Ages of the Perumals.

converted to Islam and went on a pilgrimage to Mecca. The country then divided into many small princedoms, the leaders of one of which, the Maharajas of Travancore, right up to their demise after Independence, maintained that they held office only temporarily 'until the Perumal returned from Mecca'.[10]

And that, according to myth and legend, is what happened in Kerala's early days.

CHAPTER FOUR

EARLY SETTLERS

'Thus she [Circe] lived on the island of Aeaea, and thus she has in India. Men have stood at her gate, and called to be admitted, and to all she has opened her shining doors. She has taken them in, given them seats and served food. But with the food she has mixed drugs which make them forget their country...' Nirad C. Chaudhuri, *The Continent of Circe*

'When one flying fox visits another, they sit on different branches.' Malayalam proverb

Ancient man [well, in this story, woman actually] first started on the journey out of mankind's birthplace and into the wider world about 60,000 years ago. And that first woman was Manga's ancestor! I know that that's true because we sent a sample of Manga's DNA to the National Geographic Genographic Project and found out that she belongs to a particular branch of humanity called Haplogroup M*. A gene carried by this group is passed from mother to daughter, and so Manga's female ancestors can be traced right back to the origins of modern humans in East Africa 200,000 years ago. And the exciting thing is that the M*s were believed to be the first people to leave Africa and start exploring the world! They crossed into Asia at Bab el Mandeb, between the Red Sea and the Gulf of Aden, where the sea was at its narrowest. In *The Incredible Human Journey*, Alice Roberts reckons that the strait would have been only 11km wide during the glacial period between 59,000 and 74,000 years ago, and so quite easily crossed especially as the water was very shallow too. Also the climate at that time was congenial to wandering humans, and Roberts argues that there would have been what amounted to a long oasis along the Arabian coast.[11] Manga's ancestors would, by this account, have travelled this route to the Persian Gulf and made another sea crossing at the Strait of Hormuz and so entered India. Then it seems as though the M*s left the coast. Routes can be plotted heading north to the Caspian Sea, with others following the River Indus, and the Ganges Valley and eventually reaching Bangladesh, Burma, Malaysia, Indonesia and Australia. The earliest members of

Manga's line might well have settled down in the Indus Valley, or by the shores of the Caspian Sea.

'India's long surf-beaten shore..[at]..Cape Comorin' [Kanniya Kumari]

On the basis of this theory of human migration, Manga's ancestors were not then a part of the group that Michael Wood describes in *The Story of India.* He tracks the journey made by people leaving Africa, and 'making their way barefoot down India's long, surf-beaten shore, driven as human beings have always been by chance and necessity... and surely by curiosity, that most human of qualities. In a few thousand years they skirted the Indian Ocean from the Horn of Africa to Cape Comorin.'[12] These people would have been the first to arrive in Kerala. There is genetic but not much archaeological evidence that I can find of these 'barefooted beachcombers'; Spencer Wells[13] suggests that this might be because rising sea-levels have hidden any signs of their presence. Or perhaps what little archaeological exploration there has been in Kerala has been in the wrong places. And then again things do not endure in Kerala. Nature throws down much of what man raises - persistent rain rots wooden temples however beautifully they might be carved, and however cunningly wrought. And metal and stone were not an option for builders on the Malabar coast.

There are other theories about how the first inhabitants of Kerala arrived there - that they came direct from Africa by sea for example - but of course we may never know which of the many stories best describes the incredible migration of early Homo Sapiens and there will always be just enough evidence to support the one whilst defeating the other. What is known is that by the fourth century BC the South Western coastal strip of India was home to people called the Cheras, because the empire of Ashoka Maurya traded with them and their rivals for domination of the south, the Cholas and the Pandyas, and they are mentioned in one of the great Emperor's rock-cut edicts. We shall have to wait to see if the theories of exactly how they arrived endure any better than the early artefacts that are now lost to time.

There are still today people living primitive lifestyles in Kerala and it seems reasonable to assume that they are the descendants of the earliest inhabitants. Known as the Adivasis,[i] or Tribespeople, some groups still live in separate villages in the most remote hills and forests of the region.

There has been a great deal of archeological investigation in the last few years around a group of caves at Edakkal near the town of Sultan's Battery in the north of Kerala where many of the Adivasi villages can be found. These caves and their wall paintings, possibly dating from about 5000 BC, were first discovered by the outside world when Fred Fawcett, a senior police officer and amateur archaeologist came across them in the 1890s, but they have not been extensively investigated until recently.[14] It may well be that we learn more about the history of the Adivasis from this source, and when it was that they first settled in the area. If this were to show that there was a delay in human habitation in Kerala it could have been due to its thick forests and protective mountain ranges: Ramachand Nair suggested in the 1986 *Kerala State Gazetteer*, that as long as the Deccan offered a sufficient area of easily cultivated parklands, there was little reason for people to be attracted to the jungles and wild beasts of Malabar.[15]

Again, one can only speculate about whence later immigrants came. One line will take us back north to the Indus Valley, where some of Manga's very earliest ancestors might have settled when they first entered India. Around 3000 to 1700 BC, before people made any sort of mark in Kerala, a great civilisation was flourishing in the Indus Valley and beyond in what is now Pakistan and Northwest India. The major centres and the first to

---

[i] On our visit to the Silent Valley, a protected area in the Nilgiri hills, in 2008, Adivasi villagers sold us honey they had collected from wild bees

be discovered, in the 1920s, were Mohenjo-Daro and Harappa but later finds showed that the Harappan 'empire' stretched from Jammu in the north to Gujarat, and Rajasthan. The empire's cities seem to have been carefully planned and the culture as advanced as that of the Egyptian and Sumerian nations, with which it was contemporary. There is some evidence that the Harappans traded with their better-known neighbours from the west.[16]

This is important to our particular investigations because some historians, especially South Indians, state confidently that the Harappans were ancestors of the Dravidians, and that they allegedly withdrew from their cities when the warlike Aryans invaded in the second millennium BC, and settled in the modern states of Karnataka, Andhra, Tamilnad and Kerala. Michael Wood is among the historians who support this theory, stating that the ancient language of Iran, Elamite, is 'cognate with' Dravidian languages.[17] Wood maintains that it has yet to be proved that the Harappans' language was a form of Dravidian, but the fact that a forerunner of the language is still spoken in Baluchistan, and evidence that the same language was once current in Gujarat and Maharashtra, makes it almost certain in his view that there was some form of migration from the north to the south.[18] There have, however, been no findings of Harappan-type cities being built further south. Incidentally the modern view is that the Harappans were not defeated in battle but that their culture collapsed as a result of climate change and the drying up of the water sources on which they depended.[19]

Having mentioned the 'warlike Aryans', we now need to deal with that thorny subject. First of all, we are not, of course, talking about Hitler's mythical 'master-race'. 'Aryan' was a descriptive term used to describe a people who were thought to have originated somewhere north of India. Manga and her family always believed that they were descended from Aryans and for a long time the Aryan invasion of India was an accepted fact of history. But few if any historians now espouse the invasion theory. An alternative view is that the Aryans entered northern India as travellers, explorers or refugees, rather than pouring out of central Asia as an all-conquering army, and forcing the existing inhabitants, thought of as darker-skinned and inferior, into slavery, or driving them to retreat to the south. One can imagine that Victorian Europeans liked and fostered the invasion theory because they wanted to believe that a dominant Caucasian master race was the source of all that was good in India's civilisation. Some [Indian] scholars interpret the Vedic hymns[ii] as supporting this hypothesis too. But others say that more recent translations, while certainly describing the 'Aryans' as warlike and all-conquering, do not even suggest that they came from outside India.

But not only is there no evidence of an Aryan invasion, but there is little evidence of any large-scale migration either, and indeed the very existence of Aryans is doubted. Romila Thapar wrote some time ago in the *Penguin History of India* that 'it is doubtful whether the word 'arya' was ever used in any ethnic sense',[20] but was merely an adjective describing a superior person, and further study in particular by the American anthropologist Kenneth Kennedy has produced no clear evidence of 'an Aryan biological or demographic entity'.[21] So it is not only prehistory that is the cause of speculation and confusion, but the truth about later settlements, movements and motives proves equally elusive.

Of course no one is denying that things changed in northern India at this time. But the argument is that it wasn't the aggressive movement of peoples that caused these changes, but the movement of ideas and customs. It is through this much more complex web of social interactions that change occurred. No doubt people did migrate, especially if the climate changed and their homeland became tough to live in, as does seem to have happened at this time. Maybe the movement of people was gradual and piecemeal; one can imagine the most adventurous families upping roots first, while some conservative die-hards stayed where they'd always lived until the bitter end - hoping all the time that things would get better. And you'd expect a bit of fighting too as newcomers claimed land on which to graze their herds, and that might have felt like an invasion in some cases, especially if the losing side wrote the history.

Whatever story we opt for, one thing is certain: there will be much that we will never understand for all the scientific and archaeological information that we amass.

[ii] The earliest Hindu scriptures

But let us speculate that the development of a new culture following the disappearance of the Harappan cities could have been influenced by a number of tribes moving south through the Khyber Pass from Central Asia. It is possible that the same climatic event that brought about the end of the Indus Valley civilisation - the result of a major El Nino event around 2000BC leading to a catastrophic drought[22] - caused some movement of peoples: it would be surprising if it didn't. And some groups could have found their way into India. Michael Wood argues that the homeland of these wanderers could well be Turkmenistan, on the eastern banks of the Caspian Sea. This is where some of Manga's early ancestors may have settled according to the Genographic survey. Wood points out that remains of a society have been found there with similarities to that of the Indian 'Aryans'. They didn't live in cities, were semi-nomadic, and had horses and wheeled vehicles such as chariots. They relied a lot on the cow for its milk, meat and skin, and didn't do arable farming. A further link was that they made a drink of a rare herb mixed with poppy seed and cannabis alleged to be related to 'soma', which according to the Vedas was drunk by the Aryan gods - and which was memorably sampled on television by Michael Wood![23]

So a new culture was developing on the Ganges plain, perhaps influenced by Manga's ancestors. It seems to have remained nomadic for a while, the population living in tented villages and keeping livestock. In the tradition of 'the continent of Circe' the migrants soon fell into the ways of the indigenous population, and ideas and lifestyles began to merge. In due course settled agriculture developed and people began to live in villages, which formed alliances for security and appointed kings as rulers. At first it seems that tribal assemblies kept the kings' powers in check but before long kings were regarded as having divine powers, a move fostered by the priests. From then on, priests and kings would become increasingly symbiotic. And the priests - or Brahmins - are the caste to which Manga and her family belong, so we can imagine their ancestors living a pretty good life in the corridors of power of the kingdoms of northern India.

The religion practised by the followers of this culture was based on sacred texts - the Vedas, Puranas and Upanishads - and two great epic stories, the *Mahabaratha* and the *Ramayana*. These texts were not brought down from Mount Sinai [or anywhere else] written on tablets of stone. On the contrary, they were part of an oral tradition, which developed over thousands of years into great written literature. When it was first discovered by the British in the eighteenth century, the *Geeta* [part of the *Mahabaratha*] was described by Warren Hastings, Governor General 1773-85, as 'a performance of great originality, of a sublimity of conception, reasoning and diction almost unequalled...' and he gave his opinion that the *Mahabharata* was as good a piece of literature as *The Iliad* and *The Odyssey*, and the works of Milton.[24] The Vedas are the oldest of the texts: it is said that the Rig-Veda was sung as far back as 3000 BC. They are hymns and incantations that only the learned priests, the Brahmins, knew and could recite. The Upanishads 'are the scriptures par excellence of Hinduism,' containing the most important philosophies of the religion,[25] whilst the Puranas were designed to be a more accessible way into Hinduism, 'popular traditional texts (often legends)' contributing 'to the formation of a moral code of conduct.'[26]

The Vedas are the texts that tell tales of war-like men and Gods. These Gods were a bit like those of the Romans and Greeks and were closely connected with natural phenomena. Sacrifices were at the heart of religion and 'Ideas like asceticism and renunciation', which are so important to later Hinduism, 'would have horrified them'[27] .The Vedic gods included Indra who rode on an elephant and who was armed with thunderbolts; Agni, the God of Fire; Rudra, who controlled the storms; Surya, the Sun God, and Varuna, who was associated with the moon. In the later Upanishads the members of the Hindu trinity grew in importance. These were the great gods Vishnu, Brahma and Shiva, none of whom figure much in the Vedas. Brahma was the creator, Vishnu the protector and Shiva the destroyer. Later still, Brahma's importance declined and Shiva was regarded as creator and destroyer.

The *Mahabharata* and *Ramayana* probably date from around 800-400 BC, well after the Vedas. The *Mahabharata* is a huge book,[iii] something like two million words long, and equates with the period in history when the people of the north were living in settlements if not cities and were no longer nomadic. It tells the

---

[iii] 'The Hindus have a great number of epic poems. The two most celebrated are the *Ramayana* and the *Mahabharata*. Both are of inordinate length.' The Abbe Dubois *Hindu Manners, Customs and Ceremonies.*

story of a struggle for power in the ancient kingdom of Hastinapura between two branches of its ruling family, the Kauravas under Duryodhana and the Pandavas, led by Yudhisthira. The most memorable parts are the five Pandava brothers' winning of the hand of the princess Draupadi, who becomes the wife of them all; the dice game, won by the Kauravas by cheating, and their attempt, foiled by Krishna, to humiliate the Pandavas by undressing Draupadi in public; the Pandavas' 13 years in exile; the *Bhagavad Geeta*, in which Krishna explains to Arjuna where his duty lies; the great battle of Kurukshetra, won by the Pandavas; the death of Krishna and the beginning of the amoral Age of Kali, the age in which we are still living today.

Actors portraying Rama and Hanuman

The *Ramayana* is the story of a great and good king Rama of Ayodhya, loved by his subjects, who accepts being sent into exile; of his life in the forest; of the capture of his virtuous queen Sita by the evil king of Ceylon, Ravana; of his meeting with another avatar of God, Hanuman, and of their attack on Ceylon, and Rama's ultimate victory. And unlike the *Mahabharata,* it has a happy and optimistic conclusion.[iv] But the details of the stories are of course of less importance than their messages. In fact, they teach many things, spiritual and practical: that God descends to earth in human form whenever it is necessary for example. In the *Mahabharata*, the Lord comes to earth as Krishna; in the *Ramayana*, he is Rama.

Image of the Hindu gods, Shiva, Parvathy, Ganesh and Muragan.

Both avatars are 'human' in that they make mistakes from time to time, but they are generally examples of men who live by the highest moral code. Indeed, all the 'good' characters in the books teach us how we should live. They tell us about karma - cause and effect - that good deeds will be rewarded by God; and dharma, one's duty, basically to uphold the law, to worship god in the proper way, to behave ethically. It's all-embracing - I entered 'what

[iv] On a lighter note: 'the *Mahabharatha* – a tale of cousins cheating each other… uncles killing nephews, an eldest son gambling his wife…into slavery – portrays families as they really are. The *Ramayana* shows a family as it *ought* to be'. Jonah Blank, p.307 - see endnotes for full reference.

does the *Mahabharata* teach us' into Google. The answers included: 'to accept a flawed universe'; 'the merit and vice of meat-eating'; 'what the goal of one's life should be'; 'ignoring good advice can be harmful and destructive'; 'about project management'; 'the need for a strong spiritual will'; 'follow what our elders say'; 'the importance of choosing strong allies in wartime'; 'families can do anything with unity'; 'about Indian culture'. So, just about everything really. And the *Ramayana*, says Jonah Blank is his book *Arrow of the Blue-Skinned God*, 'is not some ossified legend, it is a guidebook of life' teaching the value of devotion, duty, and relationships.[28] Incidentally, the *Ramayana* is probably the more popular story in Kerala. The *Mahabharata* takes place exclusively in the north, whereas Rama's adventures take him down to the south, all the way to Sri Lanka. And there is even a *Mappila Ramayana* - songs derived from the story sung by the Muslims of Kerala - though Rama is there portrayed as a Sultan.

CHAPTER FIVE

TEMPLE LIFE

'A door is a morsel to him who devours a temple.' Malayalam proverb

'Unique temples, built like domestic houses.' Mulk Raj Anand

The Siva temple at Trikkandiyur

Of all Parasurama's miracles, the most relevant to us is the founding of the temple at Trikkandiyur. This temple was central to the life of Manga and her family, and Manga remembers her mum having to wake her up early in the morning to go to the temple before school. This happened every weekday.

'Mangalakutty - azhuntherai! [time to get up]', she would call. 'Palle techu va; capi kondu varam.' Mum was telling me to go and clean my teeth; she would make my coffee. And again 'Mangalakutty, you must wake up now or you won't get to the temple in time!' In spite of my tardiness, Mum would never get angry with me. I was tiny and thin and often sick and they didn't think that I would survive

childhood. Do you know they never bothered to get a proper horoscope for me? That's because when I was a baby the astrologer said that he couldn't see any future for me beyond the age of nine, and who would bother to pay for a full horoscope for a girl who would not live long enough to get married? Six of my brothers and sisters died before they were any age at all, and nobody thought that I looked any stronger than they had. But Mum did think there was something special about me. I had a very fair complexion and I always showed lots of fight when I was ill. And I was very loving, even clinging. I would sleep with my Mum and cuddle up to her and I hated to be parted from her. When she had her periods, she had to sleep outside the house as was the custom and I would cry so much! Mum told me all the old stories of gods and demons and the heroes of Kerala, and I loved to go to the temple where they told these stories too. They had a professional storyteller in our temple at festival times and he would act out the tales and make us laugh and cry.

So really I was happy to get up and get ready, and I would take the burned husk of paddy [umikkari] offered by Mum and wander off from the veranda where we slept, towards the cowshed at the back of the house, and sit on the wall of the byre, slowly rubbing my teeth with it and calling to our cow. Sometimes we'd clean our teeth with a twig from a neem tree, and sometimes with ripe mango leaves, which we chewed first. Umikari was my favourite though. 'Don't be too long Manga. I'm making your coffee and your sisters are ready to go'. So I'd wander back to the house, where my beaker of coffee would be waiting on top of the stove. We cooked on a wood-burning stove and I loved the smell of the wood smoke though it did make my eyes smart. Then I had to have a bath. We always had to bath, and to put on our best clothes, before going to the temple.

In those days, our bathroom didn't have a roof or anything - it was open to the skies. The walls were palm fronds that were just to provide privacy, and new ones had to be put up every year. There were no taps of course and the bath water came in a bucket filled from the well. We dipped a tin cup into the bucket and poured the water over our heads. We never took all our clothes off, so we would still be wet when we left the house to walk to the temple. I would hold Mum's hand tightly and we'd go along the garden path, into the alleyway alongside our house and on to the road which led to the temple.'

The main road through Trikkandiyur was wide enough but unmade. It was not designed for cars and had no need to be: no cars ever came into the village. In fact Manga can't even remember seeing a car in Tirur, the nearest town, when she was little. There were no bicycles either, and for the most part if you wanted to go anywhere, you walked. Bullock carts rattled and rolled to and from the town and for the better-off there were rickshaws, the original ones, pulled most often by thin-legged, barefoot men dressed in shorts and ragged shirts. Manga never liked to use these rickshaws. She remembers a daughter of one of the local lawyers - a very fat young woman - being pulled by a particularly thin man; it just didn't seem fair. There were no cycle rickshaws in those days, and of course no putt-putts as we call them - also known as tuk-tuks [from the noise they make], auto rickshaws or scooter-taxis. Manga remembers first seeing them in north India in 1960 or thereabouts. Now they litter the roads of every town and city in the country including Tirur and its suburbs. But one shouldn't deride putt-putts. They are small and cheap to buy and run, providing opportunities for small-scale entrepreneurs to make a living. At least two of our relations owned and drove putt-putts: one of Atimbear's great-nephews in Coimbatore, and Shanta's brother-in-law in Mumbai. They are also on the way to being eco-friendly. Though their two-stroke engines belch exhaust fumes it would be much worse if they were replaced by taxis. Autos do over 80 mpg, compared with perhaps 20mpg for a car in heavy traffic. Furthermore, quite a few autos have been converted to run on LPG or CNG,[i] much cleaner fuels. Though as the 21st century progresses and more and more people can afford to buy cars, India's cities are becoming congested to an alarming degree. Perhaps the best we can say after all is that the putt-putt delayed this curse of modern urban life.

Manga, her Mum and sisters walked down the dusty track towards the temple. Turning right as they came out of the alley, they passed a tailor's shop on the corner, owned by a family friend called Appuni. Appuni's nephew kept the shop opposite - also a tailor's. Alongside Appuni's nephew there was a general store and a goldsmith's. Further along the road towards the temple was yet a third tailor. After that came houses: large, comfortable buildings,

---

[i] Compressed Natural Gas

set back from the road, with gardens, all owned and occupied by Iyer Brahmins in those days. The road was narrow here and, lined with trees and with flowers climbing over the garden walls, had a very rural feel. There were lots of butterflies and moths feeding on the nectar as well as sunbirds - the Indian equivalent of hummingbirds. And in the evenings, bats, including some really big ones, would gather in the roadside trees. I'm afraid I don't know what sort of bats they would have been - the State Gazetteer lists ten types of bat in Kerala[29] - but Manga used to find them rather spooky as they flitted silent as shadows across the darkening sky.

But now it was getting lighter as the party reached the temple after a ten-minute walk. The western tank [the temple's main pool] was already busy with people washing their clothes, bathing or swimming. In spite of all this activity, the waters were clear, and very deep. Nobody knew how deep or exactly what lay on the bottom, but on one scary day, Manga, when still very small, was swimming there when she looked down and saw...a large crocodile. Fortunately, it didn't see her, or wasn't interested; perhaps it had eaten already that day. Anyway it ignored the frightened little girl doing her best to escape with a frantic dog paddle. When Manga returned home to tell the tale of her adventure to her Mum, she only got a sharp slap for her pains, and an instruction never to swim in the tank again without her sisters! It wasn't long incidentally before many Brahmins, including Manga's Mum, stopped bathing in the tank. This was not because of crocodiles. I regret to say it was because dalits [untouchables] had been allowed to use the tank by the Temple Proclamations Act of 1947. The temple has another tank that the family sometimes used. It has a sort of shed built out over the water so that women of the Moussad caste could bathe there unseen. I use the past tense because as far as we know, the Moussads [a branch of Brahmins] don't follow this practice any longer. The Moussad women also used to carry umbrellas when they went out, so they could hide their faces if they met a stranger. One of Manga's friends comes from this caste, and she had a relation who built a house higher than the temple roof. The story goes that ever since he committed this sacrilege, he suffered terribly from verrucas!

The family passed through the gate and on into the temple. Though famous for its mythical founder, the temple building was not especially imposing. It measured about 95 feet square with a tiled srikovil - that's the centre of the temple, the sanctum sanctorum, where the idols are - but in those days only a thatched nalambalam [the cloistered building surrounding the srikovil]. The temple was constructed during what is called the 'early phase' of built temples [as opposed those carved out of rock], around the tenth century AD. The material used was laterite blocks, and the floor plan was apsidal in shape, that is, shaped like an apse or arch. Both the outer walls and inner sanctum are apsidal with their entrances on the 'base' of the 'arch'. This shape is unusual: most Kerala temples of this period are square or circular in plan. The tanks at the Trikkandiyur Temple are considered by many to be the temple's most notable feature, being particularly large and well-built. And another point of interest is that elephants are never seen there, even in processions to mark important feast days. This is because Parasurama and Ganapathi or Ganesh [the elephant-headed god] are said to have had an argument.[ii] There is though a statue of Ganapathi in the temple, so perhaps the argument was not too bitter!

Manga continues her description of the family's daily routine.

'We stood in the temple and watched as the priests closed the doors to the inner sanctum. Inside was the symbol of the god. The Trikkandiyur Temple is dedicated to Shiva[iii] so the sanctum contained a lingam, which stands for the god's creative power. The priests were Malayalee Brahmins from the Imbrathri caste and they wash the lingam every morning, cover it with sandalwood paste and decorate it with flowers. Well, you can't actually hang flowers from a lingam because of its shape, so instead the garlands are draped over beams just above it.'

You are supposed to circumambulate the srikovil, and you can do this either in the nalambalam or round the outer walls of the temple if the gates are not open. Except in Trikkandiyur you don't do a complete

---

[ii] Some say this was the argument during which Ganapati's tusk was broken as he guarded his parents' bedroom

[iii] Shiva is one of the three chief gods of the Hindu pantheon, the others being Brahma and Vishnu. The name is pronounced with a very soft 'sh' sound, so it's sometimes written 'Siva'. And the 'v' sounds more like a 'w'. Shiva is the god of creation and destruction. His body is covered with ashes and is therefore pictured as grey and he holds a trident in one of his four arms. Shiva's consort is Parvathi and his mount is Nandi, the bull.

circuit except outside: you go half way round, then back again. I don't know why. Then you pray. All the time one of the priests beats a small hand-held drum to tell you the idol is being washed and to prepare you for the opening of the shrine. Soon the priests open the doors and hand us flowers for our hair and put sandalwood on our foreheads and pour water into our hands, which we hold out like a cup. You drink a little and put the rest onto your head. The priest doesn't touch anyone, and only Brahmins have gifts actually handed to them: other castes have to take them from the floor where the priests leave them. These gifts are called prasadam and because the god has blessed them they're holy for us. If someone was offering special prayers, because it's their birthday perhaps, we might get payasam as well - sweets like rice pudding, yum. The husband of our neighbour Thangam was a Moussad, and made payasam for the temple; Thangam would do her best to make sure there was some kept for us.

The temple authorities in Trikkandiyur and all over Kerala had and indeed still have strict rules about behaviour in their holy buildings. Only in Kerala for example are non-Hindus prevented from entering temples at all. So I have never been inside our temple. The only exception of which I am aware is the temple at Trivandrum, into which it is possible for a European to enter if a fee is paid and a lungi donned. I've never felt that it's right to effectively pretend to be a Hindu, though. K.N.Pannikar writes that one can also be allowed in if one presents a certificate from a religious authority such as the Sri Ramakrishna Mission confirming that one is a 'serious student of Hinduism'. That sounds like a better policy.

For Hindus, it is essential to have a bath before going to say one's prayers, and to wear simple and clean clothes. Men should remove their shirts when they go into the Nalambalam, and must wear lungis or dhotis,[iv] not trousers. Women should wear saris and certainly not western dress. In some temples, notably

[iv] A lungi is a simple piece of cloth, about four feet wide and six feet long that is wrapped around the waist and reaches the ankles, though it can be folded to the knee. It is everyday wear for men. A dhoti in Kerala is worn in a similar fashion, but is normally made of finer cotton and often decorated with a border of zari [gold thread] and used on ceremonial occasions.

Guruvayur,[v] they cannot wear the salwar kurta[vi] either. When Manga was little, that wasn't an option anyway: this costume was unknown and unheard of until more northerners came into the state after independence. It was probably in the early fifties that a sardarji[vii] set up shop in Tirur, and began to offer salwar kurtas to a sceptical public. Now the wearing of salwar kurta is widespread, especially among the young.

So for Manga, every day started with a bath and prayers and a walk to the temple. Temples all over Kerala are, like ours, 'active centres of village life'. It's not just Brahmins who pray daily and support the temple and its priests financially and otherwise. It is now probably true to say that all sections of the Hindu community do this. But until quite recently [since the Temple Entry Act in 1947], the dalits - the untouchables - far from contributing to temple life, were not even allowed anywhere near any holy place.

Manga remembers this and other indignities imposed on the untouchable population; though I have to say that as a child she didn't see anything wrong in the way they were treated. To her young mind, it was just the way the world worked. It was natural to her that the family servant Cherumi, who was a sweeper, would not go near anyone in the family especially her father, and that neither she, nor the other servant, Kurumbai, could go into the house, nor draw water from the well.

Kurumbai was of a slightly higher caste than Cherumi. When Manga was ill - she particularly recalls having quinsy - Kurumbai would say a prayer and tie a black thread, with knots in it, round the little girl's neck. Attached to the thread there was a little silver tube containing a piece of paper, on which there was writing - Manga did not know what it said or what language it was in but it was supposed to drive away evil spirits. Kurumbai would also put ashes on Manga's head and forehead, while she sat cross-legged on the ground. If Kurumbai couldn't come, she would send her son-in-law, who also had the gift. Manga remembers him as small and

---

[v] One of the most important temples in Kerala, dedicated to Krishna.

[vi] A salwar kurta is cotton trousers and a long shirt for women. There are moves to end the ban on wearing this costume in some temples.

[vii] A Sikh. Members of this religion have set up shops all over India.

with a remarkably fair skin. And his brother would climb the coconut trees to collect the nuts for the family.

Harvesting coconuts

Manga and Kurumbai were good friends, but the only time they touched was when Manga was ill. At other times, if they brushed against each other accidentally, Manga would have to have a bath and have her clothes washed. But the family was good to Kurumbai. When she was getting old, Manga's parents employed Cherumi to help her. She would get four annas for sweeping the paths and collecting the cow dung from the byre and making dung pats for burning in the stove. Every year at Onam,[viii] Manga's mother gave Kurumbai a new dhoti, though she could scarcely afford it, and Manga and her brothers and sisters hardly ever

[viii] Kerala's most important Hindu festival

had new clothes. This does sound very paternalistic though in this case *pater* had the authority, but not the money.

Our helper pounding rice

Manga remembers also that the dhobi [washer man] wasn't allowed in the house and couldn't touch or be touched by any of the family. Not only that, but the clothes he washed had to be rinsed again and dried before they were worn. And the Parayas, members of the lowest caste, could not even come into the garden, and were not allowed to go anywhere near any Brahmin. They used to come to the gate and call out, and then go away, leaving a pot on the path. Manga's mother would fill the pot with food, herself retreat, and then the Paraya would collect it. The caste system in Kerala had far worse manifestations: some castes were not allowed to walk along public highways at all; there were rules as to how close a person was allowed to get to a Brahmin depending on his caste or sub-caste, and they could be beaten if they transgressed, and, during the Middle Ages, lower caste males might be put to death for even looking at a Brahmin woman. But I should say here that although Kerala before independence had the most complex, restrictive and cruel caste system, it is now probably one of the more caste-free states in India.

Kerala temples have a long history.[30] The earliest were cut from living rock around 700 AD. One of the best, near Kaviyur, is very similar to caves in Tamilnad, showing the influence of the Pandyas[ix] of Madurai on Kerala architecture in the eighth century. The majority of these cave temples are to be found in the south; in the northern part of Kerala the cave temples seem to have been influenced more by the Pallavas. Most of the temples are Saivist [i.e. dedicated to Shiva], the simpler ones consisting of a single room containing a lingam; but there is at least one dedicated to Vishnu.

The first great period of temple building was between 800 and 1000 A.D, during the second Chera Empire, when the Kulashekharas ruled. No intact temples remain from this period; in fact there are few really old structures of any kind in Kerala.

St George's Forane Church in Edappally

Candidates for the title of oldest might be the Padmanabhapuram Palace in Travancore and the Mattancherry Palace in Kochi, both

---

[ix] The Pandya dynasty lasted from the second century BC to the thirteenth century AD, battling for dominance of Tamilnadu with the Pallavas of Kanchipuram and the Cholas of Tanjore, and crossing swords too with the Cheras of Kerala.

dating from the sixteenth century. Most buildings were constructed mainly or entirely of wood and have either rotted away, burned down or at best been extensively and regularly repaired and renovated.[x] This is so different from the great monuments of Tamilnad - the temples in Tanjore, Mahabalipuram, Kanchipuram and above all the Meenakshi Temple of Madurai - that are made of granite and dominate the countryside for miles around, and have done so for many centuries, like the medieval cathedrals of Europe. So archaeologists can only date the earliest Kerala temples by reference to inscriptions, or sculptures, and in some cases by surviving stone basements, above which the existing temple was built. Original granite walls and foundations constructed in the ninth and tenth centuries can also be found in a number of temples still in use.

The Chettikulangara Temple is an example of how difficult it is to date Kerala's buildings. The temple's website says that the probable date of consecration is 823 AD but that the srikovil was re-built in 1540 and the adjacent chutambalam[xi] in 1827 after a fire; also that local chieftains added to or modified the structure from time to time. So very little if any of the original building is likely to be extant.

Templenet, the website devoted to Hindu religious buildings, says that Kerala temples find: '... expression in a mixed medium of stone, laterite, brick and wood; this...distinctive form of architecture lays stress on the sanctity, simplicity and a prevailing naturalism that mirrors the form of worship in these temples. This approach naturally leads to an old-world charm not seen elsewhere on the sub-continent.' To continue the comparison with Europe they are perhaps like non-conformist chapels rather than parish churches; part of the daily life of the people, not an awe-inspiring reminder of their insignificance. Mulk Raj Anand in[xii] *Splendours of*

---

[x] The same applies to Churches. We visited St. George's Forane Church in Edappally when we last stayed with my nephew Raju. I was intrigued by publicity that implied that some of the buildings dated from 1080 or even 594, but we were disappointed as they were obviously much more recent.

[xi] The chattambalam surrounds the srikovil, which houses the inner sanctum.

[xii] One of the great Indian novelists, the author of *Coolie* and *Untouchable*, books showing his concern for 'the creatures in the lower depths of Indian society who

Kerala wrote 'the fervorous imagination of passionate saints, poets, and people created a rich heritage of unique temples, built like domestic houses with ample courtyards and tiled conical roofs'.[31]

* * * * *

The *Archaeological Survey* talks of three phases of Kerala temple architecture. As we said, the Trikkandiyur Temple is an example of phase one structures. Most of these earlier temples are dedicated to Shiva or Vishnu or their avatars, such as Krishna, Rama, Parasurama or Vanama [the fifth avatar of Vishnu, involved in the story of the Kerala festival of Onam.]

The Temple dedicated to Vettakkrappammakan, son of Siva

There are rather small changes to the architecture of the middle phase, which lasted from 1000 to 1300 AD, when a 'spectacular growth' in temple building took place. The majority of Kerala temples that still exist were built in the third, late, phase between 1300 and 1800. The layout of the temples became more complicated in this era. Some temples began to be dedicated to more than one god and others temples had subsidiary shrines often outside the nalambalam. In the sixteenth and seventeenth centuries it became the fashion to build 'lofty enclosures, sculptured corridors, and ornate pillared halls',[32] untypical of Kerala temples in other generations.

---

were once men and women: the rejected who had no way to articulate their anguish against the oppressors'.

Anyone travelling in Kerala will be impressed by the vast number of temples, of all sorts and sizes, and dedicated to so many different deities. The most popular is the goddess Bhagawathi [whose forms include Devi, Durga, Parvathi, and Sastha], followed by Shiva [Mahadeva], Subramanya, Ayyapan, Rama and Krishna, to mention but a few. Trikkandiyur is an example of this profusion and variety. There are no fewer than five temples in the small village. One was until recently simply a grove of trees.

A Kavu

It has been believed for many centuries, long before the arrival of the Vedic pantheon and its successors, that gods and goddesses, divine or evil spirits and other objects of worship or fear or both, such as snakes [good if properly treated, evil if not], lived in such groves called kavu. Trees were venerated since the earliest times, especially the peepal tree, in which it was believed live the souls of the dead. And peepal[xiii] trees retain their importance today. According to K.N.Panikkar, 'not a single temple exists in Kerala which does not have an aswatha, a peepal, in its precincts.' The kavu near the road to Tirur is occupied by Devi,[xiv] the ancient mother goddess. From our house, we often hear the sound of explosions as firecrackers are let off at the kavu to propitiate the goddess. Then there is the Shiva temple that we have already described; a small temple dedicated to Krishna beside the tank - we have a photograph of our daughter Victoria praying there; and on the opposite side of the tank a walled but roofless shrine to Ayyappaswami.

And finally there is a shrine dedicated to the son of Lord Shiva as a hunter, where Manga's late cousin, her mother's brother's son, and his family came to pray annually in January. Happily the tradition continues even after Doraikutty's death.

[xiii] Ficus religiosa, the 'religious fig' aka bodhi [after Buddha, who achieved enlightenment after meditating under such a tree] or banyan, and many other aliases.

[xiv] Devi can be represented as later goddesses such as Lakshmi, Parvathi, Saraswati, Kali etc.

CHAPTER SIX

SPICY TALES

'How can it be a procession if there is no elephant?' Malayalam proverb

'Awake, O north wind; and come thou south; blow upon my garden, that the spices thereof may flow out...' The Bible, *Song of Solomon*

Bags of spice

In the past, historians often complained there was no useful evidence at all to help them unravel not only the history of Kerala but also that of India as a whole. John Keay, author of many books about the East says: 'Histories of India frequently begin with a gripe about the poverty of available resources'[33] and quotes as an example Prof. R.C.Majumdar who wrote, 'Prior to the thirteenth century AD, we possess no historical text of any kind.'[34] And William Logan wrote 'The Malayalee race has produced no historians simply because there is no history to record'![35] Keay reveals that there is plenty of history and plenty of evidence too, albeit not in documents but in 'less articulate objects like coins and charters...random inscriptions, titbits of oral tradition, literary compositions and religious texts...rocks and runes, bricks and rubrics'.[36] Nonetheless, there do seem to be more gaps and uncertainties in the story of Kerala than in other parts of India.

One period that has left us relative riches as far as sources are concerned is the time when the Romans came to Kerala in search of spices. This chapter tells of the time when the strip of land at the south west corner of India progressed to fame and fortune, and when the name of Kerala conjured up images of the exotic and wealthy Orient across the world. And our spicy tale starts in the little mountain village of Kumily.

Kumily is a village high in the Cardamom Hills in the south of Kerala. It is now a bustling holiday resort, full of hotels: expensive and very expensive ones like the Taj Group's 'tribal village'; cheap and cheerful 'budget' rooms; and a new concept to me, 'home stays' where one boards in a family home. I wonder if we, or more properly my sister Rosemary and her husband Tony, can claim any slight credit for the development of this idea in Kerala? While we were all staying at home in Trikkandiyur in the 1990s, a couple of prominent local citizens dropped in. When they heard that my sister and her husband were doctors, they occupied themselves mostly with chatting to them and might therefore have missed out rather on the family dynamic as it were. The result was a letter in the local press explaining how these two intrepid travellers were spending their holiday with an ordinary family in order to discover how real Indians lived. Surely this was how tourism in Kerala should develop, the writers proposed. The rest of us by the way were friends who were travelling with Dr. and Mrs. Birmingham.

Kumily is a typical resort really. We've mentioned the holiday accommodation; there are also numerous tourist agencies offering trips to tea plantations, elephant sanctuaries, and the wildlife park [Periyar]; and all the facilities that the modern traveller requires. But Kumily was very different when Manga and I first passed through in the 1960s. There weren't many tourists about then, and those there were stayed in the Rest House near the Lake. Kumily was more into trade in those days. Rows of dusty stores, with dilapidated lorries and bullock carts parked outside; sacks being loaded; spice powder everywhere, and spicy smells in the air; small groups of men exchanging cash and bills. There was the occasional retail outlet, and from one of them, Manga bought a big bag of black pepper to take home to Tilaiya.

The story started at Kumily because it's a spicy story, and particularly a peppery one. For it was mainly pepper, greatly prized by the rich and famous that brought the big guns of the ancient world to Kerala. And pepper grew in great quantities in the forests around places like Kumily, where it was harvested often by aboriginal forest dwellers, bartered with merchants, brought down by them to the coast and sold at great profit to sailors from the west. It was in the first century BC that traders from the biggest gun, Rome, first arrived.

Kerala had enjoyed earlier contacts with the outside world. In addition to their links with Ashoka's empire, the Cheras had received other visitors, most of them seeking spices. Arabs sailing in dhows traded all along the west coast of India, certainly reaching as far south as Kerala. Megasthenes, the famous Greek ambassador to the court of Chandragupta Maurya around 300BC, made reference to the 'Charmoe' tribe of the south west coast and also to the leading role in society and government played by women in that part of the country.[37] Egyptians, whose country became, after the breaking up of Alexander's empire, the centre of western learning, continued the trade with Kerala, opened a new port on the Red Sea coast and sailed direct to India - but only once as far as we know: the geographer Strabo wrote that such a voyage was made in 120 BC but the trip was not repeated. Normally the Egyptians relied on Arab and Phoenician ships to bring Kerala spices into their home seas, just as the Greeks had.[38]

So Arabs, Greeks, Phoenicians and Egyptians had been attracted to Kerala's peppercorns - and so had Jews. The origins of the Jewish connection are particularly interesting. In one of his more romantic passages, Logan speculates that Jews visited Malabar in the time of Moses, citing the fact that the Jewish temples in those days used cinnamon and cassia as ingredients of the holy anointing oil - and that these spices are found naturally only in Kerala and Sri Lanka. It is very likely then that the spices will have come from our region, but almost certainly bought from Phoenician or Arab traders rather than collected by the Jews themselves. Logan also does his best to connect Kerala with King Solomon [c 1000 BC]. The Bible records that ships from Tharshish arrived in Israel once in three years, bringing gold and silver, ivory, and apes and peacocks [but not spice, oddly], and Logan wonders whether Tharshish could be Tarisa, a name given, up to the ninth century AD, to the peoples living on the Malabar coast; and whether Solomon's Ophir - the source of his vast wealth in gold - could be in Malabar, because descriptions of the land fit in quite well with Beypore, a port just north of our village, famed for its wooden ships. Even if all this is speculation says Logan, 'the fact remains that Jewish colonies are settled on the coast and if their progenitors did not come with King Solomon's fleets, then they at least have traditions which carry back their arrival to the time of their escape from slavery thanks to Cyrus in the sixth century BC'.[39] The Jews had been deported from Judah in 587 BC by Nebuchadnezzar, King of Babylon. Cyrus the Great of Persia defeated Nebuchadnezzar and freed the Jews from the 'Babylonian captivity', and many of them, instead of returning home, looked for new and hopefully safer places to live, including Kerala. Of course everyone knows about the historical complexities of the expulsion and freeing of the Jews because of the work of Boney M who popularised in 1978 the reggae song *The Rivers of Babylon*!

What caused the opening up of the Malabar Coast and its precious products on a grand scale was the discovery of the monsoon winds. Sailors previously used to make their way from Kerala to the Middle East by keeping close to the west coast of India and then Persia and ending up in the Arabian Gulf, or by continuing along the Arabian coast to the Red Sea. These were very slow and therefore expensive routes, and not many ships made the whole journey, instead dropping off their cargoes at ports like Aden and Alexandria, where they would be picked up by another trader who would take them into the eastern Mediterranean. Then came Hippalos. In *Periplus Maris Erythraei* - a logbook written by a Greek sailor whose name we don't know - it is noted 'Hippalos was the pilot who first, by observing the bearings of the ports and the configuration of the sea, discovered the direct course across the ocean; whence as, at the season when our own Etesians are blowing, a periodical wind from the ocean likewise blows in the Indian sea...which is the south west...merchants committing themselves to the monsoon which blows right in the direction of their course, ...stand far out to sea leaving all gulfs...in the distance'[40]. And it was about this time that the Romans under the Emperor Augustus [30 BC to 14 AD] conquered Egypt when Cleopatra was Queen of course. The Romans were very quick to use the knowledge of the monsoon winds, and many ships sailed across the Arabian Sea to India. According to Pliny, they left 'in the middle of summer before the rising of the dog star, and arrive in about thirty days at Ocelis in Arabia... From thence they sail with the wind called Hippalos [the south west monsoon] in forty days to the first commercial station of India named Muziris[i] [called Cranganore by the British, now Kodungallor], in the kingdom of Ceroboha [Cheraputra]'.[41]

Pliny's word cannot be wholly relied upon - he believed for example a story about Hindus sailing round to the north of Asia and Europe and being shipwrecked on the north coast of Germany - but there is a lot of evidence of considerable trade between Rome and Kerala. Roman coin hoards, art objects and pottery have been found, and the author Gaius Petronius [27-66 AD] complained that Roman women were exposing their charms by wearing muslins from Kerala that were as insubstantial as 'woven wind' with 'a texture of cloud'![42] The most detailed description of this trade is again in the *Periplus*. The log refers to Muziris as being a city at the height of prosperity, frequented by ships from Egypt of a large size. Tamil epics also mention Muziris and its wealth and the fact that Roman traders [Yavanas] visited the port. Seafarers from the West brought 'great quantities of specie [coins], robes, coral, white glass, copper, brass, tin, lead, wine ['but not much'] and corn ['only for the use of the ships company, as the merchants do not sell it']. Taken home were 'pepper in great quantity, betel, transparent or precious stones, diamonds, pearls of superior quality, ivory, fine silks, jacinths [reddish-orange gems] and tortoise shell from the Golden Island'. Pliny reckoned that his countrymen paid 55 million sesterces[ii] a year to Indian merchants - and then sold their loot for ten times as much back in Rome. There is incidentally no mention of coconut being traded, which leads one to the conclusion that the tree was introduced into Kerala after the first century and unlikely therefore to be the source of the state's name, as is sometimes claimed [kera means coconut and alam means land in Malayalam].

Trade was not limited to the west coast. Kerala's imports and exports also travelled overland to and from India's east coast. This

---

[i] Muziris is the Latinisation of Muchiri, which means 'cleft' in Malayalam and refers to the splitting of the Periyar River at this point.

[ii] One sesterce would buy about a litre of wine

was more expensive than sending goods by sea, but it by-passed the pirates who waited to capture trading ships as they went round Kanniya Kumari, the southern tip of India. The main land route ran from the Malabar Coast through the Palakkad gap at the site of Coimbatore,[iii] and across the Kaveri plain to the east coast trading station at Arikamedu near Pondicherry, where the remains of a large Roman settlement were discovered in 1945.[iv] Arikamedu is described in a Tamil epic poem thus: '*The sun shone over the open terraces, over the warehouses near the harbour and over the turrets with windows like eyes of deer...the onlookers' attention was caught by the sight of the abodes of Yavanas, whose prosperity never waned. At the harbour were to be seen sailors from many lands, but to all appearances they live as one community.*'[43] From Arikamedu, trade continued with countries across the Bay of Bengal, so that south India began to spread its culture and influence to Burma, Malaya, Indonesia and points east, including the Spice Islands, which incidentally produced much more spice than Kerala itself.

Change however came to the region with the decline and fall of Rome. Trade with the empire slowed down and no other great power came forward to replace it. Kerala again slipped out of the headlines and into the footnotes of the history books. Well, those of least those of the western world. Kerala's on-going relationships with Jewish, Arab and Chinese visitors are described in chapter 26. One gets the feeling does one not, that the west's interest in Kerala is tied to a large extent to its value as a source of wealth; and indeed as we will see in chapter 28, when the trade routes to the west were re-opened, Kerala once more took a starring role in the histories of Europe.

[iii] Hordes of Roman gold coins have been found round Coimbatore.

[iv] By the well known archaeologist Sir Mortimer Wheeler

CHAPTER SEVEN

OUR VILLAGE

'You may a thousand times kiss another's child, but not once slap it' - Malayalam proverb

'Sweet auburn, loveliest village of the plain...' Oliver Goldsmith, *The Deserted Village*

A traditional Kerala house.

At the time of my first visit, Trikkandiyur was a very small village about half a mile outside the town of Tirur. The two communities have pretty well merged now and one would be hard put to say where Tirur begins and Trikkandiyur ends. No longer is the track out of the village flanked by hedgerows, with colourful butterflies visiting the hibiscus flowers, and pepper vines crawling up the blossom-laden trees. Instead, columns of shops march along on each side of the tarmacadamed road, oblivious of borders and boundaries. Back in the sixties Trikkandiyur was a distinct community, quiet and green and with quite a prosperous feel. It was, and is, rather famous too. Not only has it an important Shiva temple, but it is known as the birthplace of the 'father of the Malayalam language', with a monument and gardens to celebrate the fact.

My first few days in Trikkandiyur seem like a dream now. Manga and I slept in the living accommodation attached to my brother-in-law Balan's shop. We had to go through the shop itself to reach our rather cramped bedroom, squeezing between showcases filled with, as I remember, such cosmetic essentials as tins of 'Yardley's' talcum powder [of doubtful provenance] and our favourite guaranteed Mysore sandalwood soap, which we would take home in quantities at the end of our holidays for distribution to friends and relations. Just as the quintessentially English Yardley's powder did not seem quite the same in India, so the sandalwood soap sold in England was very tame stuff compared with the real thing. The bedroom was tiny and although Manga's sisters had done their best to make it as comfortable as possible, their efforts had been hampered by the fact that the room had to double as a store for the shop. But we did have the luxury of a bed, just a charpoy consisting of a wooden frame with coir webbing, but certainly easier on the bones than the stone floor. And we had some welcome privacy too.

I had always believed that we stayed there rather than the main house because the family was a bit worried about having a foreigner in their home and a bit afraid of what the neighbours might say - because delightful and welcoming as they were, the neighbours were certainly not above a bit of gossip from time to time, some of it not all that savoury. But Manga assures me that this was not the case. Indeed, one brother refused to see us after travelling all the way from Coimbatore because we were NOT staying in the family home. I don't know why we didn't, and Manga can't remember either. Balan's shop was called 'Apsara Fancy' and stocked a delightful mixture of goods. There was a good trade in glass bangles, beads, bindis, hair bands and other shiny things, most of the clientele being schoolgirls, but the plastic toys, many of them curled up on account of age and the hot sun were clearly not big sellers. The shop was quite modern in that it boasted a door and windows, though the latter were somewhat obscured by the brooms and buckets, children's windmills and cricket bats that hung from the beams.

Next morning we were out and about meeting Manga's old friends. This has been an important part of all our visits to Trikkandiyur and I expect that I might sometimes be confusing one visit with another. What has always been true is that we have everywhere been welcomed, whether it is just Manga and me or whether we have brought with us a tribe of eight or ten friends and relations. And we are always presented with a 'snack'. This inevitably includes a banana, usually the small sweet variety, Mysore pak, south India's favourite sweetmeat, and milky and heavily sugared tea. There might also be sweet or savoury banana chips, a salty mixture we call Bombay mix here in England, cashew nuts, different types of sweet, jelabi for example, or laddu, wada and dehi [curd] or onion bhaji, or best of all, especially if the visit was in the morning, idli or dosa and chutney. The first time we were in Trikkandiyur I recall being regaled with coconut everywhere we went, and as I didn't enjoy coconut milk then as much as I do now, and I have never liked the flesh of a young coconut [something to do with its texture I think], it was quite difficult to be enthusiastic.

One thing has changed since those first visits many years ago. Every house we went into in those days presented us with some entertainment. Usually it was a song or classical dance from the daughters of the house or a modern, film-inspired dance from the sons. Or it might be a tune on a violin or other musical instrument. I always wished we could repay in kind - but Manga, the only talented one among us and who once had a lovely singing voice, had not practised for years.

So we were pleased when our German friends Rika and Frank came with us one year. Frank sang and played his guitar beautifully, but to be honest was never appreciated that much in India. However, it is now a rarity for us to be entertained like this. More often than not the television is on, which is good, for me anyway, if a Test Match is being played, but not so good if it's a Malayalam soap opera. No one had a television on our first few visits. In fact when our family could eventually afford one, it was one of the first in the village, and the house was packed with a noisy and enthusiastic audience whenever there was a big cricket match or a film being shown. In those days there were no foreign broadcasts at all but a lot of classical, educational and 'improving' programmes: rather like the BBC under Lord Reith. Times have changed!

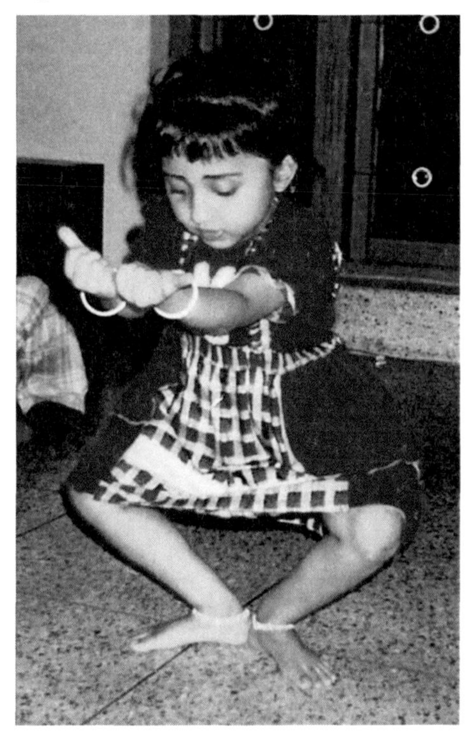

Ammu dancing for us

Next door to our house was then, and still was in 2010, the home of Baby and her family. Baby was a chubby smiley woman with a husband and three sons. At one time she had a pet monkey who would search our heads for ticks! Baby's husband Apu was a skilled goldsmith, who took us to his workshop, where we watched him make wonderful jewellery by hand. The goldsmith is a much-respected member of an Indian community because gold is so important to Indian families. A bride must wear gold ornaments at her wedding and take them with her to her husband's house, and for many families, gold jewellery is their only bank account. Apu was a very likeable and generous man. Manga and I used to share toddy with him in the privacy of his home and when Grandma visited

Apu invited us to a fish dinner washed down with whisky. Even though we had no language in common, we had a thoroughly good time, and came away thinking what a nice chap he was. Again when Tony and Rosemary and their family were in the village, another meat-eater's feast was provided. The sons of the family were a pleasant bunch and were talented musicians: Rosemary's son, Sebastian, noted in his diary that after the feast, the younger visitors enjoyed an Indian 'jam session' with them. Indira and Lakshmi's friend Lucy was with us, and she had brought her flute; I guess the rest of the English contingent sang along. The lads did not follow the family trade though and the last time we met them, one brother was trying to set up a business making decorations for temple elephants and another was seeking his fortune in the Gulf states.

Toddy by the way comes from the coconut tree; at least it does in Kerala, where the drink is known as 'kallu'. In the north there is a toddy palm *phoenix silvestris*. The drink is obtained in the same way from both trees: a slit is made in the flower stem and the sap is caught in a mud pot tied to the branch. If you drink the liquid fresh, it is delicious, refreshing, and alcohol-free, but as the day goes on and the sap becomes warm, fermentation takes place and by the time it has been delivered to the toddy shops, the drink is sour tasting and very intoxicating.

Our next visit was to Manga's old friend Thangam, now sadly dead, who lived next door to Baby. Thangam was married and had three daugh- ters and one son. Her husband was very pleased to see us and was keen to show off his pet scheme, producing and using methane from the dung of the cow he kept in his back garden. Forty years later this has become cutting edge in the fight to produce naturally generated fuel. Thangam and her daughters were charming, and we always looked forward to meeting them.

Manga's best friend at school still lives in Trikkandiyur, though on the other side of the village. Dakshayani is married to Govindakutty, an extremely tall, jovial and most agreeable gentleman who enjoys a conversation. On our second visit I remember he raced across the village to present us with several plaster Kathakali masks just as we were leaving to catch the train on our way back to England. And on another occasion, again after a discussion on the topic, he sent us, after our return to England, two large volumes containing the Puranas in Sanskrit with an

English translation. They contain the maxim 'thou shalt not have likes and dislikes'. Manga used to say this when the children didn't want to eat up their spinach but we didn't know it was written in the Hindu 'bible'. Indi managed a smile when I read it to her as she lay in bed in Trikkandiyur suffering from very severe diarrhoea one year. It was so bad that she had had to have injections at the government hospital; though after one visit to that dark and dusty edifice, Manga decided to do the injections herself at home.

Manga meeting the travelling Bangle Seller after 15 years

We had good friends too opposite our house. They had a large rather dark home on a big plot. Father always seemed to me to be a rather distinguished person - a lawyer perhaps, or education officer I thought, but he was in fact the village Postmaster. Manga maintains that this is indeed a highly respected post in India -

almost to the level of the Stationmaster. It was in their house one evening that I made an attempt on the world poori eating record. Swami mama [as he was known to his friends] had a number of sons who seemed to be doing well - medical representatives I think. They had large and noisy motorbikes - imported, not the now rather famous Indian-made Royal Enfields. The youngest son was Raju's best friend and a quiet, polite, friendly and amusing young man.

Sadly not all was sweetness and light in the many families that we knew and grew to love in the village. One young man of our acquaintance joined a political group and became involved in a violent confrontation during which an opponent was killed. And two of our friends met untimely deaths apparently because they drank too much. In each case we were shocked to see their decline between our visits. The skeletal appearance of the young man, a particularly good friend of the family, when I met him for the last time brought tears to my eyes.

Alcohol does seem to be a problem in rural India. H.K.Sharma has written a paper which suggests that the country's history of contradictory attitudes towards alcohol, with heavy drinking being quite acceptable in some eras and among some castes, alongside prohibition in many states and condemnation, especially by Brahmins, 'has produced alcohol-use patterns that include frequent high-risk, heavy and hazardous drinking.'[44] And the shame of drunkenness precludes I believe much in the way of treatment or even sympathy, in villages at least. There is now a prestigious National Drug Treatment Centre in New Delhi and a number of voluntary organisations dedicated to helping alcoholics and others, so it does appear that the problem is acknowledged at a national level anyway. My friend Ashok tells me that the current Kerala State Government has introduced limited prohibition, although toddy shops and 5-star hotels are exempt and a small number of other outlets have been temporarily licensed. Long queues snake round the streets leading to these state-owned bars and the spectacle, Ashok says with a grin, is a perfect illustration of the patience of the average Malayalee working man, standing quietly in the hot sun for hours on end until the bars open and it is their turn to be served. Until of course, someone tries to jump the queue!

Further along the alleyway lived Narayanan and his wife, Bhagyam. Narayanan, who was a big film buff and rarely missed a show at the local cinema, used to wander around the village with a happy but rather faraway expression on his face. He never worked as far as we know, but was an enthusiastic supporter of the Kerala Communist Party and had large pictures of the famous party leaders of the 1950s in his living room. He was always pleased to see us though he spoke no English. He was quite vain: used to spend a long time every evening colouring his whiskers and hair black.

Bhagyam with Victoria [foreground] and Shanta

Bhagyam was always smiling and was often in our house - she was great friends with Manga's sisters. Bhagyam used to give extra tuition in English language and I expect she was very good, though personally I found it a little difficult to switch on to her accent. It is sometimes an embarrassment when one of Manga's old acquaintances speaks to us in English and we find it hard to follow; especially embarrassing if the person in question is showing off his linguistic abilities to his wife or children! Once, in a cobblers', we met an elderly gentleman who asked me [I thought] how many pairs of **shoes** I had. I was just about to reply, '*three: one black, one brown and one white*', when I realised that what he had really said was, '*How many* ***issues****, [that is, children] do you have*?' Come to think of it, my original answer would have sufficed, more or less!!

But one evening recently when I was at home in England, our nephew Ramani rang from Bahrain. Ramani always makes sure we are kept up-to-date with the news from India. '*I have bad news for Chitti. Bhagyam died last night. I think she was Chitti's schoolmate. She had very high blood pressure and was taking pills. She was out in the village when she collapsed. Please tell Chitti; I don't want to tell her myself.*' It sounded as though she died quickly and without suffering and perhaps that was a blessing. Her children both came back from Dubai straight away. Manga of course was very upset. '*Poor Narayanan. He used to buy fresh flowers for her every day.*' I asked who would look after him now. '*O his sister is there. She never married. She did all the cooking - Bhagyam never learned how.*

Bhagyam was part of our family you know. Do you remember in the old days, whenever you got a camera out, she would be there? She's in all our family photos. Such a nice woman. She never minded being teased or anything. Once she went to see The Holy Mother, you know, that very simple woman who seems to have some healing power.[i] *She seems to be very good, not trying to make money or anything. Well, Bhagyam lined up to be blessed by Mother, and when it was her turn, Mother hugged her as she always did and asked her whether she had any problems, and Bhagyam said 'O Ma, I am all alone in the world, no-one to look after me.' That was nonsense of course but Bhagyam said she became tongue-tied and couldn't think what to*

---

[i] Mata Amritanandamayi has no particular set of beliefs and uses the money she is given to establish hospitals and colleges all over the world. She is considered modern for these reasons: 'The idea of a hugging mother figure with a universal and modern outlook on life is one that seems to have an earlier history'. See Moser, Heike and Younger, Paul, 'Kerala – Plurality and consensus' in *The Modern Anthropology of India: Ethnography, themes and theory* edited by Berger, Peter and Heldermann, Frank, p.152

say!' Bhagyam's mother had a hard life. Her mother-in-law was very mean to her, and she didn't dare do or say anything. But when the old lady died, Bhagyam's mum became suddenly dominant.

By the way, I didn't go to school with Bhagyam, but with her sister. Her sister died at the age of 13 or 14; they said it was of fright. She went near the temple, the one that Doraikutty used to go to, at night when no-one else was about, and saw something very frightening and swooned. When she woke up she told her family that it was a hunter with a bow and arrow.[ii] *But she was never the same again and developed a high fever and died after 4 or 5 days. It was very sad.'*

By the way, talking of Bhagyam's sister, if you hear a ghost coming behind you, don't look back. Just step aside to let it pass. That was what Manga's Dad used to do and he never came to any harm.

Manga is now a Nicheren Daishonin Buddhist and she and I went upstairs and sat in front of the Gohonzon. Manga said it made her feel stronger. It seemed the right thing to do

Just as I was putting the finishing touches to this book, we had further sad news from India. Our nephew Ravi had left a message on our answer phone in the night telling us what we had been fearing for some time. Rajam, his beloved chitty, Balan's beloved wife, and Manga's beloved sister, had passed away. Ravi's younger brother Raju who had been adopted and brought up by Rajam and Balan, performed the necessary rites and after the funeral, he wrote this moving and heartfelt letter.

Dear all,

Rajam chitty was, as you know, suffering from low heart pumping rate for some time. It was coming down to dangerously low rate since few weeks and we were expecting the inevitable. As usual she slept Tuesday night and Amma [Mani-akka] asked her to take her pills, for the first time she said no more pills. Then Amma told her about the oedema on her feet, legs will go with me, she replied and had a good sleep. By 5.30 am around she woke up and had chat with Amma and Chinnu [the dog]. Then she had another nap and after one hour Amma went and asked her to wake up and have the coffee. Then Amma caught her hand and it simply slipped from her hand and the doctor confirmed the worst. She had a faint smile on her face

[ii] This temple remember is dedicated to Shiva in his incarnation as a hunter.

with folded hands, closed eyes and cleanly stretched legs all showing how peaceful was the end.

Ravi called me and as Appu [his son] was in Chennai the body was placed in a mobile mortuary. Next day i.e. Thursday morning, by around 9am the priest came and the rituals done as per our custom by me. The body was taken to Nambiarparmbu, the cremation ground for Tirur Brahmins, and after the rituals there by around 12 noon the pyre was lit. The day was pleasant without even a trace of rain. Everything went so smoothly and in the evening we had plenty of rain. Yesterday the Sanchayanam, a ritual done to immerse the mortal remains, mainly few bones, took place in the river at Tirunavaya. Next week we are going to Palkkat to complete the rituals. We left Tirur today morning. I am sure it is the greatest loss in my life. May god give us all strength to overcome this loss:

with love Raju Geetha and Keerthana.

* * * * *

At the end of the alley there's a beautiful traditional Kerala house. We first went there to meet one of Raju's friends, Unni, who was going to let my mother borrow his camera. Poor Mum had been given a new camera as a Ruby Wedding present especially to use on her holiday, but left it at home. We saw a spectacular sun bird in the colourful, fragrant and flower-filled garden and admired the timbered house with its multiple tiled roofs. At a later time my sister Rosemary and her husband Tony were given a tour of the building and they loved it. There was a huge wooden pillar in the middle of the house - the trunk of what must have been a massive teak tree - and a water tank inside the building. Not long after we returned home after that visit, we heard that the house was up for sale. As far as I remember the asking price for this wonderful building and its grounds was around £20,000, when a similar house in Britain [if one existed] would I suppose have cost ten times as much. We wondered briefly whether we might buy the house. We could preserve a bit of old Kerala for all time, as other traditional houses were being pulled down, altered beyond recognition or crowded by new developments on the site; and stay there when we visited India. As it happens, it would have been a wonderful investment too. Land is at a premium in Kerala as cash-rich workers return from the Gulf, looking to spend their savings on ostentatious new houses. But we decided in the end that we were not cut out to be absentee landlords.

Another good friend of the family was Latif. He was a most engaging young man, a Muslim, with the broadest smile I have ever seen. He was very fond of my Mum. She only had to say something like 'I wonder what red bananas taste like' or 'I must get some of that sandalwood soap to take home to Rosemary', and Latif would jump onto his bicycle and scour the town for the best bananas or whatever, and bring them back to present proudly to Grandma. Although he would speak no English, he evidently could understand the language. Latif was a young lad then, and apparently a bit wild. He told us recently that Balan had 'saved' him by giving him work, and teaching him self-discipline. In later years Latif started a small haulage business and would use his truck to take us and our luggage to and from the station. When Rosemary came to Tirur, Latif asked her about his son who had a badly injured and functionally and cosmetically unsightly eye. He was being teased at school and often played truant as a result. Rosemary [who was an ophthalmologist] confirmed that nothing could be done about his sight but gave him money for an operation and a good artificial eye. During a later visit we went to see a house that Latif was building on the edge of town. We met his son Samad again - a splendid young chap who was quite unselfconscious about his eye and was studying well at college.

Several of our experiences illustrate how the village supports its own. Trikkandiyur may no longer be a village of Iyers, but it has retained a family atmosphere. On our first visit with the children, Victoria, aged eleven, became quite unwell, and had to stay in bed for a couple of days. We sat by her and were never alone. At times the whole village seemed to be around us. I have to confess that at first I found this to be a bit claustrophobic, but I soon came to appreciate that the people were there to share our concern and sadness. On another occasion, during one of the few trips that Manga and I made alone, we were awoken in the middle of the night by a cry from a neighbouring home. At once our whole household was mobilised and rushed to the scene. A new-born baby was struggling to breathe, and the mother knew that the best way to get help was by calling out rather than phoning the hospital. It was Manga who diagnosed and dealt with the problem - a minor one as it happened. Nonetheless, to be doubly sure that the baby was OK,

Ramani, who was also staying at home, rushed with the child in his arms to the home of the nearest doctor, and would not return till the baby was given a clean bill of health. Half the village spent the rest of the night commiserating with the mother. There was a similar incident on another of our visits when a young woman suffered from a convulsion.

* * * * *

I remember on my very first visit to Trikkandiyur watching parrots building a nest in a broken tree in a neighbouring garden, monkeys roosting in our trees in the evenings and waking noisily too early in the mornings, sunbirds, which we at first mistook for large butterflies, sucking nectar through their long hollow tongues from the flowers by the balcony of the house as we relaxed during the siesta. I remember too meeting a number of grave and elderly Iyer scholars, writers and lawyers as we walked through the village and struggling to keep my end up in intellectual discussion. I remember above all a magical night when Manga and I watched Kathakali till the dawn...

It was during my first time in Kerala. By good luck Manga and I arrived in Trikkandiyur in the last week in December when each year, a big literary festival is held in honour of the father of the Malayalam language, Thanjath Ezhuthachan. A cultural event is held as part of the festival, and the organisers very graciously treated us as honoured guests at the event, which was held in Thanjan Parambu, the park dedicated to Thanjath. Young poets presented their first compositions and that was followed by readings by leading Malayalam literary figures including Changambura and S.K.Pattakkadu and a tall, slim lady whose name I sadly forget and two others. They autographed our programme, as did the editor of *Madrabhumi*, a state daily newspaper. We kept the programme for ages but I'm afraid it was eaten by termites, along with several other important documents, before we left India. For the first part of the evening, we sat on a stage in front of a large and appreciative crowd, trying to look learned, as the speeches and readings proceeded.

The main attraction of the festival was the Kathakali performance, which started as night fell, announcing itself with a deafening clatter of drums. The musicians and the singers stood on the sides of the stage, bare-chested and wearing dazzlingly white dhotis. All were men of course, as indeed were all the performers. A large oil-lamp [called a kalivilakku] stood in front of the stage. The 'stage curtains' consisted of a piece of material held up by two of the cast, one at each side. You could see something of the preparations going on behind the curtain: this, Manga said, was deliberate - to whet the appetite of the audience. The evil characters pretended to try and tear the curtain down:[iii] some of the more nervous watchers took to their heels at this moment!

Then the curtain dropped and the play began. I was transfixed. The costumes were amazing - wide skirts, blouses, a sort of scarf with mirrors at each end - the make-up garishly bright, the unique masks spectacular; the singing hypnotic, the gestures and steps intriguing.[iv] Manga quickly explained the significance of the colours of the make-up and masks as we sat on the grass close to the stage. '*If the character has a green face, he is good - like Rama, for example; but if there is a streak of red on the face, the character is still noble, but has some bad in him. You'll see Ravana the demon king later with that make-up. Then the really horrible people are all red - face and beard; they are called redbeards [chuvanna thaadi]. If you see a blackbeard, he will be a wild hunter or something like that and also bad. Men playing the part of a woman will have yellow faces - look: that is Sita. And someone with a white beard will be playing the monkey god Hanuman.*'[v]

Manga said that the story came from the *Ramayana* - the tale of Rama, his wife Sita and his brother Lakshmana, and their exile in the forests. It's particularly popular in Kerala partly at least because some of the action is set in south India, unlike the other

---

[iii] This is the tiranokku or curtain-look and is 'accompanied by an exciting atmosphere created by the musicians and drummers' [David Bolland, *A Guide to Kathakali*, p.9]

[iv] In his foreword to the third edition of the *Guide,* Bolland writes of the first performance he saw: 'although it was fascinating and mesmerizing, the action on stage seemed interminable and I was soon rather bored as I had no idea what was going on'. He did not have a Manga with him of course! He later met an authority on the art and went on to enjoy over 200 more plays in the following twenty years. [*ibid,* p.v]

[v] If you would like more detail, and descriptions some of the most popular plays, do read David Bolland's excellent book.

epic - the *Mahabharatha*, which is based on the growth of a new 'Aryan' culture in the north and the battles which were supposed to have taken place among the kings of that time.

The performance went on right through the warm night. The air was fragrant from the incense burning on the stage, and up above, visible through the palm fronds, the stars were brighter than I had ever seen, and the sky blacker. Just as dawn broke, the drama concluded with good triumphing over evil and everyone was happy. Manga and I wandered home after a perfect night.

On that first visit Manga and I used to meander through the village lanes where pepper grew wild and abundantly. Pepper is expensive now, even in Kerala - and in fact because of the emphasis on exports, it's sometimes more expensive there than here in the UK. We walked over to the Muslim school, where Rajam taught; to the temples of course; and down into Tirur, passing Manga's old primary school and the government hospital. In later days we visited the former with Rosemary and she presented the pupils with pens and pencils, erasers and rulers. In the 1990s, children in India were still very grateful for such gifts. In the same year, Tony (a doctor) was given a conducted tour of the hospital. He was amazed by the antiquity of some of the equipment the doctors were using it would have been out of date even when he was training apparently - but impressed by the way they and the nurses coped with a massive workload. Not far from the government hospital, there was the private nursing home and the scout hut. Among the shops there were those of tailors sewing busily away, Ayurvedic and conventional chemists, greengrocers selling many varieties of bananas, green, yellow, brown and red, large and small, hanging in bunches, and shoe shops featuring monsoon sandals – much better than wellies for negotiating the deep puddles made by the heavy seasonal rain.

When I was first in Trikkandiyur some of the shops were less conventional. I particularly remember the mushali with his forge at the back. The mushali made and sold brass and bronze implements including the huge pans, at least six feet across, used to cook food for weddings and other celebrations. His forge was fired with umikkari - the same charcoal-like material that Manga used to clean her teeth with. The mushali isn't there now, and neither is the goldsmith who would sit at the back of his shop making bangles and necklaces to order, taking care to collect all the microscopic bits of gold which were shaved off in the manufacturing process and heating them in a small crucible so they'd coalesce.

The old village shops, including Balan's [with sign], in the 1970s

Then there were the tea-shops. There are none now but I can think of at least three on the road to Tirur in the old days. I suppose people walked more then and needed refreshment. The tea-shops were huts with walls and a roof made of palm fronds. There was a table across the front of the hut and a few wooden stools or sometimes a bench for customers. In India tea is made by boiling up water, milk, and tea-leaves, or more often tea-dust, all together in a pan, sometimes adding cloves, ginger and cardamom. In the tea stalls, so it could be used over and over again, the dust or leaves would be contained in a sort of sock in a deep jug and the boiling milk and water would be poured into the jug, and after a good stew, poured into your cup. The chai wallah would then cool it to drinking temperature by pouring the liquid from a great height from one cup into another to the admiration of all concerned - well, to my admiration anyway! But Manga's family never drank at tea-shops. They weren't run by Brahmins you see, but by Malayalees, Nairs usually, and a Muslim owned the tea shop opposite the Ambala Kulangara. That's the Devi temple, which was just a peepal tree and a sort of altar in those days. When Manga was little, her second brother, Parameswaran, who was called Rasu at home, had a coffee shop at the end of our alley for a while. He lent some money to the son of a rich man in the village, who couldn't pay him back - his father wouldn't help. So he gave Rasu-anna a silver tumbler instead, which was given to Manga, then a child, and subsequently to me as my first Christmas present in India. It sits in our showcase to this day! But the shop didn't do very well - I'm afraid that was typical of Rasu's enterprises - and it closed down quite soon.

A village shop: note the banana varieties

Of course the village and its shops have changed a lot over the years and I expect the process will continue. But we still have a lovely group of shopkeepers at the end of our alleyway. Until his death in 2011, my friend was still selling bidis, and paan for chewing as well as prayer beads bought by pilgrims on the way to the temple (his shop is the first in the picture on p.82). He always had a big smile for me and I usually found something that I could buy from him, but not bidis. These cheap cigarettes may look a bit like miniature cigars but are in fact bits of tobacco, probably the factory sweepings, wrapped in a tobacco leaf, which is tied with cotton, and are even worse for you than ordinary cigarettes. The grocer is always very pleased to see us too. We usually stop by to enjoy a glass or two of his excellent lime sodas and maybe buy a packet of exotically flavoured savoury crunches. The grocer also stocks the Malayalam calendars that we need to calculate Manga's birthday and other important dates associated with phases of the moon.

Our neighbouring community, Tirur, is a substantial town with a population of 53,000 in 2001.[vi] It is the site of one of the atrocities of the British occupation - the 'Railway Wagon Tragedy', about which there will be more detail later in this book - and is well known as a marketing centre for fish and betel nut. Geographically speaking, Tirur is as strategically placed as anywhere in Kerala. It is just less than half way down the Kerala coast, that is, about 165 miles from the state's northern border and 200 from Trivandrum in the south, and is close to two important ports. Kozhikode, which was for centuries in the Middle Ages the busiest port in Kerala, is twenty-five miles away, and Ponnani, whose harbour was also historically important, is only ten miles from Tirur and is linked to the town by river.

Tirur is the nearest railway station to Ponnani and lies on the railway line that runs between Mangalore in the north and Coimbatore and ultimately Chennai via the Palakkad Gap to the east. This was the first railway line in Kerala. The first section was Beypore to Tirur, and was opened on 12th March 1861, followed by Tirur to Kuttipuram on 1st May.[45]

Not long ago you could still find a small and barely used wooden jetty on the banks of a waterway near Tirur station. I doubt if it has survived recent developments. In days gone by the river linked the town with the backwaters of Velliyankod via the Ponnani Canal, and a boat could ultimately travel all the way down to Trivandrum. We tried to discover if this could still be done, but we could never find a boatman able to confirm it or offer us a passage. '*The waterways are often blocked these days*' said one old

---

[vi] The population of the town had increased to 56,000 in the 2011 census, 28% Hindu and 71% Moslem, with a literacy rate of 96%. www.census2011.co.in retrieved 20.7.17.

man who could remember the days when the jetty was busy with farmers taking their produce to markets further south, and travellers coming straight to the jetty from the train to continue their journeys on the country vessels. '*No one wants to go by boat; they're in too much of a hurry. So no one maintains the waterways.*' We pointed out that sailing the backwaters was now a favourite pastime for holidaymakers, but he was not impressed. '*Who'd want to come to a dirty old town like Tirur for a holiday?*' he cackled.

Actually, Tirur isn't dirty at all. Admittedly it doesn't look much like a tourist resort and doesn't pretend to be one; it is a serious working town where one can buy almost anything [especially in the 'duty-free' or 'foreign' outlets, which used to be the only places you could buy imported goods] and which has busy vegetable and fish markets.

The fish market owes its importance to Tirur's good transport connections and is a mixed blessing for the visitor at least. The platforms at the railway station are frequently packed with boxes and baskets of particularly smelly fish and the fish market in town is best given a wide berth. One can tell when it is active by counting the number of Brahminy kites circling above the site. These kites are the South Indian equivalents of vultures, and they play the essential role of keeping the streets clean of organic rubbish. Sadly, vultures have virtually disappeared from the skies above North India - and this is more than just another blow to the world's bio-diversity: it means that the threat of disease, never all that far from the poorer communities of India, is increased, as the corpses of animals lie in the streets for longer and pi dogs roam in even greater numbers in the more remote villages. The culprit is diclofenac, a drug designed as a painkiller, which can be used for humans and cows without ill effect but is fatal to the vulture. The drug is now banned for veterinary purposes in India and Nepal and until very recently it was thought a safe alternative had been discovered. International efforts are being made to find new drugs without side-effects and to re-introduce vultures and while it seems unlikely that they will ever be seen in their former profusion, a partial recovery of their numbers is possibly on its way.[46]

Vegetable market, Tirur, in the 1990s

Tirur's vegetable markets are lively, noisy, colourful, and chaotic, and the produce is of course locally grown and very fresh. You really must get your fruit and veg from the market. Ganapathi Chettiar and Rainbow, our favourite clothes shops, must not be missed either. The shopkeepers and assistants always seemed to remember us and be pleased to see us on our four-yearly visits in the old days. We would sit and drink coffee and sometimes fresh lime juice as well. We knew we shouldn't [because of the doubtful nature of the water] but we didn't want to seem ungrateful. It wasn't surprising that we were welcome I suppose - we always went out of the door weighed down by armfuls of purchases, but I hope it was also because we were happy and admired their shop and its wares. The children couldn't resist the vivid colours of the rolls of material produced for their delight; I always came away with far more lungis than I would ever use; and our particular favourites were the excitingly designed bed covers which we took home to give as presents or to use as throws to re-vitalise old chairs and settees. We didn't often buy ready-made clothes but had our shirts, skirts and blouses made up by tailors, who would copy a design and finish the garment in matter of hours. My sister Rosemary and sister-in-law Julie are very fond of housecoats, or maxis, very practical garments which they use as night dresses in England.

Tirur's main street as it was in 1979. Lakshmi, Mum, Indi and Raju in foreground.

Unni Chettiar, the goldsmith, was always a good person to visit. Again we would be offered seats and tea and would settle down to a long session examining what he had to offer and exchanging pleasantries. All the family has bought gold chains, bangles or ear-rings there over the years and we all have little leather or cloth bags advertising the shop, which we use for purses, holders for mobile telephones and cameras [before they became miniaturised], toilet bags or pencil cases. And finally there were the shops that sold stainless steel - rows of them, all stocking exactly the same products at exactly the same prices - quite baffling. We all bought plates, bowls, ladles, tiny containers, and obscure gadgets in quantity. The latter included tiffin carriers, seva makers [seva is a sort of fine spaghetti], nati pots [for washing out one's nasal passages], decoction sets [for making coffee]. Apart from the nati pot, which Manga uses whenever she catches a cold, they sit picturesquely on our kitchen shelf, slowly gathering dust.

Raju used to take us to see jelabi being made in the town, in large churns. We would then buy bagsful to bring home. We'd also buy murrukku, cashew nuts and honey in large quantities. Murrukku is a very hard, spicy biscuit made from rice flour and black gram. Honey is used as a medicine in India and sold in small bottles: no-one could believe it when we ordered pints of the nectar. And I liked the rubber slip-on sandals costing next to nothing. I still have two pairs, years old: they never wear out. The khadi shops were a big favourite. We were fond of the young man who looked after the smaller shop in the town, and would spend ages with him, buying Ayurvedic soaps, oils, carvings in sandalwood, candle-holders shaped like boats, agarbhatties, little figures of gods, and paintings on mirrors.

In the sixties we never dreamed of phoning home from India - even on such rather momentous occasions as our Wedding Day. In fact it was only when the first booths proclaiming 'STD/ ITD' [meaning Subscriber or International Trunk Dialling by the way!] arrived in town that we made our first telephone calls. I seem to remember that that was when Rosemary came with us to Raju's wedding and she wanted to ring Tony, left behind in England to look after the dogs. An attendant would ring the number and we would watch a dial spinning round indicating how much money we were spending as we spoke: a real incentive to keep your message short and to the point! These telephone booths enjoyed a rather brief heyday - in common with many households, everyone in our family now has their own phone and mobiles are commonplace.

It wasn't till recently that I knew how important paan was to Tirur's economy. This is a description of this chewable product by E.M.Forster. 'The leaf is mild enough, the crisis coming when its fibres tear and the iron pyrites fall about and get under the tongue. Now the novice rises in disorder, rushes in a panic to the courtyard, and spatters shrapnel over the bystanders; it is as if the whole mineral kingdom has invaded him under a vegetable veil, for simultaneously the lime starts singing. If he can sit still through this, a heavenly peace ensues; the ingredients salute each other, a single sensation is established, and Paan, without ceasing to be a problem becomes a pleasure.'[47] Other early visitors to India were also impressed by the humble betel leaf, including Marco Polo and Duarte Barbosa, a 16th century Portuguese official in Kochi. Barbosa's description is rather more prosaic than Forster's: the betel 'is habitually chewed by both men and women, night and day, in public places and roads by day, and in bed by night, so that their chewing thereof has no pause... It makes the mouth red and the teeth black.' [48]

Paan is chewed all over the Indian subcontinent and in Indo-China and the Pacific. It consists of various spices and herbs and other less savoury ingredients neatly wrapped [like a samosa] in a betel leaf - from a plant of the pepper family. It is used for cleaning and refreshing the mouth after eating, to help in relaxation or as a sign of hospitality. P.V.Jagadisa Ayyar in *South Indian Customs* says 'Indian physicians of bygone ages prescribed it for the overfed rich'.[49] He goes on to say that taking paan 'early in the morning checks the formation of phlegm, cleans and clears the bowels...before meal time, sharpens the appetite...after meals [it] helps digestion.' He adds cautiously, 'If people use it moderately in one or other of the above uses, though not in all, they may find it conferring on them health which is both wealth and prosperity in one.'[50] On the other hand, it is a rather messy habit, as one needs to spit out the red juice; and it doesn't seem to do teeth and gums much good. Above all it is now known to be a carcinogen - there is a high incidence of mouth and throat cancer in chewers - especially if taken with chewing tobacco.

Tirur shops old and new, and a new mosque in the background

Some say that we can blame Noorjehan, the mother of Shahjehan [who built the Taj Mahal] for making the habit popular - she liked it because it made her lips enticingly red. Manga says that paan came first from the south though, because that's where the Areca Palm grows - and the Areca 'nut' [actually it's the seed] is an important ingredient of paan. There are certainly regional differences in the delicacy. Manga says the Kerala paan leaf [vettila in Malayalam, beeda in Tamil] is big and chewy and dark-coloured, while on the east coast the leaf is small, delicate and lime-green. As well as shaved or crushed betel nut, the usual ingredients are fennel seeds, cloves and cardamom. In Bihar, white lime was a regular addition - it put me off, as it made my teeth go on edge. Perhaps I might have preferred sweet paan, which includes coconut and honey.

Most betel leaf is produced in Karnataka, but the best, because of its unique taste and durability, is from Tirur. Tirur leaf, known as 'Lanka Pana' in the trade, is particularly prized in Pakistan. Leaf is sent north by rail across the border to Karachi and Lahore, and in good times, thousands of people in the Tirur area are involved in the cultivation, preparation and transportation of betel. When, however, relations with Pakistan are strained, exports from Tirur can decline by up to forty per cent according to N.S.K. Menon, President of the Tirur Betel Traders Association.[52]

Six miles from Tirur, 20 minutes or so drive along the Kadalundi Road, or 8 minutes by rail on the Mangalore Express, lies the ancient town of Tanur. While Tirur did not come into any sort of prominence till the arrival of the railways, Tanur was important in Portuguese times. It was one of the European invaders' first settlements and it is said that Francis Xavier visited in 1546. Later it became one of the ports from which Muslim sailors harassed the Portuguese trading fleets. Also the Keraladesapuram Temple, dedicated to Vishnu, is supposed to be one of the oldest in Malabar.[53]

Empty beach at Tanur

We went to Tanur beach in Rosemary and Tony's year. These days, the beach is included on websites advertising the attractions of the Kerala coast - then it was pretty well unknown as a holiday place. One day we were feeling particularly hot and longed for a swim. We asked an old man whether there was anywhere quiet where we might take a dip. '*Tanur is quiet*,' he said. '*Leastways, it is now that the fishing fleet has moved on. But I never heard of anyone swimming there. And if you go, be careful! My granddad's brother was drowned by a tidal wave in that same place not so very long ago*!' I checked on this later. It was true - there had been a tidal wave at Tanur... one hundred years before!

Well, we set off for Tanur anyway, Rosemary, Tony, Manga and me in a jeep and Victoria, Antonia, Indi, Laksh, Lucy, and Sebastian on the back of various local lads' motorbikes, without leathers or helmets, the girls' brightly coloured skirts waving in the breeze. Parents tried to be brave, but at least one closed his eyes, and another was seen to be praying furiously. There was no-one about at first, natural for the middle of the day in high summer, but as our small motorcade advanced, more and more people came out of their houses to watch us and wave, and by the time we reached the beach there were large crowds waiting for us. Manga asked what was happening. 'The word got round that film stars were coming to Tanur for a picture shoot', said one excited young fellow. 'Are they not film stars then?' He pointed to the girls. 'They certainly look like actresses'. When told of this, the five blushed prettily; and on the way home, waved languidly to their 'public'.

Same beach after the arrival of the 'film stars'

Every January, there is a big procession, with elephants, from the mosque in Pudiyangadi, another suburb of Tirur. It's just a ten-minute walk from the house to the route of the procession, which is enjoyed by members of all religions and sects. Hindus as well as followers of Islam revere the Muslim saint who inspires the procession. And there lots of schools and colleges in Pudiyangadi and people call it the 'education capital of Tirur' - a fairly modest epithet you might think until you know that one of the schools is the Government Higher Secondary School for Girls, which Manga attended. Tourist websites mention other local attractions, evincing great enthusiasm for the Tirur village of Pachattiri - 'a place of natural beauty and calm'. This is the small group of houses just beyond Thanjan Parambu where a mosque stands beside the river, and where the ferry used to cross.

The old ferry. Laksh and Indi [pointing], and others aboard.

There is now a new bridge and the ferrymen are out of work. Once we took a trip upstream from here in a tiny fishing boat, saw many pineapples growing and watched the fishermen launching their nets into the water in skilful and picturesque arcs. The local boys enjoyed diving into the water from the small jetty. The amplified voice of the muezzin called the faithful from miles around to prayer.

Gurudankavu is 6 km out of town. It is of interest because it is the only temple in Kerala dedicated to Garuda, a kite-like bird and the mount of Vishnu, and also curiously the symbol of the national airline of Muslim Indonesia. Manga's Dad used to take her to this temple [and to many others in the neighbourhood] to pray for her good health. There is another kavu nearby, this time dedicated to

Hanuman. It is said to be at the spot where Rama sent Hanuman over to Lanka to rescue Sita. Also claimed for Tirur is Thirunavaya, the home of the Mamankam festival - a huge meeting held every twelve years in ancient times when the new Perumal or King of the Cheras was chosen; it usually involved a bloody battle. There have been attempts recently to re-introduce the festival - the funfair and market side rather than the bloodshed I should add!

Thanchathu Ezhuthchan[vii] is the most famous son of the town, but M.N.Bahttathiri, a Sanskrit poet of the sixteenth century, was born in a nearby village, as was K.T.Nambissan, a noted Kathikali musician of the mid-20th century. The astronomer and mathematician Nilakantha Somayaji, who was born and brought up in Trikkandiyur itself, lived to be one hundred and inter alia worked out a proof that several planets orbited the sun [unfortunately he still believed that the sun orbited the Earth] and that the Earth rotated on its axis.[54] These theories are included in a book of 1501, therefore pre-dating the work of Tycho Brahe [1546-1601] who is usually credited with having made these discoveries.

[vii] The founder of the Malayalam language about whom we shall read later.

CHAPTER EIGHT

PONNANI and MEMORIES OF PATTIAMMA

'*There will be no pulp in a jackfruit that looks beautiful*' - Malayalam Proverb

About ten miles from Tirur lies Ponnani, the home of Manga's mother's family, and as a young girl, Manga used to go there to visit her grandmother, or pattiamma.

No evidence has yet been uncovered to demonstrate beyond doubt that the Romans, or indeed any of the very earliest travellers landed at Ponnani, and the town does not seem to have shared in the bonanza produced by trade with the West at that time. However, standing as it does at the mouth of the great Bharatapuzha River, and being the nearest port to the Palakkad Gap into Tamilnad, it would be surprising if landfalls were not made here in early times. And the town of Tondi has been identified as Ponnani by some historians. Tondi is mentioned in an inscription written in the 2nd or 3rd century BC, and also in the *Periplus* where it is called Tyndis, an important port 500 stadia [about 55 miles] north of Muziris.[i] By the tenth century, Ponnani was well known to Arab traders, from whom in fact, the town gets its name - 'Ponnanayum' means 'gold coin' - and many Arab coins have been found in Ponnani, so the port must have been very busy.[55] Later, Ponnani became the Zamorin's[ii] second capital city after Kozhikode; and the town was caught up in wars against the Portuguese and the British, about which we'll read more later in the chapter. Logan in the 1880s said that Ponnani, 'a port of some importance'[56], imported salt from Mumbai, though the new railway routes were much reducing the volume of this trade, and rice in large quantities. Exports consisted mainly of timber, especially teak from the Western Ghats, pepper of course, and coconut and coconut

---

[i] Another possibility is that Tyndis is modern Kadalundi, where Radhika had her wedding pictures taken.

[ii] The Zamorins were the rulers of Kozhikode and the surrounding area from the thirteenth century, following the fall of the Chera Empire in 1122 AD.

products. It was mainly small coasters that carried out this trade, as larger vessels had to anchor off the coast because of the sandbanks at the river's mouth, and this was the reason for the port's decline in importance.[57] Now the main occupation is fishing.

Manga and I went to Ponnani with Raju in a borrowed car in 1999 to see Manga's grandmother's house. Sadly it had been partly demolished to make room for an extension to the Samukhamadam, the Brahmin's community centre, and the rest of the building stood dark and deserted. Through the boards nailed across the windows could be glimpsed the dust-filled rooms where Manga and her sisters used to play. Now the ceiling sags, the walls decay, the floor rots. A family of mice has taken up residence in the old chest where Pattiamma used to keep her saris, and pigeons have got in through a broken pane of glass and are building a nest on the windowsill. Manga shed a quiet tear.

Later that day in Ponnani we met Manga's cousin Hariharan, who is Doraikutty's brother and the eleventh child in the family, and their mother, whom Manga always knew as 'Mami' - auntie. She was old and frail and unable to leave her bed, but she had recognised Manga, we thought, or at least understood who she was, and for that Manga was grateful. The old lady died a few days later.

We made another visit to Ponnani in 2002, and this was altogether a happier affair. My sister-in-law, Julie was with us on that occasion, and Raju, this time with Geetha and Keerthana, as well as Ravi and Shanta, Ammu and Apu. We began our journey in a bus and then crossed the River Bharatapuzha, first by means of a rickety bridge to the sand banks in the middle of the riverbed, then by boat to the other side. This route is only possible in the dry season of course. During the monsoon both the bridge and the sandbank could be beneath at least ten feet of rushing water. We caught another bus on the other side of the river and arriving safely in Ponnani, had tea with Hariharan, and were presented with my favourite jackfruit jam (home-made, naturally, and of particularly high quality), by his wife. We sat on the veranda, some of us on a swing, and a friend came and, squatting cross-legged on the veranda wall, told us about a project to open a Brahmin school. He talked a great deal. Geetha gave him a banana to eat so he slowed down a little!

Ponnani is probably best known as a centre of Islamic learning and Kerala Muslims call the town the 'Mecca of Kerala'. Malik Ibnu Dinar, the first Islamic missionary who came to Kerala is said to have visited the place. The vast majority of the townspeople are Muslim and there are about fifty mosques in the town, the oldest of which is the Jama Masjid,[iii] which was built in the sixteenth century by a renowned scholar who wrote an early history of Kerala. Logan says that 400 students were studying at the Jama Masjid Madrassa in 1887.[58]

Boats off Ponnani

The temple near Pattiamma's home is also of wider interest. It is a Devi Temple allegedly founded by Parasurama and given to the Brahmins of Sukapuram gramam, one of the mythical 64 colonies. The temple was actually built by a merchant who vowed during a storm at sea that he would dedicate a place of worship to the God if only He would rescue him and his cargo from the waves. A report at the end of the nineteenth century maintains that the temple was plundered by Tipu Sultan, the idol being destroyed and the

---

[iii] Nearly every town has a 'Jama Masjid'. That's because it means 'the biggest mosque'

srikovil used to store gunpowder. The idol was found in the well after Tipu's departure and restored, but the local community could not afford to repair all the damage and in due course it was handed into the care of the Zamorin.

Ponnani features most often in the history books in descriptions of the Portuguese period. In 1506 for example, ships from the town were involved in a sea battle between the Zamorin and the Portuguese, and although the Portuguese destroyed the town in revenge in the following year, the Zamorin's navy continued to use Ponnani as a base from which to ambush Portuguese ships. The shallows and sandbanks at the mouth of the river suited the guerrilla tactics used by the Zamorin's Muslim allies, the Kunjalis, who had flat bottomed and narrow boats. Ponnani was frequently counter-attacked by the Portuguese, and in 1558, it was blockaded, the Portuguese hoping to make the townspeople withdraw their support for the Kunjalis. The tactic, which has been used many times before and since, did not work, even though the blockade led to famine and hardship in the town

Following the departure of the Portuguese, the Dutch and the British struggled for control of trade with India, and in the 1660s the East India Company set up a trading post near Ponnani under the protection of the Zamorin. Logan comments 'it is difficult to over-estimate the benefits of the experience thus obtained in the Company's dealings with the natives, for the factors had perforce to study native character and to adapt themselves to it; and in doing this they were unconsciously fitting themselves to become the future rulers of the Empire.'[59]

In 1776, the fort at Ponnani was taken by Hyder Ali of Mysore. Hyder, with assistance from French, British and Portuguese officers, and some French troops, as well as '10,000 sepoys and 3,000 horse', drove off the Nair[iv] rulers of the town.[60] The Europeans at this stage were supporting Mysore as a balance against the Marathas, but sixteen years later, allegiances had changed and Ponnani was ceded to the British after Hyder's son Tipu Sultan was defeated at the battle of Tiruangadi.

It was nearly two centuries later that Manga used to visit her Pattiamma there.

[iv] The Nairs are the military caste in Kerala

'I don't have very much nice memories of Ponnani. We used to go there quite often when I was a child, Mum and me and perhaps one or more of my sisters. But I never saw any special affection between Mum and Pattiamma. Perhaps it was because Mum and Dad never really knew where the next meal was coming from, whereas Mum's sister and brothers were doing well, so Mum was the only one who was bit poor.

Pattiamma was not a bad woman, but a very orthodox Hindu, and because she was a widow, wearing a white sari, I was not allowed to touch her at all. There was a sort of big veranda open to the sky, with four side parapets where people used to sit and chat with passers-by, leading to a long hall with a prayer place in the corner where Pattiamma used to sit.

She was a fairly hefty woman, with a nice prominent figure and she wore red coral beads round her neck and plenty of ashes on her forehead. We used to go and give her a namascarum and then drink a cup of tea and I would talk to Mum and that's all. I never remember them sitting and talking like British people do anyway. We used to go and pray in the temple and come. It was very close by. There was another room at the end of the hall, to the left, but I'm not sure what it was for, probably a bedroom. We slept on the floor in the hall. Behind the hall was the kitchen, very long but narrow and dark. I used to sit on the steps that led from the hall to the kitchen and watch the cooking. There was a big chest full of rice, and another where all the pots and pans were kept. The old house is derelict now. We would usually only stay at Pattiamma's for a couple of days and then go home.

One thing - if we went there by bus, which we did when Mum took us - the bus was so overcrowded and the roads were so uneven, I used to feel very sick - crying and lying down on Mum's lap - oh it was miserable.' Manga obviously preferred to go by boat and speaks animatedly about those trips. *'On the other hand, when I went with Dad, we went by the river on a punt or sometimes a motorboat. Motorboat didn't take all that long - two or three hours maybe - but the punting boat was much cheaper, cost an anna or sixpence or something so we used to go by that, in the night. It would reach there in the morning - it went overnight with one or two stops maybe. The boat was quite big, like the ones they use for tourists in the Backwaters now and they had two punters - one at each end. They knew where it was shallow enough to use their poles. They were very long. There used to be a little kerosene lamp or sometimes a petromax. It would take a load of copra or perhaps chaggeri [the coconuts' outer covering] and betel leaves, things like that. It wasn't really for passengers but that was nice. On the way back, there was probably fish or rice or salt on board, I'm not sure. Although of course we never ate any fish, I was used to the smell because a lot of fish was sent from Tirur railway station. With the motor boat, one thing worried me. People told stories about a boat getting caught in a fishing net and turned right over, tipping all the passengers into the water. I always got worried when we reached the place where the river - the Bharatapuzha - joined the Arabian Sea. The current was in great force there and if we took the wrong course, there were too much waves and the sea went ratatatata against the side of the boat - it was very frightening. So the captain had to make his way very cleverly.*

Going back to Pattiamma, she brought up three boys and two girls herself, as Pattappa died quite young. He didn't do any of the traditional Iyer jobs. He was well educated and worked for the Government I think: something to do with the land tax. Another thing I remember is that the second uncle - Doraikutty's father - was thrown out of the house. I don't know why; some misunderstanding or something. We never talked about things like that or asked questions. Anyway, he moved into another house nearby and started a business running buses and became quite rich. Another son was married to my auntie's daughter - his niece - and they had two sons. We met one of them when we went the first time to Ponnani in the car with Raju. He wasn't quite right and nor was the other son....I suppose when you get marriages within the family, these things can happen; they were both funny kids.

That auntie, who was also my cousin, we called Achummu akka and she was a very nice person. I always liked her. Her husband was a philanderer sort of chap, but he built a huge house - or it seemed so to me as a child - with three enormous rooms and you could go upstairs as well! And the rooms had great big mirrors in them - about four feet across, with a gold frame and reaching from floor to ceiling - kalkannadi we call it, proper mirrors so you could see a gap between your finger and its reflection when you touched the glass. I would stand in front of them and admire myself, and pull faces and dance! It was lovely because we only had a tiny mirror at home. And they had a pond at the end of their garden, and a tall mud wall separating the garden from the fields, and lots of coconut trees and other trees; for a child it was fascinating.

When I passed my Senior School Leaving Certificate, I went to ask my big uncle Kontha Mama if he would help with the expenses of going to college. Kontha Mama was Doraikutty's father. But while I was there I caught typhoid, and they looked after me. I had to stay in a sort of shed away from the main house. Auntie was very kind and used to make me all sorts of good things to eat and used to come and stay with me at night so I wouldn't be lonely. They gave me chloromycetin and that time it was very new and each capsule cost awful lot of money, so when I got better I didn't think I could ask for any help with college - so [Manga's voice became rather wistful] *I didn't go, and got a job instead...*

Mum's house was very close to the temple but our family didn't have anything to do with running it. That was the job of the Namboodiris, the Embranthiris [who say the prayers], the Mussads [the cooks], the Varias, and the Sharodis [who collect flowers and make them into garlands for the gods]. But there was a sort of Community Centre for Brahmins right next door to the house and Mum's family managed that. It's called Samukhamadam and all the Brahmin feasts and festivals took place there. They enlarged it just recently and knocked down part of our house to make room. We saw that when we went with Raju, do you remember? It made me cry when I saw it.

There was another sad memory about Ponnani. Mum once went to a wedding there. And someone lost their gold chain. Mum was the only poor person so they blamed her - everyone said she had stolen it. She didn't know what they were talking about and she was ever so upset. She came home saying she should never have gone to the wedding. In a few days time, my uncle - Kontha Mama - came to Trikkandiyur to say sorry: the chain had been found. Above the doorway in the big houses there is a sort of shelf, and if anyone finds anything lying about the room they will put it on this shelf. That's where they had found the chain.

Another time Doraikutty's father came to ask Mum's forgiveness. Touching Mum's feet and saying how sorry he was. One of his sons [not Doraikutty] had gone missing. Ponnani you know is a strongly Muslim town and everyone thought that the boy had gone off and converted to Islam. People said they had seen him among the Mappilas.[v] *Everybody searched for the boy, and eventually he was found. I don't know where he had been. Doraikutty's father was a good chap. I can see him quite*

[v] Kerala Muslims

clearly. He was dark-skinned and a big man. You'll have to ask Doraikutty for some more stories.

The husband of another of my aunts in Ponnani [Amakutty] was a devotee of Subramanium and he used to sit and pray and would go into a trance for fifteen, twenty minutes. He would make predictions and tell you what to do to make things right. He didn't know what he had said when he woke up. When I saw him he was an old man with a big beard, and very quiet spoken. He was a very respectworthy person. His son ran a restaurant in Madras and when I was doing my nursing training there, he made sure that I was well fed.

CHAPTER NINE

BEGUILING BIHAR

'*Out of the strong came forth sweetness*' Judges, 14.

'*If a crow baths, does it become a crane?*' - Malayalam proverb

Fatehpur Sikri

We speculated that Manga's ancestors might have been occupying the corridors of power in the palaces of the kingdoms of the Ganges valley around 400 BC. The most important of these kingdoms was Magadh, which under the Mauryans became the greatest Indian empire until that of the Mughals two thousand years later. It's ironic perhaps that the glittering Mauryan dynasty should have arisen in what is now the state of Bihar - probably the poorest and most destitute part of India in the twentieth century. And equally amazing that two great religions, Buddhism and Jainism, should have arisen in the same place and in the same period.

The domination of the Mauryans began in around 320 BC and continued for about 120 years. Chandragupta, whose religion was Jainism, was the first Mauryan ruler. He extended the Empire of the previous ruling family in Magadh, the Nandas, by conquering Panjab, Gujarat and Mumbai before he abdicated voluntarily. His son and successor was Bindusara and then came the man whom H.G.Wells called 'the greatest of kings', Ashoka. Ashoka continued the Mauryan conquests until his Empire controlled over 40 per cent of the sub- continent. One of his victories was over the nation of Kalinga [Orissa]. This event led to a turning point in Ashoka's career.[i] The tale of the conquest and its aftermath is related in one of the edicts issued at Ashoka's command:

> On conquering Kalinga, Ashoka felt remorse, for, when an independent country is conquered, the slaughter, death and deportation of the people is extremely grievous to Ashoka and weighs heavily on his mind...Even those who are fortunate to have escaped, and who's love is undiminished, suffer from the misfortunes of their friends, acquaintances, colleagues and relatives...Today if a hundredth or a thousandth part of those people who were killed or died or were deported when Kalinga was annexed were to suffer similarly, it would weigh heavily on the mind of Ashoka...This inscription of Dharma has been engraved so that any sons or great-grandsons that I may have should not think of gaining new conquests, and in whatever victories they may gain should be satisfied with patience and light punishment. They should only consider conquest by dharma[ii] to be a true conquest, and delight in dharma should be their whole delight, for this is of value in both this world and the next.[iii]

Ashoka had this and other edicts engraved on rocks and on pillars throughout his lands. They advertised his laws and rules, and his advice on how his people should behave. The principles were similar to those of Buddhism: non-violence, and proper behaviour

---

[i] The story is graphically told in a Hindi film, *Ashoka the Great* [2001]

[ii] Dharma means one's life's natural duties, but also the teachings and principles of Buddhism.

[iii] Rock edict II can be found at Dhaulagiri near Bhubaneswar in Odisha (formerly Orissa), and at Jagnda in Ganjam district, Odisha.

to one's neighbours, for example. Also, respect for all religions and all forms of life, including animals; standardisation of judicial procedures and punishments; kindness to travellers by for example planting shading trees along all roads. This is why Ashoka has been revered throughout India and the world.

Sadly, Ashoka's principles did not survive his death and his successors failed to follow his lead; in fact his Empire gradually fell apart. The last Emperor was assassinated in 180 BC and there was no single successor. The Empire split up and it was not until 500 years later that a new pan-Indian power - the Gupta dynasty - arose.

During the period of Maghad's rule over Bihar and the rest of North India, there was another notable event: Alexander the Great entered India in search of world domination. Alexander arrived in 327 BC and left a year later having made no great impact on the sub- continent, but his journey there was epic, and the tales told by his followers added to the mystique of India in the West. In T.H.White's *The Sword in the Stone* the forests round Uther Pendragon's castle were inhabited by creatures with gigantic ears in which they wrapped themselves at night; and others had one huge foot under which they could shelter from the rain, and so on.[61] These were not the products of White's imagination but contained in travellers' tales: Alexander's soldiers and Marco Polo swore they'd seen them in India.

As well as being a possible home for Manga's ancestors on their gradual passage south, Bihar is relevant to this story because I lived and worked there, latterly with Manga, during one of the state's saddest and lowest periods. That was between 1966 and 1968, when the state suffered from independent India's worst and, thank goodness, last, great famines. I still have some newspaper cuttings from that period:

> Jhumari-Telaiya, March 24th 1967: Yet another report of alleged starvation deaths has been received... Jiban Kumhar of village Nandodih, committed suicide by throwing himself under a running train to save himself from the pangs of hunger... reports of starvation and near starvation are pouring in these days... people have not tasted rice for the last three or four months. Dr.G.P.Tripathy, a prominent physician of this town, told The Indian Nation today that in the course of his professional calls he had seen a large number of people suffering from diarrhoea,

> anaemia, and swelling of face. Many people he said had died of these diseases. They would not be counted as dying of starvation, but starvation caused the diseases.[62]

Jhumri-Tilaiya, as we spelt it, was the nearest town to the school at Tilaiya Dam. Dr.Tripathy's son, Bhupendra, attended the school. He was a good cricketer.

Rain came at last, but the wrong sort and at the wrong time.

> Hazaribagh, March 28th: A furious gale with hundred-mile-an-hour speed lashed Hazaribagh and its suburbs on Sunday. Hailstones and rain accompanied the gale, which has left behind a trail of devastation. Cricket-ball-sized hailstones killed one human being and 24 cattle while 30 persons are lying in the hospital with injuries. Rabi,[iv] mango and mahua[v] had been damaged on large scale. After failure of paddy, the farmers had pinned their hopes on the Rabi crops. But now the battle is almost lost. Six buildings in Hazaribagh town and fifty huts in rural areas were battered down...[63]

My school was in Hazaribagh District and we too were affected by the storm: the corrugated iron roof of my bungalow blew off. Fortunately, the hailstones in Tilaiya were not as big as cricket balls and I was able to ward them off, huddled in my charpoy under my trusty umbrella.

The storm relieved the water shortage for a short time but made the food shortage worse. *The Indian Nation* summarised the position in its Sunday edition on April 2nd.

> Thirty-five persons in Hazaribagh alone starved to death in the first half of March. Some starvation deaths go unnoticed. This is just the beginning. Countless deaths may occur if immediate steps are not taken to give back life to the living corpses. The repeated appeals of Mr Jaya Prakash Narayan, Chairman of the Bihar Relief Society, have fallen on hard rocks...The battle against hunger seems to be a losing one in the state. People in most parts

---

[iv] Rabi is the name for the winter crop, harvested in spring – could be wheat, barley, peas, or oats for example.

[v] Mahuca longifolia, a tree grown for its seeds, wood and flowers.

> are either starving or getting food twice a week or are eating grass, roots and wild fruits...[64]

> Patna, May 5th: Story of a Dying Village by Janardan Thakur [Chief of News Bureau]. Today I write the obituary of a dying village...On a day in March about two hundred miserable human creatures trudged fifteen weary miles to the mansion in Gaya Mufassil where the district Relief Committee has its office. They were people from village Hemaidpur in Tankuppa gram panchayat of Wazirganj block. For the third successive year the crops had failed in the village, its last reserves had gone and distress emigration had started. Driven by desperation, the hungry villagers came straggling to the Committee, pleading for help. There was at hand a voluntary agency that wanted to start a relief kitchen for starving people. But this village was 'too far in the interior'...And so back went the hungry creatures into the oblivion of their desolate village. The writing on the wall had gone unheeded. Within a month from that March day a dozen human lives were lost, many houses were abandoned, many families were disrupted. Hemaidpur became a bottomless cavern of misery...We returned to Hemaidpur on April 20th...It was dark when we reached the village. Not even the twinkle of an oil lamp in the mud huts behind the scraggy date trees and bushes. Not even the stirring of a leaf...Slowly, some scrawny shapes materialised. The jeep's lights revealed a frightening sight: about twenty-five human creatures of various ages, in various stages of decay. Facing us were the gaunt frames of peasants with cadaverous eyes, tattered and distraught women, little boys and girls with spindly legs and bloated bellies...[65]

Faced with these reports, I had visions of a small child asking me some time in the future, 'What did you do in the Great Famine, Daddy?' 'Why, I taught the people to speak English, my child'. It didn't sound right. So it was in that long summer vacation that I went off to work for an organisation called CORAGS, the relief committee of the [Protestant] National Christian Council. At first I served in a Food Kitchen, literally dishing out simple meals to rows of starving souls. But later I became part of the Rice for Work scheme. This was a much more progressive operation. Villages built their own infrastructure - bunds [simple dams], roads etc. - and were paid by CORAGS according to their need. I drove round the district, through jungles, across streams, along roads for which the description 'cart-track' would have been flattery, in a jeep-truck loaded with bags of wheat donated mostly by Lutheran World Relief of America. The sacks were made of such fine material that soon, many peasants could be seen wearing vests emblazoned with the words 'A Gift from the People of the United States'. I had one myself.

Then I worked for a while with a Pump Maintenance Team. Expensive deep wells were lying unused all over the district because the electric pumps that had to be used to raise the water, had broken down and no one in the village knew how to repair them. So I drove round a van full of spares and an electrician beside me. We did a very good job.

CORAGS Famine Team; me in the centre, leaning against our jeep.

Unfortunately I was not much help except as a driver. Many villagers assumed that a European so far from home must be there to do something useful: healing their sick was a popular assumption. I fear I was a bit of a let-down. Finally I spent some time in the deep interior of Bhandaria in the forest of Chota Nagpur again delivering grain to remote villages. I stayed with a Protestant missionary, Lyle Burdett from Leicester, whose flock consisted mainly of Adivasis, and who'd been in India for twenty odd years. '*And how many people have you converted in that time?*' I asked. '*Oh that's not a priority*', he said. '*I try to meet the needs of the whole community. Of course we welcome anyone who wants to become a*

Christian, but I wouldn't say I've actually converted anyone'. He was a very good man and I wish I'd kept in touch with him. I still have the cowbell and the ceremonial axe he gave me when I left. While I was there there was a fight in the village and one man suffered a very severe head injury. I had the job of driving him to the nearest hospital, about ten miles away if I remember, along a very uneven track. At every bump, the patient screamed; but I had to get him to the hospital as quickly as possible. It was an experience I would not like to repeat.

I did take the occasional day off during the two months and would borrow the CORAGS jeep. It was rather a basic vehicle, military issue and with no concessions to comfort. The pedals, gear lever and door handles were bare metal and I'm not sure there was any covering on the seats either. This would have been a minimal problem in normal weather conditions, but in a Bihar summer, it was almost unbearable since the metal became extremely hot under the blazing sun. Also it was left hand drive. Still for us it was the height of luxury: driving instead of our usual modes of transport - walking, cycling with Manga perched on the crossbar, or squashed into crowded and bumpy buses. One weekend we set out on an educational tour and visited the ancient university town of Nalanda, and Rajgir, one of the capitals of ancient Magadh. Everything seemed to be going well when suddenly the engine coughed and gave out. We were far from any habitation and had seen nothing on the road for hours. To say we were at a loss would hardly describe our predicament. Should we abandon the jeep and start walking? If so, in which direction? But surely we needed to protect the vehicle. Should one of us therefore stay and the other walk? But that could be dangerous... All we could see was dusty scrub for miles around. We had a little water but no food. We were beginning to wonder whether we should panic, when, by great good fortune, a truck appeared in the distance. We raced into the middle of the road, and the driver had no option but to stop. Manga quickly calmed him: he had thought we might be dacoits [rather cunningly disguised presumably]. These modern highwaymen still haunted roads in the more remote parts of India in those days. Anyway, Manga persuaded him to tow us to the nearest garage. Neither of us had a tow-rope, but the driver solved the problem by unwinding the turban from his head and tying the ten feet or so long rag onto the bumper. It was nerve-wracking enough to be so close to the towing lorry, but after the rag snapped several times, the distance was down to a few inches. We eventually found a garage. I forget what the problem was now, but the repair was minor and swiftly done and we were on our way. And so we did get to see the two great ancient landmarks of Bihar. Later we made a trip to Bodh Gaya, a town full of delights: the temple, the stone seat on which it was said Siddhartha sat to meditate, the famous bodhi tree [or its descendant anyway] and the beautiful monasteries set up by various countries in their own national styles. We walked most of the seven miles from the railway station at dusty old Gaya. And we also visited Patna, the capital of Bihar where we thought we might be a little less conspicuous and where Manga bathed in the holy Ganges. I ate for the first time those tasty miniature pooris filled with very hot, bitter-sweet sauce, called golgappa. An ancient mosque built in the sixteenth century by an Afghan ruler, is there; the eighteenth century grain store, the Golghar; and the very imposing Har Mandir, the second most important Gurudwara [Sikh temple] in the world, where I learned a lot about that religion.

I spent two years of my life in Bihar and found much to admire and enjoy. But the beauty of many of its ancient buildings and the glitter of its history contrasted harshly with the widespread poverty that I observed and the apparent absence of hope and spirit among so many of its people. I could find little to persuade me that the future would hold much joy for this part of India.

CHAPTER TEN

MANGA'S MEMORIES: MEDICAL MATTERS

'Better our own gums than the teeth of other people' - Malayalee proverb

'The contribution made by Kerala to the theory and practice of Ayurveda is substantial' - A Sreedhara Menon[66]

Ayurvedic medicine seems to have become important in India at about the time that Manga's ancestors were dwelling in the Ganges Valley. So this holistic and very Indian form of healing goes back a long way.

My nephew Raju is a great advocate of Ayurveda. 'If it didn't work' he says, 'then surely by now it would be forgotten. But in fact more and more people are turning to it. New colleges are opening up mostly here in Kerala and many westerners, especially Americans, English, Germans come to learn about the cures.' Ayurveda should not be confused with herbal medicine, which has been used throughout the world for as long as people have tried to cure their ailments; or homoeopathy, a western invention, introduced in Germany in 1796. Homoeopathy is popular in India though and my great-niece Aparna is now a qualified practitioner.

Ayurveda is a holistic treatment system, and a very complex one with many different branches. Fundamentally though it is about diet and a balanced lifestyle to prevent illness, it stresses the importance of nutrition, and treats the whole person not just the symptoms. Of course sometimes an imbalance develops and action then needs to be taken. Thus Raju advised Manga when she was suffering from a spell of pneumonia and bronchitis: '*Eat food and drink fluids that are warm, almost near body temperature. When we have phlegm we should avoid cold foods, citrus fruits and grapes. Chitti* [mother's younger sister] *will be OK if she follows simple rules. Drink boiled warm water with basil leaves, pepper and dried ginger. Honey with pepper powder can be consumed five times a day.*[i] *No*

[i] More surprisingly black pepper is also used for the treatment of cholera, when mixed with opium and asofoetedfia. Aparently it includes an element identical

cold water or hair washing for a month. Lots of turmeric and boiled buttermilk with pepper - pepper is the number one for reducing phlegm. Have inhalations with de-congestant oils. If Chitti does all these, she'll have no more bronchitis or pneumonia.' Gopal, my niece's husband, broke his leg badly a few years ago and he was prescribed oil massage. The treatment seemed to us to go on for ages and be rather expensive because of the cost of the oils, but he did get better in the end.

Ayurvedic Hospital, Kottakal

I've had two experiences of traditional medicine while in India. Years ago, I had a sort of eczema in the palm of my right hand which no orthodox treatment seemed to be able to shift. When I went to India for one holiday, Raju sent me to a homoeopath. He asked many questions about my life style, and after the consultation prescribed a homoeopathic medicine [which consisted of one part of salt in many millions parts of water], but also instructed me not to drink coffee, not to take salty foods, and not to use soap, but wash

---

to morphine. Patnaik, Naveen (1993) *The Garden of Life,* London & New Delhi: Aquarian, p 92.

with green gram powder instead. The skin condition disappeared within days. It occasionally recurs and when it does I follow the same treatment [except for the medication] and it always seems to work. On another occasion I drank much more delicious fresh pineapple juice than was good for me. Result - galloping diarrhoea. Raju recommended an Ayurvedic medicine and ran into town to buy some. I duly took it. His brother Ravi said 'no, no - I have some medicine that was given to me by a pharmacist - he swears by it'. I drank a spoonful. My sister-in-law Manikutty was a fan of herbal medicine and offered arrowroot gruel. How could I refuse?

The net result was that I was constipated for the rest of the holiday!

Manga remembers her encounters with medical matters when she was a little girl.

'When we were at Infants School - we started there when we were five years old and stayed for five years before going to the High School - we had a health inspector visiting every six months. She would look at our hair and our nails and we were given a bitter - very very bitter - drink to get rid of the worms. All the pupils were anaemic and that was mainly due to the worms and of course also because we didn't have proper nourishing meals to eat. If you're anaemic you are tempted to eat all sorts of things - uncooked rice for example. Also the walls at home and school would be made of quarried stone [laterite] and they would have holes in them where there was a particular kind of yellow clay. You could dig this out with your fingers and eat it. It had a lovely earthy smell and taste. But it would give even more worms in your stomach. Sometimes when you were sick they would come out - I used to scream when I did that, and also when you go to the toilet they would come out. So we would need this medicine. Mum would sometimes take me to the Ayurvedic doctor but his cures wouldn't always work so the medicine was necessary then. Also every two or three months we would take another bitter medicine in the morning. That was made out of a seed called kadakai. You cook it in water and infuse it and the water would go very brown and that would purge you. We would do this as a family. Either you take castor oil or kadakai. This would make you go to the toilet six or seven times. You wouldn't eat much - just a kanji [gruel] made from brown broken rice. By about three o'clock, you would have cleared out your stomach and then you could have buttermilk and a bit of rice to eat. We would stand in a line to take the medicine and jump up and down to help the medicine go down quickly - it was ever so bitter. The only good thing was that we got

some jagaree, that's unrefined sugar, to go with it to sweeten the taste, and we didn't often get jagaree so that was nice!

One day we had to go to school for a smallpox vaccination. It was a big event in the village: everyone took their children to be vaccinated, because there was a lot of smallpox about that time. They had a special needle with multiple points and dipped it in the vaccine. Then pushed it into your arm. Whether it hurt or not, the thought of it made you cry out.

We had other medicines too. I had a cold and cough most of the time because I had a bit asthma. When I was wheezing badly, Dad would collect some roots and dry them and grind them up with a seed like cumin and with ginger, and then we'd go to a woman who kept goats and give her the powder and she would milk the goat directly in to the pot with the powder in it, and I would drink it - warm and fresh and frothy. I would have this for fourteen days and it would clear up the cough and cold for some time.

The other thing that helped us recover from colds and fever was a gruel made with broken rice. You know when you get paddy from the fields, you pound it to separate the chaff. Two people would often do the pounding together, one then the other in a rhythm. We used long poles held upright and brought them down quite hard on the paddy, which was in a stone bowl. Then you put the paddy onto a sack or something and tossed it in the air and the chaff would blow away and just leave the rice.

That would leave what we called red rice, because it would still have a skin on it. Most people liked polished rice though - with the brown skin taken off. So we would pound the rice again, more gently. Some of the grains would get broken though, and that was broken rice. Now the skin was really good for you and I suppose we shouldn't have polished the rice at all really. But we would collect the skin and mix it with jagaree and eat it. Lovely. It was full of vitamin B complex. We had a friend who was a Brahmin and she had some paddy fields round the village. We used to go to her and ask for broken rice when we were ill; well it was like begging really. Then mum boiled it up just like ordinary rice, in water. It was good because it was easier to swallow, especially for children. We used to use the skin of the rice seed - it's a sort of mauve colour - to make a poultice.

I was good at sewing when I was little and I once did a sampler that everyone admired, even the grown-ups in the Women's Club. Then I got a very bad boil under my arm and they said it was because the god was jealous of all the praise I was getting. It was under my arm and very painful and mum used a mustard poultice to cure it.

I was rather weak and feeble when I was little. If I saw a dead body being carried through the street, I would get so frightened that I would get a fever! They would carry the body on two poles tied together and covered with a sheet and you could see the body shape. There were two cemeteries in the village. One was for the Brahmins who would be cremated and the other for the Malayalees, who were usually buried. When we walked to school our burial ground was to the south. We would never sit facing south because that was where you went when you died. One of the things that my Dad did as a caste duty was to carry the bodies of Brahmins to their pyre and he would stay there while the body burnt. Sometimes the corpse would seem to sit up during the burning and this, not altogether surprisingly, would scare everyone, so Dad would be the person who gently pushed the torso down.

Dad's elder brother knew Ayurvedic medicine. He used to make a special tea for me with cardamom, cinnamon, pepper and so on. I had a chest complaint once and I went to stay with him and his wife in Thrissur, so he could help me. But when my sister came to visit she saw me before I'd had a bath and my clothes were a bit grubby. So she told her uncle that I looked like an orphan child, and took me home! My uncle became a sanyasin, someone who forsakes family life to pray, after his wife died.

If you had mumps in those days, people would laugh at you because you looked funny with a swollen face, so you got a coconut and tied it round your neck with a string: people believed that the badness would go into the coconut. You would go and stand by the gate and people would laugh even more. Rotten thing to do really! One person in the village had an elephant tooth; they lived where Balan's shop used to be. If we had mumps we would go there and borrow the tooth and grind it and put it on the swelling like a poultice and the swelling would tend to go down, I don't know why.

If I had a bad tummy-ache, dad would do cupping. He's put something burning in a mud pot and put the pot on my stomach and as the oxygen was used up, there'd be a vacuum, which would suck on my stomach. They thought this would get the badness out. Something that always worked was using spiders' webs to stop cuts from bleeding, and it would also heal the cut in time. Another thing that was used a lot in India, not just at home, was putting leeches on wounds that were going septic. The leeches would eat away the rotten tissue and leave the wound clean and healthy. People in the west used to laugh at us for that, but now they too use leeches. It is a funny feeling but it really works well. We used to get some fungus infection on our feet - bit like athletes' foot I think. Our feet would get wet walking everywhere without shoes or anything and the fungus would grow between the toes. Dad would grind up henna leaves and put the powder on and the fungus would clear up in no time.

Dad was famous in the village for the way he looked after people who had smallpox or chicken pox. When the pocks appeared on the skin, the sufferer would call Dad and he would go to their home and examine them. He could say how long it would take for the pocks to go and tell them that until then, they would have to stay in a darkened room and not go out; neither allow anyone outside the immediate family to come in. The patient should rest as much as possible. Dad would notify the authorities if it was a case of smallpox and once I remember he went to the owners of a travelling cinema which happened to be in the village and told them they would have to close because of the danger of spreading the highly contagious disease. Dad would prescribe a plain and simple diet avoiding fried food, meat or ghee. Buttermilk was allowed together with as much fluid as possible to drink, especially chulamvellam - water infused with chitha, ginger, cardamom, and other spices. If the patient had trouble with his bowels, Dad would suggest a drink made from pounded raisins and sultanas. He treated the pocks with the leaves of the neem tree, ground up and made into a paste: this paste could also be eaten. Dad told the patients that they must not scratch the pocks but if the itching was unbearable they could use a bunch of neem leaves. Dried leaves, powdered, could also be used to fill the pocks and this often prevented scarring; and turmeric was used to soothe the skin where the pocks had left sores. If there was infection in the eyes, Dad would wipe them with onion juice [which sounds very painful]. No bath was allowed till after the pocks had gone but if the patient had a high fever he could be washed in boiled, cooled water infused with jasmine. When a bath was allowed it was filled with leaves and flowers from all sorts of plants like the jackfruit and banyan, and cinnamon was added too.'

Prayers were offered up in the temple to the goddess of smallpox, Mariamma. Mariamma is an ancient goddess going back to times prior to the Brahminical pantheon, though she is now seen as affiliated to Parvathi. She is worshipped mainly by Tamilians, for whom she is a protector of the village, and a fertility goddess who brings children and good crops. And although she can ward off disease and death, she must be appropriately propitiated; for if she is neglected, she will bring disease to the village. In Tamil, 'maari' means rain, which is needed for the crops and also to bring relief from the diseases associated with the hot dry summer. The Goddess is less well known in Kerala although one of the stories is associated with the founder of the state. You'll remember that Parasurama killed his mother Renuka on the orders of his father. Renuka was brought back to life, but on the death of her husband threw herself on the flames of his funeral pyre. In order to save her, Varuna the rain god, sent a sudden heavy shower to put out the flames. Renuka lived but was badly burned and the villagers treated her body with turmeric powder and neem leaves and gave her buttermilk and tender coconut water to drink. The fever and skin damage she suffered are similar to the symptoms of smallpox, hence Renuka's association with Mariamma.

Manga's father was also asked to treat jaundice. People would come to him with symptoms like yellowish skin, yellow eyeballs, loss of appetite, abdominal pain and sometimes itching and he would take a sewing needle and move it round and round in front of their eyes while saying a prayer. He never told Manga or anyone else as far as she knows what prayer he said, but we think it might have come from the 'Atharva Veda' [chapter 1 verse 22], prayers associated with the Vedic culture of northern India and written around 2000 BC.

We came across the verses, described as a 'charm against jaundice', in *Sources of Indian Tradition* edited by Ainslie Embree. This is a possible translation:

> Let the golden rays of the sun soothe your pains and restore your strength
>
> Let the yellow of your skin go up to the yellow sun;
>
> Let your skin return to the colour of the brown cow which is holy and has the protection of Rohini;
>
> Let the colour of the cow envelop you and protect you.
>
> Into the golden feathers of the parrot do I deposit the yellowness of your skin;

> Let the yellow ropanaka bird absorb the colour of your skin; Into the turmeric do I send the yellowness of your skin;
>
> Let the yellowness transfer into this bowl of water.[67]

And Manga's father would then put the needle into the water and she remembers it turning yellow. If it didn't her father would have to say he couldn't help the person. That was the religious part of the healing process.

My father-in-law would then advise his patients about their diet and lifestyle. They should adopt a fat free diet, he told them. They should eat plenty of carbohydrates [rice] and drink a lot of water, with glucose. They should also pick leaves from the Amari bush and grind them and put the powder into the water. But they should drink no milk except buttermilk for seven days. It was important to take plenty of rest.

CHAPTER ELEVEN

ELSEWHERE - THE TEMPLES OF TAMILNAD

'These temples are torch-bearers of the glorious heritage of the Tamil-speakingregion...' Templenet

'*When necessity compels, a temple is a mere compound*' Malayalam proverb

The Meenakshi temple at Madurai

The imposing temples found in Tamilnad differ enormously from the modest and rather homely religious buildings of Kerala, and deservc a chapter to themselves. To quote the website *Templenet* again, the former's 'lofty towers dot the skyline of the southernmost state of India'. The Meenakshi Temple in Madurai has perhaps the best of these 'lofty towers' or gopurams. The Pandyas, rulers in the 13th and 14th centuries, and the Cholas who preceded them and built for example the great temple at Thanjavur [Tanjore], were the best-known builders of spectacular gopurams. However, although there was a Meenakshi Temple in Madurai at the time of the Pandyas, it was probably burned down by Muslim invaders, and the present temple dates from the seventeenth century when the Naiks ruled Tamilnad. As a family, we know the temple quite well. When we first saw the magnificent towers, with Grandma, my mother, in 1979, we were just overwhelmed, and each time we've seen the temple since it has been with a sense of wonder, admiration and joy. Another memorable visit was with our friends, Rika and Frank, when a sudden unseasonal storm flooded the precincts of the temple. More rain fell in an hour on that one December day than normally falls in the whole month.

Indi blessed by an elephant

We removed our shoes and waded through four inches of water to reach the shelter of the temple. The temple site is huge and contains no less than 14 gopurams, four of which, in the east, south, west and north, are of great size - around 160 feet tall. And all the way to the top, they're decorated by sculptures, telling tales of the Gods. There are many [allegedly over a million], sculptures in the temple complex, and extensive halls with so many pillars that it looks as though forests of stone have grown within.

Madurai Temple is dedicated to the goddess in the form of Meenakshi, the fish-eyed woman. The building bustles with activity, inside and out: Victoria once had a blouse made by a tailor within the temple itself during the couple of hours that she was exploring the amazing structure. The commercial activity that is a feature of many Tamil temples worries some people, and of course a similar situation in the temple in Jerusalem worried Jesus so much that he overthrew the tables of the money-changers, but I love the bustle, the acceptance that religion is part of life.

There is a temple at Kanniya Kumari [Cape Comorin] which is dedicated to another female deity, Kanniya Kumari herself in fact. *The Periplus of the Erythraean Sea,* a most valuable book dating from around the time of the birth of Christ, and from which I will quote again, says: 'After this comes another stopping place called Komar, where there is a little settlement and a port; in it men who wish to lead a holy life for the rest of their days remain there celibate; they come there and they perform ablutions. Women, too, do the same. For it is said that at one time the goddess remained there and performed ablutions.'[68] The Kanniya Kumari Temple is also known as Kumari Amman, and is what you might call uncompromising I think, rather like a fortress with its massive walls, and lacking the mighty decorated towers of other Tamil temples. There seems to have been a temple at this point, the southernmost tip of India since Vedic times, but the present structure was probably erected in the eighth century in the time of the Pandya kings and extensively altered by successive rulers thereafter. What most impresses us, and I guess most visitors, is the beautiful image of the maiden. She is carved from black stone and has a sparkling nose-ring, which, it is said, can be seen far out at sea. The temple is dark, and its pillars black, and one can imagine it being quite a frightening place if one were alone. But whenever we have been there, we have shared the experience with crowds of happy, noisy pilgrims, making their way through the gaps between market stalls and, eschewing queues, pushing their way with much good humour towards their goal, the heart of the temple.

We are also acquainted with the temples of Mamallapuram or Mahabalipuram as it used to be known. We drove there on Rosemary and Tony's first full day in India and these ancient and historic buildings formed a perfect introduction to the wonders of the East! The temple complex includes halls carved out of the living granite, complicated bas-reliefs and detailed sculptures, and the glorious shore temples looking out over the Bay of Bengal. All these magnificent structures date from the Pallava period between the sixth and ninth centuries. In the year that my sister-in-law Julie came to India with us, an excellent guide, recruited by Hari, our relation in Chennai, showed us excavations that were revealing even more ancient structures on the site. Since then the 2004 tsunami, that laid waste the coastal areas of so much of south Asia, and tragically deprived so many of their lives and livelihoods, also temporarily uncovered further stone buildings and carvings out to sea at Mamallapuram, perhaps the remains of the Seven Pagodas of which British visitors wrote in the eighteenth century. That's the trouble with building castles on the sands - they do get washed away.

We'll conclude this very quick sketch of the Temples of Tamilnad with an extract from Michael Wood's book *The Smile of Murugan*. The temple in question is at Tiruchendor, which, like Mamallapuram is on the Coramandel coast, but a little further south. It's another temple that we've seen. Our visit was a little marred as I recall by a hotel with slightly smelly drains, but we had a wonderful evening. We were busy buying stainless steel from the market in the temple precincts - there were some miniature pots and pans that the children loved - when a parade of elephants in full regalia appeared. Trumpets were blown and drums banged and the whole temple lit up with flaming torches. It seemed that for many of the crowd milling around the stalls it was just another procession; for us it was from another world. A magical and unforgettable experience

Murugan is variously known as the God of War or Victory and is the protector of the land of the Tamils. In Wood's book he is named the 'King of the Smile' and is compared to Apollo. Wood describes with real passion a scene set in Tiruchendor Temple during a Murugan festival, concluding '...the sense of excitement was quite overwhelming: the dim light, the puja flames, the damp heat, the thick, sweet smell of incense and ghee, the drenching scent of jasmine and marigolds, the sweat of our own half-naked bodies - it all combined in an intoxicating, almost sexual effect.'[69]

That's what I call religion! Very India you might say.

CHAPTER TWELVE

DOUBTING THOMAS

'This period is marked by the rare advantage of furnishing very few materials for History; which is indeed little more than a register of the crimes, follies, and misfortunes of mankind.' - Gibbon *'The Decline and Fall of the Roman Empire'*

The decline and fall of their Empire during the 4th and 5th centuries A.D. meant that the Romans no longer sailed to the spice coast. Although the occasional traveller from the west still visited Malabar - a Greek merchant known as Cosmas Indicopleustes ['Indian traveller'] arrived in 522 AD, for example - in general relatively little was heard about Kerala in the first millennium AD. But one of the most interesting debates about Kerala's history relates to this period: when did Christianity came to the Malabar coast? There is no doubt that Christians were in Kerala before Cosmas Indicopleustes. He wrote: 'In the island of Taprobane there... is a church of Christians, and clerks and the faithful...Likewise at Male where the pepper grows; and in Kalliena there is a bishop consecrated in Persia'.[70] On Logan's authority, Taprobane is Ceylon, Male is Malabar, and Kalliena a town near Udippi. But how early did Christianity first arrive in Kerala?

The Syrian Christian community, which still exists in Kerala and became rather notorious as the subject of Arundathi Roy's *The God of Small Things,* believes that the apostle St Thomas sailed across the Arabian Sea following the trade route from the Middle East to Kerala, and landed at Kodungallor [Muziris] in 52 AD. They say that he converted the local Brahmins and built seven churches, and then crossed the mountains and preached in Mylapur in Chennai, where he came into conflict with the Hindus of Tamilnad, and was eventually put to death by them, possibly after an evangelical mission to China. What is supposed to be his tomb still stands in Mylapur and is visited by Christians of all sects and indeed Hindus and Muslims too. The website of the [Syrian] Church of St.George Forane in Ernakulam district is very certain that that is what happened, and gives this account of Thomas' arrival in Kerala.

> The Apostle St. Thomas landed in Kodungallur in A.D. 52. The Greeks called this place Mousiris. While the Apostle was going to the Jewish colony nearby, he had to cross the village of Palayur, where he saw the Hindu temple and the temple tanks. Certain Namboodiris (Brahmins) were bathing in the tank. St.Thomas worked a miracle there. The Namboodiris took water in their palms and threw it upwards reciting 'mantras'. Seeing the same water falling down, the apostle asked them why their deity refused to accept their offering. He then took some water from the pond, and calling on the Name of Jesus Christ, threw it upwards. Those water drops assumed the shape of rose flowers and remained suspended in mid-air. Because of this manifestation many of the Namboodiris believed in Christ and received baptism. However, a small number of them became enraged at the incident, cursed the place, and went to another village. The place they cursed is known as 'Sapakkad,' the accursed place. Even today, the Namboodiris crossing that village refrain from bathing or eating there.

One might I believe doubt the absolute veracity of this account without being accused of bias, and many historians seem to think it unlikely that Thomas came to Kerala at all because of the absence of any written evidence. However I read an interesting article about this in *The Guardian* newspaper. It was written by William Dalrymple, traveller and author of several wonderful books about India. Dalrymple wrote of a visit he made to Putenangedi Church, south of Kochi, where Hindu and Christian worshippers 'could be found crammed together, all convinced that St Thomas was present in the building to answer the prayers of his devotees.' An old Hindu woman, Jaya, told him '*When I have difficulties, St Thomas solves them for me. Of course I go to the temple too. But any big problem I have, I come to here to pray...*' And Jaya's Christian friend, Miriam, agreed. '*In my experience, praying to St Thomas here is always effective*'.[71]

Dalrymple says that the story of St Thomas in Kerala has been known of since the sixth century when Gregory of Tours[i] was told of it

---

[i] Gregory [538-594] was Bishop of Tours, the leading bishopric in France [or, more properly, Gaul] at that time. He was a historian as well as a prelate.

by a Greek monk. Many other visitors to Kerala since, including Marco Polo and Vasco da Gama heard the tale too. But there isn't really much in the way of evidence to back it up. Indeed many western historians say there's none at all - no documents, inscriptions, contemporary accounts; indeed nothing you might call verifiable. Interestingly though, as knowledge of ancient India has grown, it has tended to provide support for the Thomas Christians.

Church of St. George Forane in Ernakulum

At one time no-one believed the saint could have travelled to India: now it is well-known that the journey could easily have been made; and substantial amounts of coins of the first century AD have recently been found near to the Thomas churches. Then there's some odd stories linking Thomas with other parts of the country. In the library of St Catherine's Monastery in the Sinai desert were found in the nineteenth century many ancient writings, saved from destruction during the Dark Ages by the inaccessibility of the building. One of these was 'The Acts of St Thomas' which told previously unknown tales: that Thomas the Carpenter was Christ's twin [Te'oma means twin in Syriac];[ii] that the

---

[ii] Language used by the Syrian Christian Church

Apostles drew lots to decide where each should spread the Gospel and that Thomas drew India. He went the court of King Gondophares, who wanted a carpenter to help build a palace. All of little interest to historians until the 1930s when coins dated 46AD were found in Peshawar bearing the name of a hitherto unknown king, Gondopherne! Incidentally, this king is also known in Armenian as Gathaspar from which comes Caspar - one of the 'Three Kings' from the Orient. Furthermore, the Kerala Syrians follow the same liturgies and practices [such as the celebration of Passover] that Thomas would have done, but not later Christians influenced by St.Paul. Then some of the services are sung in Syriac rather than Latin, and there is a substantial oral tradition too. Given all this evidence, some in India allege that the scepticism of western scholars is because they cannot bear the thought of Christianity reaching India earlier than Europe.

But if what the Syrians say is true, it's really surprising that nothing has been found in writing. Perhaps this is because everything that they found about Thomas was destroyed by the Portuguese who regarded the Syrians as heretics and did their best to obliterate all their traditions.

Or maybe the whole story is just a myth. Maybe another missionary visited Kerala at a later date. Or perhaps Doubting Thomas is himself fated to be doubted, as a punishment for his failure to believe in the Resurrection until he had tangible proof.

CHAPTER THIRTEEN

THE SANGAM AGE

'If foreign peoples and influences had not intervened it might, with almost literal truth have been said of the Malayalis that 'happy is the people who have no history'.' Logan, *Malabar Manual.*

Apart from the foreign sources referred to in an earlier chapter, it is the Sangam literature that gives most information about life in South India around the time that Christ was born. The writings do not refer particularly to Kerala - indeed the authors were based in Tamilnad - but the descriptions and stories apply as much to Kerala as they do to the rest of the south.

The word Sangam means assembly, and it was at assemblies of poets held in Madurai over long periods, that the Sangam anthologies are said to have been produced. It's not clear how useful the material is for historians. There are details of historically verifiable battles between the Cheras and Cholas, but some of the tales surrounding the works are clearly myths. For example, the gods were alleged to have attended the early sessions, and in all the works are said to have taken 9,990 years to produce. There would seem to be no reason why the descriptions of the way of life of the people who lived in these times should be inaccurate, though, and it is these sections that are the most interesting and valuable in the literature.

There were three kingdoms in Kerala at this time. In addition to the Cheras, there were the Mushikas of the Ezhimalai kingdom in the north and the Ays in the south. According to the Sangams, the Mushikas ruled the country surrounding the Eli Hills [Ezhimalai in Malayalam] near Kannur. This was the high land which Vasco da Gama's pilots said would be 'the first land to be sighted...a great mountain which is on the coast of India...they call it Mount Dely.'[72] The most famous of the kings of Ezhimalai was Nannan who is much celebrated in one Sangam poem, which describes his 'territory, its forests, hills and towns, the customs and habits of its people as well as Nannan's munificence and exploits'; and says that he was a 'warrior chieftain of insatiable ambition'.[73] He was an ally of the pirates who attacked Roman trading vessels; and won many battles before he was finally overcome and his kingdom absorbed into the Chera Empire.

The Ays were the ruling tribe of south Kerala, although they were sometimes under the control of the Cheras or Pandyas. Their most outstanding leader was Ay Andiran whose kingdom, the Sangam literature tells us, extended from Palakkad to Kanniya Kumari. Andiran made gifts of elephants to poets and scholars and was also a great warrior who thwarted the attempts of the Cheras to extend their power southward. His capital was in the hills near Kanniya Kumari and was inaccessible to his enemies. It was so large that 'but for Aykudi in the south, the flat earth would lose its equilibrium' due to the weight of the Himalayas in the north. Andiran was a devout worshipper of Shiva and on his death he 'was welcomed in the abode of the gods, and the drum in Indra's palace reverberated at his arrival'.[74]

The Cheras governed the largest part of Kerala, and their rule lasted for the longest time, too.[75] Their homeland lay between the Ays' territory and Ezhimalai and their capital city was probably near to Musiris, where the Romans carried out most of their trading. The Sangam period saw the rise of the Cheras to an established kingdom. The process was begun by the founder of the dynasty, Uthiyan Cheralathan, who ruled around 130 AD and who defeated local tribal chieftains in battles and made alliances by marriage with stronger neighbours. His reign ended in defeat though - and disgrace. During a battle against the Cholas, Uthiyan suffered a wound in the back - the inference being that he must have been in flight at the time. The shame of this was such that the king had no alternative but to commit suicide. Uthiyan was succeeded by his son Nedum, who among other things, fought against and defeated Nannan of Ezhimalai, thereby freeing the coast from piracy and helping to lead to a prosperous and peaceful reign. Eventually, however, Nedum too died in battle with the Cholas. Nedum's brother was the next king and he brought the whole of modern Kerala and Kanniya Kumari under his control, defeating the Ays en route. In his later years, he renounced all earthly pleasures. 'Like Ashoka the after his war with Kalinga, Palyanai turned away from war and carnage and came under the influence of this spirit' writes K.G.Sesha Aiyar in his history of the Chera kings.[76] The next king, like his father and uncle before him, became a great patron of poets and men of letters. His successor was said to be an 'ideal ruler and a devotee of the god of Tiruvanantapuram [Trivandrum]'[77]. Maybe this contemporary poem was describing one of his religious festivals:

> ...when the officiating priests ring their bells which send clear peals afar, the eager fasting multitude bathes in the cold waters of the sea and bustling noise rends the air, the great chakra of the Lord dazzles everyone with its brilliance, the full-orbed moon rises dispelling the black darkness of the sea to gladden these multitudes on their way home. Even as the benefaction of the moon Oh Chera King, you come to the help of suffering men of high estate and rule valorously.[78]

Some say that the next ruler, Velkezhu Kuttuvan was the greatest of the early Chera kings. He won many battles, one of which was against the king of Mokur whose chariots were said to be attached to elephants using rope made from the hair of the country's women. Velkezhu built a temple at Kodungallur, made of stone brought from the Ganges plains. Manga remembers seeing pilgrims on their way to Velkezhu's temple. It was one of the very few temples that, like the Kali temple in Calcutta, sacrificed live animals. There is a tale that the blood of the sacrificed goats was mixed with the animals' brains and then fed to the faithful, but I don't know if that is true. If it is, perhaps it explains why many of the pilgrims returned from the temple in an apparently intoxicated [or possibly ecstatic] state. In any event, Manga says, the womenfolk of the village kept well out of their way.

The Chera dynasty continued throughout the Sangam age, and its literature describes changing alliances and almost permanent war between the Chera, Chola and Pandya kings. The poetess Avvaiar[i] described one of the wars - the invasion of Kongu [now a region in western Tamilnad] by the Cheras.

> Those who see thy brigades of war elephants marching with their tusks blunted by battering thy enemies' forts, renew the strong bars with which the gates of their forts are bolted; those who see thy troops of horse whose hoofs are covered with the blood of thy foes who they have trampled to death block the entrances to their

---

[i] Poem written by one of three Tamil poets called Avvaiar, meaning 'respectable woman', who wrote during the first two centuries C.E.

> fort with stout thorny trees; those who see thy sharp lances which pierce the hardest of shields, those who see thy fierce soldiers, who bear on their body many a scar caused by sword cuts, waste not the arrow from their quivers; and though not deterred by the poisonous smoke of the seeds of the iyyavi, which thy enemies burn at their fort gates to keep off your army, seize and kill them like the god of death. Alas, who can save the fertility of thy enemies, whose fields are covered with waving corn? [79]

Towards the end of the Sangam period, the power of the Cheras went into decline and the land split into many small principalities, which were prey to each other and to the rising power of the new dynasties of the South - the Pallavas of Kanchipuram and the Chalukyas of Karnataka.

The Sangam literature does then bring some colour into the political history of the period but its most useful and interesting contribution to our understanding of early South India is its description of what life was like for the ordinary people. The kings of the three major dynasties were in overall charge in Sangam times, but in practice government was carried out by local chiefs, who owed allegiance and paid tribute to the monarch. In the villages there was a form of democracy, village affairs and policies being discussed by all at a public meeting place. Village elders settled any arguments that arose.

According to the Sangams, the religion of the early Tamils was mainly animistic - gods were thought to inhabit trees and animals and even inanimate objects. The carp, tiger and bow that were the symbols of the Pandyas, Cholas and Cheras respectively, were also worshipped, and maybe the lingam too. And in due course the gods of the animists merged with the new gods of the Brahmins. So the favourite god, associated with the phallic symbol became Shiva, and the goddess Illakami became Lakshmi. Vishnu and Garuda [or their equivalents] are also mentioned in the literature as well as Kottavai, the mother goddess of the Tamils. Now, the faithful needed somewhere to worship their idols and so they began to build the first temples. There also may have been ancestor worship, the evidence being the practice of erecting memorial stones and hero stones. The worship of natural forces such as the sun, moon, wind and rivers was also practised. The early Tamils believed in life after death and the need to perform penance to reach heaven.

Warriors who fell in battle would enjoy *'the bliss of marriage with a spotless maiden in heaven'* and it is said that any soldier dying a natural death would be *'cut asunder with a sword'* in order to qualify for the afterlife.

The books explain that people's occupations, ways of life and diet depended on the region [tinai] in which they lived. The various tinais are described in turn. So the tinai of the hill country supported primitive hunters who ate coarse red-coloured rice, millets, and honey that they reached by climbing trees with bamboo ladders. Love marriages were apparently the norm in this region and the marriage ceremony involved the man presenting his fiancée with proof of his skill in hunting, like for example, a string of tiger's teeth. Some scholars believe that this was forerunner of the tying of the tali in modern South Indian marriages.

In the wastelands men had little option but to become soldiers, especially archers, and in peacetime, I fear they turned to highway robbery. Shepherds and cowherds lived in the pastoral areas on the lower wooded slopes of the mountains. Their diet included of course dairy products, and maize too, which was grown in the region; also beans and millet boiled in milk. The better-off agricultural labourers on the plain cultivated paddy, sugar cane, and fruit trees. They ate white rice and meat, and sugar cane juice was a popular drink. Some in this region took to fishing, and dried fish and prawns were added to their diet. Their grains were bartered for salt and sea-fish, milk and milk products, and the floors of their houses were smeared with cow dung.

The final tinai was the neythal or coastal belt. The lives of the fishermen of this tinai are depicted in detail in one of the Sangam poems.

> 'The paravathas setting out for fishing in the morning at the auspicious hour, fishing at night with torches, the injuries sustained by them from the sharks, their food - fish curry, the offering of Pazhaiya women to the sea-god on full moon days, the pearl divers, the women delighting in drinking the tender palmyrah fruit juice, the fun and frolic of their children in the sea, the exchanges of salt and fish for paddy, the houses of the rich merchants, the jewels of gold embellished with gems, are among the themes of poetic fancy'. These verses are quoted in the Kerala Gazette. Verse 30 reads thus: 'When the carts, loaded

> with white salt from the unploughed fields, labour up the hill, the salt trader with his angry stick urges the bullock on and shouts the price of his salt; his beloved young daughter, who carries white salt on her head, jingling her small bracelets, shouts from street to street, 'rocksalt for paddy, measure for measure', but is frightened by the house dog, that, recognising a stranger's voice, leaps barking towards her.'[80]

Very evocative!

Descendants of the fisherpeople of the neytal tinai.

Meanwhile, the vegetarian Brahmins ate fine rice with mango pickle and pomegranate cooked with butter and the '*fragrant leaves of the karavembu*' [the curry plant]. Toddy was commonly drunk by the lower classes, women apparently preferred munnir [a sweet drink made from the palmyra nut], tender coconut and sugar cane, while the rich drank scented liqueurs made from rice and tataki flowers.[ii] The royal families enjoyed wine from Europe.

Unchanged since Sangam times

Women dressed in saris of cotton or silk, probably similar to those worn today. Men wore a piece of cotton wrapped round the waist and if they were well-off another round the shoulders. Women displayed a lot of jewellery. One of the poems gives a detailed account of the ornaments worn by an actress. They included a belt of 32 strands of pearls,'various and necklaces made of beads pendant golden leaves, ear-rings set with diamonds and sapphires, armlets of brilliant gems and pearls, bracelets of gold and coral, finger rings set with precious stones, anklets including one resembling a string of pearls extending from the ankle to the big toe, and little toe rings.' Nose ornaments are not mentioned. I wonder if it was the Iyers who introduced this now very popular fashion into South India.

[ii] The flowers of the tree the leaves of which are used to make bidi cigarettes.

* * * * *

Scholars and poets were highly respected and kings and chieftains were often their patrons.

Education seems to have been available to all if the make-up of the Sangam gatherings is anything to go by: of the 192 Sangam poets, 13 were said to be kings, 29 Brahmins, 57 vellalas [landed gentry], 36 women, 17 hill-men, 13 foresters, 7 vanigars [businessmen], 7 artisans, 1 shepherd, 1 potter etc. Fathers had a duty to teach their children to become virtuous, and education was regarded as lifelong - '*just as water springs more and more in the well as the water is drawn out so knowledge develops more only when it is used and spread to other people.*' Study was mainly confined to the three 'p's - poetry, prose and plays, and oral instruction was most significant, with memory training being therefore of great importance. Writing was done on palmyra leaves with a pointed iron stylus. The poetess Avvaiar's advice was '*learn while young; letter and number claim esteem; avoid ignorance; covet to be versed in knowledge; learn all sciences and cease not to learn*'.

Young men were trained in the use of the three 'v's - vill, vel and val - the bow, spear and sword, and military tournaments were held annually. Young women learned some of the 108 musical instruments mentioned in the Sangams so they could '*tame wild beasts by their sweet music and drive away the birds by their songs*'. There were various types of dance, one of which, the Kodukotti or Shiva dance involved '33 patterns of hand pose and a variety of expressions' [*Gazette*]. It sounds as though it could be a forerunner of Kathakali.

It's clear that festivals were an important part of the life of the people then as now. Each village had its protective goddess and festivals to honour her were held annually or on a twelve-year cycle. Other religious festivals were dedicated to Kaman, the god of love, Indiran, Aatirai, and Murugan. Murugan is still a popular deity in Tamilnad. And Pongal and Onam were celebrated. Onam is of particular interest as it remains one of the most important festivals of modern Kerala. It was originally held on the birthday of Vishnu, to celebrate the god's destruction of the demons. Pongal originated from offerings made to family gods and ancestors. At the festival of Thiruvathira, prayers were offered for the fertility of the earth; the Bharini festival was sacred to Devi, and on Karthika, when the moon was in conjunction with the constellation Karthikai, there was a festival of lights.

CHAPTER FOURTEEN

EDUCATION NORTH AND SOUTH

'A thousand words have not the weight of half a pallam ' - *Malayalam proverb*

'Education is not the filling of a pail; it is the lighting of a fire' - William Butler Yeats

We've just seen how highly education was regarded by the people of the Sangam Age, so this will be a good time to dwell for a few paragraphs on Manga's experiences in the education system in Kerala, and on mine in Bihar.

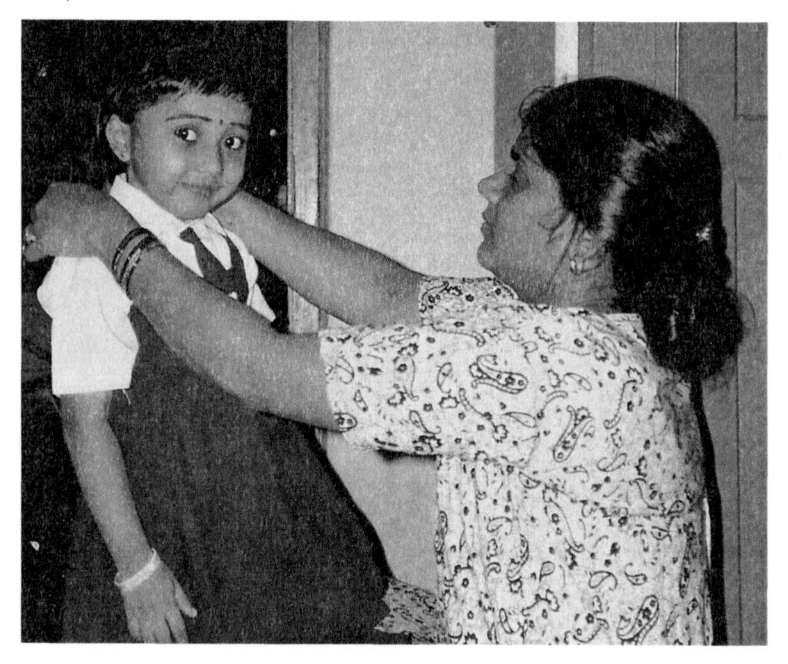

Ready for school [Ammu and her Mum, Shanta].

Kerala ranks as the most literate of Indian states by some margin, with 91% of the population being able to read in 2001.[i]

[i] These figures are reflected in the 2001 census, which can be downloaded freely from the Internet.

Apart from the mini-states of Mizoram and Goa, next comes Himachal Pradesh with 76%. Sadly, Bihar is bottom of the list with 47%. Kerala's figure is so high for a number of reasons. From early times, there were many schools teaching the Vedas [they were called saba mathams] in Kerala, and during the British era many of the large number of Christian missionaries who came to the state founded schools, and led the way for others, like the Nairs and the Muslims, to start their own educational establishments. In fact these schools have been so successful that Sreedhara Menon tells us that two-thirds of schools and 80 per cent of arts and science colleges in Kerala today are privately run.[81] Pleasingly, these private institutions are not exclusive in their intake. Many Hindus and Muslims go to Christian schools, and my great-niece Keerthana for one went to a school run by the Muslim Educational Trust. The first post-independence government of Kerala placed a great deal of importance on education and the state introduced a literacy campaign in the 1980s.

The school where my sister-in-law Rajam taught in 1979

Another factor fostering a strong educational tradition is the leading role played by women in Kerala society and it has therefore been natural for them to be offered the same educational opportunities as men. Since the decline of the spice trade until very recently, Kerala has had little work within the state to occupy the population - no large scale mining or industry for example - and so people realised that if they were to obtain employment outside the state, or indeed the country, they would need to take with them a good education.

Manga and her sisters all went to the local government-run, Malayalam-medium, schools in the village. The only one to stay on for further education was, as we have seen, Rajam, who went to teacher training college with the help of a government scholarship. Of those in the next generation who grew up in Kerala, Raju obtained a degree in science from a college in Kozhikode, and all our great-nieces and great-nephews, in Kerala and elsewhere, are attending or have been to college, some up to post-graduate level.

I taught for two years in what was then the state of Bihar. This was at a boys' boarding school called a Sainik School - literally, a school for soldiers. The pupils were not in fact soldiers - yet - but the understanding was that they would progress from our school to the National Defence Academy [NDA] in Dehra Dun and go on to become officers in one of the Indian military services, although not all did. The Principal of the school, and the Head Teacher and Registrar were serving officers, the MO an ex-captain in the Army Medical Corps, and the 'training staff' who supervised drill and PT were either current or former soldiers. But the rest of the staff, including all the teachers, was civilian. I see from one of the school magazines that I was grandly described as B.A.[Hons], P.P.E.[Oxon], G.V.S.O.

The story of the Sainik Schools as told to me by our Principal, Lt-Col. L.E.G.Smith, was that the NDA was finding that nearly all the best candidates for admission were coming from private schools, mainly those run by the churches along the lines of British public schools. Only the sons of the rich could afford to attend these schools and as a result the Academy and in turn the officer class itself were becoming skewed in their social make-up. And of course a great many potentially good officers were being lost. So it was decided, by the then Defence Minister Krishna Menon, to establish in each state a boarding school providing a first-class general education but also offering out-of-hours activities such as sports of all kinds, cultural clubs, educational outings and so on as a good British school does. Lessons would be taught in English. And most importantly, no fees would be paid. The first of these Sainik Schools to be established was in Uttar Pradesh in 1961. The Sainik School Tilaiya, then in Bihar, opened in September 1963. [Tilaiya is now in the new state of Jharkand, and Nalanda is the home of the Bihar school.] There are now 24 schools, one in each of the larger states, including Kazhakootam in Kerala. There seems now to be some controversy about the relatively small proportion of Sainik School alumni joining the NDA, and looking at the curricula vitae of some past students of the SST they do seem to have followed a remarkable variety of careers - a multi-award winning filmmaker particularly caught my eye - but I'm sure that is all to the good. When I was posted to the SST, VSO were particularly keen to quell my misgivings about teaching children destined to run the risk of killing and being killed by saying that the military was one of the most respected and stable of careers in India: no doubt very true then but perhaps less so now, so it is natural that well-educated young men will wish to scan broader horizons.

Colonel Smith was the first Principal of the Sainik School Tilaiya. He was an Anglo-Indian - that is, from the mixed-race community who trace their roots back to pre-Victorian times. Unlike many of this community, Colonel Smith had no doubt that his loyalties lay with the Republic of India, not with an idealised English 'home'. He was a good friend to me and I got on well with his family too. Connie his wife was an important part of the school community and ran the kindergarten for the children of staff. Penny their daughter was at boarding school but helped with the kindergarten during her holidays. She was lively and charming and planning to join medical school in Bangalore. I remember Col. Smith being very amused when she stood me up on a date once. She later relented and we would stroll down to the Circuit House by the Dam for an orange juice or coffee - the only activity available in Tilaiya!

The Smiths' sons were called Ernest, Robin and John, the last adopted and from Nagaland, a troubled province in the far north-east of India. He and Robin attended the National Defence Academy; Ernest had studied at SST but did not go on to military training. Then there were the 'Blacksmiths' - the two ebony labradors - the cat and the parrot. Manga and I spent a few days at the family home in Poona on our way to Kerala in the Christmas holidays 1967 as you may remember. Penny and John were the only children at home and we took a trip together to the zoo. In the evening, we visited the Shiva temple on the hill overlooking the city and watched the twinkling lights below. I remember that it reminded me of the view of Sheffield from our home in Dobbin

Hill. On the way back, we treated the Smiths to a Chinese meal, and since it was just before Christmas, we sang carols together when we reached home. Sadly, that was the last time I saw the colonel: he suffered a heart attack and died shortly afterwards. The tragedy was intensified by the fact that Connie, aged 45, was pregnant when we saw them - and looking very happy and radiant. Colonel Smith had been an excellent Principal, popular with staff and boys, and respected and loved by just about everyone. He and I played squash regularly in the early mornings in the school's open-air court before the sun grew too hot, and he dominated the games from the centre of the court, sending me racing from side to side. I was fit in those days and more than 30 years younger than the Colonel, but I only remember beating him once. His stories of the Second World War in Asia were enthralling and enlightening, and he had been present at the post-war trials of Japanese war criminals.

Penny, me, John, Connie [seated] and the dogs.

As for my experiences in Tilaiya, well, the students for the most part were great, but I'm not at all sure how good a teacher I was; I was untrained of course. But I got on well with the kids and most of the staff, undeniably helped them with their conversational English and their ability to analyse and discuss current affairs, broadening their understanding of life and the world a bit I think. Remember, in those days people didn't know as much about foreign countries as they do now - not many travelled abroad, certainly very few Indians, there was no widespread access to television in India [that didn't come till the 1980s] and the English occupation had ended before any of the young people were born. Few of the boys or their teachers had spoken with an English person let alone got to know one well, and this was reflected in their somewhat idiosyncratic grammar, syntax and pronunciation. I think I can fairly claim also that the boys did improve their cricketing skills under my aegis. There were in fact some exceedingly good players in the school, clearly capable of reaching good club standard if not more. And maybe some of those with whom I came in contact were influenced by the concept of voluntary work allegedly for the benefit of others which was inherent in my position, although most people took some convincing that my two years in India were not simply a hurdle I had to jump in order to qualify automatically for some plum post in England.

The teachers were a friendly crowd, especially when they realised that I was a 'simple' sort of chap, to use their own words. The first Principal, a cultured and charming man, I have already spoken of. He was very different from his successor, Colonel Gadeock. The Headteacher was a Muslim, who didn't always see eye-to-eye with either Principal; the Registrar, a Hindu, largely kept his head down, and we didn't really get to know him. My closest colleague I mentioned earlier - S.K.Chandra with whom I produced a performance by the boys of 'Julius Caesar'. We toured Rajasthan together during my first long vacation. My first holiday was at Christmas and I spent a few days with Shyam Das, the friend I met at the Commonwealth Club in Sheffield, in his dormitory at the Dhanbad coal mines! Interesting though - I got to go down a hell-hole of a mine, which would not have been out of place in Victorian England, with ceilings so low that I virtually had to crawl along the galleries and no lighting except for our hand-held torches. I'm glad that I was unaware at that time of the accident that had occurred in a similarly primitive neighbouring mine just

18 months earlier. An explosion of firedamp and coal dust, probably sparked by a hurricane lantern had killed 375 miners.

The Sainik School contrasted hugely with the schools that Manga attended! She started her education at the quiet little school in the village at the age of five, in the sishu [infants] class.

'I used to hate leaving my Mum to go to school. My sister used to have to carry me there and after she'd left me I'd run back and by the time she got home - talking to people on the way - I'd be with my Mum. So she'd take me again and the teacher would beat me on my hand with a tamarind stick for being late. That frightened me so after a while I used to go to school properly. Really it wasn't too bad, and I was a good student. We learned a poem about a mother carrying her child for forty weeks and what she felt, and it made me cry a bit and so did 'Mary had a Little Lamb': I was sad because the lamb couldn't go into school with Mary! Anyway I was alright at school. We used to sit on the floor to start with till fifth or sixth class. We used to have a slate and copy things from the board and when we reached fifth standard we could sit on a bench, with our books on the floor underneath; there were no tables and chairs, or desks. We had to answer questions and if we got them right we'd move up the bench towards the front of the class. Everybody wanted to be at the front. If we didn't answer the question properly, we went down the bench towards the back. And that's how the teacher ranked us. And if we were naughty we'd have to stand on the bench so all the school could see us. Sometimes I wouldn't be able to go to school because I was ill often, and sometimes I might be asked a question about something very complicated like compound interest and I couldn't get it right because I'd missed the lesson. I would have to stand outside until I got it right. I couldn't explain that I had missed the lesson, because the teacher was too busy with all the other children, so I stayed outside the room all morning. I remember we had five benches and seven children on each bench, so thirty-five children. The school was just a big hall with no walls or partitions between the classes and not much space between them either. But the children were very good and would recite their lessons without interfering with the next class.

All the learning was by rote - chanting multiplication tables, but if someone asked eight times seven no-one would know until they'd gone right through the whole table. Well sometimes you could remember. In fact I can remember still. We learned English and the alphabet in the same way. We would chant all together in a sing-song voice 'C.A.T. cat, poocha; M.A.T. mat, payya; R.A.T. rat, eli'; and so on. We did have one text book. I've got a copy in front of me now. It's tiny, about 4 inches by 3 inches and of course the pages are going brown. There are about sixteen pages and no cover - there never was. Inside are all the things we needed to know by the time we left school. The English and Hindi alphabets; all the numbers up to one crore [that's ten million] including one lakh - 100,000. Multiplication tables up to 20, and multiplication of fractions, one-eighth, one-quarter, a half and three quarters, by whole numbers. English weights and measures. The four rules - addition, subtraction, multiplication, division. We had to know the four main castes - kings, priests, businessmen, manual workers; the four stages of life, student, married man, hermit, wise man. Five metals, I'm not sure why five, but they were gold, silver, iron, copper, tin; five Pandavas, the heroes of the 'Mahabharatha' epic. Their names are Dharmaputran, Arjunan, Bhiman, Nakulan, Sahadevan. And the seven tastes that a meal prepared in the Ayurvedic way must include. There were even some cures to learn. Grind garlic and lime and put them on a bruise. For a cough, mix medicinal camphor with the juice of a betel leaf and drink it. And to make a headache better you should put oil and camphor on the forehead. All these things we learned by heart, not really understanding them at all.

After five years in the primary school, we went on to High School, so I'd be eleven I suppose though I look much younger on that school photograph. Dad gave the school authorities the wrong date of birth for me [there were no birth certificates] *- not on purpose, he just couldn't remember - April instead of February for the month, and one or two years too early - so my passport has the wrong date, and I did everything a year or so before I should have. So I was really nine or ten when I went to the big school.*

I took my lessons very seriously. I had very neat handwriting and used to make very careful notes. So my books were the best in the class, and some teachers would take them and use them as textbooks for the next year! Now of course we were writing with pen and ink. Problem was, ink used to be quite expensive and you know that we didn't have any money to spare. So Dad used to make ink for me. He took a dried fruit called kadakkai, bit like a sloe, same thing as we used for a purgative, and boiled it up. The essence was very black and flowed well and made very good ink. I've got lots of stories about High School but if I tell you them all you'll never get this book finished. One thing: we used to have to do homework of course and this was bit difficult. You see we didn't have electricity and when it got dark, we had to use lamps, with oil and wicks made of cotton wool-type and they didn't give a lot of light. It didn't seem to hurt my eyes though. I only needed glasses quite recently. Oh and I remember learning Shakespeare and poetry from the Headmaster who spoke English very well. I think so, but we didn't have anything to compare it with! But I still remember a poem about a train; an allegory of life, people getting on, finding their places, living their lives and then getting off. And one teacher, who mostly taught in Malayalam, would always say in English, 'Girls, look at the world map', rolling the 'r's in 'girls' and 'world'.'

Perhaps he was taught to speak English by a Scottish missionary.

This might be a good time to say something about Vedic Maths. One of our relations, V.S.Kalyanraman, Manga's mother's cousin, is an expert and gave us a copy of his article on the subject that was published in *New Horizons*. The article explains that Vedic mathematics is a system of calculation based on simple principles that were allegedly first expounded in the Vedic hymns. I'm afraid I didn't get beyond what Kalyanraman called the 'tricks' of this sort of calculation. Here is a very simple example. To multiply 8 by 7, you first subtract each number from 10. So that gives you [2] and [3], and you then subtract the first number in brackets from the second number which isn't in brackets, i.e. 7 minus 2 = 5. You then multiply the two bracketed numbers together, i.e. 2 times 3 = 6. Put the two results together, 5 and 6 = 56! There's a textbook for schools written by an Englishman, J.T.Glover. Although the copy I have was published in India it seems to have been intended for English schools too. The reviews of the book illustrate the different aspects of Vedic maths. On the one hand, it 'throws open a welcome opportunity for...whizz-kids [to give] one-line quick responses to mathematical calculations' [*The Hindu]*; on the other, it 'is the investigation of the real nature of the working phenomena from the origin of man up to the ultimate reality' [*S.V.U. Oriental Journal]*. No, I'm not quite sure what that means either but it's all about its being a philosophy not just an aid to adding up. Incidentally Kalyanraman has also written a pamphlet about the symbolism of the Indian wedding ceremony, and is an all-round smart guy. And very likeable with it.

A.Sreedhara Menon writes in *The Legacy of Kerala* that the library movement in Kerala started in the early part of the nineteenth century, a time when there were many cultural developments in the state. Both the British and Indian administrators were well aware of the importance of libraries for students of all ages and those who had missed out on education, as well as to enrich people's leisure. The first public library was established in Trivandrum in 1829, and there are now something like 5000 such libraries in the state. The government of Travancore was the leader in the movement, and in 1936 it had the excellent idea of attaching public libraries to its village schools.

There is much to be written about learning and culture in Kerala: the enormous number of newspapers and periodicals - including our favourite title, the *Mangalam Daily* - its museums and galleries, poetry and drama, its rich modern literature. But that's for another book, perhaps.

CHAPTER FIFTEEN

JOTTINGS ON GEOGRAPHY

'Elders' words are like amla - bitter at first but later on, sweet' - Malayalam proverb

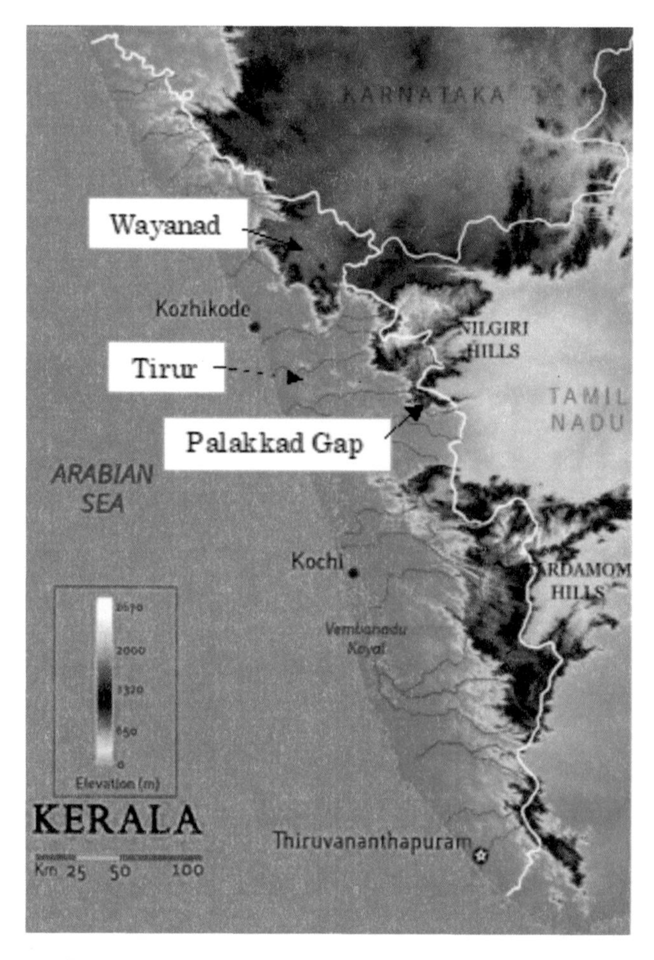

Physical map of Kerala

While European states are in many cases divided from each other by geographical features such as mountains or rivers or arms of the sea, in India most boundaries are less clearly delineated. Kerala is an exception though, and the nature of its borders has had a distinct effect on the state's history.

Kerala's eastern boundary is marked by the mountain range known as the Western Ghats, which stretches in all from Mumbai in the north, down to Kanniya Kumari at the southern tip of India. The hills are higher in the south. The mountain called Anaimudi, which means 'elephant's forehead' in Malayalam (and looks a bit like one), is in the Anamalai Hills in Kerala and is 2817 metres high. It's the highest mountain in India outside the Himalayas and lies within the Eravikalam National Park, which claims to have more elephants, tigers and bison than anywhere else. Doda Betta in the Nilgiris is close to Ootacamund and is 2637 metres high, and we've been there and seen the great views. Doda Betta means 'big mountain' in Kannada [the language of Mysore state]: originality sacrificed to accuracy! When we were there, there were farmers on its lower slopes selling carrots of prize-winning quality from handcarts, and a herbalist from whom we bought quantities of remedies in little corked bottles, which we still use occasionally to drive away coughs and sneezes and stomach complaints.. Elimbileri Peak sounds spectacular - 'a precipitous needle-shaped hill' says Logan, 'in the very heart of the best coffee producing district in Wayanad.' Kalladikodan 'is perhaps the stormiest peak in all Malabar'.[82] There is a Malayalam saying: 'If Kalladikodan grows angry, will not the Karuga River be swollen?' Further south are the Cardamom Hills and then the lower Vershanad ranges. The average height of the Ghats in Trivandrum district is only 300 metres, though one hill rises to 1869 metres.

Altogether there are fourteen peaks higher than 2000 metres in the Kerala section of the Western Ghats. Logan lists thirteen 'noteworthy peaks' in the Malabar stretch of the Ghats, including one that is haunted by a demon who lures travellers to their doom by showing them a wonderful ruby. A human bandit also once lived on this hill: he was eventually driven away and all his family killed except for one woman, whose descendants, Logan tells us, could still be identified in the nineteenth century.

These are the mountains that played an important part in often isolating Kerala from the rest of India and its wars and mighty empires, and in giving the state its own particular character. Any invaders who succeeded in getting into Kerala had to be persistent and determined, and also to know the ways through the Ghats. By far the most important pass is the Palakkad Gap. The first National Highway to cross the Ghats into Kerala came this way - the NH47 from Chennai to Ernakulam - as does the mainline railway from Coimbatore, Erode, Salem and the north and east to Tirur. Tipu Sultan[i] came in the opposite direction when he invaded Kerala and built a fort at Palakkad, which can still be seen. Given the strategic importance of the town, it is worth describing the fort.

View of the Western Ghats on the Kerala-Tamilnad border.

Tipu's Fort as it is often called is still an imposing structure. We visited it on a dark and rainy day during the second monsoon in November; and as we approached, its massive grey walls, although not especially high, presented quite a forbidding appearance, and the moat was full.

There were no 'streams of local school groups and picnickers' as threatened by the *Insight Guide to South India*:[83] the groups presumably visit in school time [we went on a Saturday] and the picnickers were perhaps put off by the weather, although it would have been a pleasant spot to eat. The grass was neatly cut, there were interesting trees, and it was all very civilised. We were surprised to find a functioning jail in the grounds; and there was

---

[i] Tipu was the leader of the Mysoreans in the eighteenth century when they were at their most prominent. He was one of the sharpest of the thorns in the flesh of the British colonists

also a small but well-presented exhibition of the Archaeological Survey's work in Kerala. Everything in and around the fort was neat and tidy, and indeed it is said to be the best-preserved fort in India. We were duly impressed, but I think I prefer my castles a bit wilder and more unkempt.

Incidentally, Logan wrote that the fort stood at north 10 degrees 46 minutes, east 76 degrees 43 minutes, on a hill 349 feet high, adding that these were not however 'the revised values found recently by the Great Trigonometrical Survey: the height however is correct.' Logan was referring to the great project to map the whole of India, an undertaking commenced in 1800, which first measured the length of the sub-continent 'from Cape Comorin to the Himalaya,' and the height of the great mountains, the tallest of which was named after the Chief Surveyor, William Everest.[84] This remarkable adventure is described in John Keay's book *The Great Arc.*

It was Hyder Ali and not his son Tipu who constructed the first fortifications here. It all started when the Palakkad Rajah asked Hyder to help him drive the Zamorin's forces from his country. Hyder did so, and in 1766, invaded Malabar through the Rajah's land. With the support of French mercenaries, he rapidly overcame all opposition. Logan says that the French were particularly successful and Hyder 'created the French commander Bahadur[ii] on the spot, and appointed him General of 10,000 horses, at the same time declaring him General-in-Chief of his artillery.' [85] Hyder then withdrew, thinking the country was subdued, but not before announcing that the Nairs of Malabar, his chief opponents, were to have all their privileges withdrawn. He 'ordained that their caste, which was the first after the Brahmins, should thereafter be the lowest of all castes, subjecting them to salute Parias [untouchables]...'[86] They could however re-establish themselves in society if they converted to Islam. Some did, but many more fled to the state of Travancore, there to cause further grief to the Mysoreans at a future date.

Hyder then proceeded to Coimbatore, giving orders en route for the construction of Palakkad fort, which, 'lying in the centre of the gap in the line of ghats, was sensibly chosen as an advanced post

---

[ii] I guess the nearest equivalent in the UK would be 'knight'

and depot to facilitate communications with the newly subdued province.'[87] The fort, which lies on the western edge of the current town, was completely re-built in 1768 after it had briefly fallen into the hands of the British and 'furnished with all the advantages of European construction and defence', says Logan.[88] The fort was subsequently captured again by the British in 1783 when a force of 1700 Europeans and 17 battalions of sepoys [native Indian troops] under the command of Colonel Fullerton was sent to relieve Mangalore, which had been attacked by a joint French and Mysorean force. According to Logan, 'the vaguest ideas regarding the topography of the country prevailed and Mangalore was found to be too distant to be reached by the force', so Palakkad, which was on the route, was seized instead 'to serve as a magazine of stores and provisions for the prosecution of our undertaking or to secure a retreat if necessary'.[89] The Mysoreans' incursions had a substantial effect on Kerala society as we will see in a later chapter.

You can't go far in Kerala without coming across a river. There are 41 of them, mostly rising in the Ghats and draining into the ocean or the backwaters. The majority of the rivers are not very long - it's not far from the mountains to the sea - but they carry an enormous volume of water during the monsoons. In the dry season, of course, the river-beds contract alarmingly and then the sometime mighty torrents can be crossed on foot.

Bharathapuzha River in the dry season. Manga and Geetha look on.

If we start in the north and travel southwards through Kerala, the first major river we meet is the Chandragiri River which originates at 1200 metres in the Ghats in Karnataka and flows for 105 kms to Kasaragod, where it winds around the town before flowing into the sea. Logan has tales of some of the creeks along this part of the coastline. They are tidal and often sluggish and 'favourable to the crocodile tribe, which here at times attain prodigious dimensions, and with increasing weight they gain an appetite for the flesh of men...the prodigious length of his ponderous jaws, armed with sharp pointed interlocking teeth, give the reptile a hold of his victim which enables him to make full use of the enormous dead weight of his ungainly carcass as well as of his immense muscular power...'.[90] But there are no crocodiles now.

The river system that drains the greatest volume of water in the Malabar region is that of the Valapattanam. It rises in the Brahmagiri Ghat Reserve Forest in Karnataka and reaches the sea at Azhikkal, a fishing village destined I understand for development, in Kannur district in the north of the state, and is 110 km in length. On the banks of the River Anjarakandy was a trading outpost of the East India Company - it is said that the best pepper grows here but it is more famous as a cinnamon-producing estate that was established by the East India company in 1767, and is still in operation.

Boats at Beypore

The Beypore River [169 kms] is one of the most important in Kerala. Its source is 2000 metres above sea-level whence it drops suddenly down to the plains in a steep waterfall near the Pass. One of its tributaries is the Gold River and very small amounts of gold can indeed be found near the confluence. The river flows through Feroke and joins the sea at Beypore. Thousands of colourful boats were moored when we visited and we also saw dhows which are built here for the Middle Eastern market. The Veliyar River, a tributary of the Kadalundi, flows through the Silent Valley on its journey westwards. We visited the Valley Nature Reserve in August 2008. This was at the end of the monsoon season and not normally a time recommended for visiting, but we were provided with a guide and had a successful trip. We saw a Green Whip Snake on the road, a [sadly] injured flying squirrel by the Forest office, a brown frog, but very few birds. Perhaps it was the time of year. Adivasis live in the valley and we saw their villages and bought some of the absolutely delicious honey they collect. And some less tasty dates - I don't know where they came from because they can't be grown in Kerala, it's too wet. We climbed an observation tower, which gave a wonderful view of trees and scrub and rivers and peaks, sometimes clear but more often shrouded in dark clouds. And this is the place where we inadvertently collected leeches. The best of the wildlife that we spotted were monkeys. My daughter Indi took excellent photos of a family of Nilgiri langurs, and our guide pointed out to me the Reserve's prize resident, a Lion-Tailed Macaque.

The next major river is the Kadalundi, which meets the sea just south of Beypore, at a well-known beauty spot, where we've been swimming, although with care for there are dangerous whirlpools associated with the estuary. A little further south still, at Ponnani, comes the river that passes close to Trikkandiyur. The Tirur as it is most often now called is only 48 km long and is famous only because it was the main highway to Ponnani when Manga was young. We too have sailed on it, both crossing on the little ferry and cruising in even smaller fishing boats! The second longest river in Kerala also reaches the sea at Ponnani. That is the Bharathapuzha, which is 209 kms long and used to best illustrate the variation in flow of rivers in different seasons. That was before a number of dams were built on the upper reaches of the river. The third longest river in the state is the Pamba [176 kms], which has to be crossed to reach the pilgrimage destination, Sabrimala.

The mouth of the Kadalundi River

Lastly, the 228 km River Periyar flows out of Periyar Lake, in the National Wildlife Park. Manga and I visited the lake resort in 1967 on our first trip after getting married, and saw among other things, a Giant Malabar Squirrel, snake-birds on the water, and a herd of elephant in the distance. We spent a most wonderful day there with my mother and the children in 1979. We enjoyed our trip on the lake; it was quite an adventure as we were not sure what if anything we might see, and the little boat did look rather rickety... and the lake awfully large! We spotted many birds to add to my mother's list, but not many animals till just before we were due to turn for home, we entered a quiet bay, and there on the bank stood a family of wild elephants! Adults and babies were right at the water's edge enjoying their evening drink. They took no notice of us as we drifted closer, engine off. All of us were struck with a mixture of awe and excitement. It was a wonderful moment and memory for Mum on her first and only visit to India. We haven't always been so lucky at Periyar. On subsequent visits a guar on the distant hills, plenty of wild pig, packs of virtually tame monkeys and grazing deer are about the sum of our sightings - but we've always enjoyed the place, with its holiday atmosphere, relative coolness [normally about 30 degrees maximum, and it can fall to 15 on a winter's day], and excellent accommodation in the Government Rest House. We climbed on to the roof of the Guest House early one morning. There was complete silence except for bird song, and the mist was just beginning to clear from the tops of the trees below us.

A wild elephant by Periyar Lake

The journey up into the hills from Kottayam railway station is a delight. In 1991, my sister Rosemary and her family came with us. Manga together with Rosemary's husband Tony did most of the organising and it was they who went off into town to look for a taxi big enough to take all ten of us. Meanwhile the rest of us chatted with other travellers, some of whom seemed surprisingly interested in English politics: '*Is Mr. Major better than Mrs.Thatcher?*' Well, yes. Rosemary put it nicely. '*He's kinder*', she said. And there were the usual enquiries about how we found India, to which we could honestly reply that everything was wonderful. Manga and Tony eventually returned with a comfortable 14-seater van and its friendly driver, Thangam, whose wife, Manga discovered, was expecting their first child, and we set off for Thekkadi. We felt a few pangs of hunger on the way up - and there was no café to be seen anywhere. But eventually we came across what might be called a lorry-stop. The proprietors were delighted to see us but didn't seem to have much to offer in the way of food, until after a hurried discussion they came up with several eggs and we enjoyed a fine snack and much happy chatter.

Our next stop was Kumily - 'fragrant Kumily, India's spice central' according to the Hairy Bikers.[iii] Here we bought a lovely souvenir - a collection of different spices in clear envelopes [one of which to this day hangs in our kitchen], together with some local coffee. It was on that trip too that we were fascinated by a monkey who had found a piece of mirror and was trying manfully to work out where the reflection came from, passing his hand behind the glass to try and touch the image.

Kaladi, the birthplace of Adi Sankara,[iv] lies on the Periyar, and the river is also famous for the Shivarathri festival, held on its banks at Aluva, close to Geetha's family home, now alas demolished. Swimming is good on this spot: the river bed is clean, sharp sand and the currents are minimal as long as you stay reasonably close to the shore. Shivarathri falls on the Krishna-chaturdasi day in the month of Makha - mid- February to mid March. Pilgrims arrive from all over Kerala - and not only devout Hindus - and used to pass by the gate to Geetha's home on the only track down to the river. Each year the family made up huge quantities of buttermilk, well diluted and flavoured with chilli, ginger and curry leaves. Tables were erected at the garden gate, and the fluid dished out to the pilgrims from great cauldrons. Some of the family kept the cauldrons topped up, others rinsed the tumblers and still more offered refreshment and blessing, calling out to the passing throng: '*Moure veno*?' [would you like some buttermilk, in Tamil] or '*Sambaram coodikyoo*' [will you drink buttermilk, in Malyalam].

This went on from the middle of the day till far into the night, during which time the narrow road outside the house saw the passage of hundreds of thousands of pilgrims, most of whom had been travelling for many hours or even days. Once Manga and I joined the family party and we can testify from personal experience that the travellers are more than ready for a spot of refreshment, especially as it's free! At the end of the day we were exhausted, but had, so we were informed, earned god's blessing for giving nourishment to the devotees. I must say I was a little surprised that

---

[iii] A BBC TV programme in which two bearded motorcyclists visit exotic venues and cook the local specialities, usually in the open air.

[iv] An internationally important religious philosopher of whom more later.

no one turned a hair at being given sambaram by a non- Hindu, with a strange accent, and a European at that.

Making sambaram at Aluva

Everyone knows about the Kerala backwaters and everyone who goes for a holiday there includes a boat trip in their itinerary. These water features are formed by sand brought down by the rivers from the mountains. Instead of being deposited on the ocean floor, the silt is swept into long banks parallel with the shore. In due course, the banks form barriers against the rivers that created them, and the latter become broad and shallow slow-flowing channels or great lakes of fresh water that only become brackish in the dry season. The backwaters have had a big effect on Kerala life. People use them to travel from place to place in small boats, and to transport heavy cargoes in barges; they fish in them and keep ducks there.

The sandbanks shift sometimes and can destroy ports - most notably the ancient harbour of Muziris, silted up by the Periyar in flood in the fourteenth century, and consigned to history as a result - or form them. The backwaters measure about 260 square miles in area and the largest is the Vembanad Kayal. We had a lovely day on the backwaters with Julie, Raju, Geetha and Kitty. We hired a workaday boat, with a friendly driver from Alappuzha [Alleppey] and cruised along a canal next to the road before reaching the lake and passing the big thatched barges mainly used by tourists now, river buses packed with commuters, wild water birds, and domestic ducks corralled in enclosures from which they were either unable or disinclined to escape.

The Backwaters, near Alappuzha

Human activities of all sorts continue in the back yards of thatched houses and on the adjacent river banks - desultory fishing mainly by old men and children using the absolute minimum of equipment, washing, bathing, swimming, tending gardens - most of which contained a conical haystack - cooking and dozing. Few people were interested in the passing tourists like us and they did not allow us to disturb their normal way of life. We bought some half-ripe mangoes from one house, and some fresh toddy from another and took tea in a small lakeside café. Kitty was allowed to drive the boat but we couldn't swim: too much water-weed we were told, it would catch our feet and drown us. Raju and Geetha sat on the roof of the boat with handkerchiefs wound round their heads - 'just like mappilas' said Manga. We shared our picnic - rice and yoghurt and wadai - with the driver, and then said goodbye and went down to the excellent beach. Kitty played on some swings and I had a swim. We bought some roasted peanuts and Indian soft drinks [difficult to find: Coca Cola seemed to have taken over everything, including 'Thums Up', a locally owned cola, the spelling of the name of which never failed to amuse us]. And we had another lovely day on the

Backwaters again in 2008 when our daughters Indi and Laksh managed to get a bit of a tan from sunbathing on the boat's roof, and we saw weaver-birds and their nests, and the longest metal snakeboat in the world!

Weaver birds' nests

There are some more good beaches in Kerala. The most famous are at Kovalam, which has become more commercialised since we first went there with Rosemary and Tony in 1991 but hadn't been entirely transformed by the time of our last visit. On the earlier occasion we stayed in a rather posh hotel made up of separate bungalows - very nice: ours looked over the bay and had a shaded garden for the hot afternoons. We swam during the day and went out on a boat hollowed out from a tree trunk to do some snorkelling, which was a wonderful experience. Unfortunately though I cut my foot on a rock; the wound went septic and a few days later I was lying in a delirium on Hassan Railway Station, and would likely not have been here to tell the tale had it not been for the fact that Tony's voluminous medical bag included the right antibiotic.

There's some interesting geology in Kerala. In south-east Wayanad the quartz country is auriferous - and at one time gold was mined, but no longer, though in Logan's time 'some of the lower classes of the population try to eke out a precarious living by washing the sands after each annual flood.'[91] The laterite from which our house in Trikkandiyur and the garden wall are made, is formed where the water table goes up and down during the year and iron ores are deposited into the upper layer of the soil [in this case decayed gneiss]. Laterite is soft and crumbly while under the ground. While it's still in this state, it can be shaped into blocks, which will then harden in the open air and mostly stay hard even when wet. Finally, the varied colours of many sandy beaches are caused by grains of garnets [red], sapphires [blue], jacinths [yellow], iron ore [black] and silica [white] washed down from the mountains, or brought from farther afield by ocean currents. The best example is the beach at Kanniya Kumari, which is however just within the boundaries of Tamil Nadu.

Kerala's climate is generally described as equable. It's not very often too hot and never too cold. The only thing that isn't equable is the heavy monsoon rainfall. The Kerala *Gazetteer* divides the year into three climatic seasons, thus: 'The period March to May is the hot season. This is followed by the south-west monsoon season, which starts on or about 1st June and continues till the middle of October. Then the north-east monsoon season begins and lasts up to the end of February, although the rain associated with the monsoon ceases by December.'[92] During the hot season, the mean maximum temperature is up to 5 degrees higher than it is in the south-west monsoon season. From the end of October, Kerala begins to be much drier, and from then until March it rains on average for only 14 days altogether. [see Table One, below].

Table One: Average monthly rainfall in mm. Top row: mean of all districts; second row: mean of Malappuram District.

Jan	Feb	Mar	Apr	May	Jun	Jul	Aug	Sep	Oct	Nov	Dec	Tot
18	17	43	112	245	676	695	417	235	305	188	49	3001
7	6	19	79	211	702	787	405	199	209	164	31	2900

Table Two: Average maximum and minimum temperatures

Jan	Feb	Mar	Apr	May	Jun	Jul	Aug	Sep	Oct	Nov	Dec	Av
32	32	33	33	32	29	28	29	29	30	31	31	31
22	23	25	25	25	24	23	23	24	24	23	23	24

As you can see, average temperatures don't vary that much from season to season, especially the average minimum temperatures. And there's not that much variation from place to place either. The hottest area is Palakkad, with a yearly average max of 32.3 and the coolest, Fort Kochi with 29.8. The highest temperature ever recorded is 41.7 degrees Celsius at Palakkad on 26th April 1950 and the lowest, 12.9 at Punalur on 8th Jan 1965.[93]

Rainfall on the other hand varies hugely from month to month and also from place to place. The greatest amount of rain falls in Kozhikode District (3796 mm) and the least in Tiruvanantapuram (1833 mm). And the wettest month anywhere is Kozhikode's 1,117.4 mm in July, compared with that district's figure of 7.6 mm in February! The reason that Kozhikode's figure is so high is that the district includes Wayanad, where the high land is extensive; in Trivandrum, the Western Ghats are at their lowest and are nearest the sea. The most rain falling in one day was recorded on 27th July 1967: 645 mm! That was when I was in Bihar and we were gasping for even ten mill of rain to end the drought there. The *Gazette* reported [in 1986] that rainfall is reliable in Kerala and droughts occur very rarely. However, in his book *Chasing the Monsoon,* Alexander Frater wrote that the monsoon did fail badly in the early nineteen nineties, and as a result, tankers were supplying drinking water, engineers were installing over 11,000 street hydrants, 500 tube wells and 400 bore wells had been sunk, but still the poor went thirsty.

This is certainly unusual, but it does seem that in recent years, there is increasing uncertainty about when the monsoon will arrive. And sometimes it rains when it shouldn't. In the year that our German friends Rika and Frank journeyed with us, they were greeted on their arrival in Kochi by grey clouds instead of the blue skies that are expected at Christmas time. Worse, there was something approaching a freezing fog in the highlands at Kodaikanal; and worst of all, more rain fell in one hour when we were in Madurai than usually occurs in the whole season. Humidity is high in Kerala, especially of course during the monsoon. In Kozhikode, the average morning humidity is 82%, evening 75%, with the highest figure of 92% on July and August mornings.

Water shortage!

These bare facts and figures are gleaned from the *Gazette*. A rather more romantic view of the seasons is included in a collection of Indian poems from the British Museum, edited by A.L.Dalapiccola. [94] I have given the names of the months in Hindi, Tamil, Malayalam and the nearest English equivalent, respectively.

Chaitre - Chiththirai - Medam - April/May

The charming creepers are in bloom and once more the trees are young, covered in blossoms. Flowers fill streams and pools; elegantly dressed women, burning with passion, abandon themselves in the enjoyment of love. The parrot, the mynah and the cuckoo warble songs of love. In such a charming season, no one should embrace the thorns of separation, abandoning the flower of union. [Keshava Dasa of Orchha, a Rajput court poet of the 16th/17th century. Translated from the original Hindi]

Vaishaka - Vaikasi - Edavam - May/June

The earth and sky are filled with fragrance; a gentle sweet-smelling breeze blows softly. Beauty is everywhere and perfume pervades the air, inebriating the bee and filling with longing the heart of the lover far from home. I beseech you, who have made me so happy, not to leave me in the month of Vaishaka. The arrows of the love-god Kama are difficult to bear during separation. [Keshava]

Jyestha - Aana - Mithunam - June/July

Air, water, ether, earth and fire - all these five elements become one: a blazing fire. The wayfarers are exhausted and the elephants become tame, seeing the dried up pool. The cobra slithers up the elephant's trunk and the tiger lies in its shade. All creatures on earth and in the water are restless and weak. This is why the wise enjoin lovers not to leave home in this season. [Keshava]

The poet Kalidasa has this to say about Jyestha: *The sun is blazing and we look forward to the coolness of the moon. Continuous bathing exhausts the water reservoirs, the sunset is lovely and brings thoughts of languorous love.* In Kerala, however, the monsoon season begins in Mithunam.

Asadha - Aadi - Karkidakam - July/August

There don't seem to be any poems describing love in July – perhaps it's too hot for that sort of thing. In Kerala of course the monsoon is in full swing.

Shravana - Aavani - Chingam - August.

During the month of Shravana the streams filled by the monsoon rains look lovely while rushing along to unite with the sea. The creepers clinging lovingly to the trees delight the eye. The restless lightning flashes all around while flirting with the clouds. The peacocks with their shrill cries announce the union of earth and sky. - Keshava

The mighty rain cloud is his charging elephant, the lightning is his banner, the rumbling thunder his kettle drums.–Kalidasa

The great Kerala festival of Onam takes place in the month of Chingam.

Bhadra - Purattasi - Kanni -September/October

No poems for this month but the nine-day Navratri festival and Vijayadashami day [when the young start to learn to read and write] take place in Kerala.

Ashvin - Aippassi - Thulam - October/November

During this month the spirits of the ancestors descend to earth to be propitiated. It is time to worship the nine Durgas[v] *for prosperity in this life and future salvation. The kings and their pandits set out to visit their territory. After the monsoon the sky is clear and in the pools the lotuses are in full bloom. The moon brightens the night, and Lord Vishnu and his consort Lakshmi engage in their celestial dance.* - Keshava

The Temple festival in Trikkandiyur comes in the month of Thula

Kartik - Karthikai - Vrischikam - November/December

Woods, gardens, rivers, earth and sky are bright, illuminated by the lamps of Diwali; merriment reigns supreme over days and nights. Lovers spend their time in festive gambling. Rich and poor vie with one another to decorate their houses for the arrival of the goddess Lakshmi. A clear light pervades the whole of creation; men and women are under the spell of love. This is the month to cleanse oneself in the holy river, to give alms, and to worship god. - Keshava

Agrahayana - Markazhi - Dhanu - December/January

The Sabarimala Mandala Pooja takes place in Dhanu.

Pausha - Thai - Makaram - January/February

During the month of Pausha no-one likes icy water, cold food, light dresses or an unheated house. Frost pervades earth and sky. This is the time when rich and poor alike enjoy a massage with oil, cotton padded clothes, pan, fire in the room, and the company of young women. Days are short, nights are long: it is not the time to quarrel with one's lover.

I have to say that this is not descriptive of the climate in Kerala, where the temperature is likely to reach 32 degrees! It is a bit chilly in Delhi, but you would have to go up into the foothills of the Himalayas before you'd need to wear padded clothes.

Magha - Maasi - Kumbhan - February/March

---

[v] These are the nine forms of the Mother Goddess, most often known as Devi in the south at least

Kumbhan is Manga's birth month. Her true birthday falls on the day before the new moon; the western date might be anything between 6th February and 5th March, because the Malayalam calendar is related to the phases of the moon rather than the march of the sun. We have to refer to the Malayalam almanac each year to be sure of the timing of the new moon, then we know that the birthday is the previous day.

Phalguna - Panguni - Meenam - March/April

Rich and poor make merry together without a care for social conventions. They speak freely without restraint or sense of shame. In every home young men and women play Holi with great abandon and gusto: they knot their garments together in mock wedding ceremony and rub gulala on each other's faces. The perfume of scented powders fills the air.

The most exciting month in Kerala as far as the climate is concerned is Karkidakam - July - when the south-west monsoon is at its height. 'The monsoon buffets the people but replenishes the land;' says Shashi Tharoor, 'it affirms life even as it sweeps away the frail and the weak before it'[95]

Alexander Frater, in his book *Chasing the Monsoon* adds some further colour in his description of the arrival of the monsoon at Kovalam. Excited tourists are watching the dark skies and the sea foaming 'like champagne'. Flashes of lightning illuminate the scene and thunder reverberates. Suddenly the wind crashes into the crowd and then comes the rain. Frater says he felt as if he was imprisoned inside a waterfall.

Manga's memories of the monsoon are a little more prosaic.

'The roof of our house was made of coconut leaves - not the fresh green fronds but the dead brown ones. We used to pay some men to climb the trees to get them for us. It was a difficult and dangerous job, but they shinned up the bare trunk really quickly - they used a rope made of coir of course tied between their ankles to keep a foothold and another one between their hands to pull themselves up. - and made it look very easy. Anyway after they had thrown the nuts [and they did this very carefully, for if a coconut fell on your head it could knock your brains out], they would pull off the dead fronds and throw them down to us too. Dad and our servant Kurumbai used to sit and weave the leaves into mats and

put them on the roof. They were very good at keeping the rain out at first but the trouble came when they got old. We should have put a new roof twice a year - before and after the monsoon - and we didn't have enough coconut trees for that, and couldn't afford to buy any. So during the hot season, the fronds became brittle and weren't waterproof any longer. It was alright for light rain but when the monsoon came, water would pour into the house. We would sit inside holding our sleeping mats over our heads to try and keep dry, and all the pots and pans from the kitchen were put around the rooms to catch the leaks. Insects like centipedes and millipedes would fall from the roof too. If you touched them with a stick they would curl around it and you could put them outside. We would never hurt them. But if they crawled on you, they would burn your skin and leave a mark and it would itch badly and go sore. So we were a bit scared of them.

But we had some good times in the monsoon season too. We quite liked the hot season at first because that is when the best fruit come and we would have lots of treats like really sweet mangoes, as well as papaya, jackfruit, guava, supporta[vi] *- all sorts of things. There were brightly coloured flowers in the garden too. It was lovely to sit outside in the evening when it was cool and because it was dry, there were no mosquitoes to worry us. But soon the earth dried up and the blooms began to fade and dust got everywhere - in our hair and in our clothes - and we weren't allowed to bath more than twice a day, to save water. We were very lucky to have a good well in our garden and that never dried up but we had to be careful anyway. The best time was early morning. We would get up and put waste water from washing round the coconut trees. We would build a sort of dam round the tree to keep the water in until it soaked into the ground. Dad also had a series of little channels taking water to all the plants - like a small irrigation scheme.*

Anyway, when the rain came, everything changed ever so quickly. First it would get very dark and then we would see lightning flashes all over the sky. Then the thunder would start - kudda-kudda-kudda: rolling thunder you call it I think. When we were little we would put our hands over our ears and hide behind mum. Sometimes there would be just thunder and lightning and no rain, but if it suddenly got cooler and there was a breeze, we knew rain was coming. We'd rush outside and put our faces up to the sky and the rain would go in our eyes and our mouths and

---

[vi] Also called chicu. Very sweet, rather like kiwi fruit.

down our backs and the ground would get muddy and we would squelch our toes in it.

And really you could almost see things growing. One minute plants would be drab and brown and after an hour they would wake up and start going green. And fresh shoots would suddenly appear, out of the mud. Snakes that had been hiding anywhere that was dark or cooler came out in the open: mostly, they'd be harmless ones we called chera but sometimes there were cobras too. We knew they wouldn't harm us but we kept well away from them anyway. They were supposed to eat the frogs but I never saw them even chase them. The frogs came when the pools around the coconut trees grew deep. They were big frogs - bullfrogs I think you call them and when they croaked, their throats would blow up like balloons. They said 'Thara pillaru; kadam vanghia, kodukilla', which means 'I'll give it to you, children; if he borrowed it, he won't give it back.' Insects came too of course and all sorts of bugs - some big black flying beetles that would fly towards the lights and bump into your face. But we didn't mind. It was just good to feel cool and clean again.'

CHAPTER SIXTEEN

PRINCIPALLY PALLAVAS

'An enemy who is near is more use than a relation who is far away' - Malayalam proverb.

The Shore Temples

In the seventh and eighth centuries, the leading power in the south of India was the Pallava dynasty - the Pallavas of Kanchipuram. They impinged little on Kerala but are worth reading about mainly on account of their architecture, and also because the Cheras of Kerala fought on their side from side to time; and, later, against them alongside the Cholas. The Pallavas' main rivals were the Chalukyas from Karnataka [who invaded Kerala at one stage] and the battles between them were fierce, with the city of Kanchipuram being lost and regained at regular intervals. All this fighting did not stop the Pallavas from building the wonderful temples on the seashore at Mamallapuram, however.

Mamallapuram was the Pallavas' major port and was named after one of their great kings, whose nickname was 'Mamalla', meaning great wrestler. The shore temples and the temples-carved-from-a-single- stone were completed during the rule of his successor, and the Kailasanatha Temple at Kanchipuram shortly afterwards. This is one of thirteen Shiva temples in Kanchipuram. In addition there are sixteen Vishnu temples in a town with a population of only 150,000. The Pallavas' influence stretched beyond India. They had a powerful navy and close ties with 'Greater India', countries such as Burma, Thailand and Cambodia. In Sri Lanka and Indo-China there are many temples including Angkor Wat that are very similar to those in Mamallapuram. There is some speculation that the ruling houses of the kingdom of Angkor and of the Pallavas were related.[96]

A rock carving, Mamallapuram

I have already described Mamallapuram [or Mahabalipuram as it was called until recently, before reverting to the original name]; it is a wondrous place. We've been there a couple of times. When Tony and Rosemary came with us to India, we flew direct to Madras [now called Chennai of course], which was a much more relaxed place to land than Mumbai or Delhi used to be. We stayed at the Connemara, one of the city's top hotels, formerly a palace. In the 1990s, before the rise of the Indian middle-class, the hotel was quite affordable out of season [it was Easter - too hot for most tourists] and we enjoyed the luxury of a large, floodlit swimming pool in the courtyard that had originally been part of the palace harem. We ate a sumptuous buffet meal in the gardens with classical dancing as cabaret. My nephew Raju, who was travelling with us, professed to be unimpressed by both the dancing and the food, doubting their authenticity, but I caught him writing to a friend that he was 'living the life of a rajah.' We hired a minivan to get to Mamallapuram and admired the shore temples before bathing in the sea. When Julie came with us ten years later, we couldn't swim because there lots of signs prohibiting it: apparently a family had drowned there recently. But on both occasions we found the architecture of the Pallavas particularly impressive.

Incidentally, there was no final victor in the wars between the Pallavas and the Chalyukas. The latter were defeated by the Rastrakutyas in 755 and the former by the Cholas of Tanjore 140 years later. These stories belong however to the next era in Kerala history, the Age of the Second Chera Empire.

CHAPTER SEVENTEEN

MANGA'S MEMORIES: WILDLIFE

'*To an elephant, a horse is only a footstool*' Malayalam proverb.

Before considering the next era in Kerala's history, we can learn something about local wildlife, as seen through Manga's eyes.

> *'There was a lot of wildlife in the village when I was little. Snakes and insects and lizards as well as birds and few animals. We just took them for granted most of the time and didn't go bird spotting or anything like that. One thing – we would never hurt any creatures, even poisonous snakes or insects. But snakes would never attack anyone in our family anyway because one of our ancestors had once saved a snake. That's what we believed anyway. But we were still careful if we saw one. These days things are bit different though we try not to hurt anything. But I remember Balan finding a small snake in the garden once and killing it. We all told him not to but he said it was a very dangerous one. He didn't really believe that we were safe!*
>
> *We saw a lovely long green snake when we went to the Silent Valley. It was on the road and its head was reared up to try to scare us. Christopher looked it up and it was a Green Whip Snake, which is very mildly poisonous. Malayalam name is pachila pambu, or kankuti pambu in Tamil, which means 'snake that goes for the eyes'. We had a lot of long grass growing at home when I was young and so there were plenty snakes and also we would see mongoose, which preyed on them. There are not many snakes now and I haven't seen a mongoose alive since I was a child.*

In the two years I was working in Bihar, far from any towns and with forest and scrub nearby, I only ever came across two snakes. One was in my bathroom and it escaped as quickly as I did when we saw each other; and another was a tree snake of some type in the forest. I also met a scorpion in my bungalow. It raced off and hid in my shoe. For many years afterwards even in England I knocked out my shoes before putting them on. And don't mention termites, which chewed through some of my books, or red spiders, which had me clambering onto the kitchen table, because Manga told me some terrifying tales of their powers!

Whipsnake

The best-known snakes of India are probably the cobra and the krait. The Indian Cobra should not be confused with the King Cobra. The latter is the largest poisonous snake in the world and a truly formidable creature. It can be over 18 feet long, mainly eats other snakes, including very poisonous ones like the krait and very large ones like the python, and can easily kill a human with a single bite. Not surprisingly it is revered, especially in Tamilnad. The town of Nagercoil is named after a temple in the town dedicated to the snake king. Fortunately, King Cobras [Rajahvembalan in Malayalam] are shy and humans don't come across them much. The Indian Cobra [Moorkhan] on the other hand grows to only six feet long and only kills about ten per cent of the people it bites. But it is seen more often, especially as it likes to live in rice fields. The Krait [Vellikettan] and Russell's Viper are also poisonous and living as they do near humans [because that's where their main prey, rats, are to be found] they are regarded as particularly dangerous: with good reason, since The Russell's Viper [Mandali] kills more people than any other snake in India, though estimates of how many die from its bite vary widely. The official figure for deaths for all snake bites in India is 2,000, but the American Society of Tropical Medicine and Hygeine says that the figure is 46,000.[97]

As a small child, I used to enjoy Kipling's story about a mongoose called 'Rikki-Tikki-Tavi', which protected a family in India from the local snakes. It made me rather scared though. What would happen if we had to go to India [a fairly unlikely eventuality admittedly!]? We would surely all die of snakebites, because we didn't have a pet mongoose to look after us.

Manga continues.

'The birds I mainly remember are the tiny little sunbirds - ever so colourful. They take nectar from the flowers, like hummingbirds. When Mum first came from Sheffield to our house in Trikkandiyur, she was really thrilled when she saw one just by the doorway. We looked it up in the bird book[i] *and we thought it was a yellow backed sun bird. Mum used to sit in the garden with the bird book and binoculars and make a list of the species she saw. One funny thing was that Ravi - who was a bit naughty in those days - used to wait till she was settled comfortably in the front garden and then shout 'Grandma, there's a big bird in the back garden!' She'd get up and hurry round to the back and Ravi would say, 'Oh, bad luck, you just missed it!' And when she was back in her chair, he'd call out again!'*

On the same holiday, a neighbour came round to say that there was an interesting bird in his garden. We followed him to his house, and were thrilled to see a little silvery-white bird with a black head and a crest and a long white tail. It was a paradise flycatcher, and it soon flew off in search of its lunch. Salim Ali describes the bird beautifully: 'The agile fairy-like movements of the male as he twists and turns in the air after flies, with his tail-ribbons looping or trailing behind, is a spectacle of exquisite charm.'[98] I don't think we've seen such an attractive bird before or since. We used to see a lot of parrots - rose-ringed parakeets. A pair was nesting in a rotten tree trunk in another neighbour's garden when Mum was there. When we got back to England, she gave a talk to her birdwatching society in Sheffield about the birds she had spotted.

The biggest birds to be found in most gardens are the koel, chambothu or crow pheasant and the house crow. The koel is glossy black, and is about the same size as a crow but slimmer. The best thing about the bird is its call, which 'begins with a low 'kuoo', rises in scale with each successive 'kuoo' until it reaches fever pitch at the seventh or eighth, and breaks off abruptly.'[99] The crow pheasant is very pretty with chestnut coloured wings but is very destructive, eating the eggs and fledglings of smaller birds.

---

[i] Salim Ali's *Book of Indian Birds* which I had bought in Calcutta New Market in November 1966.

Manga says,

'You seem to be able to hear it all the time in summer - its call is sort of echoing - coo, coo, coo, lots of times. And the crow is very important to us. It's just like an English crow - eats anything, noisy, bullying, but good fun really. There are so many stories about crows in India. It is connected with the god of death, Yama, and also the ancient god of wisdom, Varuna. So if you put out food for the crow, Yama will be good to your dead ancestors and to you when you come to die. So at home we would always throw some rice into the garden before we started our meal. It's also supposed to be a wise bird, like the owl in England. For us, the owl is a bird of ill omen. If we heard it hoot, we had to quickly put a knife in the fire as protection, otherwise there would be a death in the family. We often seemed to hear of a death in the neighbourhood after an owl had been hooting.[ii] *Some people think the crow is evil, but they still have to treat it well so it doesn't do evil things to them. I never did anything bad to a crow but one was horrible to me once. It seemed a real disaster at the time.*

You know we didn't have much money at home, so I didn't have many treats. But one day I had saved a few paisa which people had given me for running errands or at festivals, and I bought myself my favourite sweet. I decided not to eat it straight away, but to carry it home so I could enjoy it in comfort. I carried it very carefully so as not to drop it on the floor. Once I opened my fist to have a look at it, and...whoosh - down came an old crow, snatched it from my hand and flew away with it into a tree, and gobbled it up. I cried all the way home and even now my eyes water a bit when I think of that poor thin child losing her precious treat! So I can't say I really like crows! Mum (that's Christopher's Mum of course) loved to spot birds from the train also. In those days you could see lots of birds sitting on the telephone wires or in the trees or in the fields'

Kingfishers were quite common. They often perched on the wires looking for prey in pools and ditches. There are lots of different types of kingfisher - the common, which is like ours in England; the pied, which is black and white of course and bigger, and the very colourful white-breasted kingfisher. Also on the wires you see little bee-eaters and striking blue jays or rollers; glossy black

---

[ii] Hearing an owl hoot can be a bad omen in the west too, and again the response should be to put an iron in the fire, or throw salt into the flames.

drongos with forked tails and if you're lucky, racket-tailed drongos - they have two very long thin tail feathers with broad tips and Salim Ali says they 'give the illusion of the bird being pursued by a pair of large bumble bees.'[100]

Brahminy Kite

In the fields there are all sorts of egrets: you can see the little egret in England now that the climate is changing - there's often one by the sea here in Whitstable - and cattle egrets too I think. And there are bulbuls, weaver birds with their wonderfully constructed nests, babblers, hoopoes, barbets, mynahs - which like starlings are very good at imitating, including human speech - owls, some, like the great horned owl, quite scary if you see its eyes peering at you through dense foliage as I did one day, and kites. The kites circle the Fish Market in Tirur; they are very useful birds because they clear up any carrion left in the roads and fields, like vultures used to in North India. The most spectacular Indian bird is probably the peacock of course, and it is the national bird of India. There is a Peacock Reserve in Kerala at Choolannur near Palakkad, but our best experience of them was in Jaipur when we stayed at a hotel annexe, surrounded by these splendid creatures.

Vikky with some monkeys

Manga continues. *'You don't come across that many animals in villages in India now. Mostly they are in protected areas as far away from people as they can get. When I was little, there were monkeys in the garden, and they were still there when I first went home after being married, but now you only see them in tourist places where they beg or steal from visitors. One of the stories about monkeys that Christopher likes very much is the one about tamarind. You know tamarind is the spice that we use to make sambar taste very sour. Well the pods of tamarind grow high in very tall trees and you can't reach them. So what we used to do is to throw stones up at the monkeys in those trees. They would get angry and want to throw things at you. So they would take the pods and throw them! And we would go away with plenty tamarind! My sister was very naughty. If there was a band playing she would take some tamarind and go and stand in front of the trumpet player. He would see her sucking the sour spice and his mouth would water so much that he couldn't play properly! But back to monkeys. Our neighbour Baby had a pet monkey for a while and we would stand and let it take nits from our hair. Monkeys are well looked after in India. That's because Hanuman, the monkey god, helped Rama defeat the demon king Ravana in the Ramayana story.'*

One of the varieties seen all over in India is called the Hanuman langur - which Malayalees call korungu, which just means 'monkey'.

It is the sacred monkey, but the other varieties should never be hurt either. The most widespread in the south certainly is the bonnet macaque. Malayalees call it vella [white] korungu, because it has a white face; the langur's face is black. Manga remembers common langurs, the ones with black faces, stealing papaya from the trees in her garden - her father's remedy was to get all the family to come out and bang on saucepans. That usually did the trick!

Nilgiri langurs in the Silent Valley

In some cities monkeys have become a great nuisance, damaging overhead power lines, holding up traffic - and worse. In New Delhi in 2007 a mob of macaques reportedly attacked and killed the Deputy Mayor, though in fact he fell from a balcony while fighting them off, so manslaughter perhaps rather than murder. Still the monkeys cannot be hurt. The authorities have however trained langurs, which are larger, to frighten the macaques away. We've recently seen the Nilgiri langur, an endangered species, in the Silent Valley, a protected environment in the Western Ghats; our guide also pointed out to us a rare lion-tailed macaque. Another quite rare creature we have seen is a Malabar squirrel. This was when I first went to Kerala and we made the inevitable journey to Thekkadi.

That was a good trip. Lake Periyar didn't have so many visitors in those faraway days and there were more animals. We saw plenty of wild elephants, pig and deer and while strolling by the banks of the lake heard a sound above us and looking up saw what looked at first like a rather large red bear-like creature. On inspection, we could see its squirrel face, but its body must have been well over a foot long and its tail perhaps two feet. Well is it called the giant squirrel. It was certainly nothing like the little striped palm squirrels we were used to. These charming characters are said to have stripes where Lord Rama stroked them after they had collected stones for him to build a bridge to Lanka in the *Ramayana*. We've seen gaur at Thekkadi and heard its surprising call, which sounds to me like a dog howling: strange for the largest of the cow family. Away from Periyar, we came across a herd of wild elephants on a trip to Wayanad one year. When the herd saw us they gathered protectively around two youngsters. And samba [mane in Malayalam] and spotted deer [chital] have crossed our path occasionally. None of us have ever seen a tiger or even its prints, but I think I might have heard one late one evening on the Chotanagpur plateau in Bihar as I was driving home after a long and tiring day delivering food to remote villages. Probably I imagined it! I certainly used to hear the howls of wolves and the yelps of jackals at night in my bungalow right on the edge of the school compound in Tilaiya. That was very eerie especially as I was reading at the time Jim Corbett's book about man-eating leopards and tigers, which would walk into villagers' huts and take their pick of the humans present for their dinner!

Manga says,

'Of course, elephants are my favourites. So nice creatures. I learned a story at school. An elephant used to go to a temple every day and he went past a tailor's shop. The tailor would always pat his trunk and perhaps give him a banana. Then one day, the tailor was in a bad mood. Something had happened, don't know what. Anyway, when the elephant came for his pat or treat, instead the tailor pricked his trunk with a needle. The elephant didn't do anything, just walked on. Next day, the elephant walked by again. He was prepared; he had filled his trunk with water, and squirted it all over the tailor's work - which was an important job he was doing for a rich man. So the tailor learned two lessons. The first is, if you're angry about something, you shouldn't take it out on someone else. And the second is - always be kind to

animals. And - no, there are three lessons - the third is, an elephant never forgets!'

Elephant travelling in style

There are still plenty of working elephants in Kerala - either in temples or the timber trade. These days they are carried to their workplaces on the back of lorries to protect their feet from the hard roads. They do look rather comical; we always hope that they are not scared by the experience.

We haven't mentioned lizards, but when Manga was little, there were hundreds of them living in the thatched roof. She and the family had to be careful because if a lizard fell on their head, it foretold death. P.V.Jagadisa Ayyar in his book *South Indian Customs* refines this belief to an extraordinary extent giving different outcomes depending on which exact part of the head the lizard falls. One of the possibilities is apparently coronation![101] I think the lizard concerned is the house gecko; they also inhabited my bungalow in Bihar and were very good at keeping down the insects! I grew very fond of them. We see lizards in the garden in Trikkandiyur bigger than the gecko and capable of blending in with their surroundings, but the most impressive lizard I ever saw was in the forests of Chotanagpur - I was driving my jeep truck along a barely used track in the jungle when I saw a dragon-like creature in the scrub alongside the road. It must have been four feet long and I thought it was a small crocodile at first. It must have been a monitor lizard. I think I'd have been quite scared if I'd been on foot! We did see a crocodile when we were taking Mum for a bird-watching trip in 1979. We were in a small rowing boat looking for water birds, and we saw a big reptile in the distance. I don't suppose we were in any danger but it was coming our way and we had very little freeboard, the boat being as usual overcrowded...so we returned smartly to shore!

Wild elephants in Wayanad Forest

But nowadays wildlife is in trouble in Kerala as in all parts of India. Rapidly increasing population, road building and industrialisation, all of this robs animals of their natural habitat and food supply. Especially tragic is poaching, in particular of tigers, the body parts of which are used in Chinese medicine, and can be sold for large amounts of money. There were something like 40,000 tigers in India at the end of the nineteenth century in spite of the depredations of princely and/or British hunters. By 1972, continued hunting and habitat destruction had reduced the number to 1,800. Enter Project Tiger - Indira Gandhi was shocked by the situation and introduced legislation to ban hunting, open new tiger reserves, and increase protection. Until recently Project Tiger was regarded as a huge success. The census of 1997 put the numbers at over 3,500 and the number of tiger reserves had increased from 9 to 28. But a more recent count, which took place in 2006, estimated that only 1,411 tigers remained in India. In Kerala the estimated number has fallen from 75 to 46 in the 15,000 square kilometers of forest in the state. Of these 20 to 27 might be in Periyar. Park officials are surprised at this figure, believing that the number might be 30% higher. In fact more recent estimates put the number of tigers up to 2,500 in India as a whole. If true, this is encouraging, but doubts have been expressed about the accuracy of the calculation and more evidence is needed before it can be said with confidence that the truly wild tiger has any future in India.

CHAPTER EIGHTEEN

JAINS, BUDDHISTS AND BRAHMINS IN KERALA

'He who has lost a great many arrows becomes a good archer; he who has spoiled a great many cadjans,[i] *a good writer.'* Malayalam proverb

There's a period between the first and second Chera Empires in Kerala that seems like the Dark Ages, with no-one apparently knowing much about what happened. It's possible that it was in fact a time of some bliss in 'God's Own Country'. This is certainly the view of Logan who writes of the period in the preface to volume one of the *Malabar Manual*, 'Progress in the modern sense it is true was impossible...but what after all has been the goal of all modern legislation but as Bentham's great dictum puts it, 'the greatest possible happiness of the greatest possible number'? To anyone who has studied the history of the Malayalees it will become apparent that the race had advanced far towards the attainment of this modern aim.'[102] Other historians however describe the period as 'The Kalabhra Interregnum', and the Kalabhras seem to be thought of as a pretty evil lot who, in the words of the *Gazette* '...exterminated many of the smaller chieftains and even plundered the temples.'[103] However there is little hard evidence of a major Kalabhran presence, evil or otherwise, and perhaps there were no dominant dynasties at all in a constantly changing and unstable political scene. There were invasions of Kerala at the end of the period by the Chalukyas [543-755 AD]; by their successors as the strongest power in southern Karnataka, the Rashtrakutas, and by the Pallavas of Kanchipuram and there seems to have been in fact a great deal of commotion and confusion at this period in the history of Kerala. So perhaps it was not so happy a society as Logan surmised after all. On the other hand it is perfectly possible that the common people were barely touched by the comings and goings of the ruling classes.

Away from the political scene, it does appear that the northern Vedic culture began to influence the Dravidian peoples of the south

---

[i] Palm leaves that can be written on, using a metal stylus.

in the early centuries BC. This will have been partly through the movement of peoples from the north, including Manga's Brahmin ancestors, and partly the migration of ideas. Cattle, horses and chariots arrived in the south, as well as changes in religious practices. Priests grew in importance, Brahmins became the dominant group and caste became fixed - no longer would a man be able to say 'a bard [or priest] am I, my father is a leech [doctor], my mother grinds corn.' Only priests 'could bestow divinity on the king [which was by now essential to kingship] ... [and] also give religious sanction to caste division'.[104] This was the state of Hinduism as the Vedic culture moved south. And we know that the Sangam literature says that Brahmins were established in Tamilakam, by which is meant Tamil country, by the third century AD, and that they were beginning to make their presence felt. The Brahmins to the west of the Ghats were Namboodiris, and may have been of northern origin as they themselves claim [descendants perhaps of the 64 families brought into Kerala by Parasurama], or may have been Keralans, formerly Nairs, who became priests in order to take advantage of the way society was moving. Those to the east, in present day Tamilnad, included Iyers, who had not yet migrated into Kerala and would not do so for many centuries.

Buddhism moved south with Ashoka the Great's Mauryan Empire. The founder of this new religion was Siddhartha Gautama, who was born the son of a raja on the borders of India and Nepal some time in the mid-fifth century BC. He was shocked by the suffering he saw in the world and concluded that this was due to people's appetites and desires: their greed. He was one of many reformers who were opposed to the extravagant sacrifices practiced by Hindus and he rejected the Vedic gods and disliked the growing power of the Brahmins. Gautama meditated under the Bodhi tree in Buddh Gaya and achieved enlightenment there. His solution to life's woes was 'the middle way'. One should overcome one's desires, and not indulge oneself, yet avoid extreme asceticism, and thereby at length attain nirvana and break the cycle of re-birth. Ashoka's predecessor as Emperor was a follower of Buddhism and its influence spread with the growth of the Empire.

Buddhist monks came to Kerala to spread the word, and seem to have been successful because the Chinese traveller Hsuan Tsang noted that Buddhism was flourishing in Kerala in 642 AD, and the later Ay kings in the south of Kerala, though themselves Hindus, were patrons of Buddhism.

It is pretty astonishing that Jainism should have begun in the same place and at the same time as Buddhism. Its leader - Jains do not describe him as founder of the religion - took the name Mahavira, which means great hero [his birth name was Nataputta]. He preached in what is now Bihar and Uttar Pradesh in the sixth to fifth centuries BC. Like Buddha, Mahavira believed you should suppress the enemies inside you like anger, greed and passion, and also like Buddha, following many years of meditation, he became spiritually pure and when he died his soul was liberated. Jainism differed from Buddhism in that the right way for a Jain to live was more extreme: non-violence meant causing no harm to any living being, and this included even insects. To achieve this they wore masks so they couldn't breathe in tiny creatures, and employed sweepers to to clear any living things from their path. It was also important not to indulge in sensual pleasure, and to practise complete detachment from people and any material things. Mahavira was opposed to the worship of gods and did not believe in god as creator, protector or destroyer. The important thing was human life. Jain monks travelled south to spread their beliefs, and like the Buddhists, were successful in drawing people away from Hinduism. 'The spiritual power and moral grandeur of Mahavira's teachings impressed the masses' says a Jain website. 'He made religion simple and natural, free from elaborate ritual complexities. His teachings reflected the popular impulse towards internal beauty and harmony of the soul.'[105] Jainism entered Kerala in the early years AD and it seems that some of the Chera kings were Jains.

There are few Buddhist or Jain remains in Kerala to remind one of the presence of these religions during the 'Dark Ages', but one of them is the wonderful temple at Kallil, which we've visited with our nephew Raju twice. Kallil was built [or excavated] as a place of worship for Jains but it is now a Bhagavathi Hindu temple although still apparently visited by Jains. There is a carving of Mahavira on the back wall of the cave and an incomplete figure on the facade of the shelter.

We asked a local resident about this. He said that ghosts come down at night to finish the sculpture. '*Have you seen them*?' asked Raju. '*What, do you expect me to come out here at night*?' he replied, '*I'm not crazy you know*'. What I couldn't understand was why, if these ghosts came with their hammers and chisels every night, they hadn't finished the sculpture by now. The villager could not enlighten me.

Rear of the rock hewn temple at Kallil

Kallil is a great place to visit. When we went with Julie, we soon felt we were far away from anywhere. The temple is some way from the village and can be reached only by climbing along a steep and rocky path. We found cashew nut trees: but we were not interested in the external nut but the thirst-quenching fruit. We took care not to get the juice onto our clothes for we knew it would never wash off. Then we walked down into a glen where there was a lone cottage with what looked like bedsheets hanging out to dry. But these were in fact sheets of rubber produced by a very small-scale industry. No-one was about while we were there but we could see the various pieces of low tech machinery, mangles and the like, used in the production of the rubber. And alongside the cottage was the temple pool, and in it a resident snake. The walls and pillars surrounding the pool had collapsed. It reminded me of Kipling's *Jungle Book* and the story of Mowgli finding treasure guarded by a sinister cobra among the ruins of an ancient temple in the jungle.[106] Above the pool was a flight of 42 steps that led up to the temple itself. We seemed to be in such a remote spot that it was a surprise to find someone selling tickets when we reached the top of the steps, but it did not spoil the atmosphere - views across dusty scrub land, bats hanging in the caves, paths worn by the feet of pilgrims over a thousand years.

The first Jain temple I ever saw was in Calcutta. When the new VSOs for the north-east of the country arrived in India in 1966, we were invited to a reception at the British Council on the first evening and on the following day were taken for a tour of the city. We were taken to Mother Theresa's hostel, not so famous in those days. That was a hard introduction to India, and contrasted sharply with our next venue - the Jain temple. I was moved by that remarkable building - perhaps because it was so unexpected. In the middle of dusty Calcutta, a mirage of mirrors and marble, carvings and colours, a lot of gold and what looked like precious stones, even flowers and gardens. I'm not quite sure how this fits in with Jain austerity, though.

There is nothing like that temple in Kerala and the fact that so little remains there of the once flourishing religions of both the Jains and Buddhists prepares us for the fact that changes were to come, viz. the Reformation of Hinduism

CHAPTER NINETEEN

OUR GARDEN

'Do not plant a tree head downwards' Malayalam proverb

'Sow Carrets in your Gardens, and humbly praise God for them, as for a singular and great blessing.' Richard Gardiner, *Profitable Instructions for the Manuring, Sowing and Planting of Kitchen gardens. C 1533*

Lakshmi in the garden, 1979

'When I was little', says Manga, *'our garden was very colourful and really big, with only one small house, and a barn for the cow. We had lots of flowers. What we called mandaram, kollambi, and konnai were growing, and jasmine, bougainvillea by the gate, a lot of lantana, canna alongside the path to the house, mirabilis, aloe vera, and a six-petalled flower, green at first and then going lemony, on a rather straggly plant, which smells like you hope it will. Ranjitham*[i] *I think it was called. Then we had Himalayan balsam, which we*

---

[i] Artabotrys hexapetalus aka ylang ylang..

never thought of as a pest as people do here, and the yellow muthira. We used that in the centre of flower decorations for the Onam festival: several circles are made with flowers and leaves and petals, with different patterns and colour schemes. Ashoka thechi had big bunches of flowers for poojas. Dad used to make oil out of the flowers of the thechipoo and mix it with the bark from various trees and with leaves to make a special Ayurvedic oil for Mum for her head. We used it too - twice a week. We had to leave it on our hair for half an hour and then wash it off. It was green but had a lovely smell so we didn't mind at all. Dad used the oil in other medicines as well I think; and the fruit was good for you too.

Hibiscus flower

We used to put aloe vera, which we called kachu vazha on our hair too, as a tonic, and sometimes the leaves of hibiscus too. Hibiscus flowers made a good drink when steeped in hot water, especially the red ones. We took konnai flowers to the temple - they were red and yellow. The books say that konnai is a type of laburnum but this was bit different. You can use the fruit as a mild laxative but you mustn't take too much. The kollambi flowers were yellow and shaped like kollambi - a spittoon. It's called a cup and saucer plant in England. Mundaram[ii] *has pale yellow flowers and leaves shaped bit like hearts and is in full bloom in the rainy season. Arali had thick waxy leaves that we used to twist*

[ii] Bauhina tomentosa

round to make into flower shapes, and a mild scent. It was used in medicine too. And we grew oleander bushes like the one we once used for a Christmas tree in Whitstable.

Rosema holding a cashew nut

Coconut palms, cashew nut trees, guava, tamarind, mango, areca nut, and teak trees all grew in the compound, and bamboo in the corner near Bhagyam's house. Someone used to come to harvest the fruit trees and they kept 10% and we ate the rest. Or if we were desperate for money, we sold them. You know the nut of the cashew grows OUTSIDE the fruit. The fruit juice is good to drink though it stains your clothes very badly - but the flesh is an irritant, so you have to be very careful how you treat this plant.

One year my brother brought home a sambangi plant, a sort of creeper like Morning Glory, from Coimbatore. Its flowers had a really strong nice perfume that attracted the bees. So Dad asked a neighbour who was a bee-keeper to help and he put a hive in our garden and collected the honey for us. The plant died after only one year, though.

Crops didn't do so well in our garden; the soil was too sandy. But Dad used to plant cassava, arabi, chenai, and chembu. The cassavas make your hands itch so dad used to put them in whitewashing lime to take away the itchiness. What we called arabi was a root, sort of slimy: we cook it in sambar. Chenai is like yam and chembu a bit like Jerusalem artichoke.

There was a very tall cotton tree in the garden then. It had fruits that looked just like loofahs. When they were ripe they would fall down, and dad would collect them. He took off the hard skin and out came very soft cotton, which he would dry in the sun and then stuff it into pillows. Unfortunately, the cotton didn't stay soft when it was crushed into pillow cases - and it felt as though we were sleeping on stones!

Bamboo plant

I told you before that Dad planted a henna tree so that Mum could have daughters - and it worked! So you can see what a wonderful plant it is. We used the leaves to make henna dye. You grind the leaves with turmeric and it makes a lovely red colour. We made patterns on our hands and feet and showed them to our friends at school and see whose was best. One particular bush in the village gave the best colour, better than ours, so all us girls would crowd round to that house and pick the leaves. It was fun.

I used to love helping Dad in the garden. Plants that are cultivated indoors in England, like wandering Jew or zabrina, grew like weeds in our garden and I used to collect them and things like chickweed, wash them and feed them to the cow. And I specially loved watering the garden in summer. We would raise and lower a bucket into the well on the end of a long bamboo pole, and empty the water into a channel that took it to the trees one by one. As soon as the depression round one tree filled up my job was to divert the water along another channel to the next tree. Once Rajam was doing this job when she fell into the well! The water had nearly all gone so she landed on the sand at the bottom, about 12 feet. She was about 14 years old and quite chubby, so my brother had to ask for help to pull her out!

We didn't use any fertilisers or compost. We just swept the leaves under the trees. The kitchen waste went to the cow to eat. I could never understand how people in Britain could feed cows with meat. It's not surprising they caught that horrible thing, mad cow disease. We did sprinkle some of the cow dung mixed with water over the spinach, cheerai [or keera in Malayalam] - two types - a tall plant with red stalks and a small green 'cut and come' variety, but most of the dung we made into a sort of pancake and put it on the walls or on the roof to dry, then used it as fuel. Or we sprinkled it on the floor of the house, or outside the front door as an antiseptic. People wrinkle their noses when I tell them this. But dried cow dung is very clean and it does stop smells. And some we burned to make ash for prayers.'

Rosemary recalls the time when we were travelling back from Luxembourg by car after Rika's funeral. *'Her daughters had started asking Manga about life in her village as a child. 'Our cow of course needed to have a calf every year', she told them. 'If it was a girl calf there were plenty of people who would take her'. We wondered what happened to the boy calves ... 'Oh Dad knew where to find a good home for them', she said confidently and we privately thought a little naively!'*

CHAPTER TWENTY

KULASHEKHARAS - THE SECOND CHERA EMPIRE

'*Better to see one sovereign than a thousand ministers*' Malayalam proverb

'*Another year! - another deadly blow! / Another mighty Empire overthrown!*' William Wordsworth, *Sonnets*

The *Gazette* tells us that 'a new epoch in Kerala history dawned in the ninth century AD with the revival of Chera power under Kulashekhara Varman'. This second wave of Cheras was certainly not a mythical dynasty - there are plenty of surviving relics and records including copper plates - but no-one seems to know where they came from. Notwithstanding the mystery about their origins, much was achieved in Kerala in the time of the Kulashekhara kings: according to the *Gazette,* the era marked 'an all-pervasive transformation in the political, social and cultural fields'.[107]

The founder of the dynasty was Kulashekhara Alwar, who reigned it is believed from 800 to 820 AD. His capital city was close to the old port of Muziris. No trace of the city remains today, though an unknown writer in the sixteenth century found the ruins of a palace on the site. Kulashekhara Alwar was said to be 'skilled in the arts of kingship and learned in spiritual matters',[108] and a playwright to boot. Next came Rajashekhara Varman [820-844], contemporary of Sankaracharya and a devotee of Lord Shiva. Many Shiva temples were built in Kerala during his reign, including the one at Trikkandiyur. He was so loved that legend says that many of his subjects were said to have committed suicide when they learned of his death. There are a number of temple inscriptions on copper plate referring to the next king, Sthanu Ravi Varma. The date on which he came to the throne has been established in a rather clever and complex way. 'A certain year in which [the planets] Jupiter and Saturn were together in the house of Sagittarius is mentioned [in temple records] as being the 25th year of Sthanu

Ravi. Since Jupiter takes 12 years and Saturn 30 years to complete an orbit, only once in 60 years do the two planets come together in a House. Between AD 825 and 925 these planets came together in Sagittarius only in 869. Therefore it follows that Sthanu ascended the throne in 844'.[109] Sthanu Ravi sent an army to help Aditya Chola in his fight against the Pallavas, and led a prosperous country with a well-fortified capital known as a centre of learning and culture. He knew a lot about astronomy, and arranged for his observatory to sound a bell every twenty-four minutes so people would know what time it was. The king was Hindu but he gave land and privileges to the Christians and it's possible that the church of St Thomas at Kodungallur was established at this time.

Vivekananda Rock viewed from Kanniyakuma

It was under Kothi Ravi Varma [917-947] that the Nemesis of the Cheras, the Chola Empire, again began to harass its neighbours. First the Cholas defeated the Pandyas. One of the copper plates says of this battle, 'Encircled by the fire of Parantaka Chola, the Pandya, as if desirous of cooling the heat caused by it, quickly entered the sea [en route for safety in Ceylon], abandoning his royal state and the kingdom inherited from his ancestors'! [The king was incidentally welcomed by the King of Lanka, but not by his nobles, who "stirred up a sorry strife to the undoing of the Pandu king.'[110] He therefore fled again, this time to Kerala]. Then the Cholas deposed the Ay kings, although most of their lands fell into the hands of the Cheras. Both these outcomes caused friction between Cholas and Cheras and their conflict rumbled on for another 150 years. At this stage, the Chola Empire stretched from Kanchipuram [near Chennai and now famous for its silk] to Kanniya Kumari, but it was not able to defeat the Chera army, which was particularly strong. Then the Cholas tried their luck against the Rashtrakutas, but were heavily defeated, and as a result, for the next thirty years the Cheras were left in peace. The growth in power of the Namboodiris and the construction of temples proceeded apace.

Bhaskara Ravi I [962-1013] is famous for the 'Jewish Grant' - he gave honours and revenue rights to the Jewish settlers - and notorious for being defeated by Rajendra Chola, who sacked the Chera's capital city. Fortunately, the Cholas then seemed to lose interest in Kerala and embarked instead on a doomed attempt to conquer North India, Malaya and Sumatra; but raids were soon resumed. In one battle, a Chera king was trampled to death by an elephant; one of his successors 'weakly' [or wisely perhaps] submitted to Chola rule and wrote plays instead. Bhaskara Ravi III who reigned from 1043 till 1082 seems to have been more warlike and to have decided that steps had to be taken if the Chera army was ever to stand up to the Cholas. So he introduced suicide squads made up of Nair Chaver warriors, and a military training system called Kalaripayuttu.[i] Kalaripayuttu is still practiced today though not for military purposes and it still requires enormous application.

Here's how the training was described by the Portuguese traveller Duarte Barbosa in the 16th century.

> The more part of these warriors when they are seven years of age are sent to schools where they are taught many tricks of nimbleness and dexterity; there they teach them to dance and turn about and to twist on the ground, to take royal leaps, and other leaps, and this they learn twice a day as long as they are children, and they become so loose-jointed and supple that they make them turn their bodies contrary to nature; and when they are fully accomplished in this, they teach them to play with the weapon to which they are most

[i] Tradition says that kalaripayattu is much more ancient, and indeed the forerunner of all the oriental martial arts.

> inclined, some with bows and arrows, some with poles to become spearmen, but most with swords and bucklers, which is most used among them, and in this fencing they are ever practising. The masters who teach them are called Panikars. [111]

The last Kulashekhara king was Rama Varma Kulashekhara [1090 - 1102]. The *Gazette* says that he 'occupies a unique place in Kerala history as the founder of the illustrious royal house of Venad', and that he 'finally erased the Chola menace.' At first sight, this does not fit in well with a CV that includes a retreat from his capital Mahodyapuram to Quilon in the south, and then a further withdrawal so that only the land between Kanyakumari and Trivandrum remained under his control. However it is a fact that the Cholas were seriously weakened too, and indeed never invaded Chera country again.

All the local histories I've read describe this period, whether it's known as the Age of the Perumals, the Second Chera Empire, or the Kulashekhara Dynasty, as being a glorious phase of Kerala history. The *Gazette* says: 'formative period saw the socio-political dominance of Aryan Brahmins, the unique caste system, matriliny, plurality and peaceful co-existence of various faiths, the evolution of Malayalam, the rise of temples and ritual-orientated Hinduism, and the decline of Buddhism and Jainism, the birth of great seers like Sankara, and the rise of merchant guilds and progress in the field of trade and commerce'.[112]

We are particularly interested in the continuing rise of the Brahmins, though it is important to remember that they were not Iyers, but the Namboodiris. We'll be coming to the arrival of the Iyers in Kerala in due course! At the moment they are we think in Tamilnad, Karnataka and Andhra, doing much the same as the Namboodiris are doing in Kerala; and that, we remember, is building up dominance over all other castes by their validation of kings. One can see parallels with the way that church and state operated in Europe. The religious leaders in both continents told the people that the kings had a divine right to rule; then crowned them, and if they went off course threatened to excommunicate them, the worst thing that could happen to anyone in those days. Kings were also expected to support the priests in getting rid of heretics; but in both continents, this became a bit of a struggle. As we've seen,

Hinduism was rocked by the rise of reformers like Buddha and Mahavira, and so was Catholicism by Luther, Calvin and Zwingli. But both the established faiths in due course fought back in a counter-reformation. In India, one of the leading counter-reformers was the Kerala-born philosopher Adi Sankara, regarded, at least by many south Indian scholars, as one of the greatest of the Indian philosophers, and possibly one of the greatest in the history of the world.

Adi Sankara was born in the village of Kaladi to Namboodiri parents who had long been childless.[ii] They were however a pious couple, and in due course, god offered them the choice of having one son who would be exceptional, but would have only a short life, or many ordinary sons who would all live for a long time.

Not having been given the option of having three exceptional daughters, they chose to have the one son. When he was very young, Sankara not only performed miracles but also worried about problems in the country. He believed that 'kings at war and intolerant priests' were destroying the land and that the people needed spiritual unity. He wanted the whole world to be peaceful and happy and decided he could best help by becoming a sanyasi, a holy man, dependent upon alms. His mother was opposed to this but relented when the twelve year-old boy, caught by a crocodile when swimming in the River Periyar which ran by their house, asked for her blessing on his ambition as his dying wish. As soon as she had agreed, the crocodile disappeared. Sankara duly became a sanyasi and roamed the country, doing good deeds and debating Hinduism with all. He founded a monastic order and centres of learning at Badrinath in the north, Puri in the east, Dvarka in the west and Sringeri in the south.[iii] He and his disciples believed that 'True happiness does not lie in practising mere rituals, but in the pursuit of knowledge and understanding through the Vedas'. There are many stories about Sankara's travels. One that I like in particular concerns his meeting with an 'outcaste'. He was returning with his disciples from bathing in the River Ganga when the outcaste was seen. '*Move away and do not sully the purity of our master*', the disciples called out. '*And what shall I move*',

---

[ii] Generally accepted dating places this in the early 8th century

[iii] In the Himalayas, Orissa, Gujarat and Karnataka respectively

responded the unclean one, '*my body of common clay, or my soul of all-pervading consciousness?*' '*This man has seen the one reality in all*', cried Sankara. '*He is indeed my guru,*[iv] *regardless of his low birth.*'[v]

Adi Sankara continued on his travels, visiting Kashmir, Assam, Nepal and Tibet in the north as well as all points of the compass in India, returning home only to be with his mother as she died. He wanted to perform the funeral rites but the orthodox Namboodiri community would have nothing to do with the ceremony for it was not proper for a sanyasi to cremate the body of a householder. So Sankara had to hold the funeral in his back garden - and this tradition is still maintained among the Namboodiri caste. Sankara finally died at the age of only 32 years.

Sankara's philosophy is known as Advaita, which means literally 'non-dualism' or 'monoism'. As the Advaita website states, it is not an easy philosophy to explain briefly. All Hindus believe that man's life is full of suffering and that he is condemned to a constant round of death and re-birth until and unless he attains moksha or liberation. The debate is, how does one achieve such liberation? And the Advaita answer is that one must understand the true nature of oneself. This true nature is one's essence or soul or Atman. And the Atman is the same as the Brahman, the all-pervading god. 'Nothing other than God really exists - He alone is real; the world is maya [a dream].'[113] Though it is not purely an illusion. Sankara compared God to a rope that in the darkness can be confused with a snake. The snake [the world] does not exist, but of course it is not entirely a dream either; something is there. But it is only in the light [of knowledge] that one can see that it is only a rope [God] that exists. Sankara also said 'The world is filled with attachments and aversions and is changing like a dream; it appears to be real as long as one is ignorant but becomes unreal when one is awake. 'He who knows this, not merely as bookish knowledge, but through his own experience, is liberated even when living. Such a man is a

[iv] Teacher, master or pandit. One whose example one tries to follow.

[v] The quotations in this paragraph are taken from *Adi Shankara,* an Amar Chitra Katha publication [1974]. This is not a learned work but the extracts seem to me to give a good picture of Adi Sankara's life and philosophy.

jivanmukta, and he does not return to the cycle of re-births'. The Advaita path to salvation is, then, the path of knowledge - jnana.

Logan is most complimentary about what he calls Vedanta. 'It is ill-adapted for a work-a-day world where fields have to be ploughed to gain bread, where children have to be born to continue the human race, and where the good and evil things of this world meet the passer-by at every corner of life's journey. But it is an ideal always present in the mind of a devout Hindu, and its deep refining influence on the people cannot be exaggerated - an influence, which, in their inner life, is productive of many most admirable qualities.' [114] A rather different viewpoint from that of the Abbé Dubois, the French Christian missionary, writing less than 80 years earlier: 'The Vedanta school is distinguished by the obscurity of its doctrine... most of the Brahmins who wish to pass themselves off as learned men blindly embrace its principles without understanding them.'[115]

There are a number of monuments to Adi Sankara in his native village, Kalady: a Sri Krishna temple, founded in his lifetime, a Vedic school, Sankara's shrine, and the most magnificent, the Sri Adi Sankara Keerthi Sthambam, an eight storey tower which dominates the surrounding country-side and is painted a brilliant pink. The tower contains relief paintings that illustrate various incidents in Adi Sankara's career. Judging by the huge car park opposite [virtually empty at the time of our visit], the Sthambam is a popular attraction. After climbing the tower and listening to Raju's careful interpretation of the paintings, we retreated to a café. The owner [whose brother we gathered lives in Streatham] said, '*Many pilgrims come here, especially for the Sankara Jayanti festival in May, but also for Lord Krishna's festival when they bathe in the Holy Ghat. And for Navaratri of course.*' We enjoyed an excellent meal, Raju's daughter Kitty being particularly satisfied with her 'bulls' eyes', eggs fried sunny-side up. Our next visit was to Adi Sankara's shrine, of special interest because Iyers rather than Namboodiris perform the prayers. We asked the priest where it was that the young Sankara had been caught by a crocodile. '*Muthala Kadavu is close by*' he said gesturing towards the river on whose bank the temple stood. '*But take care if you intend to bathe. There may be no crocodiles here now, but the current is strong and there are weeds waiting to pull you under*!' We swam anyway. It was too hot not to, and it was very refreshing!

Adi Sankara Mandapam, Kalady

So Sankara was one of the leaders of the Counter-Reformation. But as usual nothing is straightforward in Indian history. We suggested in an earlier chapter that Buddhism and Jainism flourished because of the people's distaste for the complex rituals and sacrifices of Brahminism; and as we have seen, Adi Sankara was critical of intolerant priests for whom ritual was all-important. Yet the *Gazette* in common indeed with all the histories I have read talks of the 'rise of...ritual- orientated Hinduism' in this period, as well as the increasing influence of the Brahmins. So if ritual remained important in spite of the work of Sankara, why did Buddhism largely disappear from Kerala? In a sense, says K.M.Sen [*Hinduism*], it did not. 'Most of its tenets came to be accepted by large sections of the Hindus, and Hinduism ...revealed its remarkable power of assimilation by making Buddhism a part of itself.' In fact Buddha is accepted by some as one of the Hindu avatars 'spreading enlightenment to all creatures'.[116] [The confusion is even greater in south-east Asia where the Thai court 'employs to this day Brahmins from India for all court ceremonies; yet the state religion of Thailand is Buddhism' writes Romila Thapar.[117]] The Abbé Dubois gives another reason for their decline. Buddhists, he says, are 'human monsters so detestable and so opposed to all considerations of social well-being [that they] became objects of general execration, and were almost exterminated in India where, it appears, they were once so powerful'![118] [The British editor of Dubois' work by the way adds in a footnote written in 1905: 'this description of Buddhism conveys an altogether false impression.']

In any event, Adi Sankara's gospel was not the only one that was reforming Hinduism. The Bhakti movement, which urged the path of devotion rather than knowledge or action, was very popular. Bhakti is less demanding than Buddhism [especially in its Theravada[vi] form], and Jainism, and less abstract than Advaita; and it involves 'the adoration of a supreme being [rather than an all-pervading abstraction]' particularly in the form of Shiva or Vishnu, and is not greatly concerned with the 'intricacies of theology'[119]. And a further attraction for the mass of South Indians was that they regarded it as 'home-grown' since both Shiva [in particular] and Vishnu [to some extent] were seen to be Dravidian products rather than imports from the north. [On this point, Sen has a delightful footnote, viz., 'like most other propositions about ancient Indian history, this may be questionable'!].[120] It is easy to be confused over the Bhakti movement. Sen says that it was opposed by Brahmins 'because of its disregard of traditional ceremonies and its indifference to caste divisions.'[121] But it seems that Kerala was different, as is often the case! For Gangadharan points out that in Kerala, the movement 'wanted to establish the growing authority of the temples upon the common man as well as the ruler' [who was already in thrall to the priests who gave his position religious legitimacy]. Its aim was thus to 'spread the Vedic religion among the masses with all its ritual and customs'[122] in order to resist the growth of Buddhism and Jainism. Peter Reffell tells me that the debate in Christendom between Iconoclasts and Iconophiles was similar.

[vi] The less strict form of Buddhism is Hinayana

And royal patronage was important, too. At the height of their popularity, Jainism and Buddhism were adopted by numerous kings, but in time many lost power, or 'lost interest' [Thapar] perhaps because of the asceticism involved. Brahminism was re-established as the state religion, and the Brahmin priests were rewarded with grants of land, which increased their economic power and influence.

It looks as though it was probably a combination of factors that caused the decline of Buddhism. And although some of these factors do not seem to explain directly how it was that the Brahmins flourished, the support of the popular Bhakti cult was of particular importance. The leaders of the official religion consolidated their hold over kings and people, and found themselves at the head of a religion made stronger and more popular by its battle against the new faiths and by the changes made by the reformers even though they might not have agreed with them all. For example, though what Adi Sankara called 'unnecessary ritual' may well have been expunged, some rituals remained and Brahmins were still needed to carry them out. It is probable that in this period, more and more priests migrated from the north to join in the debates with Buddhist monks. And no doubt the Namboodiris in Kerala began to accept the reformed practices and modify them to fit in more closely with their own beliefs.

* * * * *

People are fascinated by the matrilineal system of inheritance that was practiced by many castes in Kerala until its abolition after independence. In the *Malabar Manual*, Logan acknowledges the surprise that people from Europe experienced when told that a 'father can stand in no recognised legal relation to his own children, and that a father's property does not as a matter of course descend to his own offspring' - an even more amazing state of affairs no doubt for Victorians than for us. Logan goes on to say 'this law of inheritance, usually styled Marumakathyam, may be *shortly* described thus…' [my italics]. This is followed by two pages of closely typed text with examples and diagrams![123] It is described more succinctly by Woodcock as 'a joint family system which…governs the inheritance of ancestral as distinct from personal property: a daughter and all her children inherit equal shares in such property, but the son only inherits his share and his children must inherit through their mother's family'.[124] The practice was characteristic of the Nair caste, but was also adopted by others, including 'seventeen Brahman illams [households] in the village of Payanur'; but not otherwise by Namboodiris or 'Pattars' [Iyers].

Marumakathyam seems to have occurred among certain of the aboriginal peoples of Kerala and to have been resurrected by the Nairs at some time during the Kulashekhara period. Some say that this was because so many men went away to fight in the Chera-Chola wars, that they were in no position to act as heads of families. And because of the necessarily transient nature of marriage to a member of a suicide squad, the Nair women were very likely to have a number of partners during their lives. In some Nair families, polyandry was practiced. The anthropologist Kathleen Gough says that in Kochi, 'a woman might have six or eight husbands of her own or a higher caste... spouses lived separately in their natal homes and a husband visited his wife in her home at night. Exact physiological paternity was clearly often unknown and anyway a man had neither rights nor obligations to his children'.[125] K.N.Pannikar adds that brothers might have a common wife, and indeed sisters a common husband. The Nairs lived in Taravads, homesteads, consisting of a female ancestor, her children and all the descendants in the female line. Within this family group, 'women had great personal freedom to take decisions regarding marital and sexual relations, and played a crucial role in making household decisions'. Although marumakathyam has largely disappeared it seems likely that this lifestyle laid the foundation for the gender equality found in modern Kerala leading to, for example, 'the positive and confident approach of Kerala women to their men.' Which is something I can vouch for! And speaking of who's in charge in an Indian household, although the menfolk have the appearance of superiority, it's often the women who hold the power. Men often hand over their wages to their wives or others and are told what to buy from the markets. I have a friend who compares the position of men in the east [his experience is in Thailand] to that of constitutional monarchs - they have the trappings of power but no authority.[vii] I do not of course mean for

---

[vii] This is Jason, son of our neighbour. He lived in Thailand and says that there it is customary to pay labourers in beer as well as cash, because the women can't lay their hands on the former!

a moment to imply that married life is an unalloyed delight for all or even most Indian women. There are far too many incidents of bullying and worse, often by the womenfolk into whose home the new wife moves, and the dowry system is open to terrible abuse. But their situation is different in Kerala, as evidenced by so many writers from Kathleen Gough [quoted above], through Shashi Kapoor and M.F.Husain's *Kerala: God's Own Country* ['...the resilience of Kerala, the defiance of the Indian stereotype...and above all its empowerment of women'[126]] to Anne Mustoe - 'Kerala is a place where women really count' - in *Two Wheels in the Dust.*[127]

The Namboodiri Brahmins had a rule that only the eldest son could marry a woman of his own caste. This, together with the practice of makkathayam [inheritance through the father] helped to keep the Namboodiri landholdings undivided. Younger sons had to find women from other castes - normally Nairs - and in this way the interests of both castes were served, for the Nairs felt honoured to have their daughters married to men from a higher caste and welcomed their enhanced social standing as well as the growth in influence and power which came as a result. And this was in spite of the fact that the Sambandham marriage, as the arrangement was called, was not regarded as a true union in the sense that a caste marriage was.

Echoes of this lifestyle among our family and friends in Trikkandiyur in the mid-twentieth century are noted in the next chapter.

It was during the reign of the Kulashekharas that Malayalam evolved into a clearly separate language. Like Kannada, spoken in Karnataka, Telugu in Andhra Pradesh, and Tamil in Tamilnad, Malayalam is a Dravidian language. These languages are quite different from those of the Indo-European family spoken in the north of India. They developed from proto-Dravidian, which was spoken through most of India prior to the spread of the Arya culture. As we have learned, some say that the language of the ancient North Indian empire of Harappa was Dravidian, and indeed a Dravidian language is still spoken in that part of the world - Baluchistan, which is on the Pakistan-Iran border.

Malayalam most resembles Tamil and it used to be thought that it was merely an offshoot of that language. It may be though that they were separate though similar languages even in prehistoric times. The differences became most marked from the ninth century onwards when Malayalam began to absorb more Sanskrit words while Tamil remained 'pure', but it did not become a totally distinct language until the sixteenth century through the work of Thunchatu Ramanjan Ezhuthachan, known as the founder of modern Malayalam.[128] And where did Thanchatu come from? Why, from Trikkandiyur of course! More of him later.

Malayalam, Hindi and English on Tirur railway station

Tamil and Malayalam do still share many similar features though, including for example, the awfully difficult-to-pronounce consonant 'zh', which is present in no other language in the world. [I was taught that the best way to pronounce this consonant was by trying to produce a rolled 'r' without touching the top of the palate with one's tongue. It seems to work]. And Tamil and Malayalam speakers can often understand each other. Manga says that one of the main differences between the two languages is that in Malayalam it is not the form of the verbs themselves that change according to who performs the action. Instead personal pronouns are used. So in Tamil one would say [the example is taken from Logan]: '*adittu*, to beat: *aditten* = I beat, *adittay* = you beat, *adittan* = he beats'; in Malayalam, the equivalent verb adichu is used throughout...with the prefixed pronouns I, you, he etc., i.e. *nyan adichu, ni adichu, avan adichu.*'[129] And as we said earlier, Malayalam includes more words related to Sanskrit - and also other Indo-European languages, Arabic, Chinese and Pali [the sacred language of Buddhism] than the more 'purely Dravidian' Tamil, mainly it is thought because of the influence of the dominant Namboodiris and of foreign traders and invaders on the west coast. Some examples are *narenga* [Mal] / *naranja* [Spanish] = orange; *mesha* [Mal] / *mesa* [Sp] / *mensa* [Latin] = table; *atma* [Mal] / *alma* [Sp] = soul; *kursi* [Mal] / *karesa* [Arabic] = chair.

Spoken Dravidian developed much earlier in India than the Indo-European languages from the north, but the earliest specimens of Dravidian writing that have been discovered post-date the earliest Aryan documents by hundreds of years. The latter are written in Brahmi, the ancestor of the Hindi script that is called Devanagari and other North Indian scripts. And although they look very different from their northern equivalents, South Indian scripts might also have originated from Brahmi, though they now look similar to the South Indian ancestral script - much less ancient then Brahmi - called Grantha. The Tamil 'n' and 't' are identical to those in this script, and the overall rounder appearance of Tamil and Malayalam seems to be almost certainly inherited from Grantha. Grantha was used in India, and indeed other parts of South Asia, to record Sanskrit works in the days when writing was done on palm leaves. It is incidentally quite a surprise to learn that Manga's mother could read Grantha, which by the twentieth century was a very dead language. We don't know whether she learned it at school, whether her parents taught her, or whether she taught herself so as to be able to read old devotional texts.

It is a mystery to me too why Dravidian languages, spoken before the Indo-Europeans in the sub-continent, were not apparently written down until much later. And why, when the spoken languages were similar, should there be different scripts at all for Tamil and Malayalam. It's the same in North India: similar spoken languages, different scripts. In Europe as we know the spoken languages are quite different but the scripts pretty well all the same.

The earliest writing that is known of in Malayalam is an inscription written around 830 AD and the earliest known literature is a song from the twelfth century. When she was at school, Manga had to learn by heart ancient Malayalam poetry which included lots of Sanskrit words, called Manipravalam. I guess this would be similar to English-speaking children learning Chaucer. The most popular early literature seems to have been folk ballads describing the deeds of heroes such as Tachcholi Othenan. Logan devoted six pages of the *Malabar Manual* to a translation of the Ballad of Tachcholi, whom he called the 'Robin Hood of north Malabar'.[130] He mentioned too ballads about Tipu Sultan, the Tiger of Mysore and scourge of the British, and about the 'mythical feats' of Veikeleri Kunhi Kelappan, and wrote that the 'common people still compose ballads in memory of passing events'. He gave as an example a song about one of the Mappila 'outrages' of his time, which 'recalls with graphic power and a great deal of exaggeration *of course* [my italics], the chief incidents that occurred'.[131]

The boundaries of the modern state of Kerala were drawn up on linguistic lines after independence, and Malayalam is the first language of nearly all its population. Only 'foreigners' such as our family, Tamil Brahmins, who have lived in Kerala for at least 200 years, are exceptions. Our family does of course speak Malayalam but only outside the house or to Malayalees; their native tongue is Tamil, which they still speak at home and to other Pattars. They do mostly use Malayalam script though, even when writing in Tamil.

Malayalam is spoken by about 35 million people as their first language and is one of over 1,600 mother tongues spoken in India, 850 of which are in daily use. And it is one of the country's fifteen national languages, the others being Assamese [spoken by 15 million people as their first language], Bengali [70 m], Gujarati [45 m], Hindi [180m], Kannada [35m], Kashmiri [4m], Marathi [68m], Oriya [31m], Panjabi [27m], Sindhi [3m], Tamil [61m], Telugu [69m], and Urdu [48m, most of whom are Muslims].

There are about 30 other languages each spoken by more than a million people as a first language. Before leaving for India on VSO, I was told that Bihari was the language spoken in Bihar and I was discouraged from learning Hindi as a result. And indeed 42 million people in the state as it was before it was partitioned [out of a total population of about 90 million] described Bihari languages such as Magadhi or Maithali as their first language. But it would have been surprising had I come across anyone who did not speak fluent Hindi in Bihar - only the most isolated groups would have understood only their mother tongue; and in any event, 'Bihari' has much in common with Hindi.

However, it is not surprising given the diversity of languages spoken, that in the early years after independence in 1947, much thought was given to establishing a single national language for the new country in order to assist in uniting its people. Hindi was the obvious first choice. It is spoken fluently by over half the population and many of the other languages of North India are closely related. Urdu is very similar in its spoken form. And it was the threat of Hindi being imposed as the national language that led to the riots described in the Introduction to this book. For as we have seen, the Southern Indian languages are very different from Hindi, which has more in common for example with English than with Malayalam. So South Indians believed that if Hindi became the national language, they would be at a severe disadvantage as far as education and jobs were concerned, and this, combined with their own national / regional sensitivities, is why the serious rioting resulting in deaths, disruption and destruction of property occurred. After 5 years of discord during the 1960s, the proposal to have a single national language was dropped, and a 'three-part' solution reached - schools and government would use Hindi, English and the local language. The main language issue today, as more and more people value English as an international means of communication, is probably that of 'Indian English' and whether it is of any concern that the English spoken by many in India is developing its own vocabulary and grammar. My own experience leads me to believe that it is certainly of no concern to the younger generation of Indians, and that they no more consider that the way they speak English is 'wrong' than do Americans.

And one final point of interest about Malayalam: it is the longest single-word palindrome in the English language!

CHAPTER TWENTY-ONE

MANGA'S MEMORIES: FAMILY AFFAIRS

'She who leaves her husband, falling in love with a King, gets neither' - Malayalam proverb

Manga remembers the relationships between people of different castes in the village during her childhood.

Parakutty and her daughter

'Parakutty was our servant when my second brother Parameswaran fell in love with her. Even though we were very poor and often had only just enough money to feed ourselves, we always had a servant - that was expected of a Brahmin family. There were no other luxuries such as new clothes, books, toys, or special food,

except perhaps at festival time; but always a servant. That is what India was like in those days. Some people would always be servants; that was their dharma, their fate, their duty. Others would have the duty of employing them, come what may. Things are so much better now of course and there's nothing to stop anyone from doing any job they want, at least in theory. But I suppose there were some advantages in the old system. People always knew who they were and what was expected of them. It was believed that there was nothing wrong in being a servant and nobody felt bad about it.[i]

Anyway, we didn't treat Parakutty like a servant. She couldn't come into the house, but that was because of her caste, not her occupation. Otherwise she was an equal - she ate the same food as us and we were always kind to her. She didn't do a lot of work - she did the sweeping around the house, washed the clothes and pounded the rice - things like that, and would spend a lot of time chatting to Mum or one of us girls. It was funny to watch her when Parameswaran came home. She would go very coy and hold the edge of her sari over her face, just glancing sideways at him. Parameswaran would get a bit flustered and pretend not to notice her. Of course I didn't know what was going on - I was very small - but the adults did, and they didn't seem to mind.

Since Parakutty was a Nair, the lovers couldn't get married, but they remained faithful to each other for the whole of their lives. They had what we called a samantham marriage but it wasn't quite the same as the Namboodiri's samantham. It wasn't the custom for our men to marry Nairs, and there was no wedding ceremony, just an understanding. The children of these marriages stay with the mother in both castes, however.

We had a neighbour who was like a brother to us all and we called him Mani-anna. He worked in a hotel near to the railway station in Tirur and would bring us Mysore pak, laddu and other good things to eat. Mani-anna also had a samantham wife, and she lived in Muttur, not far from Parakutty's house. In the evenings he and my brother would take a torch and slink off together, not saying where they were going. But Mum would say, 'there they go: off to see their acchis!'' They would walk three miles to see their 'wives' and not come home till

---

[i] Jonah Blank describes this situation cleverly in *Arrow of the Blue-Skinned God.* For example 'India is starting to trade stagnation and peace of mind for opportunity and frustration.'

morning. Then they would take a shower, have breakfast and set off to work as if nothing had happened. Until her recent death, Parakutty lived in the same house in Muttur. You know we used to visit her every time we went home and she was always very moved to see me, wasn't she. She had a nice place with a big garden and all sorts of different trees - plenty cashew nuts. The house had hardly changed since I was a child. The kitchen was separate from the house. She moved to her daughter's home in Kadampuzha near the temple there for a while, but then returned to her old house. Parakutty had some bad luck in her life. Her son-in-law was killed while working abroad - there was something strange about the circumstances. That was bad enough but they didn't want to give any compensation, and the family were very badly off at this stage.' Things seemed to improve financially, but when we visited in 2011 it was to learn that her granddaughter had been killed in a car accident. The virtually blind old lady took my hand and was worried because she said I'd lost weight. Parakutty died shortly afterwards.

Of course, my father had an acchi too. My Mum knew all about her and accepted the arrangement. I don't think she minded - it was just part of life, nothing unusual. But we never talked about her and I don't even remember her name or where she lived. I do know that they had a daughter and I think I might have met her once, but we had no curiosity about Dad's other family. He would go off and see his acchi but no-one ever said anything. I don't think I knew anything about it till I was older.

Mani-anna had a sister, Thangakka, the mother of Thangam, my friend who lived in the same house until she died. Anyway, Thangakka (that just means Thangam-elder-sister) - she's in the only family picture we ever had taken, must have been when I was about twenty - was married, but her husband, Krishnamama, who was a bank employee, went to live with another of our neighbours, Ammu, one of twins. The other twin was called Nani. They were Malayalees and because they were twins they were supposed to have special powers. So whenever we had a sprained ankle or something like that, we would call them and they would come and give a massage with some oil. What was in it was a closely guarded secret. We would always get better soon.

Anyway, after her husband left her, Thangakka got friendly with Velayathan who was the brother of Raghavan, Unni's father - the Unni who lent our Mum his camera when she came to India. They had a lovely old house and a beautiful garden where we saw that paradise flycatcher.

Velayathan used to come to Thangakka in the night. She thought no-one knew, but my Mum knew. You see Velayathan's mother died young so he used to tell all sorts of things to my Mum instead and would come and talk to her when he came back from work. My Mum used to say to him,' It's all very well carrying on with Thangakka now but once you get married you must give all this up - or you will hurt your wife.' I used to know all about it too because I used to go to Thangakka's house to sleep when I had periods and I wasn't allowed in my own bedroom. I saw Velayathan coming and could hear him and Thangakka, but I pretended to be asleep. Thangakka was a bit vain. I remember she had some grey hair on one side of her head and she used to pull hair from the other side to cover it!

This all sounds as if we were a terribly immoral lot. But nobody ever felt that - it was all very discreet and on the surface we were very strait-laced. Certainly nobody had sex with their partner before marriage. I don't think that there are any goings-on in the village these days. The custom of samantham has finished and there are no bars to inter-caste marriage.'

CHAPTER TWENTY-TWO

TEMPLE ARTS

'Will a goat know anything of the merchandise in a bazaar?' Malayalam proverb

It was during the reign of the Kulashekharas that temples became the centre of people's lives in Kerala. The growing importance of ritual meant that people started to prefer to worship in temples, where the experts in rituals, the priests, were based, rather than at their personal shrines at home. And the temples became more attractive too because the priests revived or introduced temple festivals with all the fun that they involved. Pilgrims and traders were attracted to these events, which further enhanced the standing of the Namboodiri Brahmins who were the temple priests, and at the same time fed more and more wealth into their hands.

This was good for the Namboodiris of course but there were valuable spin-offs for the rest of society too. For their new-found wealth enabled the priests to introduce art forms into the temples both to enhance the worship of the gods and also to attract still more devotees. Dance-drama was particularly popular, and took place in the temple theatre [koothambalam], which K.V.Soundaranrajan [*Temple Architecture in Kerala*] describes as 'one of those religio-cultural adjuncts of Kerala temple life, introduced by the genius of the local people who are adepts in gesture drama...'[132]

Kathakali is the most famous of these dance-dramas. The structure of the dance and of the music developed from folk patterns, and the stories were taken from the great Hindu epics, the *Mahabharatha* and *Ramayana*. Kalari, the martial art of Kerala, influenced many Kathakali dance movements including the basic stance and the Chuzhippu or whirling of the body. You have to be very flexible to do either of these activities and the training is long and hard and you have to begin when you're very young. There are a number of different aspects to Kathakali - facial expression or natyam; dance or nritham; acting or nrithyam; singing [geetha]; and instrumental music, called vadyam.

Kathakali dancers representing Rama and Sita

I described my first experience of Kathakali on a magical night in 1967 in chapter seven. Since then, we've watched Kathakali as often as possible. A dance company came to Newcastle when we lived there, and we went to see them twice. And there have been two shows at the Gulbenkian Theatre as part of the Canterbury Festival, and another at the Little Theatre in Margate. The company that performed down here had a make-up artist who was an Englishwoman from Manchester. It was funny to hear Malayalam spoken with a strong Lancashire accent - but I'm not being critical. After all I can hardly speak the language at all. We chatted to her and were introduced to her husband, the leading player, and other members of the cast. They are based in a village quite near to Tirur and we have intended to visit them, but haven't quite managed it yet.

We've also watched Kathakali twice more in India. One was a display put on for tourists in a tent in a car park in Kochi. It did not pretend to be a performance, just a demonstration of some of the techniques, and as such was most interesting. We also got to see the actors putting on their complex make-up. The event did not of course have the same atmosphere as one enacted for religious purposes and I was reminded of it when I read *The God of Small Things*, the Booker-award winning novel by Arundhati Roy. There is a passage that describes the feelings of a Kathakali troupe that has been reduced to giving 'truncated' displays of their art to tourists for money. They have become 'unviable' in their original form and are now 'a Regional flavour' instead of 'dancers for god'.[133]

Bharata Natyam dancers

I think we might also have seen a glimpse of 'unviability' in a performance we saw at Aluva. This was when Juliema was with us and we went to Aluva, where Geetha has her ancestral home, for Shivaratri. It was pure serendipity that when we went down to the temple one evening, a Kathakali performance was just beginning. This was the real thing - there were no tourists to pander to. Again I was enthralled and so were Manga and Julie. Manga told us the story - it was the one about how Ganesh got his elephant head, and it included Mariamma, the bringer and/or curer of smallpox, being chased into the audience. But very few people were watching. Are modern Keralites suffering from 'imported attention spans'? I fear it may be so.

There is of course very much more to be said about Kathakali. It is surprisingly accessible, but to an expert there is much more to be enjoyed - the subtleties of the eye and hand movements, the dance steps and so on - and as we have said it is first of all a religious celebration. It is only one of many Kerala dances and dramas which originated or were perfected in the temple: Theyyam, Kolamthullal, Kalamezhuthu, Chakyarkoothu, Mohiniyattam, to name but five.

Ottamthullal - a Kerala dance form created in the seventeenth century.

The best known and most often performed today, mostly by women, is probably Bharata Natyam. Manga learned Bharata Natyam but I never saw her dance. Radhikar was very good as a little girl and she performed for us on Grandma's visit. It is believed that the dance originated in the fifth century BC, and that it developed with the growth of the temples. Bharata Natyam is associated with the devadasis, temple dancers who seem to have become widespread in South India in the seventh century AD, and were introduced into Kerala by the Cholas by the tenth century. They were at that time honoured and honourable women; professional artistes who promoted dance, music and other fine arts in the community, who gave their earnings to the temples, and who enjoyed high status in society. In fact, daughters of the Kulashekhara kings Alwar and Stanu Ravi Varma were devadasis, and Kerala Varma of Venad married one. However from the thirteenth century onwards the devadasi system suffered from 'moral degeneration' to quote the coy words of the *Gazette.*[134] It may be that as the Kulashekharas declined, the devadasis lost their patrons and had to turn to what was basically prostitution.

Abbé Dubois is very interesting on the subject of devadasis. He at first refers to them as 'lewd women' but he seems to have some degree of admiration for their abilities and even character.

> They employ all the resources and artifices of coquetry. Perfumes, elegant costumes, coiffures best suited to set off the beauty of their hair, which they entwine with sweet-scented flowers; a profusion of jewels worn with much taste on various parts of their body; graceful and voluptuous attitudes: such are the snares with which these sirens allure the Hindus, who, it must be confessed, rarely display in such cases the prudence and constancy of a Ulysses.
>
> Nevertheless, to the discredit of Europeans it must be confessed that the quiet seductions which Hindu prostitutes know how to exercise with so much skill resemble in no way the disgraceful methods of the wretched beings who give themselves up to a similar profession in Europe...The man who behaved familiarly with [a devadasi] in public would be censured and despised by everybody who witnessed the scandal. Is it the same among ourselves?[135]

The European colonists did their best to get rid of the system. They seem to have been in no doubt that devadasis were merely common prostitutes and the system just another example of Oriental depravity to be despised and demolished. Others argue that because they engaged in sex outside the Christian idea of marriage, this does not make them immoral. Yet others believe that the devadasis were not prostitutes at all but closer to the Japanese Geishas. Whichever view one has, it is clear that the devadasis were important in the development of temple arts.

Manga remembers with pleasure the temple story-tellers, who came to the village for the Temple Festival in the month of Thulam, after Onam. The story-tellers were from the Chakiar community and their art was called Chakiar Koothu. They arrived for the Temple festival and every afternoon, from 2 to 4 pm for seven days, they would tell their tales for an excited and appreciative audience of all ages. '*The stories would always be religious, from the Ramayana or Mahabharata or the Puranas*', Manga says, '*but they would choose the nice jolly ones. They used different voices and expressions and poses and they would roll their eyes and do all sorts of things to make us laugh. We would sit in a semi circle in the entrance to the temple and the adults would stand at the back. The story-telling was in the afternoon, and in the morning there was some more fun - called Ottam Thullai. A boy or young man comes in wearing a mask like a Kathakali dancer's, mid-length red trousers, a broad belt and a neck decoration with mirrors, and with bells round his ankles, and dances to the beat of a drum while a story is told. They say that this came about because once when the Chakiar was telling his story in the afternoon, the boy who played the drum for him fell asleep. The Chakiar was very cross and mocked the boy in front of the whole audience. The boy gained his revenge next day. He dressed up in bright colours, came to the temple and danced very energetically and noisily. All the people listening to the story turned to watch him and the story was spoiled. So the Chakiar made his peace with the boy and it was agreed that he would continue to tell his stories in the afternoon, and the boy would do his dance in the morning.'* So the Temple festival had two entertainers - or more properly, preachers, for through their acts, they were teaching the people religious stories and the importance of devotion.

* * * * *

The plastic arts of South India are widely admired, especially the Chola School, named after the Chola Emperors of Tanjore. This was the subject of a recent exhibition at the Royal Academy. Writing in *The Guardian* about the exhibition, William Dalrymple explained that the fine bronze Chola statues emerged when it became the fashion to carry images of the gods around the village and fields, or to be bathed in a sacred river. The stone statues of early temple art were impossible to move, and more portable idols were needed. This was in the tenth century when, Dalrymple points out, the Vikings were settling in Northern England and 'Turkish warlords from Afghanistan' were invading the Ganges Valley. Bronze casting began in southern India in the eighth century under the Pallavas, but was perfected when the Cholas of Tanjore gave their patronage to these sculptors. Dalrymple describes the bronzes as follows:

> Exquisitely poised and supple, these bronze deities stand silent on their plinths, yet with their hands they speak gently to their devotees through the noiseless lingua franca of the

> gestures [or mudras] of South Indian dance: their hands are raised in blessing and reassurance, promising boons and protection, and above all, marriage, fertility and fecundity, in return for the veneration that is so clearly their divine right.

Dalrymple believes that 'only Donatello or Rodin from the west can equal the Chola sculptors when it comes to evoking the sensuality and beauty of the human body.'[136]

Chola art came to Kerala in the eleventh or twelfth centuries and the Trivandrum Museum has some examples of bronzes of this period which impressed us greatly. The museum also houses some bronze images of Vishnu, which were sculpted in the early ninth century. But the most important plastic art truly indigenous to Kerala is probably wood sculpture. There are wood carvings all over Kerala temples. The temples are of course mostly made of wood, so there are plenty of opportunities for the wood sculptors to practise their craft. Walls, ceilings, pillars, rafters and beams are decorated with carved patterns or more often, with scenes from the Puranas or the great Hindu epics. Many of the sculptures are painted with bright colours and there are full three-dimensional figures as well as bas-reliefs. There are bronzes cast in a typical Kerala style from the sixteenth century in Trichur museum and the Survey says the one of Vishnu is typical of the period, being 'marked by heavy modelling, elaborate ornamentation and stylised features.'[137] At about the same time, stone sculpture was apparently being influenced by the 'exuberant' style of Vijayanagar. The Kerala School of painting provided temples with murals from the middle of the seventeenth to the middle of the nineteenth centuries: Mattancheri Palace in Kochi has some of the best examples.

CHAPTER TWENTY-THREE

FOOD, FEASTS AND FESTIVALS: EATING AND ENJOYING IN KERALA

'In eating and bathing be first, and in war, umbrella and mud, take the middle' Malayalam proverb

'Will you not be satisfied with eating the bread? Why should you count the air-holes in it?' Malayalam proverb

'Cause them to partake gradually and slowly [of each dish] and repeatedly invite them to eat by offering the food and proclaiming its qualities.

All the food must be very hot and the guests should eat in silence.

Having addressed the question 'Have you dined well?' to his guests, let him give water for sipping and dismiss them with the words 'Rest [either here or at home]'. From *The Laws of Manu* as quoted by Skelton and Rao in *South Indian Cookery.*

'It is in the remote East, and especially in India, that we may expect to find the living representation of ancient observances, and the still existing solemnisations which delighted the nations of antiquity...' from *Hindu and Mahammadan* [sic] *Festivals* by John Murdoch, 1904, quoted in *South Indian Festivities* by P.V.Jagadisa Ayyar.

The day starts [in our home in Trikkandiyur at least] with a hot cup of coffee as soon as we wake up. Shanta will have been up at about five and will hear us stirring and bring us our drink. She now knows we like a big mug of strong coffee in the morning to get us moving!

After a while breakfast comes. There are strict combinations of foods. So if we have appam, it will be with ishtu as a side dish. Idli, which is a steamed cake made of rice flour and black gram, or dosa, a rice flour pancake, will be accompanied by coconut chutney and/or sambar, or mullaga podi; masala goes with poori or chapatti; and puttu can only be properly appreciated if eaten with chickpeas, banana [the big ones, not so sweet] and poppadam [or pappad].

Radhika grinding rice for idli

Appam is similar to dosa but thicker and the batter rises a little because the mixture includes yeast. Ishtu is very tasty - chunks of potato with lots of coconut milk, chilli and ginger. Sambar is a hearty vegetable stew flavoured with tamarind and coconut, and Mullaga podi a powder you moisten with oil on the side of your plate. It's made of chillies and ginger and tamarind and pepper, all the hot stuff, and other bits and pieces too no doubt. Puttu is a dry rice flour and coconut mix, cooked in a cylindrical container called a puttu kutti. Sometimes powdered ragi is used instead of rice; it is more nutritious as it includes methionine, an essential animo acid lacking in starchy foodstuffs.

We eat lunch too, so it's not surprising we gain weight while we are in Trikkandiyur! It's usually a rice meal with curry or uperi [potato or banana perhaps with onion and coconut]. Whenever there is rice, there is also curds or buttermilk, sometimes with the meal and always at the end. And rasam, a thin tamarind sauce, very sour, is never far away. In the evening we eat again. At home this is often chapatti and curry because Shanta comes from Sholapur in Maharastra where wheat dishes rather than rice are the main staple. There's always sambar for one meal - Balan insists. In fact if he had his way, every meal would be sambar.

Manga remembers some of the vegetables that were available when she was little.

> *'On Sundays we had a market near the hospital on a large patch of land there. We call it 'chandu'. Dad used to go every week and used to bring all our vegetables. One was what we call 'wadiliku', which is like a big cucumber or gherkin, but not always green - they can be yellowy, orangey - a mixture of colours. They were very watery, almost like melons and delicious in sambar. Dad used to bring three or four and we had to keep them cool, so Dad would tie them in palm tree leaves and hang them in the eaves till we were ready to cook them. He did the same with ash- gourds, which were grey and had thick skins but were very nice.*
>
> *We had another vegetable like a long green snake. Mum made dry curry out of that. It had a wonderful smell. What we used to do as children was - the plant had a flower and before it opened there was a tiny little bud. If you picked it, the sap was very sticky and we stuck it on our nose as an ornament. After a while it would fall off, but it was fun especially as it had a lovely smell. And of course we had bitter gourd, which was very good for your digestion, and so was the leaf from the neem tree. So Dad would get all these things from the market when they were available. We tried to grow vegetables in the garden but the soil was very poor. Fruit trees grew well though - we had papaya, two types of jackfruit (one the goats ate the leaves) and of course banana, coconut and mango.*

In those days by the way, women always used to eat separately from, and after, men. They would serve all the males in the household, standing patiently by the table and not until all had finished and left the table did they themselves eat. This still happened, rather surprisingly, in our Indian family until quite recently, though there was absolutely no element of servility at all. I think it was just a habit.

Lakshmi displaying a jackfruit

Children start to eat solid food at about six months. A party is held and special food offered to the child: milk and curds, with dried and powdered banana. Also the mothers will grind ragi [finger millet] to make a custard. Doctors recommend that for children because it has a high calcium content. The staple food for children of this age is kuzhu, which is ground rice and milk.

Snacks are a big part of eating in Kerala! When you make a visit to another house, as I've mentioned earlier, a selection is almost always put before you. It might be simply banana [best if just taken from a tree in the garden] and/or sweet or salt tapioca or banana chips, which might be home-made. If you're lucky it might be vadai [made from urad dahl] or vadam, like poppadam but made of sago or rice. Or a home-made sweet. Lakshmi's favourite is neyyappam - like appam but with jagaree and ghee [dalda or coconut oil for vegans]. A lot of sweets are made with milk or ghee or both so they're no good for Victoria, Indi or Lakshmi, who are vegan, and that includes the best and most Keralite of sweets, payasam. Payasam is also a holy food - that is, one that is offered to the Gods as a prasadam - a gift - before being eaten by devotees. Payasam is a sort of milk pudding to which you can add almonds, cashew, and/ or coconut. Sometimes it can be made with coconut milk squeezed from the flesh of the coconut instead of cows' milk. There are all sorts of different types. Rice payasam is made with rice and chana dahl fried in ghee; and there are others made with moong dahl, rava [which is creamed wheat], sevia [vermicelli], or sago as the main ingredient. Manga makes pal-payasam, very milky, and it's very popular in England. Rosema will eat it for breakfast, lunch and dinner! Manga also uses soya milk sometimes so the vegans can eat it. Mysore pak [a bit like fudge], laddu [fried balls of channa dahl, with spices] and jalebi [made from deep-fried batter] are not really Kerala dishes, but they are popular in the south. I've missed out barfi [coloured sweets made of coconut and almond], gulab jamun [another of my favourites], poli [a sweet poori]- I could go on and on.

I said at the beginning of this rather long chapter that we always start the day with coffee when we're in Trikkandiyur. The family do drink tea later in the day, but you wouldn't call it a Brahmin drink. When Manga and I were travelling in the sixties she would always look for a Brahmin restaurant if we wanted coffee, but a Christian one for tea. But of course tea is very important to the economy of Kerala.

The tea-fields of Munnar in the hills near to Anamundi, the highest Indian mountain south of the Himalayas, produce Nilgiri tea - the best there is in some people's opinion. A great aroma, full of taste, and the most expensive in the world - a kg of orange pekoe sold for $600 in 2006, Wikipedia tells us. But that sort of tea normally finds its way overseas - at home we drink gunpowder tea, named after its appearance. It's boiled up in milk-and-water, heavily sweetened and often includes a touch of spice. You get to really enjoy it, even if you wouldn't dream of putting sugar in your tea in England.

The tea-plant had been known since ancient times in India, but it was not till the 1840s that the East India Company started to cultivate tea commercially in the sub-continent, up in Assam. Production rocketed only after the Company was largely marginalised in the sub-continent after 1857, and Assam soon became the largest producer of tea in the world. Now India has been overtaken by China though.

A tea plantation in Munnar

Coffee's important too - India is the world's sixth largest producer and most of it is grown in Kerala, with Munnar again being the most important centre. It's grown in Wayanad also, and we once walked through a plantation there - the scent of the coffee flowers was intoxicating. Again it is very good quality and if the drink is made properly, it has an excellent and memorable taste. Manga remembers that when she went to India for the wedding of her niece, Radhikar. Radhi would wake her in the morning with a cup of 'proper Brahmin coffee' - made by the decoction method. In good times when she was young, thc family would buy coffee beans and grind them with butter to produce a great beverage. But she was not always so lucky: often they couldn't afford the beans and had to make do with roasted coriander.

These days most people take their meals off plates and sit at tables, but this was not the case in Kerala in the 1960s - then in nearly all the homes we visited it was a case of squatting on the floor and eating off banana leaves. And everyone still eats off banana leaves at a proper feast, maybe at a festival, wedding or another special occasion. The last feast we ate was at a ceremony to celebrate the completion of a new house at the end of our alleyway. We sat at a long table with a large leaf in front of us, and water with which to wash it. No knives and forks of course because we were to eat by hand: by far the best way to eat Indian food anyway, as long as you're sure your hands are clean, and of course you must use your right hand only, and slide the food into your mouth with your thumb.

A family meal – Shanta at the head of the table.

Then the food is served. In Kerala it's all done quickly and efficiently and always in a particular order - so for example, payasam arrives first and should be the first thing you eat. It will be placed on the right hand side of the leaf, nearest to you. The other dishes are put in particular places on the leaf too. They should provide six types of flavour sweet, sour, salty, that's easy enough - but also 'bitter', which might be a preparation including a neem leaf for example, which, says Manga, has the dual role of enhancing the other tastes and driving away evil. And 'pungent', meaning hot, like chilli; and finally astringent. According to the Ayurvedic philosophy, the astringent taste is dry and light, and astringent foods absorb fat. Examples are vegetables like bindi and broccoli, fruit such as cranberry, and spices like turmeric.

So on your leaf goes raitha [curd with usually something like cucumber and onion added], chutney, banana chips, pickles, salt, and curries. Then comes a substantial pile of rice, followed by dahl, and one eats these with the curries etc. That course finished and more rice arrives, this time followed by sambar; then rice and rasam; and the last course is always rice with curd. That really is a meal - and it is also nutritious, and balanced according to the Ayurvedic rules.

As we've said, feasts such as this are often a part of a religious festival. The most important such festival in Kerala is Onam. Onam is the day on which the mythical ancient king of Kerala called Mahabali or Maveli is allowed to return to earth to visit his people. The reason the gods gave him this boon is that when he was ruling he passed a test of his steadfastness by allowing Vishnu in the guise of the dwarf Vamana to put his foot on his, Maveli's, head when there was no other place to put it. Vamana did so and thereby pushed the king into the underworld. Mahabali was by one tradition a wonderful king, though others say that he suffered from the sin of pride, which is why Vamana came to punish him - or perhaps the gods were jealous of him. Kerala people however have no doubt about Maveli's qualities and sing the following song about him, ['freely translated' by Manga and me!]

When King Maveli ruled our land, we were indeed a happy band.

All our people equal were, and there was naught for them to fear.

Youngest children never died and older people never lied;

Sickness was not there at all and everybody, large or small

Was honest as the day was long. And so I end this happy song.

Onam falls in the month of Chingham [August/September] and is also the Malayalee harvest festival. It is celebrated with a traditional feast and of course prayers in the Temple, and by gifts of new clothes from the head of the household to friends and relations. Special to Onam are the Snake Boat Races including the Nehru Cup, which would be great to see one day. Kathakali and other dances are performed and women make patterns with flowers - Onapookalam they are called.

There are so many festivals in Kerala. You could probably go to one every day of the year if you travelled from village to village. Those best known to us in England are probably Diwali or Deepavali, the Festival of Lights, and Holi, the Festival of Colours. Holi is a North Indian festival hardly known until recently in Kerala, except at a Konkani Temple in Kochi, though it is played for fun in some colleges.

Onam flowers- photograph

The festival is called manjal kuli [means literally turmeric shower] in Malayalam. Holi marks the end of winter and the beginning of spring, and in Bihar at least it celebrates the defeat of a demon by Vishnu in the form of Narashima, the half-lion. The name Holi comes from the demon's daughter Holika who is burned in the story and bonfires are lit to commemorate this. I think probably the great majority enjoy the festival because of the fun and games, and people of all religions, not just Hindus, play. The boys at the Sainik School loved it. They had a licence to throw coloured water and powder over their teachers and took full advantage of their opportunity! We finished up drenched and multi-coloured but we made sure the boys did too. And the other good thing was that all the men would go from house to house in the campus and be served with delicacies like kalakund [another of my favourites, soft and creamy, made of milk, and a speciality of Kodarma in Bihar] and pakoras. Outside the campus it seems things were a bit wilder. *Wikipedia* says that in Bihar 'vast quantities of liquor are consumed alongside ganja and bhang [forms of cannabis], which is sometimes added to foodstuffs.' But I missed all that. Diwali was another festival that we celebrated enthusiastically at the school. All the bungalows were decorated with oil lamps, the drill sergeants supervised huge bonfires and fireworks and the boys were issued with sparklers and bangers. Again paying visits to neighbours and sharing goodies was a big part of the festival. Diwali commemorates Rama's return to his home in Ayodhya after defeating Ravana. There are other stories but all of them concern the victory of good over evil. The stories serve to illustrate that this is the time when we must defeat the evil that is inside us, and cleanse our atman or soul. Bodies, clothes and houses must be clean too or Lakshmi the Goddess of Wealth will not visit you; and this could mean financial problems in the year to come. Those really serious about money will perform Lakshmi Puja, and start their financial year at this time. People celebrate Diwali in all parts of India - and it's a religious festival for Jains and Sikhs as well as Hindus - so it's an official national holiday.

The Mahasiva Ksheetram festival, Trikkandiyur

Manga remembers putting two terracotta oil lamps at the gate of the house in Trikkandiyur and four or six more on the veranda.

> *'We couldn't afford to buy the oil to have more lamps'*, Manga says. *'And Dad couldn't always afford to buy us new clothes for the festival either. But sometimes we did get a new gawun or frock.'* We think 'gawun' is a corruption of the English 'gown' by the way. *'What I liked specially were the different things there were to eat. There was a sweet made of puffed rice, very ripe coconut, ginger and jagaree. You know that jagaree is unrefined sugar? Well it's*

mostly cane sugar but the best comes from a palm tree. And there's coconut jagaree too. Anyway this puffed rice was delicious and we didn't have it any other time. Apart from that we went to the temple but we didn't have fireworks or anything like that.'

Manga thinks her favourite festival when she was a little girl was Vishu. This is New Year's Day in the Kerala calendar - the first day of the month of Medam, which falls in April or May. This is when the sun enters the constellation of Mesha Rashi, the equivalent of Aries, and the first Zodiac sign in Hindu astrology. One of the features of Vishu is that the first thing you see in the morning will influence what happens for the rest of the year. It's similar I guess to 'first-footing' in Britain, where the first person to enter your house after midnight on New Year's Eve is preferably of dark complexion [I've no idea why] and bears an auspicious gift. In our case at home in Cleethorpes, the first-footer was usually brother Rob, carrying a lump of coal.

Manga remembers:

'For Vishu, we had to have a big jackfruit. And we needed all sorts of vegetables and nine types of grain, like rice, gram, millet and so on - I can't think of all nine just now. All this was laid out by Mum on the floor on a tray I think, and there would be a clean cloth and little gold tokens that she put on top of a half coconut. Yellow flowers like the ones you get on a laburnum tree, and neem leaves would be used for decoration and there would be oil lamps and all sorts of good things. It was called kani. Mum would do this on the night before Vishu after we had all gone to bed and she would make the tray as pretty as she could. Next morning, she would wake us up and put her hand over our eyes and lead us to the tray. Then we would open our eyes and look at the tray and all the things on it and say prayers. This was all very exciting for us. We believed that what we saw was a sort of visualisation of the year to come. We saw all good things and hoped that the New Year would bring things like that into our lives.' The nine grains would be rice, wheat, maize, sorghum and two types of millet; and and three types of gram - green, black and horse gram. 'Also it was a time when adults should give children money [that's called kattam or kaniattam]. So you go up to everyone you know and show your hand, and if you were lucky, they would give you an anna. They were silver coins in those days - not now though.' An anna was one-

sixteenth of a rupee, so about six new paisa. The anna itself was divided into 12 pice or 4 paisa'.

Another celebration that Manga remembers with pleasure is the Trikkandiyur temple Ulsavam. The festival lasts nine days during the month of Thulam [October/November], and prayers were said to the presiding deity, Shiva of course.

'What I remember about our Ulsavam,' says Manga, *'is that travelling salesmen set up shops selling bangles and chains and all sorts of things like that for children, and they brought with them a sort of mini fairground. One of the rides was a wheel with four cradles like boxes attached to it. Four or five people would get into each box and then two men would turn the wheel manually. Just like a miniature London eye. It wasn't very big but it was very exciting for us, because we didn't have anything like that.'* Manga says the wheel was three times my height, which sounds very high to me! *'There was a band playing - called a panchavaidyam, five instruments - and story-tellers came to the temple in the morning and the evening. Dad always had a food stall on that day so we had to work but we found time to have fun as well. It was a wonderful holiday. There was a parade with an elephant but of course he didn't go into our temple. The colour of the elephant's costume made us gasp! Lots of gold on his face and trunk especially. Really bright in the sunshine. One man was sitting on the elephant with a decorated fan made of peacock feathers and another waved what looked like a mop made of threads like hair. A third carried an image of the deity. The procession went up the hill past the hospital to the kavu to Bhagwati. This was the kavu where women went to pray if they wanted a child. Amakutty went there, but it didn't work for her. You have to leave a doll there called maramkutty. Sometimes Dad would go to the kavu and bring back one of the dolls for us to play with because we didn't have any toys of our own. It was just a face and ears and no shape to the body or arms or anything but we loved it. They put red and blue markings on it.'*

We saw the Ayyappaswamy Festival in the village with Rika and Frank. Manga explains:

'There is a procession with a devotee of the God carrying a decorated yoke with containers of milk and water attached. He and others in the procession might put needles through their cheeks and so on [they did when we were there - tongues, lips, all sorts: it was very

exotic]. They might have promised the god they would do this if he granted them some favour. One dancer represents Ayyappan and carries a sword with a curved tip. As he dances he will hit himself with the sword on the chest and shoulders and he'll bleed. His friend, the Muslim Wavaru, will try and stop him from hurting himself. Malayalee girls with pretty dresses will line the road and move along with the procession, carrying silver trays with oil lamps and someone will carry a supply of the fuel and make sure that the lamps are kept topped up.'

I must mention Krishna's birthday, called Ashtamurti because he was the eighth son (Ashta means eight in Sanskrit). The festival takes place at the end of September or beginning of October, and Manga remembers a special kolam being drawn on the steps of the house - kolam are the geometric pictures made of rice flour - and the house being specially cleaned. All the family had to fast and recite [or listen to] religious texts during the day, and at midnight came the treats! There would be freshly cooked seedai [hard little balls of deep-fried rice and dahl flour], crunchy, coiled murukku, and all sorts of other goodies.

Durga Puja was a big event in the community near my school in Bihar in north India, where the villagers made statues of the Goddess riding a lion, and, with her foot on an evil demon and armed to the teeth, represented a woman's fierce protective side. The ten days of the Puja, also called Dusshera, celebrate Durga's fight with and defeat of a demon the familiar tale of good defeating evil.

The equivalent of Durga Puja in the south is Navarathri, when the Goddess is worshipped in several forms. Women in particular visit the temple every evening to pray for the safety of their families and the well-being of the community. Navarathri means nine nights, and events take place each evening. Indi was in Trikkandiyur for the festival in 1999. In her letters home, she wrote,

'I helped to set up Boommakkolu [decorations, especially dolls, for the festival]. Incredible decorations including all the things we brought out when we came here with Grandma - Pierrot stuff, teapots made of shells. I can't touch them at the moment because of my period...' In her next letter Indi added, 'Rajam periamma says she'll cry when I leave' I think everyone is a bit soft at the moment because today is 'Boommakkolu' - and we have set up the Pooja decorations with lots of family treasures, lights and

tinsel. Last night Shantamani and I got dressed up and went to all the Nair families to ask them to come and see the decorations and do pooja. I had to ask them to come in Malayalam, which caused great amusement. I had to take off all my silver jewellery and put on gold and glitter glass bangles on my arms, a beautiful heavy gold chain, big ear-rings with a chain over the ear, red sari, powder, eyetex and bindi. This morning it's a green sari and the Iyer community.'

On the last three days of Navarathri, Saraswati is worshipped. Saraswati is the Goddess of Learning and so in the evenings, books, pens and musical instruments are placed before the goddess, and thanks are given to teachers.

One final festival - Vinayaga Chaturthi. On this day, in late August or early September, Ganesh is worshipped. The elephant god is a great favourite in Kerala and elsewhere and is known to help remove impediments to the success of projects, and to promote harmony and goodwill. Figures of Ganapati, as he is most often known in the south, are made out of clay and offerings made to them. A delicacy called modakam is supposed to be his favourite, so it's important to offer it to the statue. This is a sweet made of coconut and jagaree covered in dough and steamed - or the filling can be savoury, with dahl, chilli and again, coconut.

Those were Manga's favourite festivals, but while we're thinking about fun times in Kerala, we must remember The Cinema. The arrival of the travelling Movie Theatre in the village was a great day for everyone. Even the elders who in theory disapproved of this newfangled technology that would doubtless corrupt the young and divert them from more healthy pursuits, could be found in the packed audiences for the few performances that were offered. Manga says:

'The theatre was a bit like a circus. There was a flat piece of ground quite near our house where the 'Big Top' was erected. The two or three young chaps who came with the Theatre got all the strong men in the village to haul on the ropes and there was ever so much anticipation and excitement as the tent went up. It was the biggest we had ever seen and although it happened every year we were always amazed. Although we were not supposed to, we would hang about around the tent and watch all that was happening. I got friendly with the man who worked the generator for the electricity - we didn't have any power in the village that time - and he would

explain how it all worked. He prayed every morning to the goddess Saraswati to make sure that the generator didn't break down. The projectionist was a very important fellow - and he knew it. He didn't think much of unsophisticated villagers, except that he came to our house to eat. He would give us children boiled sweets and sometimes free tickets. Otherwise we would have to pay one anna. I think it was two or three annas to sit on a chair, which we could never afford. We would clap and cheer and boo throughout the performance and it was great fun. When I first came to England, people stayed quiet in cinemas and I would sometimes disgrace myself by calling out as if I was watching a pantomime. So I didn't enjoy going to the cinema much here, until I came to Sheffield and the Indian nurses would go off to Bradford to see matinees in a cinema there. All the audience would be from India or Pakistan and there'd be lots of shouting. English people weren't interested in Bollywood then, and I must say that most of the films were just entertainment and quite similar to each other. There were some good ones though - 'Mother India' was one of my favourites and 'Anarkali' [who was the Mughal Emperor Jehangir's girl-friend].

But I must get back to Trikkandiyur. We would sit at the front eating peanuts and boiled sweets...with wide eyes watching all the scenes. We loved to see mountains and snow, and cities and other countries, and of course stories of the gods that Mum had told us. We'd all boo the bad characters and cheer when the hero appeared. We used to laugh, because when a God came on the screen some of the old women would wail and get out of their seats and kneel down and put their foreheads on the ground. The cinema would come once a year in summer and sometimes stay for quite a while. It was such a happy time for us.'

CHAPTER TWENTY-FOUR

CHRISTIANS, JEWS AND MUSLIMS

One of the charming things about Kerala and its peoples is the way they've always embraced diversity, and welcomed visitors from different cultures and backgrounds whether they came to stay or to trade or just explore. The early Jewish and Christian settlers in Kerala were, like most incomers to the State, treated very generously and quickly absorbed into society; their exotic religious beliefs were not a barrier. For the most part the same hospitality still seems to me to apply today. I hope it lasts for another thousand years. As far as our family is concerned, well, Manga married a chap who was brought up as a Christian of course; the Mumbai branch of the family lived for many years in a Christian enclave; and our great niece's mother-in-law is Jewish. And incidentally, Manga's sister Rajam for most of her working life taught in a Muslim school. So all that is quite impressively multicultural.

To go back to the ninth century, both Jewish and Christian communities were well settled in Kerala and indeed thriving. We saw in an earlier chapter how Jewish merchants had been rewarded for their loyalty to the crown in the Chera-Chola wars. The Christians were equally well integrated into society during the Kulashekhara period and had flourished, so that when Vasco da Gama landed in Kozhikode in 1498, he found 200,000 Syrian Christians in Kerala.

The Christian Community

'We pray...that all who profess and call themselves Christians may be led into the way of truth'. The Book of Common Prayer 1662

The Kerala Christians came from all sorts of different places and backgrounds. Some had become Christians at the time that Doubting Thomas was in Kerala, in the early years AD; then there were the Christian refugees from Persian persecution who arrived in Kodungallor in 345 AD. Other immigrants came from the Gulf in the eighth and ninth centuries seeking freedom to practice their religion in Kollam and received support and comfort from the king of that land. A lot more conversions happened while the Kulashekharas were in power, although prior to the arrival of the Jesuits, there would have been no particular pressure on people to convert, and it seems to have often been higher caste Hindus who turned to Jesus. This is a contrast with later years when it was those of lower or no caste who sought Christianity, hoping I think to improve their prospects and social standing. But in this period Christians were pretty prosperous, involved in trade and money-lending; they were 'embarking on those commercial and financial activities which, in the absence of a Vaushya [Vaishya] caste of merchants and money-lenders in Kerala, became in later years the particular province of the Syrian community'.[138] So I'm not surprised that people were happy to join the community, irrespective of any question of faith. Bishops were celibate but priests were not, and many of the community were vegetarian. Certainly they seem to have absorbed some of the customs of their hosts - there is evidence of a caste structure, and weddings for example were a bit like Hindu ceremonies. As late as 1891, this comment was included in the Mysore census report: 'Christians continue undisturbed in the rites which had guided them in their pre-conversion existence. They still pay worship to the Kalasam at marriages and festivals, call in the Brahmin astrologer and purohita [a teacher of religious procedures], use the Hindu religious marks, and conform to various other amenities, which have the advantage of minimising friction in their daily intercourse with Hindu fellow-caste brethren'.[139] No doubt the writer is correct in suggesting that inter-community relations were helped by the 'Indianisation' of their practices, but there is no evidence that Christian communities were discouraged from doing their own thing, and they seem largely to have enjoyed the same privileges and were expected to bear the same responsibilities as Hindus. They were allowed to carry weapons, for example, but also expected to help in the defence of the country. The Syrian Christians of Kerala were well integrated and in affairs of faith went their own way, isolated from the rest of the Christian world until 1480, when the Patriarch of Babylon became their leader. Their big shake-up did not occur till 20 years later, however, with the arrival of Vasco da Gama.

There were Roman Catholics in Kerala before da Gama. John of Monte Corvino came to Kerala in 1294 and founded a church in

Kollam in 1330, the year after the Pope called for the Syrians to 'abandon their schism'. But Roman Catholicism did not establish itself until the Portuguese arrived. At first the two Christian communities lived together peacefully, for the Franciscan monks who accompanied da Gama on his journey hoped to be able to bring the heretics back into the fold through debate and persuasion. It was however a rather different story when Francis Xavier and his Jesuits appeared forty years later. They were impatient at the slow progress of conversion both of Syrians and Hindus and, in the words of the *RC Encyclopaedia* 'continued the good work with such earnestness and zeal that most of the Nestorians were converted before 1600'.[140] Other sources are inclined to ascribe the Jesuits' success to the methods of the Inquisition.[141] The problem seems to have been that the Portuguese thought that the Syrians were deliberately flouting the authority of the Pope, while the Syrians said they had simply not heard of him. Thomas Yeates in *Indian Church History* is one of a number of writers who describe the meeting of east and west in a similar vein: 'These Christians met the Portuguese as natural friends and allies, and rejoiced at their coming - but the Portuguese were much disappointed at finding the St Thomas Christians firmly fixed in the tenets of a Primitive church...'[142] St Francis complained of 'Jewish wickedness' among the Syrians, including the refusal to eat pork or treat Sunday as the Sabbath, for example, and many were allegedly burned for such sins. The Jesuits were also keen to get rid of any Jews they came across of course, but a contemporary witness remarked, 'The judges of the Holy Office might readily ascertain the truth or falsehood of the charge of Judaism, would they take the trouble to investigate the matter without prejudice, and to consider, that of an hundred persons condemned to be burnt as Jews, there are scarcely four who profess that faith at their death. The rest exclaiming and protesting to their last grasp, that they are Christians, and have been so during their whole lives, that they worship our Savior as their only true God, and that on his mercy, and the merits of his adorable sacrifice'.[143] For their part, the Roman Catholic historians speak of conversions being achieved because they made sure that anyone converted was promised protection and full civil rights and an improvement in their social standing; although some add that the 'vicious habits' of the Portuguese soldiers did not set a good Christian example! But for whatever reason, there is no doubt that 'the harvest of souls was rich', especially among the poor fishing communities.[144]

We met some Christian fisher folk near Mumbai on one of our visits to that city, and they took us to an island just off the coast where a cross had been raised 'for the souls of the drowned'. They were very poor and their houses and way of life was little different from the Hindus in the same area. Gaudy coloured pictures taken from calendars supplied by local tradesmen crowded the walls and they had a prayer corner with idols just like any Hindu house. They told us that they were quite happy to ask favours of Hindu gods if it worked, and said Hindus would come to their churches to worship the Christian God in times of crisis. So the Indianisation of Christianity seems to be healthy and happy still!

A Christian home in a fishing community near Mumbai

I wrote about festivals in the previous chapter and this is a description of one of the most important Christian festivals as celebrated in Kerala and which incidentally illustrates my point about Indianisation. It is an extract from a recording I made in 2008 for the Whitstable Echo magazine for visually impaired people. I am indebted to my friend Ashok for most of the content.

'I said there weren't many Christians in India - but that's only in comparison with the total population. There are in fact 24 million Christians there, more than the number who practise in England perhaps? That's less than one person in forty, but in Kerala the ratio is much higher [19%], and that's where we're going for an experience of a Roman Catholic Christmas celebration in India. Like everyone else in India, Kerala Christians are very keen on their festivals, especially of course, Christmas. But they celebrate the festival quite differently from most of us in Britain. First and foremost it is for everyone a fundamentally religious occasion. There is no orgy of buying presents in the weeks up to the 25th - on the contrary, there is fasting, prayer and serious contemplation. Only plain food is eaten and no meat. Very much like Lent. Shops are not decorated, and there are no advertisements trying to encourage people to buy things they can't afford. Children do not present lists of demands, and pressurise adults into agreeing to them to avoid scenes and tears. Malayalee children by and large look forward to the big day only because of the promise of good food, two days holiday and the chance of meeting their aunts and uncles, grandmas and grandpas.

So after three weeks quiet meditation, Christmas Eve arrives, and the fun begins. Everyone must have a star hanging outside their front door. This is usually made of paper or card with a candle inside it. In fact families vie for the greatest number of stars hanging from the house. There's no record of how many fires are started in this way, but it must be plenty. It does look very pretty though. And as most Christians' houses are clustered together, the overall effect is spectacular. Then there is the carolling. The priest, together with a small group of singers from the church start going round the houses of local Christians singing hymns about the birth of Christ at their doors. The priest carries with him an image of the infant Jesus and when the choir is welcomed into the home, the priest places the image into the crib that each family has prepared in advance, and all kneel and pray. Oddly enough, one of the carollers is always dressed as Santa Claus, fur-trimmed red coat, white whiskers, boots and all! He must be a fairly recent innovation I think. After the prayers, each member of the family comes forward to kiss the Christ figure, and then Father Christmas will give chocolate to the children. Then the carollers move on, now joined by the members of the household that has been visited. Next house - carols - crib - prayers - chocolate and more people join the group. Eventually all the Christian families are in the choir - tough on the last house to be visited it seems! – and all process to the church at

11 pm to take part in the midnight Mass. The priest reads the chapter describing the birth of Christ and at the stroke of midnight, fire crackers are set off to welcome Jesus into the world – really loud crackers, waking the whole village, and no doubt the Christians are cursed by members of other religions trying to get a good night's sleep. Mind you, Hindus are fond of firecrackers too, and get their own back many times during the year!

Christian church, Kanniya Kumari

There is a big crib in the church and here the peripatetic figure of the infant Christ takes his place. There's also a Christmas tree with parcels hanging from it. Everyone who's paid a rupee [just over a penny] to the church can go and take a parcel. Some have small gifts in them; others do not. But nobody minds too much. And the priest announces the winner of the much coveted 'best crib' award from all those in the houses the carollers have visited. Some people spend weeks making their crib, using wood and straw and surrounding the hut with paddy fields and miniature coconut trees.

On the following morning, everyone breaks their fast, eating appam and meat curry - usually chicken, not turkey - and visit friends and family and have a restful, joyous day. No alcohol, no presents, no arguments over who does the washing up. Christmas is a religious and family occasion and, many would say, all the better for that.'

The Jewish Community

'Hath not a Jew eyes? hath not a Jew hands, organs, dimensions, senses, affections, passions? fed with the same food, hurt with the same weapons, subject to the same diseases, healed by the same means, warmed and cooled by the same winter and summer, as a Christian is?' William Shakespeare, *The Merchant of Venice*

In chapter six, we reported on a number of theories about the origins of the Jewish community in Kerala. It is possible that some Jewish sailors from King Solomon's fleets settled in Malabar as far back as a thousand years BC; and it is likely that many more Jews came to Kerala to escape a series of persecutions: the Babylonian Captivity in the sixth century BC, the wrath of Titus, son of Vespasian in 70 AD, and the Emperor Hadrian's torments in 136 AD. And there was immigration too of Jews from Spain and Portugal fleeing from the Inquisition. Many of these groups formed distinct clans within the community in India. The Meyuhassim were the first settlers; the Pardisi were the later immigrants; and the 'black' Jews were probably descended from former slaves or servants in Jewish households who were converted and freed. There appears to have been very little social contact and no inter-marriage between the 'black' and 'white' Jews.

The Jews were respected and well-rewarded traders and citizens in the Kulashekhara era. As in very few other places in the world, Kerala welcomed the Jews of the Diaspora, a fact of which Malayalees should be very proud. And although there were terrible troubles to come, at this point in history the Jewish community enjoyed peace and prosperity in the lands granted to them by Bhaskara Ravi Varman the First. Ravi Varman granted them not only just land, but also, according to contempoary copper plate inscriptions, '*tolls on boats and carts, the revenue and the title of the village of Anjuvannam...land tax, and weight tax...freedom from paying dues to the royal Palace*' and various ceremonial rights such as the right to be borne in a Palanquin.

The Jews called this land 'Shingly', probably adapted from 'Cyngilin', the name by which Cranganore was known to some medieval travellers. There is a rather emotional little verse written by Rabbi Nissim, a fourteenth century poet and traveller which illustrates the importance of this place to all Jews:

I have travelled from Spain,

I had heard of a city of Shingly

I longed to see an Israeli king

Him I saw with my own eyes! [145]

And their attachment to the place was so strong that in the words of *Kerala and her Jews* 'till recently, a handful of Shingly sand found a place in the coffin of every Jew alongside that from the Holy Land'. But a hill called Juda Kunnu, a tank called Juda Kulam and the copper plates are all that remains of Shingly - 'this forgotten outpost of the Jewish world'. For in 1524, 'following an argument between Muslim and Jewish merchants about the pepper trade, the Muslim community 'burned [the Jews'] houses and synagogues', and left nothing standing'.[146] When the Portuguese came to Shingly at the beginning of the sixteenth century, they found only a few destitute Jews there, the rest having fled to Kochi where the Hindu ruler granted them his protection, and land on which to build. But destitute or not, the Portuguese were not going to leave the Shingly Jews in peace. 'The nation that was helped to discover a new sea route by Jewish astronomers, travellers and interpreters soon forgot their services and subjected them to persecution and torture.'[147] Their leader Albuquerque told the king of Portugal that there were a number of Portuguese and Castilian Jews in Malabar, and asked for permission [readily granted] to exterminate them one by one as they were found. The destruction was complete, and it is said that even today, Jews avoid visiting the place, and 'if business brings a Jew thither, he hurriedly leaves before sunset.'[148]

Later, Kochi's Jew Town, founded in 1567, was also sacked and burned by the European invaders, though the synagogue partly survived and was later re-built. So it is not surprising that when the Dutch came to Kochi in 1661, the Jews gave then their support, for which they suffered again when the Portuguese drove the Dutch out. Two years later the Dutch returned and throughout the period of their dominance [1663- 1795], then that of the British and finally in the independent Republic of India, the Jews enjoyed another period of prosperity and stability. It was particularly pleasing to the community that Indira Gandhi joined them to celebrate the four hundredth anniversary of the construction of the Kochi Synagogue. But in 2010, there were only 52 Jews left practising in Kerala, while 8000 of their brethren had emigrated to Israel.[149]

The Synagogue in Kochi

The Muslim Community

'O you who believe! Enter absolutely into peace [Islam].Do not follow in the footsteps of Satan. He is an outright enemy to you'. The Holy Quran

After the Prophet Mohammed died in 632 AD, it took only twenty years for Islam, aided it has to be said by force of arms, to spread to Syria, Egypt, Iraq and Iran.[150] The new religion then conquered the whole of the Middle East, North Africa, Spain, and central Asia and by 700, the Islamic armies under their Caliph had reached the borders of India. The Caliph seemed inclined to call a halt at this point and consolidate his gains, but raids on Arab shipping carried out by pirates based in the Rann of Kutch were an irritant. The Buddhist ruler of Sind claimed that he could do nothing to restrain the pirates but the Caliph's viceroy could not agree and following a particularly daring raid by the pirates on a vessel bringing him gifts from the king of Sri Lanka, he ordered the invasion of Sind in 707. The General appointed to lead the invasion was the charismatic Muhammad ibn Qasim, and he took Debal [modern Karachi], the main town of Sind, 'by assault and the carnage endured for three days' according to the chronicler al-Biladduri.[151] Qasim marched on, winning further victories, all seemingly ending as 'the idolaters fled and the Mussalmans glutted themselves with massacre'.[152] Nonetheless Qasim built a reputation as a fair conqueror who honoured his promises and allowed Buddhists and Hindus to continue to worship where they were co-operative. Indeed it is said that when he was relieved of his command 'the people of Hind wept'.[153*] With good reason, for much worse was to follow in later centuries under the rule of the man that Hindus describe as the devil incarnate, Mahmud of Ghazni [c1030], and the Delhi Sultans of the twelfth and thirteenth centuries.

It was all very different in Kerala. Arabs had been visiting the Kerala coast for centuries to trade, and for the most part enjoyed good relations with their hosts. And nothing changed after the Arabs had been converted to Islam. The Chera kings were happy to allow them to set up mosques and preach their religion and some conversions were made - mostly of lower caste Hindus but also of some local chiefs. The legend of the Last Perumal and his pilgrimage to Mecca dates from this period, and the Keralolpatti also tells stories showing how the honesty of the Kerala kings fostered close ties with Muslim merchants*.

The great Muslim traveller Sheik Ibn Batuta visited Kerala in the middle of the fourteenth century and wrote of what he found there.

> We next came to the country of Malabar which is the country of black pepper. Its length is a journey of two months along the coast of Sindabur *[Goa]* to Kawlam *[Kollam]*. The whole of the way by land lies under the shade of trees and at the distances of every half mile there is a house made of wood, in which there are chambers fitted up for the reception of comers and goers, whether they be Muslims or infidels. To each of these there is a well, out of which they drink, and over each of these is an infidel appointed to give drink... to the Muslim, he pours the water into

> their hands, for they do not allow Muslims to touch their vessels, or to enter into their apartments... but in most of the districts the Mussalman merchants have houses and are greatly respected so that Muslims who are strangers whether they be merchants or poor may lodge among them. But at any town where no Muslim resides, upon anyone's arriving they cook, and pour out drink for him, upon the leaf of the banana; and whatever he happens to leave, they give to the dogs. And in all this space of two months journey, there is not a span free from cultivation. For everybody has a garden, and his house is placed in the middle of it, and round the whole of this there is a fence of wood.[154]

Logan observes that this description of Malabar in 1340 could serve as an account of the countryside in his day too - and neither is it unlike Kerala as I first saw it in 1967.

There were raids into the south by the Muslim conquerors of north India during the fourteenth century, Malik Kafur reaching as far as Madurai in 1311. Keay describes their relationship with India as being similar to that of the 'the white sahibs of European colonialism', that is, 'a source of wealth, a scene of adventure, and a subject of for moral indignation spiked with prurient fantasy.'[155] The latter reactions were fuelled partly by the Hindu form of dress especially in the south, a subject commented on by Christian travellers like Marco Polo [1290] and the Russian Athanasius Nikitin in 1470 as well as Muslim writers. Marco Polo was amazed to find no tailors in South India; that was because the only dress worn by women as well as men including the king himself, was a length of unstitched cloth wrapped around the waist. Marco Polo concluded (illogically) from this choice of clothing that the people 'regard no form of lechery or sensual indulgence as sin.'[156] Nikitin was shocked that women went about with their 'breast bare and their heads uncovered' [157] but his contemporary Abdu-r-Razzak could see the point - when he met the local kings, they remained cool, dressed as they were in little except jewellery, while he himself 'in consequence of the heat and the great number of robes in which he was dressed, drowned in perspiration'.[158] But Muslims in general were shocked and horrified by what they saw as the lax behaviour of the Hindus of Kerala.

Mosque at Annara, near Trikkandiyur

Keay comments that this was not just about differences in religion or race, but in what was considered proper and correct behaviour. He describes the Islamic code as being 'universal, inflexible, authoritarian and obligatory which upheld the equality of individual believers and theoretically promoted a strong sense of community' while the Hindu was 'India-specific, sectional, discriminatory and hierarchical which denied equality and revelled in diversity'.[159] This was reflected in the clothes worn by the followers of the two religions. Muslims wore 'stiff brocade kaftans and ankle-tight trousers' and their women's clothes and way of life were designed to conceal while the cotton loincloths, lungis, and jewellery worn by Hindus were seen by Muslims as 'disgustingly indecent'.[160] But as time went on, as has been the way for centuries in the continent of Circe, cultures began to merge. In due course, Hindus began to hide their women folk away in the home; Muslim women wore saris and their men lungis, and Hindu women adopted the salwar kurta; caste distinctions began to creep into Islam, Hindus were attracted to Sufi saints and Muslims supported Hindu artists and craftsmen.

Many of the Arab traders settled in Kerala either bringing their families or marrying Malayalee women, and this early Muslim community was joined by Hindus who had converted. They were known as Mappilas or Moplahs, and still are. Mixed views about the community as it existed towards the end of the nineteenth century are noted in Logan's *Malabar Manual*. The author quotes one of his colleagues as having reported thus: 'On the coast they are industrious, skilful in trade, crafty, avaricious, rigid observers of the injunction of the prophet in abstaining from the use of spirituous liquors, particular in their attendance to the forms rather than the spirit of their religion, being regular in worship but at the same time hypocritical rogues and zealous in their attempts to gain proselytes.' Logan himself as usual is much more generous. He describes the Mappilas as frugal and thrifty; and says approvingly that they marry as a rule but one wife and live with her and their family on affectionate terms. They are very scrupulous about the chastity of their women, who nonetheless appear in public without veils, and enjoy much freedom. Logan observes that the men are reliable workers when treated with kindness - but 'the hand that controls them must be firm'. They are though largely illiterate and because of their ignorance and bigotry easily led by 'designing persons'.[161]

The Mappilas were a very important force in Kerala during the period of resistance to European colonisation and we will return to them later.

CHAPTER TWENTY-FIVE

MEANWHILE ...CHIEFLY CHOLAS

'If you subdue your anger, it will turn out nectar; but if you fail to use your weapon, you will not keep up your manliness' - Malayalam proverb

Temple Elephants processing

During the latter part of the Kulashekhara period in Kerala, the most powerful Empire in the whole of India was that of the Cholas. They are important to this story, even though they were a dynasty based in Tamilnad, partly because of their dealings with our own Cheras over many centuries, and partly because it's possible that at the time we're writing about, Manga's ancestors might well have been living under their jurisdiction. Their rise from one of three minor squabbling dynasties in the remote south to the greatest power in the whole of India within two generations, further justifies their inclusion in this book. They are not widely recognized as one of the great empires, possibly because they are from the south. As John Keay says, they turned 'the supposed hegemony of North India on its head'.[162]

The rise of the Cholas began with King Aditya who defeated the Pallavas [in 897] and then the Pandyas, occupying first Mamallapuram and Kanchipuram, and then Madurai. But a victory over Aditya's son by the Rashtrakutas delayed further Chola expansion until the arrival of Rajaraja. He first of all pacified the Cheras and Pandyas, and then turned his attention overseas. At this time, Arabs controlled the east- west trade routes, but by occupying the north of Sri Lanka and 'the thousand islands', probably the Maldives, the Cholas were able to take a slice of the action. Like the Pallavas before them, the Cholas' influence also extended to 'Greater India' - Indo-China and Indonesia. Then came the expeditions into the north, when the Cholas famously 'watered their war-elephants in the Ganges', and ruled over a third of India.

Sad to say, this Tamil power has the reputation of great brutality against its enemies. Keay reports that the Buddhist Sri Lanka's capital, Anuradhapura, 'was sacked and its stupas plundered with a rapacity worthy of the great Mahmud' [of Ghazni]. And in Bijapur, the Chola army 'behaved with exceptional brutality'.[163] But the Cholas are best known for their wondrous plastic arts, to which I referred in chapter 22.

The greatest memorial to the Cholas is perhaps Tanjore Temple, known at the time that it was built as the largest and tallest temple in all of India. The temple included sixty bronzes, many frescoes in its pillared cloister, and a particularly serene Nandi statue. The Vimana [main tower] is 65 metres tall and is surmounted by a 'crown' allegedly made from a single piece of stone and weighing 80 tons. The temple was completed in the year 1010 and is typical of Tamil temple architecture. And according to Francis Watson's *Concise History of India* 'it provided among other things for four hundred dancing girls, exponents of the exacting art of Bharata Natyam and not yet degraded from ritualistic to promiscuous sexuality'.[164]

But artistic brilliance did not save the Cholas: their Empire in its turn declined and fell. In the twelfth century the Hoysalas from Mysore and the resurgent Pandyas of Madurai undermined Chola power and a new era emerged. The Hoysalas, who drove the Cholas out of Karnataka, were themselves famed for their artistry - particularly of their temples. Well-known examples of what are described as their elaborate and delicately carved temple buildings remain at Belur and Halebid in Karnataka, and also Somnathpur which some of our family took a trip to see under Raju's leadership in Rosemary's year and returned full of admiration. I meanwhile was sweating out a fever in a hotel bed in Mysore, Manga changing my soaking bedsheets hourly.

One of the dominant dynasties in the south in earlier times had been the Pandyas. They were admired for building the Meenakshi Temple in Madurai and for their sculptures - 'characterised by their slim and soft elegance', says the *Indian Mirror,* but lacking the 'warmth' of the Chola masterpieces.[165] Their revival began around 1150 and they quickly dispossessed the Cholas and then pushed the Hoysalas out of Tamilnad. By 1250 the 'later' Pandyas had not only wiped out the Cholas altogether but conquered Orissa in the north and Sri Lanka in the south, and were the masters of their region. However, within a generation the invincible armies of the Sultan of Delhi would be marching into the south country.

CHAPTER TWENTY-SIX

TRADE AND COMMERCE

'*Danger follows avarice*' - Malayalam proverb

As the Roman Empire declined, and the Turks blocked off the route from Europe to India, Kerala's direct trade with the west went into decline. However, that did not mean the end of her trading activities. There was still a big market for spices, and Arab merchants took over the job of buying the 'black gold' and Arab travellers grew to know Kerala well.

One of these intrepid adventurers, Al Adrisi, was the first to refer to Kerala as Malabar, and another, Istakhri, reported on Malabar's exports into Persia via the port of Siraf: 'aloes wood for burning, amber, camphor, precious gems, bamboos, ivory, ebony, sandalwood, and all kinds of Indian perfumes, drugs and condiments'.[166] The most important commodity travelling in the opposite direction were Arab horses. The Kerala kings were well-known for being honest and fair and as a result, Muslim merchants trusted them and trade flourished. There's a story in the *Keralolpatti* about a merchant of Muscat who was said to have visited various countries and given presents to their rulers. The presents consisted of pickle boxes filled with gold, but to test their honesty, he told the kings that the boxes did indeed contain only pickles. All those whom he visited, on discovering what the boxes really contained, concealed the fact and took the gold, but when the test was applied to the Keralan ruler [the Zamorin of Calicut in this case], the latter at once called for the merchant and said, '*You have made a mistake. This is not pickles but gold!*' The *Keralolpatti* says 'the traveller thereupon concluded that here at last was a trustworthy king, and so he settled down at Calicut and became the Koya [Muslim priest] of that city'.[167] One must remember that the *Keralolpatti* is a work designed to enhance the reputation of high caste Hindus - but it is a good story.

Jewish traders were also important, although if a contemporary writer is to be believed, their cargoes seem to have been somewhat less savoury. 'They take from the west eunuchs, female slaves, boys, silks, furs and swords. On their return they bring musk, aloes, camphor, cinnamon, and other products of the east.' Benjamin, a rabbi from Tudela in Spain visited Kollam as part of his travels all over Asia in the twelfth century. He sailed for seventeen days from Iraq and reaching Kollam described the inhabitants as

> descendants of Khush[i] who are addicted to astrology and are all black. During the summer, the heat is extreme. From the third hour of the day [nine o'clock in the morning], people shut themselves up in their houses until the evening at which time everyone goes out. The streets and markets are lighted up and the inhabitants employ all the night upon their business, which they are prevented from doing in the day time, in consequence of the excessive heat.[168]

Rabbi Benjamin was another traveller who noted the positive attitude of the local rulers to international trade.

> This nation is very trustworthy in matters of trade, and whenever foreign merchants enter their port three secretaries of the king immediately repair on board the vessels, write down their names and report them to him. The king thereupon grants them security for their property, which they may even leave in the open fields, without any guard. One of the king's officers sits in the market and receives goods that may have been found anywhere, and which he returns to those applicants who can minutely describe them. This custom is observed throughout the whole realm of the king...[169]

A third group of trading partners were the Chinese, although during the T'ang [618-907] and Sung [960-1279] dynasties, contacts were relatively rare as the Chinese governments did not encourage trade, apparently because of the high cost in particular of the jewels they imported and the consequent drain on coinage. [The Romans were similarly exercised by this problem].

Furthermore, the Chinese rulers were more interested in keeping safe at home and didn't trust merchants, whether they were

---

[i] It appears that Khush is another name for Abyssinia, as referred to by Benjamin later in the *Itinerary*.

Chinese or foreign. The trade that existed was carefully controlled. In the tenth century, however, various independent kingdoms arose in South China and though they were all short-lived, they did welcome contact with India. Ships from Kerala visited the Srivijayan cities of Sumatra and the Malay Peninsula and the ports of the Khmer Empire, and along with other Indian traders helped spread Hindu culture all over South-east Asia. And the Chinese brought their culture to Kerala too: the Chinese fishing nets of Kochi are well-known, and the design of various wooden palaces of this period are supposed to be influenced by Chinese architecture.

Fishing nets: A legacy of the trade with China

The big expansion in Sino-Kerala trade arrived after the end of the Kulashekhara period when China had been conquered by the Mongols during the early thirteenth century. The Mongols encouraged contact with foreigners, and Marco Polo, the great Venetian traveller in the east, said that the Chinese were by the end of the thirteenth century, by far the most important of Kerala's trading partners. In 1290 Polo wrote, '*ships come hither* [to 'Melibar'] *from many quarters, but especially from Manzi* [southern China]. *Coarse spices are exported from hence both to Manzi and to the west, and that which is carried to Aden goes on to Alexandria, but the ships that go in the latter direction are not one in ten of those that go to the eastward...*'[170] Products traded included the inevitable pepper, ginger and cinnamon, and also 'turbit'[ii] and '*very delicate and beautiful buckrams;*[iii] *cloths of silk and gold and sandals; also gold and silver, cloves and spikenard...*'[iv]

Marco Polo first visited India on a mission from the Chinese Emperor Kublai Khan. 'When you leave the island of Ceylon', he wrote, 'and sail westward for about sixty miles, you come to the great province of Maabar, the Coromandel coast of South-East India, which is styled India the greater; it is the best of the Indies, and is on the mainland.' He described the kingdom of Coilum [Kollam], the country called Comari [Kanniya Kumari] and the kingdom of Deli [Ezhi]. 'We will tell you particularly about their manners and products because we are now drawing near to places that are not so outlandish. There is no proper harbour in that country, but there are many great rivers with good estuaries, wide and deep. Pepper and ginger grow there, and other spices in quantities. The king is rich in treasure but not very strong in forces. The approach to his kingdom is, however, so strong that no one can attack him, so he is afraid of nobody.'

Apparently Polo did not find that the people of this part of the coast quite so trustworthy as those further south in Kozhikode. Here he says, your cargo may easily be plundered if '*a ship be driven by stress of weather into some other port than that to which it was bound*'. He wrote that this 'naughty custom' was widespread, though no other traveller has mentioned it.

Ibn Batuta, writing of his visits to Malabar between 1342 and 1347 maintains that the ships of China sailed as far north as Ezhimala, but no further; and that they entered only the harbours of Kozhikode and Kollam. Logan thinks that Kollam might have been a Chinese trading post at this time, for the Muslim geographer Al Kazwini in a moment of confusion no doubt states in his account of India in 1263-75 that the king of Kollam was Chinese.

[ii] Could be an Indian spiny turbot, a tasty fish caught off the Kerala coast; or a fancy pigeon.

[iii] A stiff cotton cloth used to bind books

[iv] This is the oil that the Bible says was used by Mary to anoint Jesus' feet after the Last Supper. It comes from a plant a bit like Valerian that grows mainly in India.

Al Kazwini also wrote incidentally that the people of Kollam 'do not eat fish, nor slaughter animals, but they eat carrion'. I don't know where the last bit came from. So back to the more reliable Batuta on the subject of the Chinese merchants.

> There is only one season in which the Sea of China is navigable. Nor then is the voyage undertaken except in vessels of the three descriptions which follow: the greatest is called a junk, the middling size a zaw, the least a kakam. The sails of these vessels are made of cane-reeds, woven together like a mat...In some of these vessels there will be employed a thousand men, 600 sailors and 400 soldiers. Each of the larger ships is followed by three others, a middle sized, a third, and a fourth sized. They row in these ships with large oars, which may be compared to great masts, over some of which 25 men will be stationed, who work standing. In the large ships too, they sow garden herbs and ginger, which they cultivate in cisterns. In these are also houses made of wood in which the higher officers reside with their wives. Every vessel therefore is like an independent city. Of such ships like these Chinese individuals will sometimes have great numbers and generally, the Chinese are the richest people in the world.[171]

The trading dominance of the Chinese does not appear to have lasted very long however. It seems that the alliance between the ruler of Kozhikode [the Zamorin] and the Muslim traders began to drive the Chinese away and no mention is made by Abdur Razzaq during his visit to Calicut in 1442 of Chinese merchants or fleets.

As an aside, Marco Polo's other observations on life in South India are amusing to read, being a 'hectic blend of correct, careful information and the wildest fantasy' [*Penguin Great Journeys*]. He was accurate, for example, about suttee: '*when a man is dead and his body cremated, his wife flings herself into the same fire and lets herself be burnt with her husband*'; and '*Most of* [the people] *worship the ox, because they say that it is a very good thing. No one would eat beef for anything in the world, and no-one would kill an ox on any account*'; and other customs: '*Let me tell you further that they daub all their houses with cow-dung'*; and *'you must know that in eating they use only the right hand; they would never touch food with their left...the function of the left hand is confined to such needful tasks as are unclean and foul, such as wiping the nose or the breach and suchlike*'. And finally, '*as soon as a child is born, whether girl or boy, the father or mother have a record made in writing of his nativity, that is, the day of his birth, the month, the lunar cycle and the hour. This they do because they guide all their actions by the counsel of astrologers and diviners who are skilled in enchantment and magic and geomancy*'.[172] All these customs [with the exception of suttee of course] still survive.

On the other hand, the method Marco Polo describes for the collection of diamonds sounds a little unlikely:

> Men take many lumps of flesh imbued with blood and fling them down into the depths of the valley. And the lumps flung down pick up great numbers of diamonds, which become embedded in the flesh. Now it so happens that these mountains are inhabited by a great many white eagles...[which] swoop and seize the lumps and carry them off. The men observe attentively where the eagles go, and as soon as they see that a bird has alighted and is swallowing the flesh, they rush to the spot as fast as they can. Scared by their sudden approach, the eagles fly away, leaving the flesh behind. And when they get hold of it, they find diamonds in plenty embedded in it...

What on earth persuaded him that this story was accurate?

Kerala's next trading 'partner', if that is a possible description in this case, brought the wheel round full circle, for it was a European nation, Portugal, which would soon rule the waves. Spain and Portugal led the European age of discovery, and to prevent these two great Catholic Empires from clashing, the Pope ruled that the Spaniards could colonise the Western hemisphere and the Portuguese the eastern. This left Spain free to ravage most of South and Central America, while the Portuguese were only allowed Brazil. So it was imperative that their sailors and navigators found a sea route to the east. And the leader in this enterprise was Vasco da Gama, and his first ally in the east was the Raja of Cochi.

CHAPTER TWENTY-SEVEN

KOCHI, QUEEN OF THE ARABIAN SEA

'...the opening of the shutters let in...the dust and the tumult of boats in Cochin harbour, the horns of freighters and tugboat chugs, the fishermen's dirty jokes and the throb of their jellyfish stings, the sunlight as sharp as a knife, the heat that could choke you like a damp cloth pulled tightly around your head, the calls of floating hawkers...'
Salman Rushdie, *The Moor's Last Sigh.*

Modern Kochi

Kochi [Cochin is its Anglicised version] was one of the great spice-exporting ports at the time that the Portuguese arrived in India at the end of the fifteenth century. It is now one of the biggest attractions for tourists in Kerala, and is known as 'The Queen of the Arabian Sea' and 'The Venice of the East'. It's still famous for its spices, and for its Chinese fishing nets and Jewish, Dutch and Portuguese architecture. But it has also become an important industrial centre. The city has a population of about 600,000, less than half of whom are Hindus, and with the very high proportion of 35% Christians - a legacy of the Portuguese occupation. It is part of a conurbation including Ernakulam and Eloor which is the largest in Kerala, and which has the characteristic urban problems of pollution and traffic congestion. The latter is being tackled imaginatively by a rapid transit overhead railway. In photographs it looks amazing, another symbol of the new India unrecognisable to anyone who has not visited the country in the last few years.[i]

Kochi fishing nets

Information Technology is an important engine of growth of the economy and there are a number of new industrial parks as well as the government-built 'Info Centre'. One of the biggest employers has been FACT [Fertilisers And Chemicals Travancore] where Raju works. Raju, his wife Geetha and their daughter Keerthana [or Kitty] also live in the firm's housing complex, in Udyogamandal. The accommodation is rented, but Raju built a house on the family land in Trikkandiyur, which he planned to use in his retirement, though he now owns a modern flat in Ernakulum too: how our Indian family has prospered in the last twenty years! The FACT housing estate is a good place to live - clean [although the reports of air pollution caused by the chemical works worry us rather] and peaceful with good schools, little traffic and lots of greenery.

---

[i] My nephew Raju is not so impressed as I am. He says it consists of 3 coaches and he's not sure how far it will ease traffic congestion, but it has of course changed the face of his beloved Kochi.

Raju has been at FACT all his working life since graduating as an engineer, and he is still friendly with his colleagues - his 'batch' - who graduated and joined the firm at the same time. He married Geetha in 1993 and we went to the grand marriage ceremony at Aluva, Geetha's home town.

Kochi certainly has lots of history, especially since 1341 when it succeeded Muziris [now Kodungallur] as Kerala's major port. A flood deposited silt at the entrance to the ancient harbour at Muziris in that year, effectively closing it off for ever, but at the same time, produced the conditions for a better harbour further south at Kochi. The city's sights illustrate its history very well.

It was spices that made the city rich and you can still see and visit warehouses filled with locally grown pepper and cardamom, and other exotic products awaiting export. Then there are reminders of the Far East connection, especially the fascinating fishing nets, which are used nowhere else outside China. The *Insight Guide to South India* describes in detail the way in which the nets operate. The whole contraption is constructed on decks built on wooden supports at the water's edge, and the net is tied to poles and lowered and raised into and out of the water using various weights and balances. Especially when viewed against the background of the orange-red setting sun, it is a truly exotic sight. The clay storage jars you can see in the city are also of Chinese style, and the turned-up roofs of some buildings may have Chinese origins.

One of the curiosities of the era of the rajahs is the Veliyatta Parambil temple, which stands on Vypeen Island. Trial by Ordeal was practised in this temple from the twelfth century right up to two hundred years ago. Ordeal by water involved the accused having to swim across the temple pond, the problem being that it was full of crocodiles. To survive ordeal by fire or poison one had to dip one's fingers into a jar of boiling oil or one containing a poisonous snake without ill effect and the worst of all must have been the hanging test. Brahmins however had the rather painless 'ordeal' of merely being weighed, then having a list of their alleged wrongdoings tied on to them. If their weight then increased they were pronounced guilty, but might only be ostracised or fined, whereas members of other castes could be put to death even for relatively minor offences.

The Portuguese were the first people from the west to come to Kochi, in 1500. They settled in the area now called Fort Kochi and a number of buildings remain as memorials to their occupation. The leader of the first Portuguese expedition was Vasco da Gama and his house survives, as does the church of St Francis [possibly the oldest in India] where he was buried. There were Christians in Kochi long before the Portuguese arrived, possibly converted by St Thomas, Christ's disciple, but the Jesuits wanted them to be absorbed into the Roman Catholic Church. The Thomas Christians tied themselves to the still-surviving Coonen Cross in protest.

Jews once played a big part in Kochi's prosperity, acting as soldiers and above all successful merchants, but now they've nearly all left. Their synagogue still stands in Jew Town, though, and is a very interesting place. The building is full of glitter inside. There are gold crowns, crystal chandeliers and brass columns. The ancient copper plates on which are written the grants made to the Jews by the Kochi rajahs are stored there and the 45-foot clock tower has numerals in Hebrew, Latin, Malayalam and Arabic. The floor of the synagogue is covered with blue ceramic tiles from China about which there are many spooky stories: it is said that the pictures change to represent the continuing history of the Jewish community, and that those in the know can read the future in the tiles. Jew Town still thrives, but now only as a tourist centre.

The Dutch period is represented by Mattancherry or the 'Dutch Palace', and by Bolghatty Palace, now a hotel. The Mattancherry Palace was in fact built by the Portuguese, but modified by the Dutch in the seventeenth century. It is a wonderful place to visit, though not especially impressive from outside. Only the upper of the two floors is open to the public and this is reached by a flight of steps. They are rather steep and on a hot day, I almost persuaded myself not to bother to attempt the climb. But I was glad I had done once we got inside, partly because the wood panelling made the rooms seem cool, even though I was not allowed to sit on the inviting chairs, which were either exhibits or reserved for staff. There are lots of the rajahs' possessions including palanquins and weapons, ceremonial clothes and furniture. And there are some wonderful traditional Kerala floors, looking like black marble but which *Webindia* tells us are made from 'a mixture of burnt coconut shells, charcoal, lime, plant juices and egg whites.'[173] But the best bits are perhaps the painted murals. There are portraits of the rajahs of Kochi, and scenes from the *Puranas*, the *Mahabharata* and the *Ramayana.* The king's bedroom is the most heavily decorated. It has a low ceiling and on its walls are 48 paintings from the sixteenth century. Manga as always took a lot of time and showed great interest in everything in the Palace, but examined particularly carefully the paintings of scenes from the *Krishna Lila,* which she translated as 'the playful acts of Krishna'. The paintings are described by *Webindia* as follows: 'a cheerful God Krishna using his six hands and two feet to engage in foreplay with eight happy milkmaids'.[174]

The British influence is perhaps best illustrated by Marine Drive and Willingdon Island, the latter made from sand dredged from the harbour, enabling the port to provide shelter and harbour facilities for the largest ships. Prior to that, Logan said, it had 'failed to come up to the requirements of modern trade in the matter of harbour accommodation for the large ocean-going steamers now used'.[175] It had nonetheless been of importance as 'the centre of an immense area of rich country, tapped in all directions by inland waters and navigable creeks...' Willingdon Island became both a major naval and air force base during the war, and after independence the aerodrome was converted into a civilian airport. The new international airport is now on the mainland. It is modern, clean, cool and efficient, but has lost its old character. You can't buy cheap Indian whisky with names like Bagpiper, Royal Challenge and Officers' Choice; or Nilgiri tea direct from the hills packed in wooden boxes; or glass bangles. The island has some of the best hotels in Kochi [and one of the worst, if the cockroach-ridden place in which we stayed with Rika and Frank still stands!] and many important office buildings.

We've been to Kochi quite a few times. The first time I remember stopping there was to search for a shop that stocked film for my camera - such things were difficult to find in India in those days - and we bought a huge bag of cashew nuts. I'm afraid we'd never be able to afford so many cashews at today's prices; on the other hand, film became very much cheaper as time went by. I think I'd prefer the exotic to be cheap and technology to be expensive, but then I don't live there. Once we arrived by boat. There is a ferry service from Ernakulam and we sailed through the backwaters picking up and setting down passengers at jetties looking just like bus stops. One of the oddest places we've visited is the Mangalavanam Bird

Sanctuary. It is right in the middle of the city next to the High Court, and herein lay its problem. Knowing how much we loved birdwatching, Raju took us there one year. It is basically quite a small area of mangroves in a shallow tidal lake, home to up to 40 species, but above all it is a quiet and fresh oasis in the noisy and polluted desert of Kochi city. The Warden said visitors were not allowed because it was the breeding season but Raju managed to persuade him that we were serious students and so he let us in. It was dusk and we saw communities of large bats hanging in the trees as well as numbers of Little Cormorant and Black-crowned Night Heron. On the way out, Raju asked the young warden why he was looking so glum. He replied that the Reserve would disappear soon: the High Court wanted more room for car parking and what the High Court wanted, the High Court got. Manga wanted to know what he was going to do about it, and he shrugged his shoulders. 'What can I do' he replied dolefully. Manga got rather cross and told him he would certainly lose his Reserve if he just stood around looking miserable. He could ask the lawyers in the Court to stand up against it. Didn't they enjoy coming to watch the birds as a relaxation in their busy and stressful days? And were there not environmental and birding groups in the City that could be mobilised? A few months later, Raju sent us a cutting from *The Hindu* , dateline Kochi, Jan 29 and headlined 'Eco- activists take pledge to protect Mangalavanam'. It read: '*Environmentalists today pledged to protect the Mangalavanam Bird Sanctuary against encroachments including the proposed construction of a parking bay at its buffer zone for the High Court building...The widespread protest against the proposed parking lot symbolises the growing concern of the common man for protecting water sources, fresh air and the right to live...*' And a month later, another cutting arrived with the headline, 'Lawyers' Plea': '*A memorandum signed by 73 lawyers of the Kerala High Court, has urged the Chief Justice to drop the proposal to convert the buffer zone of Mangalavanam, a bird sanctuary, into a car parking slot for the High Court complex.*' And in August a year later, the paper carried news of a development plan for the Sanctuary that would be included in the City Plan. Mangalavanam is now in the forefront of people's minds and will not be taken over by stealth. It has also become an integral part of the City's tourist programme.

CHAPTER TWENTY-EIGHT

KOZHIKODE, GATEWAY TO MALABAR

'*How can a man with no clothes use a clothes line*?' Malayalam proverb

At the start of the next era in Kerala history, the town of Kozhikode took centre stage. Following the collapse of the Kulashekhara Empire, no new unifying force emerged and the region divided into small groups of villages called Nadus. They had existed before as part of the Empire's administrative structure, but now they became independent. The names of four of the Nadus are worth noting: Kochi is one of them and we've already read about that city. The others are Kozhikode, Kolathandu and Venad..

Kolathandu was ruled by the Kolathiri rajahs. Its major port was Mount Deli or Ezhimala often the first land seen by sailors coming from Arabia. An ancient lighthouse, now maintained by the Indian Navy, still stands on the hill. Kolathandu fell in due course under the control of Kozhikode.

Venad [modern Travancore] grew prosperous as a result of overseas trade through the port of Kollam. The descendants of the last Kulashekhara ruled Venad and their most famous rajah, Ravi Varma, who ruled from 1299 to 1314, occupied Madurai and declared himself King of South India. Venad's power did not however survive Ravi Varma's death. Somewhat confusingly, another Ravi Varma was on the throne of Venad at the time of the arrival of the Portuguese in 1498. But he was of little consequence. The centre of attention on the day in May on which the Portuguese fleet hove into view on the western horizon was Kozhikode.

The state website, *Kerala.com,* says the town had always attracted travellers because of its 'charming physical features and prosperity' and goes on to say that the glory of Kozhikode has not faded to this day. One traveller who was not particularly impressed however was a *New Internationalist* correspondent who described her arrival in the town thus: '...the bus dips down into a hot, traffic-jammed bowl called Calicut.[i] The dust, pollution and spasmodically overpowering drainage problems come as a shock...'

A working beach at Kozhikode

I think we would have recognised the latter description rather than the former on our first visit to Kozhikode in 1979. Although we as always enjoyed the train journey to the city, especially as we passed the centre of the Kerala tile trade at Feroze, with its huge kilns which always reminded me of miniature Mayan temples, I certainly can't remember our being greatly impressed on our arrival. Kozhikode seemed to us to lack anything in the way of spectacular buildings [we missed the interesting mosques and houses with their tiered roofs in the main square], elegant avenues, attractive suburbs or even characterful slums.

It was a very hot day and we decided to walk down to the seaside in the hope of a refreshing dip. Indi and Laksh aged seven at the time were carried for most of the distance by Raju and his friend Prem. Victoria, Grandma and I were not so lucky and soon fell some way behind. When we finally reached the sea, we did not sadly find a classic golden strand fringed by nodding palm trees and with clear blue water lapping at our feet.

---

[i] Calicut is the Anglicised version of Kozhikode of course, Kozhikode being a word that it's hard to get one's tongue round. Calico [a plain cotton fabric] is named after the city.

No, it was more of a working beach. We were of course very interested to see the 'country' fishing boats pulled up onto the sand and to appreciate their rugged rough-hewn charm; and to note the larger ocean-going ships beyond them moored by the old Victorian jetties, but somehow we didn't feel disposed to swim among them. The beach was if truth be told a bit grubby. I fear that Grandma was bitten by a particularly hungry species of sand fly, which set her scratching for much of the rest of the holiday. We understood where the local was coming from when he said that lots of tourists came to Kozhikode, but *'they stay one night, see there is nothing for them and move on'*. On later visits however we became increasingly fond of the town. There's a good park with people selling ice creams [which like good tourists we never bought], and savoury snacks [which we did eat and enjoy], and, when we were there, an enormous number of students. The town is an important centre for education. Raju went there to study chemistry at the Malabar Christian College and even more famous are the Engineering College and the Medical School. Everyone seems very friendly and Raju says the taxi drivers are very trustworthy, which, he maintains, is not the case everywhere. During one visit, we were tempted to give the main shopping street a miss when we read that it was called 'Sweat Meat Street', but from the prevalence of shops selling local halwa we realised that there was a typing error somewhere. And we were glad we had taken the risk because we came across some really good quality postcards in the days when such things were very hard to come by. Then Victoria found a little shop selling metal toys. The best were tin-plate boats powered by a candle and we know they worked because one subsequently sailed successfully across Rob and Juliema's garden pond. The bookshop had a good atlas and a history of Kerala written by a local professor T.K.Gangadharan, and the first supermarket we had been into in Kerala was there: quite a novelty at the time.

Also there *are* good beaches. Kappad where Vasco da Gama landed is a little way out of town but well worth the ten-mile bus ride along the bumpy Kannur road and the walk along a track to the sea. There is a small and unobtrusive monument to the Portuguese adventurer [why would they want anything big and glossy anyway? - he hardly proved to be a welcome guest]. The swimming is excellent and made much more fun as the sea is shared with fishermen throwing their nets skilfully into the water. And there used to be a splendid little café selling tea and all sorts of mouth-watering goodies. However the whole sea-front has now been developed for tourists.

The Kadalundi Bird Sanctuary is nearby, with its unusual visitors, grulls, trens and whimberels. No, not exotic tropical sea-birds but the tourist guide's typewriter slipping up again. Other places to visit on our next trip are the Krishna Menon museum, including, apparently, as well as memorabilia from the great statesman's life, paintings by yet a third rajah Ravi Varma, a very highly thought of artist of the late nineteenth century who was a prince of the Royal Family of Travancore. Manga is very fond of his pictures. The Planetarium and fun-sounding Science museum should be worth seeing too, as well as the planned eco- tourism project should it be completed.

The Portuguese were not attracted to Kozhikode by such delights however. For them, Kozhikode offered opportunities for profitable trade in the most desirable of products - spices - and, according to reports they had received, a friendly welcome for visitors. And this was in addition to the equally desirable opportunities to save souls by converting the population to Roman Catholicism.

The Zamorin was the most influential king on the south west coast. His dynasty had started by becoming the leaders of Ernad, a small Nadu that had fought its neighbours for years to obtain an outlet to the sea. There they had built a fort and founded Kozhikode [koyil = palace, kodu = fortified], and became known by the respectful title of Swami Thirippad, which changed over the years to Samuthiri, or, as the Europeans pronounced it, Zamorin. In a series of battles with other local Nadus, the Samuthiri rajahs took control of Thirunavaya, which was symbolically important as the venue of the Mamankom festival, during which, according to legend, the Perumal, or King of Kerala, had been elected every 12 years. They built a fort at Ponnani and soon dominated the whole of the Kerala coast north of Kochi. So on May 18th 1498 it was Rajah Manivikraman, the Zamorin of Kozhikode who welcomed Vasco da Gama to India.

It is fascinating to read from the official ship's log how da Gama described the people of Kozhikode at that time. '*The city of Calicut is inhabited by Christians.* [He thought the Hindus must be

Christians since they were evidently not Muslims or Jews, and he knew of no other religions].

> They are of tawny complexion. Some have big beards and long hair, whilst others clip their hair short or shave their head, merely allowing a tuft to remain on the crown as a sign they are Christians [!]. They also wear moustaches. They pierce their ears and wear much gold in them. They go naked to the waist, cover their lower limbs with very fine cotton. But it is only the most respectable who do this, for the others manage as best they can. The women of this country, as a rule, are ugly and of small stature. They wear necklaces of gold, numerous bracelets round their arms, and rings set with precious stones on their toes. All these people are well disposed and apparently of mild temper. At first sight they seem covetous and ignorant.[176]

Most neutral observers would I think be more inclined to ascribe these last two adjectives to the Portuguese themselves. And their taste must really be called into question already, even allowing for my partiality: they were the first, and probably only, visitors to Kerala to describe the women as 'ugly'. Not a good start to Indo-Portuguese relations!

But let's accompany da Gama a little further on his journey through Kozhikode.

> The road was crowded with a multitude anxious to see us' [Well, that rings a bell!]. 'Even the women came out of their houses with their children to follow us. They took us to a large church [actually it was a temple] and this is what we saw. The body of the church is as large as a monastery, all built of hewn stone and covered with tiles. At the main entrance rises a pillar of bronze as high as a mast on the top of which was perched a bird, apparently a cock [probably Garuda]. In the centre of the body of the church rose a chapel, all built of hewn stone, with a bronze door and stone steps leading up to it [sounds like the sanctum]. Within this sanctuary stood a small image which they said represented Our Lady [presumably Devi]. Along the walls by the main entrance hung seven small bells. In this church the captain major said his prayers, and we with him.

Amusing to think of da Gama praying to Devi!

> We did not go within the chapel, for it is the custom that only certain servants of the church, called quafees [evidently Brahmin priests] should enter. These quafees wore some threads over the left shoulder and under the right arm [the sacred thread of course] as our deacons wear the stole. They threw holy water over us, and gave us some white earth, which the Christians of this country are in the habit of putting on their foreheads...Many other saints were painted on the walls of the church, wearing crowns. They were painted variously with teeth protruding an inch from the mouth, and four or five arms...[177]

And in the next chapter we'll see how the Portuguese behaved after that first curious day.

CHAPTER TWENTY-NINE

VASCO DA GAMA PAYS A VISIT [THE PORTUGUESE 1498 - 1663]

'Inwardly malicious, but pious outwardly' Malayalam proverb

'To choose to sail in the middle of the sixteenth century from Lisbon to Goa... in a creaking carrack... presupposed an excessive zeal for one of two things: money or God' - Stephen Batchelor, *The Awakening of the West'*

Vasco da Gama's capital - Old Goa

The story of Portugal's attempted colonisation of South India is well-known. Vasco da Gama arrived at Kozhikode in May 1498 after a voyage lasting for 316 days. He was welcomed by the king of Kozhikode, known as the Zamorin, but fell out with him when he refused to give the Portuguese a monopoly of trading rights. The Portuguese then decamped to Kochi where the rajah was more accommodating [and not so powerful] and an era of military struggle and intrigue among the local rajahs, the Portuguese, French, British and Dutch ensued, ending with the British East India Company on top.

At first it must have seemed from the Indian viewpoint that Vasco da Gama was just another merchant eager to make his fortune and incidentally add to that of the Zamorin and his people through trade and barter. But in fact the Portuguese were very different from those who had come before, from Romans to Chinese, Greeks to Arabs, Venetians to Jews. Not only had they discovered an all-sea route to the East but they had come with a different agenda. They were for example acting partly in response to a Papal bull which urged all 'Christian Princes' to find out new countries and to bring their sad and deluded peoples into God's fold. The Portuguese were given the Eastern Hemisphere to explore and after Bartholomew Diaz had found a way to Asia round the Cape of Good Hope, Vasco da Gama soon followed, in search of 'Christians and spices'.[178]

The Muslim merchants and seamen were hostile to the Portuguese from the start. Since the decline of the Venetians, and the Chinese retreat into their own waters, most of the spice trade had been in Muslim hands, and they were never going to welcome a rival. The local Muslims had been important allies of Kozhikode in its defeat of the other Kerala Nadus, and so the Zamorin didn't take kindly to the Portuguese either. But to make it more unlikely that the Zamorin and the Europeans would become friendly, the Muslim merchants bribed government officials to treat da Gama with disrespect, to keep him waiting, mislead him about meetings and so on - the idea being to try da Gama's patience and make him go away or behave badly. The Portuguese did not help themselves, for the goods they had brought for barter were it is generally reported 'rubbish, and scanty even with that'. Though the gifts brought for the Zamorin himself sound quite appropriate if they were indeed as listed by Logan: a piece of very fine scarlet cloth, piece crimson velvet, piece yellow satin, chair with brocade of much nap studded with silver gilt nails, cushion of crimson satin with tassels of gold thread, cushion of red satin for the feet, a hand basin chased and gilt with ewer, a very large and splendid gilt mirror, fifty scarlet caps with buttons and tassels of crimson twisted silk and gold thread, fifty Flanders knives with ivory handles and gilt sheaths. [179] The presents were apparently all wrapped in napkins and all in very good order. Although I guess it might seem paltry enough if one were used to receiving as presents elephants, maidens and solid gold chariots, as the Zamorin was! Nonetheless some sort of trade was eventually performed before da Gama left Kozhikode on 4th November 1498. He called in on his way home at Cannanore

[Kannur], where the Kolattiri rajah, who was supposed to be loyal to the Zamorin, presented gifts, sympathised with the poor treatment the Portuguese had received at the hands of the Zamorin and in general ingratiated himself with them. Da Gama finally left India on 20th November. His voyage home was a disaster, and by the time he landed again in Portugal, he had lost at least half of his crews including his brother Paulo. Neither had he brought home much in the way of riches. However, he was fortunate in his timing, because there had been wars in the Mediterranean, which had interrupted the supply of pepper, so it had become very expensive. The king could see that da Gama had opened up a new opportunity for trade and welcomed him as a hero. And indeed all the spice from the Indies soon came by the sea route, by-passing the Mediterranean ports and driving great medieval powers like Venice into obscurity.

The next fleet to leave Portugal was well prepared for trouble. Its leader Cabral was under orders to have 'the Moors' banished from the Zamorin's kingdom and to establish a factory [trading post] by fair means if possible but otherwise 'to carry fire and sword into the country'.[180] Also, the fleet was blessed by the Bishop of Visen and included five Franciscan Friars. Cabral arrived in Kozhikode in September 1500. The Zamorin allowed him to establish a factory but refused to exclude the Arabs, and argument soon turned to violence. It's not clear who exactly started the inevitable killing or what was the precise reason, and no doubt both sides were at fault. But Logan says that Cabral, though 'protesting that truth and honour were alike unknown' in Kozhikode, was 'perfectly regardless of the sacrifice of human life, being quite ready to slaughter Moors and Nairs indiscriminately, with or without provocation...'[181] Not surprisingly he failed to carry out any trade with the Zamorin and sailed south down the coast to Kochi. The rajah was as we have seen antagonistic to the Zamorin, and saw the Portuguese as possible allies, so he was happy to engage in trade as a first step, and as a result, Cabral was able to return to Portugal with a substantial profit.

Da Gama led the next voyage to the east and it was obvious that the Portuguese had colonisation in mind, because one of the passengers bore the title Viceroy for the Estadio da India. On this expedition, da Gama seems to have displayed 'unscrupulous might and great cruelty' according to the *Catholic Encyclopaedia*.[182] Logan says that da Gama's acts against any ally of the Zamorin were 'those of a fiend in human form over which it is well to draw a veil'.[183] Other historians are less sensitive and described in lurid detail the appalling savagery which was characteristic of da Gama's expedition. During his campaign against largely unarmed Arab trading vessels, he came across a ship with pilgrims on board returning from a journey to Mecca. Da Gama captured the ship and set it alight. There were some 400 men, women and children aboard and da Gama kept the fire blazing until all of them were burned to death. He then captured a group of fishermen working off Kozhikode, cut off their limbs and threw them into the sea so that their bodies floated in to the shore and to their awaiting families. It is not, incidentally, in the writings of their enemies that these atrocities are detailed but in those of the torturers themselves.[184] The Portuguese seem to have been proud of their cruelty. Keay muses on this in his book *The Spice Route*. 'It was as they say a brutal age especially where religion was concerned...the Dutch, Spanish and British no less than the Portuguese delighted in casual mutilation and took torture for granted...'[185] The Portuguese seem to have been special though in that their victims were innocent civilians with no involvement in any war.

During his voyage da Gama effectively established the Rajah of Kochi as a Portuguese puppet and made a favourable treaty with the Rajah of Kollam. Both kings were pleased to welcome the Portuguese as allies against the Zamorin - the pattern of European invaders taking advantage of local feuds was taking shape. And the Portuguese viceroy, Francisco de Almeida, built at Kochi the first European fort in India. Portugal seemed well on the way towards establishing colonial government in Kerala.

Only Kozhikode stood in their way. The two powers were at war for most of the sixteenth century, broken only by occasional strategic withdrawals and treaties. The Zamorins were surprisingly successful in these conflicts, partly at least due to the support they received from the Muslim fleet, in particular from a clan known as the Kunjali Marrakkars. These sailors have been described as the first freedom fighters against European colonialists; or as mere pirates; or as opportunists seeking an independent Muslim kingdom on the west coast.[i] But there is little doubt that by their harassment of the Portuguese ships they stood as a major obstacle to the Europeans' ambitions.[186] There is a small museum dedicated to the Kunjalis in a hut in Quilandy near Kottikal. Inside there is a dusty collection of sixteenth century weaponry. The equally dusty retainer who looks after the museum told us that his family had been serving the Kunjalis for twenty generations. He had no time for the revisionist historians who claim that his masters were not patriots, or were not Malabar Mappilas, but came from Coramandel [on the east coast] or even Cairo. '*Not that anyone seems to care these days*' he added. '*You are the first visitors we have had here for more than a week. Yet if it were not for the Kunjalis, we could still be slaves of the Portuguese*'. I hope that the old man lived long enough to see the postage stamp issued by the Indian government in the year 2000, which commemorated the achievements of the Kunjalis. The three-rupee stamp shows a small boat with seven oars a side and two flimsy sails. These vessels were used by the Kunjalis to make surprise attacks on Portuguese shipping: they could hide in the shallow backwaters, attack the enemy ships and slip quickly back out of sight.

Between 1506 and 1508, Kozhikode seemed to be gaining the upper hand in the struggle against the European invaders. Together with his allies the Sultan of Bijapur and the Sultan's trading partner the Sultan of Cairo, the Zamorin kept up an attack on the Portuguese ships, and in 1508 inflicted a heavy defeat on them at the Battle of Chaul, at which the Viceroy's son, Laurenco Almeida, was killed. That however was a high point for Kozhikode. A year later, the Portuguese hit back, defeating the Zamorin's navy at the Battle of Diu and driving the Sultans away for good.

The Portuguese now effectively controlled the whole of India's south-west coast from Gujarat to Kollam. They built forts all along the coast including one at Chaliyum at the mouth of the river Beypore, only a few miles south of Kozhikode. They were not much bothered by the Zamorin any longer, though the Kunjalis continued to be an irritant: the Portuguese responded by sacking Ponnani, their home port, from time to time. They later managed to drive a wedge between the Zamorin and the Kunjalis, which led to the defeat of the

---

[i] According to the founder of the CPI[Marxist] A.K.Gopalan, only 'imperialist historians' describe the kunjalis as pirates.

latter and the execution of their leader. The Viceroy then moved his headquarters from Kochi to Goa, which had been taken from the Bijapur Sultanate in 1510. Diu, Daman and Vasai [Bassein] also fell to the Portuguese in the early years of the century. And the Portuguese were still in Goa, Diu and Daman over four hundred and fifty years later: it was not until 1961 that the Indian government regained its territory from the colonial power - and even then Nehru was criticised in the west for sending the Indian army in to drive the reluctant Portuguese away!

Panaji, the capital of Goa, still has some resemblance to a city in southern Europe. The streets are lined with trees, and the houses and churches are similar to those in Spain and Portugal, while the local language, Konkani, still has a few Portuguese words. I suppose the territory is most famous in the west as a holiday resort - at first in the mid 1970s as venue for hippies, and by the 1990s for mainstream tourists. It always saddens us that Europeans can spend a holiday in a resort like the exclusive Taj Village in Goa that provides food, drink, entertainment and its own beach and have no need to venture into town at all. They very probably will never see any Indians except servants. And those servants previously possibly tended the land on which the hotel was built, and fished from its now exclusive beach. And of course most of the money spent by the visitors will not go towards helping the dispossessed but into the hands of foreign investors. I have to admit that we stayed in a bungalow in the Taj village during our tour with Rosemary and Tony. We included Goa in our itinerary in preference to Mumbai largely to provide some rest and relaxation especially for the younger members of the party and they did indeed enjoy the resort's famous beaches. The rest of us paid a visit to the town, called in on some relations and took a trip out to Velha [Old] Goa, about 5 miles inland from Panaji. Old Goa is now a really odd place. It was always extraordinary. In the sixteenth century the Portuguese built a number of massive churches, cathedrals, monasteries and convents, and travellers reported that the city was one of the greatest in the world. Then the area was struck by epidemics of malaria and cholera, and most of the survivors moved to the coast. By 1990 Old Goa had declined to a village, and an almost deserted one at that, with huge white buildings from a foreign land towering above it. The *Insiders Guide to India* describes it well as a 'Christian Angkor Wat'.

The churches are undeniably magnificent. The Basilica of Bom Jesus completed in 1604 is the largest. Inside is the body of St Francis Xavier, contained in a silver and glass casket, so that his skull and feet can be seen. Very close by is the Church of St Catherine, a majestic building inside which the air and stone is so cool that I can testify that on a scorching hot day, the temptation to lie down on the bare floor is irresistible. And neither can one easily avoid lingering under the sprays of water that keep the lawns around the church a vivid green even in the middle of summer.

Vasai Fort [also known as Bassein] is another poignant reminder of Portuguese rule. The fort, which was built originally by Bahadur Shah, the Sultan of Gujarat, is about 35 miles from the centre of Mumbai. The Sultan had scarcely completed the Fort before it was captured by the Portuguese, who re-built and expanded the fortifications, so that they could contain a substantial settlement. You can climb onto the walls and can see how strategically important the site was: it overlooks a dock at the mouth of a nearby creek and defends both the access to Thane and to the islands of Mumbai to the south. The massive walls are still imposing, but decaying, and there are demands that the Archaeological Survey of India take over the site and save its buildings. No doubt that would be the correct thing to do, but for me, it would spoil the mystery of the place, which we have enjoyed on several occasions. Our first exploration took place during our trip to India with my mother. Our stay in Mumbai at that time was the first experience of India for her as well as for Victoria, Lakshmi and Indira, and was quite an eye opener. We all had a wonderful time and the newcomers showed considerable sang-froid when faced by outside toilets, open drains and numerous rats. The mosquitoes caused them most grief I think. The journey to the fort by putt-putt was a bit scary, but peace if not quiet ruled after we went through its great gates. Swifts swooped and soared, shrieking shrilly as they chased airborne insects around the fort's romantic ruins; brightly coloured flowers stood in for curtains at gaping windows; trees and bushes, their roots sunk into crumbling walls, displayed their blossom where flags might have flown in earlier days. Grandma identified the birds as house swifts; there is an entry on the appropriate page of our copy of Salim Ali's *Book of Indian Birds* that reads '*seen, and heard, Vasai, 2.XII.79*' in her unmistakable handwriting.

Vasai Fort

On later visits we explored further and found the remains of at least three churches and other public buildings within the walls. The nave of one of the churches was being used for cricket practice. '*The tombstones in the floor make a nice true wicket*' said one batsman after a sweet off-drive ricocheted into the bushes off one of the carved columns. We found mysterious staircases leading to watchtowers or roof gardens, clearances in the untended grounds used for drying fishing nets, and cellars and stone huts with suspiciously new-looking doors. '*The place is still a centre of smuggling*' my nephew Ramani told us. '*The authorities turn a blind eye*'. On one particularly hot day we drank from an old well, taking the precaution of filtering the water first, and it was notably sweet and refreshing.

Portugal remained in virtually total control of trade with Kerala throughout the sixteenth century, although Kozhikode's fleet continued to be a thorn in their side. There were harbingers of collapse though: the arrival of the first British mariner on the coast [Ralph Fitch] in 1588; the foundation of the Dutch East India Company in 1594; the formation of the British East India Company in 1600 and the building of its first factory [at Surat] in 1612; and the Zamorin's treaty with the Dutch in 1604. The ruler of Kozhikode preferred the Dutch to the Portuguese because they were only in India for trade and tried [not always successfully] to keep out of local politics. The Dutch practised religious toleration and also made no attempt to stop the Arabs from trading. They did inevitably come into contact with the Portuguese of course, and after various battles finally defeated them in 1663, when Kochi fell.

The Portuguese occupation has generally had a rather bad press, but some good did come from their brief visit. The Canadian historian, Woodcock, points out that they encouraged systematic and scientific farming and discovered new uses for coconut fibre. [187] They also introduced new crops to the region - a better strain of coconut [from Africa], papaya, pineapples and cashew nuts [Paragi Maru, which means Frankish Mango] - town planning and attractive public buildings. The Portuguese were free from racial prejudice and as in Brazil for example, encouraged colonists to marry local women. It is uncertain however whether in this instance miscegenation is evidence of racial tolerance or simply a practical policy to increase the number of pro-Portuguese inhabitants. And one unfortunate policy of the Portuguese was the cultivation of cash crops for export at the expense of food for home consumption. Already by 1600, Keralans were having to buy rice from outside its boundaries. Ralph Fitch, an early English traveller noted in 1583 that food was scarce - 'for here grow neither corn nor rice, the greater part cometh from Bengala'.[188]

Whatever their long term legacy, the Portuguese too often showed themselves to be cruel and arrogant rulers during the time that they dominated Kerala, and when they finally left the country , driven out by the Dutch in 1663, they did so largely unloved and unlamented.[189]

CHAPTER THIRTY

THE IYERS MOVE SOUTH

'If there is no-one else, then give me a Pattar. If there is nothing else to eat, then give me Tal[i] - Malayalam proverb

'It remains only to add that ideas, as well as armies, swept south, south, south from the northern heights...' - Salman Rushdie, *Midnight's Children*

The Iyers are relatively recent immigrants into Kerala. They came from Tamilnad, but were not native to that state either, having migrated from the north over many centuries. As they made their way south, caste rules notwithstanding, the Iyers' genes will have undergone plenty of mixing, and plenty of the people they came across will have adopted the beliefs, occupations and life-styles of the immigrants. And many of the northerners themselves will have decided to stop travelling and to settle down long before they got as far as Tamilnad. Two things are certain – one, that Manga's ancestors once lived in the north of India and central Asia [which is not to say that this applies to all Iyers]; and, two, there are no clues to indicate that the ethnicity of these people has survived: in the south today you will seek in vain for tall, fair 'Aryan' Iyers, standing out from smaller, darker, native Dravidians.

The Iyers as far as is known were little different from other Brahmins: they were priests, and experts in the rituals essential to successful worship. They probably arrived in Tamilnad before 300 AD [they are mentioned in Sangam literature], where they met the need for religious leadership. Manga's ancestors earned their name - probably a version of arya or ayya, from the Sanskrit, or the old Tamil Iyya, meaning 'respected person', because of their learning and particularly their understanding of those most important skills for priests – astronomy and astrology.

Migration continued on and off over the years, its volume depending upon things like the extent of persecution of Brahmins

---

[i] We think this might be sesame seed, not a very desirable foodstuff.

by invaders in the north, or when the confident and expanding southern empires of the Cholas and Vijayanagar sought out people well versed in Vedic ritual to grace and enlighten their court. There are now about two million Brahmin Iyers, most of them in Tamilnad.

Precisely when the Tamil Iyers first crossed the mountains into Kerala is uncertain. The Kerala Iyers website says that almost all the 'old famous families' [I don't think this includes ours] know their family histories up to 6 or 7 generations back, but in most cases all these forefathers lived in Kerala. The only exceptions are some isolated migrations in the last couple of centuries that don't represent a pattern. None of Manga's friends in Trikkandiyur seem to know the answer. Some are convinced that Iyers have been in Kerala for a thousand years, but can't point to any evidence for this; nor for the belief that the Iyer temples in the Kalpathy villages near Palakkad are 700 years old.

Kalpathy is a fascinating place. It is no surprise that migrating Iyers would have settled here, for the majority of them will certainly have found their way across the Western Ghats from Tamilnad through the Palakkad Gap, the easiest route by which to cross the mountains. What is amazing is that the settlement has survived as an Iyer stronghold for at least 500 years. An Iyer village is called a gramam or agraharam and no fewer than ninety-six of them were built in the Palakkad area by the immigrants. Sixteen are in Kalpathy. One of them is called Vaidyanthapuram, and since the year 2000 has been protected as a heritage site, so no alterations can be made to the street or the houses in it. So we'll always know what an Iyer village looked like: a long single street with a row of terraced houses on each side and a temple at each end. Each house has red tiles on its two-tier roof, one over the single-storey porch and entrance hall and another behind that, over the puja room and kitchen and the sleeping room and store above. We visited the village and its temples, dedicated to Ganapathy and Shiva, just before the annual *Ratholsavam* or 'car festival' when stone sculptures of the temples' gods are hauled round the villages in massive wooden chariots called therus. Worshippers throng into the street to try to help to pull the cars, while an elephant pushes from behind, and huge crowds watch the spectacle from the houses on either side. When we were there, the chariots were being prepared for the big day. An army of mainly young volunteers were cleaning, repairing and re-painting the theru in the pouring rain. They posed happily for Indi's camera.

Traditional Iyer houses at Kalpathy

It was in Kalpathy that the last rites for the father of Ravi, Raju and Radhi were held, as there are no longer any properly qualified Iyer priests nearer home. We went down to the river behind the Shiva temple to watch the water flow by and to think of Atimbear…

We missed the Kalpathy festival, but Raju has described the similar Kizhakkanchery theru for me.

'Ever since we got married, Geetha's brother-in-law has invited us for the theru in his village. As it falls on Christmas Day I can never get leave to go there. This year, as the plant was shut down, I got a chance of going. The theru, or chariot, is about fifteen feet high with huge wooden wheels and is pulled through the street by hundreds of devotees. Once it reaches one end of the street, food will be served. Never in my life have I eaten such delicious food. The menu is very simple. Sambar with big pieces of yam and pumpkin, as big as a cricket ball, no exaggeration, with olan made with pumpkin not

smaller in size, and an excellent gooseberry pickle. They use big spoons to serve the curry. I ate the curries with a little rice [boiled]. After feeding is over - it takes about four hours – the theru will be pulled back to its original position again, which marks the end of the procession.'

So to recap, Manga's ancestors came perhaps from Turkmenistan to the Ganges plain; thence to Tamilnad, and finally to Kerala, where they might have been living for anything between 100 and 1000 years. Why did they end up in God's Own Country? It might have been because they were invited to settle in Kerala by various rajahs. Iyers had a reputation of being bright, hard working and well educated, and though they weren't needed as priests in Kerala [the Namboodiris had that area buttoned up] they were sought after, according to *Keralaiyers* 'to promote priestly traditions'. Manga says that when she was young, Iyers were still needed to advise the Namboodiri priests on astrology and astronomy, such as when there would be an eclipse; this would no doubt be one of the priestly traditions referred to. And the Iyers' learning meant that they were also in demand for administrative and clerical posts.But the Iyers also came as merchants, trading particularly in cotton goods. Cotton was not, and is not grown in Kerala, so cotton cloth was bought in from Tamilnad, especially Madurai. Some of the Iyer merchants settled in Kerala. Another group of immigrants worked as plain manual workers[190]. They might well have come to Kerala when the Vijayanagar Empire met its sudden end in the 1560s, after which Muslims then ruled in Tanjore, and impoverished Brahmins suffering as a result of famine migrated across the mountains through the Palakkad Gap, in search of the free food available to Brahmins in Hindu-ruled countries. There were other famines in later centuries that also led to migrations.

There are also tales of rajahs who having argued with their Namboodiri priests, brought in Iyers to perform the rites and duties that the Namboodiris objected to. For example, a Palakkad rajah once fell in love with an Adivasi woman. When the Priests refused to carry out the marriage ceremony, the rajah turned to the Iyers. And similarly Iyers were prepared to absolve another rajah of his sins when the Namboodiris would not. The Tamils were rewarded with grants of land and jobs for coming to the aid of the kings. Namboodiris refused to cremate Adi Sankara's mother and one story says Sankara brought Iyers from Tanjore to undertake the task, and that they remained in Kerala. Thanchath Ezhuthachan, the father of the Malayalam language, also appears in stories about the migrations. Allegedly, he was impressed by the Iyers he met on a trip into Tamilnad and encouraged them to move into Kerala and settle. And finally, Iyer musicians from Tanjore were employed in the court of the music-loving Swati Thirunal, Rajah of Travancore; once more, some of them made Kerala their permanent home.

We do not of course know where in Tamilnad Manga's ancestors might have stayed. They are Vadamas, the most common sub-group of Kerala Iyers, but this does not necessarily help since it is uncertain whether the description Vadama, which probably comes from the Tamil word for 'north', should be taken to mean that they came from the north of Tamilnad, or the north of India, where the Sanskrit language and the rituals with which the Vadamas were adept originated. I'd like to think that they were living in Tanjore, centre of one of India's greatest Empires, and that would not be a bad assumption since more Iyers seem to have migrated from there than anywhere else. And there is a better reason for guessing that that's where my nephew's wife Geetha's family come from, because they [and incidentally in many cases their partners too] all seem to be excellent musicians.

There is a tradition that the Vadamas came direct into Kerala escaping from the armies of Alauddin Khilji as he invaded peninsula India in the fourteenth century. But either way, we might fairly conjecture that our ancestors paused for a while in Palakkad, where most did. Perhaps it was trade that led them to move west towards the coast or perhaps they were encouraged to do so because of their knowledge of religious ritual; and maybe they settled in Trikkandiyur because that is where their skills were needed or because the famous Shiva Temple promoted an aura of sanctity. We will never know precisely why, but settle they did, and became citizens of Kerala.

CHAPTER THIRTY-ONE

THE BRITISH ARE COMING 1600 – 1800

''Tis the sunset of life gives me mystical lore, / And coming events cast their shadows before .' Thomas Campbell [1777-1844], *Lochiel's Warning*

The Siva temple at Trikkandiyur.

The biggest Empire in India prior to that of the British was the Mughal Empire. The Mughals first invaded India from the north in 1505. They were led by Babur who was a descendant of Genghis Khan and Timur the Lame, also known as Tamburlaine. Successive Emperors conquered more and more of the sub-continent and nearly 90 per cent of India was under their control during the rule of Aurangzeb in 1658-1707, although they never conquered Kerala or attempted to. The first recorded British visitor to India, Thomas Stephens, arrived some twenty years after the accession of the mightiest of the Mughals, Akbar the Great, to the Imperial throne in 1556. Akbar was known for his religious tolerance and encouragement of the arts, and his policy was to make those he conquered feel part of his empire rather than defeated subjects. And in his time 'the average Indian peasant enjoyed a relatively higher income and lower taxation than his descendants ever would again'. [191]

Stephens seems to have been less tolerant, in that he was in India to take part in the Goan Inquisition. He appears briefly in the story of Ralph Fitch, the first Englishman to land in Kerala.

Fitch was a London merchant who sailed in his ship the *Tyger* to the eastern Mediterranean in 1583, and whose first claim to fame is that his voyage is mentioned in Shakespeare. [The first witch in *Macbeth* says: 'Her husband's to Aleppo gone, master of the "*Tyger*"'. One might infer that the voyage was quite famous at the time]. From Aleppo, Fitch went on to modern Iraq where he visited places we now know all too well – Fallujah, Baghdad and Basra – before sailing down the Persian Gulf; only to be arrested by the Portuguese and imprisoned in Goa. Here Father Stephens intervened: it was he who stood surety for Fitch and his companions, and as a result they were able continue their journey, which included a visit to Akbar the Great, and proceeded along the Ganges and across the Bay of Bengal to Burma and Thailand. At length Fitch turned for home, landing en route in Bengal and, in 1588, in Kochi, and reaching London after many further adventures three years later.[192] He didn't have much of interest to say about Malabar even though he stayed there 8 months. '*Here groweth the pepper*' he says '*and it springeth up by a tree or a pole...all the inhabitants here have very little houses covered with the leaves of the coco-trees...The men be of reasonable stature; the women litle [sic]; all blacke with a cloth bound about their middle hanging down to their hammes... they have horrible great eares...*' Nothing new there, apart from the ears perhaps. He also grumbled that if he'd only arrived in Cochin 3 days earlier he could have '*found a passage to Goa presently*', and would not have had to stay in Malabar at all. Well he was coming towards the end of his travels and eager to get home I expect.[193]

Captain William Keeling was the first Englishman to come to Kerala for trade. He sailed under the auspices of the British East India Company, formed to foster commerce with India, and he landed in Kozhikode in 1615, signing a treaty with the Zamorin.[i] The latter was really only looking for military help against the Portuguese however, so not much trade in fact took place. Keeling was an interesting man. He was the first European to land on the Cocos Islands – Indeed they are officially known as the Cocos

---

[i] The treaty is reproduced in Day's *Land of the Perumals*

[Keeling] Islands to differentiate them from Cocos Island, off the coast of Costa Rica - and he carried a copy of the works of Shakespeare with him wherever he went, directing his ship's crew in on-board performances of *Hamlet* and *Richard II.*

The British East India Company had been formed in London in 1599; it received the Royal Charter a year later and in 1624 'was invested with the powers of Government'. But it achieved little until a treaty was signed with Portugal in 1635 giving the Company access into Portuguese ports. As a result, 'pepper was for the first time exported to England direct from Malabar'.[194] In the words of Gangadharan, 'their beginning was humble and cordial'.

Britain was not the only European nation interested in taking a share of Portugal's trade with Kerala. The Dutch East India Company came into being six years earlier than the English one and it had ten times as much money, and many more ships - heavily armed ones to boot. As far as Kerala was concerned, the great coup for the Dutch was their support for the right side in the war of succession for the crown of Kochi in 1661. As a result, they were able to drive the Portuguese out of this important port. The Dutch soon had bases at Kollam, Kodungallur and Kannur too, while the Portuguese no longer had a single settlement in the state. In addition the Dutch had signed treaties with the rulers of four important Nadus, and with the Kolathiri Rajah, the Rajah of Kannur and the Rani of Attingal. And Portugal's cause was not helped by what was happening in Europe either: King Philip of Spain had taken their throne, at the same time as the northern provinces of the Netherlands declared their independence from Spain.

Then there was France, but like Britain she had few footholds in Kerala at this time. The British were following the advice of Sir Thomas Roe, envoy to the Mughal court – '*War and trade are incompatible. Do not engage save at sea. Wars have been the beggaring of the Portuguese and have been an error too of the Dutch. Let this be the rule: if you will profit, take it at sea and in quiet trade; for it is incontrovertibly an error to affect garrisons and land wars in India*'.[ii] In truth, the English were so weak on the ground that they had no alternative but to follow this advice; as for the French, they,

---

[ii] This or something similar is 'often...quoted' [Watson *op cit* p.120], but I havent been able to discover the exact source

like the Danes who had a settlement in Tranquebar on the Kaveri estuary, were late arrivals, and were concentrating on the east coast and their headquarters at Pondicherry. The Zamorin remained the leading Indian ruler, claiming supremacy from 'the northernmost part of Malabar to the southernmost extremity of Travancore.'[195] However, his rule was probably little more than nominal: certainly the Rajah of Kochi was totally independent of him, and most other rajahs were effectively their own masters. The Zamorin was no longer the powerful individual who had welcomed Vasco da Gama to his shores in 1498.

This then was the situation in 1663. The Dutch were clearly in control in Kerala, though their interest was in trade rather than colonization, the Indian rulers were divided, and other European countries were minor players. In the rest of India, the Mughal Empire remained dominant and the Emperor seemed unworried by the activities of the Europeans. But the balance of power soon began to change again. The Dutch were possibly more interested in their colonies in the East Indies than those in India. They also began to make enemies in Kochi by interfering too closely in the government [they appointed a chief minister to 'advise' the rajah without his consent], and they fell out with the Zamorin too.

In their *History of India,* Kulke and Rothermund have some interesting things to say about international maritime trade at this time. They point out that the Dutch Company's huge fleet, which had helped them in gaining the upper hand in Kerala, began to prove rather cumbersome and was expensive to maintain.[196] Meanwhile the British Company had adopted the method of leasing ships from private individuals, which meant it could more easily cope with fluctuations in trade, and the profits that could be made by these private merchants led them to develop highly specialised vessels and to attract a group of enterprising sea captains who shared in the profits of their voyages. The French still concentrated for the most part on the east coast, but their leader Francois Martin was outstanding. It was 'only due to the quiet endeavour of one man, that the French East India Company gained a foothold in India at all' declare Kulke and Rothermund.[197] Martin arrived in India in 1668 and stayed in the country until his death in 1706. Meanwhile, the Mughal Empire was showing signs of beginning to decay, doing nothing to prevent new independent powers from beginning to arise, for example in Mysore and Travancore.

In spite of the fact that the British and Dutch were rivals in India, and the fact that that there were several Anglo-Dutch wars in Europe, the struggle between the two powers in Kerala was an economic rather than a military one. In 1680 for example, according to Logan, the Dutch began seriously to consider destroying some of their forts, or even selling them back to Portugal! The garrisons were becoming so expensive to maintain that the whole profitability of the Dutch East India Company was under threat.[198] And they were drawn into another expensive conflict when the Zamorin attacked Kochi. He was beaten off but the Dutch decided never again to get involved in 'native wars'. This was in accordance with Roe's advice to early British adventurers, but the fact is that without help from local kings, traders could not establish themselves in the country, and if they did not support the ambitions of local rulers, such help would not be forthcoming.

Meanwhile, the English Company was beginning to grow, although it was not helped by the British decision to start a war against the Mughal Empire in 1686, the end result of which was that the Company was expelled by Aurungazeb from its headquarters at Hooghly in Bengal[iii]. However they had already built their first factory[iv] in Kerala [1693] at Anjengo [now Anchuthengu] in Travancore, on land granted by the Rani of Attingal. The Rani is said to have agreed to the lease of land because she had fallen in love with an English agent.[199] But unlike the Dutch and Portuguese, the British, again influenced by the wise Sir Thomas, did not fill the fort with costly soldiery and armaments and did not withdraw from the community. Sir Thomas Roe: 'The Portuguese, notwithstanding their many rich residences, are beggared by the keeping of soldiers...they never made advantage of the Indies since they defended them...It has also been an error of the Dutch who seek plantations here by the sword. They turn a wonderful stock; they possess some of the best, yet their dead pay

---

[iii] The Company was reduced to trading from a small village in the mudflats called Kalikata, or Calcutta by the British!

[iv] A factory was a centre for the export of goods and consisted of offices, warehouses, residences etc

consumes all the gain'.[200] Logan explains: 'they [the British] established manufactures; they attracted spinners and weavers and wealthy men to settle in their limits; the settlers were liberally treated and their religious prejudices were tolerated...no compulsory efforts were made to spread Christianity...'[201] No doubt all was not as rosy in the British settlements as Logan describes, but the Company's policy seems likely to have been one reason for the advance of their trade and the decline of that of their rivals.

In 1699, the Company opened another factory at Tellicherry in the north of Kerala. They would probably have preferred a base at Kozhikode but the Zamorin would not agree. He had had enough of Europeans on his doorstep! At Tellicherry, the company was faced by hostility from a local Nair chieftain. When the latter was defeated and gave up some land in the vicinity he did so in the following statement [translated from the Portuguese]: '*Having behaved ill towards the Honourable Company without any cause I cede and give the following as reparation...*' He then describes the land in question and concludes '*the said writing will undergo no change till the sun and moon last.*'[202] It was felt that a fort was needed in case of any future disagreements and one was offered by another chieftain. The treaty begins: 'To acknowledge the love and friendship that the Company bears towards me and my palace...'[203] It seems that the British were sought after allies at this time.

The French began their attempt to exploit the wealth of Kerala rather late and it seems with less than overwhelming enthusiasm for the project. The Compagnie des Indes was not formed until 1664, and wealthy Frenchmen were reluctant to invest in the venture until an edict issued by Louis XIV assured them that it was socially acceptable for the nobility to be involved in trading with India. And their factory at Surat was described by a British observer [a Mr. Fryer] as '*better stored with monsieurs than cash; they live well, borrow money, and make a show*'[204]. Perhaps there's a touch of national stereotyping here, but it does produce a lovely image! In 1725, the French did however seize Mahe in a brilliant action led by Captain Labourdonnais.[v] Mahe was rather too close to Tellicherry for the peace of mind of the British. They tried to enrol

---

[v] According to C.P.Brown of the Madras Civil Service, Mahe was named for the Captain, one of whose Christian names was such. Previously the town was known as Mahi, or Mayyali in Malayalam.

the local rajah into helping them drive out the newcomers, but negotiations failed and soon it was the French who were receiving help. There were various confrontations until the home governments of the two countries demanded a ceasefire.

But the two Companies were soon at each other's throats again when the Seven Years War began in Europe [1754]. This time, Mahe was taken by the British and as a result, the French left Kerala alone, though they still remained a major player in the colonial drama elsewhere. Mahe incidentally still retains a French flavour. Three centuries after their departure, it is still the place to go to in Kerala to enjoy or purchase a good bottle of wine.

Travancore, in the south of Kerala, began to become important when Rajah Marthanda Varma ascended to the throne in 1729 at the age of 23. His victories included an important one against the Dutch in August 1741 when General De Lenoy was captured. De Lenoy's life was spared on condition that he led and trained the Travancore army, and he transformed it into a very efficient force. Marthanda's reputation became such that the leaders of other Nadus accepted his rule, and by the middle of the century his kingdom stretched right up to the city of Kochi. And Kochi came effectively under the control of Travancore after 1762 when at the request of the Kochi rajah, Marthanda drove the Zamorin out. He introduced a centralised administrative system, with taxes and a budget; built dams, canals, reservoirs and roads, and established a postal service. And he renovated the 8th century temple of Sri Padmanabha in Trivandrum and dedicated his kingdom to the god: a good move because it meant that opposing the king was the same as opposing Sri Padmanabha himself. Well is he known as 'The Maker of Modern Travancore'.

Meanwhile, further north, Mysore was also becoming a force to be reckoned with. When the future ruler of that state, Hyder Naik, was a boy, he told his mother that he would become a great soldier but that he would have a son who would be even greater and would drive the Ghoris [white men] out of India. From an early age he was interested in military affairs, and helped his brother who commanded a brigade in the Mysore Army. He also learned about modern fighting tactics by studying the methods of the great French general Dupleix, Governor of Pondicherry. Hyder's skill as a soldier was recognised by the Government and he was given a small command himself. After this, his strength grew so much that in twelve years time he became the effective ruler of Mysore, though he never called himself the rajah.

Hyder Ali as he was known was a clever politician too. His first aim was to conquer Malabar and he used the divisions and jealousies among the Malabar rulers to help him achieve this. Gangadharan says that the Naduvazhis would accept help from anyone – foreigners, potential conquerors, anyone – to support them against their neighbours.[205] So, Hyder was invited to assist the Rajah of Kannur against the Kolathiri, and the Palakkad Rajah against the Zamorin - who on his defeat committed suicide by burning down his palace with himself inside - and became before long the boss of Malabar.

Now he had his first clash with the British. The East India Company in Chennai was becoming a bit envious of colleagues in the north of India who under the leadership of Robert Clive were making themselves rich and powerful by taking over territory – the whole of Bengal in fact. So, when The Nizam of Hyderabad suggested an alliance against Mysore, the East India Company's officers in Chennai saw that such a venture might open up a chance for them to conquer and rule too, and the first of four Mysore Wars began in 1767. Keay and others say that this was the way in which the British conquest of India progressed[vi]. It wasn't necessarily premeditated. 'The four Mysore wars, the three Maratha wars, the two Sikh wars, not to mention a host of lesser campaigns, hint at piecemeal policies and uncoordinated direction...yet a pattern of conquest, a progression of arms, does emerge'.[206] In this case however, the Nizam changed sides and the British were beaten back, suffering their first defeat at the hands of an Indian army, in no small measure due to Hyder's generalship.

By the terms of the peace treaty of 1769, the British agreed to come to the aid of Mysore should she be attacked. So, when the Maratha army moved into Mysore from central India a year or two later, Hyder called for British aid, as he himself returned from the fighting in Malabar. But Hyder's pleas were ignored; and his

---

[vi] I particularly like Jonah Blank's description of how the British gradually took over the governing of Awadh: 'Year after year the British had to be bought off with chunks of sovereignty, slices of privilege, parcels of land...' *Arrow of the Blue-Skinned God* (Grove Press, 2000)

dormant hatred of the British was awakened, and he swore vengeance. The opportunity came in 1780 when the French and British started fighting again. Hyder joined the French side and his son Tipu Sultan defeated the British at the battle of Polilur [near Kanchipuram], thereby at least in part realising his father's prophesy. This was perhaps the biggest victory by Indians over any British force. Apparently Tipu used rockets to great effect, making them with iron shafts instead of bamboo as had been the practice previously, and tipping them with sword blades. It must have been extremely frightening for the British troops to look up and see swirling swords descending on them when the enemy was over a mile distant! This successful engagement didn't lead to very much, however. According to one historian of the British conquest, Sir Penderel Moon, all that followed was four years of 'profitless and uninteresting war' before the Peace of Mangalore in 1784 largely restored the status quo ante bellum.[207] Tipu, who had become the ruler of Mysore two years before on the death of Hyder, was disappointed with the outcome of the war, even though the British felt humiliated by having to agree a treaty at all, and, in spite of both sides officially swearing perpetual peace and friendship, each secretly determined to destroy the other at the first opportunity. Tipu's plan was to work towards an alliance with France.

Tipu Sultan is an interesting and controversial character. To some historians and to my nephew Raju, he is a great patriot, one of the first Indians who stood up to the British and who was at least their equal, militarily and in the arts of diplomacy and good government. To others he was a warrior for Islam, a champion of the faith, a successful saviour of souls through the many non-believers that he converted. And to a third group he is nothing but a brutal murderer of innocents, and a scourge of Hinduism who would stop at nothing to attain his goal, to be conqueror of South India.

Tipu was born near to Bangalore around 1750 and grew up to share his father's hatred of the British and with an equal determination to drive them out of India. He fought against the British in the first Mysore War at the age of fifteen, and also in the first Anglo-Maratha War of 1775-9, and enjoyed great success in the second Mysore War. Tipu – now known as the Lion of Mysore – became ruler of his country in 1782 and signed the Treaty of Mangalore two years later. During the peace that followed, Tipu appointed Arshadbeg Khan to be Governor of Malabar. There were increases in land tax under Khan and as a result, a revolt among the local farmers, reaching its height in 1785-6, under Kurrikkal, the leader of the Mappilas. Tipu had to return to Malabar in person to crush the revolt, which he did with some difficulty, and had to come back again a year later before the local Muslims and their allies the Nairs of Kozhikode could be suppressed. The rebels had been helped by the rajah of Travancore, and Tipu demanded that Travancore must be weakened by giving up their forts on the border of Kochi. Rajah Marthanda Varma's successor, after confirming that the British would back him up, refused. In fact, he lost the forts to Tipu, before the British intervened by attacking Mysore. Meanwhile the deposed rajahs of Malabar reclaimed their lost territories, receiving British aid in return for their acceptance of the overlordship of the East India Company. The Rajah of Kochi also acknowledged British supremacy, and Company forces captured the strategic forts of Palakkad, Vaipin and Kodungallur. Then Tipu was defeated in the Third Mysore War instigated by the Governor General Lord Cornwallis; and by the Treaty of Srirangapatnam, ceded Malabar to the British.

In spite of these reversals, Mysore remained a threat to the British and as late as 1798, Tipu was corresponding with Napoleon Bonaparte, who had landed troops in Egypt and was confident of throwing the East India Company out of India with the help of Mysore.[208] But the danger passed. Napoleon's fleet was defeated by Nelson at the battle of the Nile, and Hyderabad, in spite of Tipu's warnings about perfidious Albion, threw in its lot with the British. Richard Wellesley became Governor General, and in accordance with his policy of conquest and occupation, authorised a huge force of Europeans and Indians including ten battalions provided by the Nizam, and a large number of Marathas, to march against Mysore. Tipu was driven back into his fortress at Srirangapatnam. Tipu's fortress had been designed by the famous military architect Sebastien de Vauban[vii] and his soldiers were well trained by French officers, but the odds against the Mysoreans were overwhelming. The assault was led by a former prisoner of Tipu, General Baird; Arthur Wellesley, brother of the Governor General

---

[vii] Rika Staedtler points out that Vauban designed and built 'the perfect example' of a fort at Neu- Breisach in Germany; and also the defences for the city of Luxembourg.

and the future Lord Wellington, led a reserve battallion. The defenders fought bravely and Tipu died a hero's death, but the fort was captured and Srirangapatnam was sacked 'with an ardour which would not have disgraced Attila... and the settlement that followed left the British unchallenged throughout the peninsula'.[209]

Gangadharan argues that the Mysorean occupation had a substantial effect on Kerala society.[210] Tipu hated the caste system and tried to undermine it by ending the exemption from land tax hitherto enjoyed by the Namboodiris and the temples; and by ending the monopoly of the best jobs in the government and the army that had been held by the Nairs. In particular, Tipu despised the concept of untouchability. He wasn't able to get rid of this or other detested customs but he did shake the dominance and security of the Kerala elite. Tipu improved agriculture, industry, transport and trade. He had a number of major roads built, ended the European monopoly of trade and opened warehouses on the European pattern. Keay compares Tipu to the eighteenth century monarchs and landowners of the 'Age of Improvement' in Britain: introducing new crops and agricultural practices, establishing small-scale industry and the like.[211] In Tipu's case, this included the introduction of silk-worms, for example, and the manufacture of weapons so as to end dependence on unreliable external sources. The merchants of Palakkad were quoted as saying that the volume of trade in Tipu's time was much greater than it had been before he arrived or after he left.

It is hard of course to be sure whether Tipu was a merciless conqueror or a liberal reformer, and the answer as usual probably lies somewhere between the two extremes. Dr.Raja is perhaps typical of those who hate his memory. He wrote to the Minister for Information and Broadcasting, on May 23 1990 in the following terms: '*I am a member of the Zamorin's family...I am constrained to send this letter specifically with the intent to stop the telecasting by the Doordashan*[viii] *authorities of the proposed serial 'The Sword of Tipu Sultan'. The net result of the permission granted to telecast the serial would be to make out that Tipu Sultan was a great and benevolent martyr...a citadel of all virtues and good qualities...The average viewer would be left with the impression that Tipu Sultan*

[viii] The state-owned broadcasting company of India

was an ideal ruler especially when several deliberate and grave omissions [have been made] relating to the terrible and inhuman atrocities that were really perpetrated by Tipu Sultan during his infamous march into Malabar...

As a member of the Zamorin's family, my blood gets boiled even today when I hear the very mention of Tipu's name...' etc. etc. [212] [The programme went ahead nonetheless and was extremely popular.]

Even up to Manga's generation, recalcitrant Malabar children were threatened with Tipu, the embodiment of evil, rather as Napoleon was once used to frighten English children. It is indeed probable that some temples were destroyed and some unwilling conversions made; but that wasn't unusual in those days, and it is certain that Tipu did for example employ Hindus in important jobs in his administration. He himself probably exaggerated the extent to which conversions were made to ingratiate himself with other Islamic leaders; and British historians and observers will certainly have exaggerated any instance of cruelty in order to justify their conquest of Mysore. Whatever one's view is of his character, Tipu is for sure an extremely important figure in the story of Kerala.

CHAPTER THIRTY-TWO

MYSORE, CITY OF PALACES AND GARDENS

'*In Mysore it is easy to become enthusiastic...*' - Rosita Forbes, *India of the Princes*.

Mysore Palace, 1979. L to R, Victoria, Manga, Lakshmi, Mum.

Mysore is a lovely city and as it's just a day's journey across the mountains from Tirur, we've been there quite a lot.

Very different visits they were too. The first time was in 1967 when Manga and I stopped off on our way from Bihar to meet her family in Kerala. We arrived by train late in the evening and had no time to look round for a place to stay. We asked at the ticket office whether there was a decent hotel nearby. Manga speaks Kannada, the language of Mysore, a little, but it turned out that the clerk spoke English anyway. '*Why – there's the Retiring Room*', he volunteered. Thinking he was talking about the Waiting Room, I politely declined: both of us had had enough of sleeping rough. '*But it is a very fine room sir, very fine*'. Railway Retiring Rooms in India still exist and are, or were in the mid-sixties, like hotel rooms within the station building. There were only usually one or two first class rooms per station, mostly used by travelling Railway dignitaries, together with dormitories for 20 to 50 people. Luckily, the first class accommodation at Mysore was vacant. We went upstairs and found a large rather dark room, clean, and furnished with solid wooden furniture consisting of two comfortable, well-padded easy chairs, a coffee table, an enormous dark brown wardrobe which could have devoured the accoutrements of a small army, and a king-sized bed with a frame for a mosquito net; and all for a very small fee. The accommodation was so superior to anything else we had experienced in our permanently impecunious state that we were a little intimidated at first, but it wasn't too long before we adapted to our luxurious surroundings and greatly enjoyed our stay. The next morning our breakfast was idli and coconut chutney and excellent coffee in the station restaurant, and we set off for a busy day of sightseeing well rested and well fed. We stopped at the Nandi statue before climbing 1300 feet to the top of Chamundi Hill so Manga could say a prayer at the famous temple, and managed to fit in a short tour of the gorgeous Mysore Palace before spending the rest of the day at Brindavan Gardens beneath the Krishnarajah Sagar Dam. The Dam is surrounded by attractive flower-beds and bushes and I remember feeling cool and at peace. We bought a little wooden dancing doll from a young man who demonstrated it most effectively to us as we sat on some steps. I'm afraid I could never make the wretched toy work though! We had lunch in a Workers' Restaurant, a big room with trestle tables offering as much rice and vegetables as you could eat for five rupees. It was a great day, even though Manga's most abiding memory is of leaving her best silk sari in the Retiring Room.

Our second visit was nearly twelve years later, when we hired a Jeep and driver to take us from Trikkandiyur across the Ghats into Karnataka. It was quite a tight fit. That was the year of Grandma's visit, and in addition to Grandma herself, Manga and me, and the children, Raju came of course [although a young man of only eighteen, he led the expedition], and Ravi and Radhika, and at the last minute Rajam agreed to join the party. That made ten of us, for a six-seater. Then there was our luggage, and food for the day, which didn't mean a few sandwiches, but a simple though substantial meal. Rajam and Manikutty had risen early in the morning and prepared dahi-rice [rice with yoghurt] that was wrapped in coconut leaves and tied with cotton. Lemon pickle and mango pickle were carried in aluminium containers. Sometimes we took chapatis for our picnics, occasionally spread with my favourite jackfruit jam. (Manga and I lived off this delicious and quite nutritious fare for days as we returned to Tilaiya by train along the east coast via Kanniya Kumari following my first visit to Kerala). Victoria loved Indian food even then, but Laksh and Indi weren't particularly keen on rice and curry in those days so they had their own packs: pooris and Marmite [the latter brought from England] and tomatoes and oranges, and some malt biscuits. We stopped en route to buy a big bunch of bananas from a stall by the road; and then we saw a huge pile of green water melons, and stopped again to buy one. It was a very large specimen and cost such a very few paisa that we were rather sorry for the vendor: but as usual we were reminded that we should not pay over the odds as this would lead to the locals being charged higher prices and not everyone would be able to pay. I was never entirely persuaded of this, but we followed our hosts' advice of course. Raju chopped the melon into chunks for us and we happily slaked our thirst.

It was a wonderful drive. I remember at one stage seeing a road zigzagging up through the teak trees on the opposite side of the steep valley, with hairpin bends on the edges of precipices, and rather hoping that wasn't the road that we were going to have to take. Of course it was, but our driver and already our friend, Yousuf, was careful if not slow and we had few alarms and no excursions – certainly fewer alarms than the passengers in a bus must have had when its driver tried to overtake us on a tight bend. Once we had to stop for Grandma to examine the poinsettia and bougainvillea bushes by the roadside – she couldn't believe they were growing wild. We also saw a group of aboriginal people in one of the hill villages, their features quite different from those of other Malayalees.

The road took us across the Nilgiri Hills through Manjeri and Nilambur across the border into Tamilnad for a few miles and then into Karnataka and the Bandipur Wild Life Park. There was a large and slightly scary but rather exciting notice warning us that we were entering tiger country, and we kept our eyes peeled. Soon we came across a forest ranger and Raju asked him if we were likely to see any interesting animals. Raju translated his reply as '*Well not at this time of day certainly; and not close to the road. But at dawn and dusk, up in the hills where the travellers' bungalow is, there'd be a good chance of seeing something. The number of tigers here is on the increase – there are about 60 of them now, and we're really hopeful about the future.*' Sadly, the Ranger's optimism has not been justified. The Ranger also told Raju that elephants, gaur, chital and sambar were on the increase, and that there were a few of the rare sloth bears, and fearsome dhole or red dogs. Things were looking rosy but inevitably there were problems. An awful lot of domestic cattle grazed in the park and sometimes passed on diseases to the wild animals as well as causing clashes between villagers and the Rangers if predators killed any of their stock. And, rather like rhododendrons in English National Parks, lantanas were spreading. '*Useless plants*' said the Ranger. '*No animal will eat them. The only things that like them are the damned mosquitoes. They're ruining the place. And do you know who planted them here? Don't tell your friends, but it was the damned British*!'

As the ranger had predicted we saw no animals in the Reserve but enjoyed travelling through the forest, and before long we were in Mysore. As usual, our hotel was, if not the cheapest in the city, certainly in that range. Men in one room, women in the other, which was not to my taste, but it was clean. Anyway, we had a great time and visited all the main tourist attractions. We spent one morning around the hotel as Yousuf wouldn't take us out without Indi, who was going to stay back with Manga because she wasn't feeling well.

The third time we went to Mysore was during our trip with my sister Rosemary and her husband Tony and their family. Believe it or not, we stayed at the Lalitha Mahal. Allow me to quote from the Hotel's publicity leaflet. '*The Lalitha Mahal offers an experience of princely living in a real Maharajah's palace...it was built by the Maharajah to house his most important guests...it is a splendid Italianate palazzo double-columned and domed - set in sprawling terraced and landscaped gardens.*'

Lalitha Mahal Hotel

They're not wrong about its magnificence and impact. The palace rises above the city and its bright white dome can be seen for miles. Unfortunately I was in the middle of a major fever when we stayed there, the one that I contracted after grazing my foot while snorkelling in Kovalam. So while the rest of the family cooled off in the pool, I lay on my bed sweating so profusely that my bedsheets had to be changed hourly. Raju then took everybody off to see Chamundeswari Temple and the rather garish statue of the demon Mahishasura; and then the thirteenth century Hoysala temple at Somnathpur, half an hour's bus ride out of the city, before they all enjoyed sumptuous meals in the hotel, served by armies of flunkeys. Poor Manga had to stay with me. We were at the hotel on Easter Sunday and Victoria went off with Raju to buy sweets [instead of chocolate eggs], including of course Mysore Pak, and I was just well enough to enjoy them! I also recovered sufficiently by the end of our stay to visit with Tony the Railway Museum, one of the highlights of which was the Maharajah's railway carriage.

Statue of Nandi at Mysore; Manga, Julie and Doraikutty 2002

The last time we saw Mysore was in company with Doraikutty, Manga's cousin on her mother's side, a man we really loved. We had a wonderful time when he and his wife Parvathi came to England during his post-retirement world tour, and he was determined to show us everything when we made a return visit to his home in Bangalore. In one day we drove to Mysore and back and visited Srirangapatanam - which included a boat trip in a country-made coracle - the glittering Ambavilas Palace, the Temple, the massive carved Mysore Bull, the Dam and the Gardens next to it. Very sadly, it was the last time we saw DK before he died.

A few memories surviving across the years are of Victoria, Raju and I ascending Chamundi Hill by a flight of steps rather than the road. We lost count of how many steps there were but it must have been close on a thousand. I don't remember seeing the monkeys on that occasion, but they provided a lot of entertainment when we went with Doraikutty. On that occasion, we had a picnic lunch and watched the monkey families playing around the temple tank. A whirlwind blew up while we there and a score of colourful saris were whipped from their drying lines and blown skywards: it was as if a flock of peacocks had suddenly taken to the air or a display of silent fireworks set off for our delight. On our second visit, we temporarily lost Lakshmi and hurried back through the dazzling rooms of the Palace, to find her transfixed by the decorations on a massive golden door. And that was the year that Grandma's papaya was stolen from her hand by a passing cow outside Chamundeswari Temple.

CHAPTER THIRTY-THREE

A LOCAL HERO - THANCHATH EZHUTHACHAN

'The Hero can be Poet, Prophet, King, Priest, according to the kind of world he finds himself born into.' Thomas Carlyle 1795-1881

At about the same time as the first Briton arrived in India, there was born in Trikkandiyur a baby who became a very important person. This was Thanchath Ramanujan Ezhuthachan.[i]

Gateway to Thanjan Parambu, with Juliema, Radhi, and Manga

Thanchath is a really big name in Kerala history. You can't say that he actually invented the Malayalam language of course because it had been spoken for many centuries before Thanchath lived, but it was he who made it into a proper respected language. The booklet about Thanchath produced by the Thanchan Memorial Research Centre bemoans the absence of an 'authentic biography' of the great man. It is known though that he was born into an underprivileged caste and unusually for one who was not a priest, he studied the Vedas and the Upanishads and went on to

[i] Ezhuthachan means 'learned person, one who writes'

translate the epics into Malayalam, using a blend of Sanskrit and the local language. The booklet goes on:

> Ezhuthachan's accomplishment is distinguished not only for the excellence of his transcreations of the Ramayana and the Mahabharatha, but by the versatile talent which the whole achievement displays. In his hands Malayalam attained a remarkable simplicity, and proved to be an instrument capable of interpreting different moods and nuances of feeling; a language that is free and flowing and uncluttered by the verbosities of Sanskritised diction. His followers could not achieve his simplicity of style, that depth of expressing or breadth of vision... His poetry achieved a perfect integration of devotional sublimity and aesthetic sensibility. Ezhuthachan, regarded as the father of the Malayalam language is a veritable symbol of India's cultural heritage and emotional integration. [213]

Thanchath had a progressive effect on Kerala society because he made the epics and other great literature available directly to everyone, by-passing the Namboodiri Brahmins. Not only did Thanchath translate the works but his disciples copied the translations onto palmyra leaves, using an iron stylus, so that many people could have access to the works. Dr Burnell, a Victorian linguist said, 'The Sanskrit literature was after this [i.e. Thanchath's translations], no longer a secret and there was perhaps no part of South India where it was more studied [than in Kerala] by people of many castes during the eighteenth century'[214]. Our hero also broke the Namboodiris' stranglehold on education, opening a school where lower castes could study the Vedas, and was the first literary figure not only to criticise the caste system, but also do something about it. All this of course made him rather unpopular with the priests and according to the linguist F. W. Ellis, quoted by Logan, they are said to have 'seduced him by the arts of sorcery into the habit of ebriety [which I take to mean drunkenness], wishing to overshadow the mental powers that they feared.'[215] But he fared better than William Tyndale, who in some ways foreshadowed Thanchath by translating The Bible from Latin into English in Europe two centuries earlier. Tyndale was not only vilified for this act but also tried for heresy, 'strangled to death while tied to a stake and his dead body burned in ritualistic fashion.' [216]

Logan says of Thanchath, 'the site of his house is still pointed out at Trikkandiyur near Vetattpudiangali ...and as usual among Malayalees when a man has risen a bit above his fellows in good or in bad qualities, something of superstitious awe attaches to the place of his dwelling'.[217]

The Mandappam in Thanjan Parambu

Thanchath's birthplace is more than just 'pointed out' these days. When I first went to Thanchan Parambu [meaning Thanchath's compound] it was just an open area where literary functions took place and where children were introduced to the art of writing. A few years after that a large and imposing granite open pillared hall, or Mandapan, was built on the very site of Thanchath's house; and when we last visited there was an extremely impressive brick gateway, a study centre, library, museum and auditorium.

We almost always stroll down to Thanchan Parambu when we're in Trikkandiyur. We taste the fruit of the ancient kanjira tree *nux vomica* under which Thanchath would often rest and work. Normally kanjira tree leaves are very bitter but here, they taste sweet! We visit the pool where Thanchath bathed and wonder at the statue of the parrot that he allegedly taught to recite the *Ramayana.*

Incidentally, Manga's Mum had a parrot which used to call out '*Anikkum kulikanam*' ('I want a bath') when she went to wash, and '*Ponnukutti inge wa*' ('Come here Ponnukutti'). Ponnukutti means golden nugget – that was what Manga's Dad called his wife.

Thousands of children go with their parents to the Parambu to be initiated into education on Vidhyarambham Day. The Acharya, a sort of religious teacher, writes the words 'Hari Sri Ganapathaye Namaha' on the children's tongues with a golden ring. Later the children are guided to write the words in the sand with their forefingers. And I'm sure you'll be interested in the following extract from the Malayalam weekly *Mathru Bhumi,* dated Friday 15 October 1999:

> Tirur: Indira Clare Banner has written 'Hari Sri' in the sacred sand of Thanchan Parambu. She came to write her first letters in Malayalam under the Kanjira tree, the leaves of which never go bitter, only because of the love of her mother's language.
>
> Having been awarded a Ph.D. in biology in England, Indira is working temporarily in a bank. She has wanted to learn Malayalam for ten years and she recently wrote to her mother's sister, Parvathy-teacher. Parvathy-teacher told her she must follow the proper path, starting by writing in the sand in the temple of Thanchan, the father of the language and taking part in the special Brahmin festival of Navarathri, and seeing Boommakkolu. Without a second thought, she took leave from her job, and came to Tirur by herself. In case she was called back by the University, she could not wait till the end of the festival, so she started writing in the sand on Thursday.
>
> Indira's connection with Malayalam started in 1966. The story is that the youngest daughter of Parameswara of Trikkandiyur went to England to work as a nurse. There, her head nurse was Victoria [sic] and she had a son who was helping fight the famine that was raging in the state of Bihar. Victoria suggested that she might get in touch with her son when she returned to India, and the nurse did as she was bid. A friendship developed and in due course this led to marriage. Mangalam and Christopher (for those were their names) returned to England where they had three daughters. The first, Victoria, is a computer consultant currently employed in Kuwait; the second Lakshmi is a student of

> mass communication; and the third daughter is the Indira of whom we write.
>
> Because she is not yet familiar with the language, Indira is helped and accompanied on her outings by her cousin Ravi.
>
> When we met her, Indira was wearing a pink salwar kurta, glass bangles, flowers in her hair, and a bindi on her forehead and looked every inch an Indian girl. Not only that but she has been going round the alleys enjoying the festival.'

Sadly but not untypically, there was one reader who was not impressed by this story. '*Why was she not wearing a sari? Why was she wearing shoes*?' Oh well, you can't win them all over, especially in Malabar!

CHAPTER THIRTY-FOUR

THE TREES OF KERALA

'Orpheus with his flute made trees, / And the mountain tops that freeze, / Bow themselves when he did sing'. Shakespeare, Henry VIII.

William Logan describes Kerala's trees in a rather imaginative way – in the *Malabar Manual* , he takes a virtual journey from Kozhikode across the lowlands and foothills into the mountains on the Kerala/Mysore border, telling us about the trees he passes en route. This is a journey that our family has made quite often so I don't think it will be cheating if I follow him up the road a short distance but a hundred and twenty years behind. Logan was riding a horse, but we'll be driving a jeep.[218]

We start the journey close to the sea where the most conspicuous trees are the various types of palm. And I might say to the children:

'Look at those tall, graceful trees, swaying in the sea breeze. Don't their green fronds look picturesque against the deep blue of the sky? Why is the sky so blue here, did you say? – oh dear, not sure I'm afraid. We'll look it up when we get home. I think the group of trees on the edge of the paddy fields over there are areca nut palms; you know, their nuts are used in paan. You can recognise them because they're really thin and not all that tall, The trees in the forest are much taller. I think those will be Palmyra and Sago[i] palms. I reckon that some of them must be 100 feet high! They look a lot more substantial than the areca nuts too. There's one with a really thick trunk. Mum [ie Manga] says it's a kudu pana, what we call a talipot.[ii] You can see those amazing palmate leaves – they might be 15 feet across. Palmate means like the palm of your hand – the leaves come out separately from the base.

Oh. I don't know if the tree was called a palm because it looks like a hand. That's another thing to look up. Here's a bit of interesting

---

[i] Palmyra [borassus flabelliformis] Sago [caryota urens]

[ii] Corypha umbraculifera

information: the talipot only flowers once in its lifetime and then produces the biggest flower of any plant, and dies as soon as the fruits have formed. You can't really eat them but some people use them for flavouring gin. Yes, like sloe I suppose: we've done that haven't we? Now there's another tall tree but with quite a slim trunk. And at the top of the tree, the foliage makes a round shape. Can you make out the shape of the individual leaves? If they look like big fans, the tree will be a palmyra. Mum says that we've eaten the seeds of that tree – they're small and jelly-like, three or four of them in the round, brown fruit. Called nungu. The leaves were used for writing on before they had paper, and to make baskets, mats and roofs. In fact all of the tree can be used for something or other, and because it so valuable, it's the state tree of Tamilnad. I don't know what the state tree of Kerala is. O yes – must be coconut, you're right. And England? Erm, the oak I expect, if we have one. There's another palm that looks different. The leaves on most of the palms only sprout from the top of the tree– but on this one they're branching out from the trunk for some way down. That means it's a sago palm. Manga doesn't know why it's called that because the sago she ate came from the tapioca plant. Maybe that's just a Brahmin thing.I can't see it from here but the leaves are supposed to look like fish tails, and some people call the trees fish-tail palms. Mum says you can get jaggari from the sap.

We're coming to some houses now. What do you think the palms are in their gardens? Coconuts[iii] *of course. The tree is called keram in Malayalam and some say the state was named after the tree, though Mum says people spoke of the tenga tree, tenga being the name of the fruit. Anyway, the name Kerala existed before the coconut tree arrived.*

Oh from Africa I think. Just sailed across the sea - they float very well. About half India's coconuts are produced in Kerala. Around 60 feet tall [they can be bigger]. Curved trunk. Big green leaves like feathers. The proper word is pinnate. People say that coconuts are the most useful trees that there are. The nut gives you drink, which can be milk, water or toddy; and you can eat its flesh, fresh or cooked, ground or grated. I know, we seem to have it in most meals one way or another. The coir makes mats, ropes and baskets, and these days you can use it for potting compost

---

[iii] Cocus nucifera

instead of peat. Copra, the sun-dried flesh, can be made into coconut oil or mum used to feed it to her cows; and she likes eating it with jaggari. The husk is used like a flannel - we had some at home that we bought from the fair at Aluva - or you can burn it, and the shells can be burned too - or even made into containers. Manga didn't use them at home, but we did buy a tea-set made from coconut shells once: that was strictly for tourists of course! You can build with a coconut tree's trunk and its roots make dyes or medicine. Brooms, thatch, baskets and shelters can be made from the leaves. Also, it is used in Ayurvedic medicine 'for a variety of cures, from the treatment of burns and the restoration of hair growth, to the dissolving of kidney stones and treatments for the heart and blood pressure'.[219] No, sorry I don't know why it's called coconut. I did read somewhere that 'coco' means 'grinning face' in Portuguese, and Vasco da Gama's men thought that the three marks at the top of the fruit looked like a face. But coco also means ghost, and some people say that's what the hairy husk looks like. Nothing to do with the cocoa we drink anyway.'

At this point in the journey we have to slow down – the monsoon rains have washed away the road surface here. Too many of the trees that Logan saw on his journey over a century ago have been chopped down to make way for grand houses paid for by Gulf money - money sent home from the Gulf states by people working there - and the water pours down the hills uncontrolled. But there are still quite a lot of big old trees around. Mangoes - evergreens with stout, black branches, dense and dark, though the young leaves are pink before they go red and then dark green. And a thick and corky bark. In January they have small white flowers. Nearly 18 million tons of mangoes are picked every year in India, according to figures from 2013![220] Another evergreen in the forests is the jackfruit, a different shape altogether from the mango: taller and slimmer. It's another very valuable tree; so many are and it's a major tragedy that we are intent on destroying them so enthusiastically all over the world. The jackfruit is known for its timber, which, being termite proof is excellent for building, and making furniture. The fruit are the biggest in the world – they can be 3 feet long and weigh up to 100 lbs each according to Mrs D.V.Cowen.[221] That's not much less than Manga! You cook the fruit in curries but according to Mrs.Cowen, the smell puts off

Europeans. Not this one! One of my favourite things ever is Jackfruit Jam...I might have mentioned this before. Manga says you have to be careful when you're preparing jackfruit because the skin is spiky and also produces a very sticky latex. You have to cover your hands in oil or you'll never get them clean. The fruit gets its name from the Malayalam word chakka; the tree is pilavu in that language. One other thing – you won't see many growing close to rivers or paddy fields because the fruit won't be produced if the roots are in water.

We are now approaching the hills and the roads are lined with different trees. It's a pity it's not summer because many of them would look lovely in flower. That boring looking one with grey branches is a Poinciania Regia; alasippu in Malayalam. From April onwards it will be covered with feathery leaves and red or orange flowers. And the one next to it doesn't look up to much either – twisted branches, ragged leaves. But in summer, it will have been covered with pale green leaves and lavender flowers. It's called The Pride of India.[iv] I wish we could see that Indian Laburnum[v] in full bloom too; its flowers are much bigger and brighter than the English variety and it can grow to 40 feet. Logan praises its 'pendulous racemes of golden flowers and long dark brown legumes'.[222] The trees by the roadside are White Damor, resin from which is used as incense and in Ayurvedic medicine, and poongas. Poongas or Indian beeches seem set to become a very important trees in India. The oil has been used since ancient times for soap, lamp oil etc.; and might soon be an important bio-fuel. Also the tree is drought resistant. There are also banyans and peepals.[vi] You can't miss the banyan – the roots are in the air instead of under the ground! They wrap round each other till they look like tree trunks and just keep on spreading. Mrs Cowen says she's seen a picture of a whole village sheltering under the branches of a really big specimen. And she quotes Milton: *Branching so broad and long that in the ground/ The bending twigs take root and daughters grow/ About the mother tree, a pillared shade/ High over-arched with echoing walks between. Paradise Lost, Book 8.*

[iv] Lagerstroemia reginae

[v] Cassia fistula

[vi] Ficus indica and ficus religiosa respectively

The peepal is related to the banyan but it doesn't look anything like it. It is also a very holy tree as its botanical name implies. It's particularly revered by Hindus and Buddhists. The leaves are lovely, like big hearts and the tree can live for many centuries. We've sat beneath the famous bodhi tree in Bodh Gaya. The bodhi tree is a peepal, and strictly speaking the specimen at Bodh Gaya should be the only one that is so called, though other holy trees are sometimes given the same title.

As we climb higher into the mountains, we can find cashew nut trees[vii], maybe 30 feet tall. They're native to Brazil apparently, brought to Goa by the Portuguese. We drank feni while we were in Goa – that's an alcoholic drink made from the cashew fruit. Very thirst quenching, the fruit: we picked and ate some on a very hot day up near Kallil Temple. When she was little, Manga used to cut the fruit into small pieces and eat it with chilli, salt and a pinch of sugar, and it really packed a punch like horse-radish or the Chinese mustard leaves we grow in our garden in England. Unlike horse-radish etc., too much would make you tipsy! And the cashew is the best nut there is – external of course, so you can't mistake it for anything else. There's some lantana – just like we grow in our garden except bigger. There are no trees though; the laterite must be near the surface. Further up there's a casuarina, an evergreen between six and thirty-five metres high; katodi in Malayalam, which looks a bit like a conifer with a straight trunk and little cones. And there's some frangipani, and euphorbia like the ones in our garden, but they're shrubs really, and a cotton tree! There's one just like that outside Tirur station - tall and straight.

Let Logan take over for a bit at this point

> Growing in this fringe of jungle, the Cerbera odallum claims our attention with its green fruit, looking for all the world like mangoes but in fact deadly poisonous. This is the othalanga, or suicide tree.. It's been estimated that in a ten- year period at the end of the twentieth century over 500 people died from eating the fruit – on purpose or by accident ...[223]
>
> The mountains of the Western Ghats rise right before us clothed with forest from base to summit...we enter the forest. There to

---

[vii] Anacardium occidentale

our right is a timber depot...There are logs of all sizes. Ebony,[viii] Irool,[ix] Mutti,[x] Poomaraday[xi] and a few logs of red and white Cedar. All these will be floated down the little stream when it is in flood into the main stream at Kuttiyadi, and from there they will be rafted to Calicut.[224]

The forest has now grown denser; everywhere we see the quaint stems of Cycas circinalis, which is spared for the sake of the nuts it bears...they are green, and as large as a pigeon's egg; but one or two are golden- yellow,andmustberipe.[225]

Rubber trees

[viii] Ebony is a dense black wood that comes from a medium sized evergreen tree, a native of south India. It is threatened because of its value for making ornaments and as firewood – it will burn even when damp.

[ix] Very durable wood from the *xylia xylocarpa.*

[x] From a tall tree native to southwest India used in shipbuilding. *Terminalia tomentosa*

[xi] The word means 'flowering [poo] tree [mara]'. It is a type of terminalia – probably paniculata.

We haven't seen anywhere near all the important trees of Kerala on our journey, but we did see many rubber trees[xii] unlike Logan who wouldn't have spotted any, because they weren't introduced until 1902, after which the product was called India rubber in England. The plantations are not huge and are often parts of mixed orchards with areca nut and cashew. Coconut shells are often used as cups to catch the white latex as it seeps from the slashed bark. Our friend Ashok's father had rubber trees on his land in Kerala.

We must mention the economically important teak trees that dominate the roadside forests on the way to Thekkady, a town named after the tree, which is thekku in Malayalam. The teak is a tropical hardwood much grown in plantations because of its value for making furniture and use in house- and boat-building. The wood is full of natural oils that resist termites and weathering. The patriotic song '*Hearts of Oak are our ships, jolly tars are our men, / We always are ready, Steady, boys, steady,*' etc. was written in the eighteenth century about 'Our wonderful year' [1759] and is still the Royal Navy's official marching song; but in fact as the century proceeded, good quality oak was rapidly running out and the British navy increasingly relied on teak from Kerala [and particularly Burma] for their ships. So that when British sailors stood up to sing before the Battle of Trafalgar, the words that should have used were '*Hearts of Teak are our ships...*' Teak was used not only because of the over-exploitation of the alternative – 2000 oak logs were needed to build just one ship of the line – but also because teak was a greatly superior timber for building warships. Resistant to woodworm, a pest from which oak-built ships suffered a lot, as well as termites, it was also much less likely to splinter when struck by cannon balls – an extremely important property, as splinter wounds were common in naval warfare at the time. And teak lasts and lasts – teak beams allegedly 1000 years old can still be found in use![226]

So the British were very keen to develop teak plantations. And the very first of these is in our own Malappuram District – at Nilambur. 'Conolly's Plot', founded by the eponymous Collector of Malabar, in 1846, is in fact the oldest teak plantation in the world. A memorandum about the plantation written by another Collector, Athol MacGregor, M.C.S., is included in Appendix XXI of Logan's

---

[xii] *Havea brasilensius.* Introduced by the Dutch. Kerala is the biggest producer of rubber of all the Indian states

Malabar Manual. Mr.MacGregor starts by relating the problems Conolly experienced, firstly in getting the teak seeds to germinate - it seems to have taken 4 years to come across a foolproof method - and then in obtaining good sites for the plantations. The local landowners were not prepared to sell or lease land to the government, and MacGregor says that 'the plantations owed their existence to the accident that one of the many religious bodies holding temple lands happened to be in want of funds…'[227] Then some sites were found to be unhealthy, and others [laterite hills] unsuitable for planting. But the climate was ideal and communications were excellent, especially in the form of a navigable river to 'Calicut Bazaar, the best timber market on the west coast', and in the ten years after 1844, seedlings were planted on over 1000 acres of forest land.[228]

For the rest of his memorandum Mr.MacGregor writes in extraordinary detail of the costs and income involved in the operation, noting, for example, that weeding and hoeing round plants cost 2 rupees and 8 annas per acre, and thinnings of an average diameter of 2 to 3 inches, and an average length of 3 to 4 feet, could be sold for between 12 annas and 1 rupee 4 annas. The conclusion drawn after this exhaustive cost-benefit analysis was that 'it seems impossible to resist the conclusion that eventually the result of the plantations must be to contribute to the wants of the country an immense stock of useful material, realising such a revenue as fully to reimburse the state for their outlay even after compound interest for the unproductive period is allowed. This result must be deemed a satisfactory outcome of the exertions of Mr.Conolly…'[229] The Plot is now said to contain the oldest living teak tree, planted by Conolly's men and nearly 50 metres high: though I have heard recent reports that the tree is dying. On one of our most recent visits to India, we spent a very happy day with Ravi and his family at Nilambur, which has been very attractively developed for visitors. There was none of the sometimes charming but more often irritating shoddiness that might have characterized such a development in the past.

Another group of trees we can't ignore are those whose fruit is vital to the Malayalee diet, that is the trees that give us tamarind[xiii],

---

[xiii] Tamarindius Indica.

bananas,[xiv] drumsticks[xv] and papaya![xvi] The tamarind tree, vaalam puli in Malayalam, has seeds that are used of course to provide the sweet/sourness in sambar. It is a bushy single-trunked evergreen, shaped like a vase, with bright-green pinnate leaves, and is 40 to 60 feet high. The banana isn't really a tree at all, but a herb, and its fruit is officially a berry. You can't fail to recognise it - though most people are surprised to see the fruit growing 'upside down'. May I recommend Julia Morton's contribution to *Fruits of Warm Climates* for much fascinating detail about this plant?[230]

A drumstick tree in town

Manga reckons there are over 200 types of banana or plantain in India - the ones we mostly see are small sweet ones, fat red ones, 'ordinary' yellow ones, and big green ones to go into curries.

[xiv] *Musa balbisiania* is the wild variety of the banana, and has seeds. There are hundreds of cultivated ones; the one seen most often in the UK is the 'Cavendish' banana, valued for its lasting qualities rather than its taste. India produces 22 million tons of bananas a year, out of a total world production of 72 million tons [http://www.fao.org/docrep/007/y5102e/y5102e04.htm]

[xv] *Moringa oleifera;* muringa in Malayalam.

[xvi] *Carica papaya.* Omakka in Malayalam. A native of tropical America.

[Those for eating are called collectively warapazham by Manga, those you boil and eat for breakfast are called nandram pazham in Malayalam]. The drumstick is yet another candidate for Most Useful Plant. Wikipedia says it 'has potential to improve nutrition, boost food security, foster rural development, and support sustainable landcare'.[231] It's used as a medicine too. The tree is about 30 feet high, has weeping branches and a thin trunk. We, especially Indi, value it for its drumsticks, which are the immature bean pods. The luscious fruit of the papaya was my Mother's favourite. The tree looks a bit [though not much, come to think of it] like a giant Brussels sprout plant, 15 to 30 feet high.

Bananas growing upwards

Finally I must mention the old booklet we picked up in the Oxfam bookshop in Canterbury issued by the Chief of the General Staff in India, printed by the *Daily Post Press* in Bangalore, and distributed to army units in India during World War Two. Its purpose was 'to provide the individual soldier with some knowledge of jungle trees, so that he will be able to exist, if he should unfortunately be cut off from his supplies and companions...'[232] So, the bark and roots of *Barringtonia acutanglia* can be 'pounded and thrown into dammed up streams to intoxicate fish' so they can be caught easily.[233] The unripe fruit of the *Randia dumetorium* [madu karray in Tamil] can be used in the same way. The *Randia uliginosa* [or Tamilnadia] sounds very useful. The seeds can be roasted and eaten, rope can be made from the stem and the leaves used for thatching or plates! The fruit of the *Gmelina arborea* can be eaten and the wood used for making rafts; the *Dillneia indica* has similar properties. The *Cordia* is another good one: the wood can be used for raft making and as an excellent fuel; the bark makes rope; the fruit and kernel can be eaten and the pulp makes birdlime to catch birds. The persimmon – panicha in Malayalam - has edible fruit, the pulp of which when unripe makes a good glue, and has oily seeds that can be used as candles. I could go on. Trees or parts of them can be used as dyes, barbed wire, sources of drinking water, sails, flour, laxatives, stuffing [for pillows], caulk, floats, sleepers, bait. You'll need to read the booklet if you want more detail. I wonder how many of the trees can still be found today.

And last but not least, the lemon tree. Manga uses the leaves for cooking – and the thorns for piercing her own nose, and Victoria's ears, for rings! And Rosemary had her ears pierced with a lemon thorn, after numbing with the leaves of a type of basil, when she visited Kerala for Raju's wedding: there was no infection or problem at all [unlike her first piercing in England when a teenager] and Rosema says the holes remain patent to this day.

CHAPTER THIRTY-FIVE

THE BRITISH IN MALABAR

'The 180 years of British rule in India were just one of the unhappy interludes in her long history.' Nehru

'I think it would be a good idea.' Mahatma Gandhi, when asked what he thought of Western civilisation.

An enormous amount has been written about British Rule in India – The Raj, the Pax Britannia and so on – but most books concentrate on the north of the country. Less is known about the British in Kerala.

The first thing that the Honourable East India Company did after Malabar came under their control in 1792 was of course to review and assess their new territory. The Joint Commissioners [from the governments of Bombay and Bengal], described the province as disintegrated and shattered – very different from the wealthy and relatively settled region that had existed for centuries prior to the arrival first of the Europeans and then the Mysoreans. According to Woodcock, Malabar has remained [at least up to the time he was writing in 1967] 'the poorest and most restless region of Kerala' ever since.[234] Logan [who might not be the most impartial of historians in this case] says that the country was 'split into a number of kingdoms and principalities, a prey to the bigotry of its late Muhammedan conquerors, abandoned by its principal landowners, and distracted by the depredation and rapacity of the Mappila banditti'.[235] So, the British, in the guise of the East India Company, felt there was much to be done. The Company's priority of course was to raise revenue, and as a means to that end they needed to re-establish peace and order and prosperity. The following extract from the Governor-General's instructions to the Commissioners confirms this. It is only part of an extraordinarily long sentence.

> ...you shall enter into full investigation with a view to ascertain with as much accuracy as possible the general and particular situation of this Ceded country, in respect as well to its former as its late and present Governments, as far as may be requisite to enable

> you to point out in what manner justice has heretofore been and may in future be more advantageously administered to all classes of the natives, the nature of whose several tenures and more especially those of the Zamorin of Calicut and of the principal rajahs and Nayars and Mappilas throughout that and the other parts of the country are to be specified, accompanied with Estimates and statements, formed on the best materials you may be able to procure, of the amount of Revenue which these several districts are capable of paying; together with the particulars of their interior and foreign trade, on which subject you will form and report your opinion as to the best means of improving them both, in such manner as shall have the greatest tendency to conciliate the Commercial Interest of the Company with those of the natives, and best promote the internal prosperity of the Country at large.[236]

Note which common nouns are given capital first letters!

> The Governor General wisely adds later in his instructions: '... with a view to conciliate the native rajahs, Landowners and cultivators to the Company's Government, and encourage them to improve their respective districts and increase their productiveness, more especially by replanting the pepper vines wherever they have of late years been destroyed, their Burthen, that is, the revenue assessed on them, should in the beginning at least, be in general lighter than that exacted from them by Tipu...

Many landlords had escaped into Travancore when Tipu invaded. Now they returned and the company made separate agreements with them. The landlords were to be responsible for actual revenue collection, and they were to hand over to the company a fixed amount each year. Unfortunately, many of the returning chieftains persecuted the peasants, especially the Mappilas, whom they accused of supporting the Mysorean invaders. This led to many localised revolts among the Mappilas, and contributed to the first big rebellion against the British, led by the Hindu rajah of Kottayam, Kerala Varma Pazhassi. Pazhassi Raja had helped the British in their fight against Tipu on the understanding that his lands would be returned to him after the conflict. Instead, the British decided that his relation, the Kurmbranad Raja, should administer the region, since he seemed to be a more 'passive' ruler. Pazhassi found allies from among the tribesmen whose traditional way of life had been disrupted by British rules and regulations and they, together with Nairs and Mappilas, formed a strong army. They had a tough opponent though - Colonel Arthur Wellesley, the future Duke of Wellington, whom we met earlier playing a minor role in the defeat of Tipu Sultan. Other duties prevented Wellesley from leading the Company's forces but he planned the campaign. Pazhassi cleverly avoided open conflict and at first inflicted losses on the British through guerrilla warfare in his stronghold of Wayanad. The Company then imposed Military Rule in the province in 1803, put a price of 3,000 pagodas [a gold coin worth about 8 shillings] on Pazhassi's head and recruited 'loyal' natives, Kolkarans, into their army. In November 1805, Pazhassi was surprised and killed by soldiers under the command of the North Malabar sub-Collector Harvey Baber.

Mr Baber wrote a detailed and atmospheric account of the action to the Principal Collector. The significant moments he described as follows:

> After proceeding about a mile and a half through very high grass and thick teak forests, Cheran Subedar [Sergeant] who was leading the advanced party, suddenly halted, and beckoning to me, said that he had heard voices. I immediately ran to the spot and having advanced a few steps I saw distinctly to the left about ten persons, unsuspecting of danger on the banks of the nulla [a mountain stream] to our left. Although Captain Clapham and the sepoys, as well as the greater part of the Kolkars were in the rear, I still deemed it prudent to proceed, apprehensive lest we be discovered and all hopes of surprise thereby frustrated. I accordingly ordered the advance, which consisted of about thirty men, to dash on, which they did with great gallantry with Cheran Subedar at their head. In a moment the advance was in the midst of the enemy, fighting most bravely. The contest was but of short duration. Several of the rebels had fallen and a running fight was kept up with the rest ...I later learnt that the Pazhassi rajah was among those we had first seen and was among the first who had fallen. It fell to the lot of one of my cutcherry [law court] servants, Canara Menon, to arrest the flight of the rajah, which he did at the hazard of his life...and it is worthy of mention that this extraordinary personage, though in the moment of death, called out in the most dignified and

commanding manner to the Menon not to approach and defile his person...[237]

Pazhassi Raja's burial place, Mananthvadi, Wayanad.

After the raja's death and the capture of his leading supporters, resistance to the British faded and by 1806, the Pazhassi revolt had been completely crushed. Gangadharan comments that the revolt has particular significance since it was the 'first organised popular resistance against the British occupation in Kerala...'[238] and paved the way for future freedom fighters.

Wayanad is still a place of jungle and mountains and unspoilt corners. Tribal people still live in the remote hills and there are wild animal reserves that still reputedly are the home of tigers and other rare creatures. It's a place where one could walk and camp, and I guess one of these days might become quite popular with more adventurous tourists. We've been there twice; each time in a somewhat overcrowded jeep packed with food and jollity. On the first occasion, Victoria, Indira and Lakshmi were with us, as well as Raju, Rajam and Manikutty. We were bound for Tirunelli Temple, which is in the far north of Wayanad. Tirunelli is sometimes called the 'Kashi of the south' [Kashi, pronounced with a very soft *sh*, is another name for Varanasi]. That's because people go there to perform the last rites for their loved ones. So it is a very important temple and an impressive one too for those allowed inside. There are, Manga tells me, thirty columns of granite surrounding the shrine and the floor is made of huge granite paving slabs. And the idol of Vishnu is supposed to have been installed by Brahma himself. There is beauty outside the Temple too. The river that runs through the grounds is sparkling and cool and can, it is believed, wash away one's sins. The pools that occur along its route are therefore very popular with pilgrims.

We came across few pilgrims on this first visit back in the 1980s, though sadly the concentration of rubbish, especially the ubiquitous pink plastic bags and plastic teacups, showed that plenty of people had been there before.[i] I went with Raju to the upper stretches of the stream. He bathed, then apologised for the mess. 'We are not so advanced as you people' he said. 'We still throw things willy-nilly on the ground. In the old days when we used mud cups and paper packages it was OK to throw them away because they simply returned to the earth.' I told him that regrettably in England at least in the 'civilised' West there were plenty of people who littered the countryside wherever they went.

And when we came away from the favoured bathing ghat, the countryside took over again. We spotted plenty of birds including babblers, barbets, bee-eaters, and bulbuls to mention only the 'B's! There were lots of parakeets, mainly rose-ringed, but we thought we might have seen a blossom headed one as well. There is a bird-watching centre not far away but it takes a good hike to reach it. And we stumbled across a modest shrine hidden in the undergrowth. Manga thinks it might have been dedicated to Brahma. There was also a small café where we could get nothing more than a cup of tea, and a little shop where the children were delighted to find fridge magnets and stickers of the gods.

During the drive to Tirunelli, we spotted wild elephants in the jungle. We leapt from the jeep and walked carefully among the trees towards them. To our great delight we could see the little group clearly. They had a tiny baby with them and when they heard us coming, formed a protective circle around it. We managed to get close enough for Indi to take a good photo. We also saw chital [spotted

---

[i] In many parts of India, the sale of plastic bags is now prohibited

deer] and of course monkeys, and on the way back a big samba was caught in our headlights for a moment.

Manga's sisters at Tirunelli

We must have been lucky because we didn't see any wild animals on our second trip. This was in the new century. Manga's nephew Ramani, on leave from his job in Kuwait, was with us, together with his wife Pushpa, and their son Ritesh, as well as the Kerala family and my sister-in-law, Juliema. We hired a good-sized minibus and stopped off at Pookot Lake on the way, as we had during our first trip to the temple, and enjoyed boating and cups of tea. Raju helped the chai-wallah who was a bit overwhelmed by the number of people seeking his wares. The lake had become quite a tourist trap since we were last there – perhaps because one website says it has 'salacious weather' and 'hypnotising scenic beauty'. Not too sure about that; but it is pleasantly cool, especially on the water. On our first visit, Manga and I rowed round the lake; this time we were not allowed to – Health and Safety seemed to have reached the sub continent – and we either had to hire someone to take the oars, or alternatively, use a pedalo. We chose the latter, but it was hard work even when you got the knack, which some of our party never did! We saw a jacana or Jesus bird skipping along the water lily pads. It was very enjoyable.

We were in for a bit of a surprise when we arrived at Tirunelli. Instead of the temple being tucked away in the woods, it was surrounded by a swathe of new buildings – a substantial brick-built hotel, shops and meeting halls. However once into the temple grounds, peace was regained. We all had a bath in the river this time; I climbed a tree to collect wild figs ['Grandpa – be careful, you're not a jaiwan [young man] any longer'], and we found the overgrown shrine again.

There seem to be lots of good places to visit in Wayanad. The Pazhassi Raja's tomb is in Manathavady; although he led a revolt against them, the British buried him with full military honours. There is now a Tourist Resort there. The Eddakal Caves near Sulthan Bathery have Neolithic drawings on the wall. The Wayanad Wild Life Sanctuary has bison, wild cats, panthers, and tigers in addition to the elephants we saw, and the Muthunga Sanctuary has bear as well. At Koottamunda, there is the Glass Temple dedicated to a Jain saint, with mirrors reflecting wonderful patterns. There are lakes and waterfalls, islands and dams [including the largest earth dam in India] and rock climbs. Mount Chembra, the highest peak in Wayanad 'is a risky mountaineering endeavour'. I do wish we'd spent more time there.

Wayanad was also the centre of the second significant revolt against the British; significant because it was the first uprising of tribal people. Tribesmen had supported the Pazhassi Raja, and as a result had been subjected to tight control that interfered with their historical way of life. The last straw according to both Logan and Gangadharan was the ruling by the collector Thomas Warden that taxes had to be paid in cash. The Kuruchias and Kurumbras were used to paying taxes, but had always done so in kind. According to the clearly sympathetic Logan they were 'unable to find a market for their produce, and had to part with their grain at ruinous prices to pay the revenue'.[239] Failure to pay led to evictions and confiscations and harassment, and drove the tribal people to violent reaction. The Kuruchia Revolt began on 25 March 1812, and enjoyed some success even though the battles were between bows and arrows on one side and guns on the other. In the end, however, the Company was able to suppress the uprising in three months. The main opposition to British rule came from the Mappilas. There were isolated Mappila uprisings, mostly in south Malabar, throughout the nineteenth century – the British called them 'outrages' - mainly precipitated by land policy and taxes. Only five percent of the land was owned by Muslims and most members of that community were agricultural labourers or tenants of the Hindus. They were often subjected to high rents and oppression. The revolts were mainly aimed at the Jenmis [landowners] and were ruthlessly put down by the army and police.

An example quoted by Logan of one of the clashes between the Mappilas and the security forces is described here by Major Dennis of His Majesty's 94th Regiment based in Kannur. The encounter took place on the Great Western Road out of Kozhikode. '*Major Dennis drew up his men - 6 officers, 2 of whom were European, 9 naigues,*[ii] *2 buglers and 132 privates - in column of sections, right in front, so as to occupy the whole breadth of the road, when the enemy came on with the most desperate courage, throwing themselves on our bayonets; after firing off their matchlocks, they took to their war knives, swords and spears, and when struck down to the ground, renewed the fight even on their knees... I am happy to say that through the steadiness, correct and low firing of the men, our loss has not been so considerable as might have been expected...*' [240] The engagement left 64 Mappilas dead; on the British side, two privates were killed, and three others and a sergeant wounded; one officer received a deep flesh wound and Major Dennis himself experienced a near miss.

The Indian Mutiny, or Sepoy Revolt, or as it is often known in India, the First War of Independence, seems hardly to have caused a ripple in Kerala. Gangadharan mentions it not at all; Logan only very much in passing: in describing one of the 'outrages', he wrote: 'About the latter end of 1857, Puvadan Kunyappa Haji and seven other Mappilas of Ernad taluk, the hot-bed at that time of fanaticism and disaffection, were suspected of conspiring to revenge the supposed insult offered to their religion by the relapse of a Nair convert, and to make an attempt to rid the country of the Kafirs

---

[ii] The most junior NCO, equivalent to Corporal or Lance-Corporal

[Europeans], representing that the Government was weakened by the mutiny in Northern India'.[241] Nothing resulted from this. The conspirators were reported to the police and arrested.

But the Mappilas remained militant and the British, concerned to know why, commissioned a report from a Judge called Mr.T.L.Strange. Strange researched one particular incident and found that of those involved 'but fourteen [had] any personal cause of provocation; nine persons were instigated to engage in crime by others; and the remaining 144 were without any personal provocations whatever'. His solution was repression. Logan says, 'the policy advocated by Mr Strange has signally failed to fulfil what was expected of it.' And he goes on:

> Fanaticism of the violent type flourishes only upon sterile soil. When the people are poor and discontented, it flourishes apace. The grievous insecurity to which the working ryots [landless labourers] are exposed by the existing system of land tenure is undoubtedly largely to blame for the impoverished and discontented state of the peasantry, and a measure to protect the working ryot, of whatever class, is the means which seems to commend itself the most for the amelioration of their condition. With settled homesteads and an assured income ...it is certain that fanaticism would die a natural death.'[242]

Another example of Logan's generous spirit and love of Malabar and its peoples.

At this time, the land that is now known as Kerala was divided into three parts and of these only Malabar was under direct British rule, coming under the jurisdiction of the Madras Presidency. Travancore and Kochi were officially independent states ruled by their rajahs, but they were very much under the control of the British, who appointed 'Residents' to advise and monitor the rulers' actions. External affairs were totally the concern of the colonial power, and if he decided to, the Governor of Madras could at any time enforce his wishes concerning internal policy too. This was a pattern incidentally that occurred all over the sub-continent. Direct rule operated in the areas then known as Burma, in Bengal, Bihar and parts of Orissa; the United Provinces, Panjab and Lower Sind; Bombay, Madras and Ceylon. And rajas reigned if not ruled in Nepal, Kashmir, Baluchistan, Rajputana, Mysore and Hyderabad as well as in hundreds of minor princedoms.

The princely State of Kochi immediately to the south of Malabar consisted at this time of little more than the city and its surroundings. It had its own flag, three broad horizontal stripes of pink, yellow and pale blue [!], and its own currency: the 'chakra', Vishnu's weapon, the image of which appeared on its postage stamps. After the defeat of Tipu Sultan, the British inherited the suzerainty of the state, and the Company assessed the level of financial tribute to be paid and how much power the rajah could retain. In 1809, the treaty was revised, for the hereditary Chief Minister of Kochi had joined with his opposite number in Travancore to rise against British rule, attempting to involve the French in Mauritius as well. The uprising in Kochi was swiftly defeated, and, as a punishment, the state's tribute was increased, its leaders were banned from contacting any foreigners, and its fortresses were opened for occupation by the Company's forces, or even destroyed.

The revolt continued for a longer period in Travancore. Travancore extended south of Kochi to Kanniya Kumari, at the tip of the sub-continent, and it too had its own flag, a conch shell on a red field, and currency, the cash, from which the English word is possibly derived.[iii] Travancore had resisted Tipu but only with assistance of the British, and one of the Company's earliest forts and its largest had been on the Travancore coast, at Angadi [Anjengo]. Travancore accepted British protection in 1805 after civil disturbances in the state. But the British resident and the state's chief minister argued, and the latter, Velu Thampi, issued a call to arms to the people – 'the Kundara Proclamation' - urging revolt against the British. It included the following insightful phrase: 'It is the nature of the English nation to get possession of countries by treacherous means...'[243] But Thampi was defeated in battle, and when the Company's forces had captured Padmanabhapuram Fort and were marching on Thiruvananthapuram itself, he committed suicide. The uprising has been referred to as a national rebellion but it does not seem to have had significance beyond Travancore. In any event, the immediate consequence was that British control over Kerala tightened.

Gangadharan, no friend of the Colonial power, does concede that the British did introduce some progressive reforms during its take-over of Kerala. A proclamation prohibiting the slave trade was issued

---

[iii] There are a number of other, possibly more likely, suggested derivations.

as soon as British rule commenced in 1792. It was intended to stop the practice of the capture of children, especially those of the 'most useful inhabitants the cultivators'.[244] If caught, the kidnapper was to be fined five times the value of the slave, and the buyer would be similarly treated. Anyone transporting slaves would be 'severely flogged and fined at the rate of 10 rupees per slave'. The measure was not very successful as captives could still be sold in French or Dutch controlled areas. Additionally, it was not until 1819 that orders were issued stopping landowners from accepting the children of tenants and others in lieu of rent arrears. As the century proceeded, slavery became an important issue in Britain and so more had to be done in Kerala.

Slaves working on Government land were freed in 1836; though it was kept quiet 'so as not to create any unnecessary alarm or aversion to it on the part of other proprietors, or premature hopes of emancipation on that of other slaves.'![245] The Collector at that time did not seem to be specially interested in this problem, claiming in 1839 that there 'few or no slaves' in North Malabar. But the Judge at Kozhikode, Mr. E.B. Thomas, was well aware from the cases that came before him that slavery was rife in the state. He noted that in some places, women were being purchased by landowners to breed slaves; that boys were bought and sold for 3 rupees 8 annas, girls for somewhat less, and the going price for a baby was 1 rupee 10 annas and 6 pice. Numbers of slaves had gone up from 144,000 in 1835 to 159,000 in 1842. The Collector's indifference notwithstanding, there were plenty of Britons who found this abhorrent, and in 1843 the Government of India passed an Act abolishing slavery once and for all. In fact, it was not until 1862 when heavy penalties were exacted on slave owners that the decisive blow was struck. Logan commented [in the 1880s] however that 'slaves as a caste will not know what real freedom means until measures are adopted to give them indefeasible rights in the small orchards occupied by them as house sites'.[246] Sounds rather like tied cottages in Hardy's England, or freed slaves being paid by tokens in America.

The Government also began to introduce a modern judicial system, based on evidence, and outlawing primitive punishments such as amputation, and capital punishment for untouchables who polluted Brahmins.

One reform resulting from a court case brought by a Christian missionary led to the 'Channar Rebellion' in Travancore. The women of the Channar caste [Dalits mainly involved in working with leather] historically were not allowed wear anything to cover their breasts, but this did not of course apply when they became Christians as some did. The fact that converted Channars could wear bodices made the Hindu Channars want the same thing. The courts agreed but upper caste Hindus would not accept the ruling and various scuffles resulted, in one case involving the burning of a church and Channar houses. Lord Harris [sometime captain of the County of Kent Cricket Club, but in this case in his capacity of Governor of Madras] instructed the Travancore government to permit Channar women to wear 'jacket and pinafore' though I guess as a sop to the Brahmins, they had to be made of raw cotton, rather than cloth.

There was no printing in Kerala until the Europeans came, presses being started in Vaipin and Kochi by Portuguese missionaries. The first book about Kerala was an encyclopaedia of local plants written by the Dutch with the help of traditional medical practitioners. The first complete book in Malayalam was written by a Jesuit missionary; it was about Christian doctrine. The most famous and important English – Malayalam dictionary was published in 1872 by Herman Gundert [a German missionary] who also produced the first Malayalam newspapers.[iv]

Missionaries, notably the London Mission Society and Christian Mission Society, were also responsible for introducing western-style education to Kerala, especially Travancore. Education was offered to all, irrespective of caste, and as the best educated people were the ones who got government jobs, western education was much sought after. The first European-style school that opened in Malabar was in 1841 in Kannur and the first primary school, in Kozhikode. The first non-religious school was opened by the government in Trivandrum in 1834, and by the second half of the century, western education was widespread in Kerala. So were the seeds sown for the current enviable situation in the state: it has the most widely and highly educated population in all India.

[iv] Gundert was the grandfather of the novelist Herman Hesse

Raju's college in Kozhikode 1979

Education and the growth of stable jobs especially in government service now began to affect the Marumakkathayam joint family system with inheritance through the female line. The Nairs were the caste that took advantage most enthusiastically both of western education and of the availability of government employment; and it was this community which first decided it would be advantageous to adopt 'Makkathaya' – a nuclear family with the father having responsibility for his children, who would inherit from him. They no longer had need of sambandham [informal] marriages either. Various rulings by the Chennai High Court, Commissions, and laws passed by the Chennai Legislative Council throughout the end of the nineteenth and the first half of the twentieth century culminated in the Maramakkathayam Act of 1933, which legalised Makkathayam in Malabar and gave rights to the children of sambandham marriage; soon to be followed by similar legislation in the 'Princely States' of Kochi and Travancore.

Local reformers were active too, the best known being Sri Narayana Guru. The high castes, particularly the Brahmins and Nairs, dominated social life in Kerala even after the arrival of the British. The British, you won't be surprised to learn, were more interested in maintaining law and order than in social fairness, and therefore bolstered the power of the landowners. Sri Narayana championed the lower castes, particularly his own Ezhava[v] community, and his message was 'One religion, one caste, and one God'. Sri Narayana was born in Trivandrum in 1855, and in 1887 he defied convention and tradition by establishing in the city a Shiva temple, which only Brahmins were really allowed to do; he defended himself against the priests by saying the temple was dedicated to an Ezhava Shiva, not a Brahmana Shiva. Other similar temples were founded throughout Kerala. They had Ezhava priests and welcomed untouchables as worshippers.

A contemporary of Sri Narayana, Ayyankali, a member of the Pulaya[vi] caste, also devoted himself to reforming caste oppression. The Pulayas and other low caste communities were regarded as 'untouchable' and indeed unapproachable by higher castes in Kerala. Ayyankali strove to get untouchables the right to use public roads and to attend government schools. He used strikes to advance his case and in 1907 the Travancore government 'issued orders favouring the lower castes'.[247] Members of the upper castes succeeded in delaying the implementation of the orders for three years; and even then, discrimination continued, and does, some would say, to this day. I have to say though that some Brahmins that I know feel that the provisions of affirmative action legislation discriminate against them. Ayyankali became the first Pulaya member of the Travancore assembly in 1911, and began to spread the word beyond his native state, to Kochi in 1913 and Kozhikode in 1927.

Other names to conjure with are: Vaghbatananda, born in Kannur, and another implacable opponent of caste. He believed that the important part of all religions was that they taught love and universal brotherhood and rejected idol worship. His social policies included opposition to the drinking of alcohol, and he argued that 'any rich person is directly or indirectly responsible for poverty'.[248] Vakkom Abdul Qadir Moulavi worked to improve the condition of Muslims in Kerala. He also started a newspaper, *Swadesabhimani*

---

[v] The Ezhavas [called Thiyyas in Malabar] were traditionally known as toddy-tappers, but as the biggest caste in Kerala – about 40% of Hindus – they have many other historical occupations including soldiering and farming.

[vi] Pulayas were the lowest caste, effectively slaves. In Tamil they are called paraiyars

[meaning *Patriot*] that fought against corruption in the Travancore government. Chattampi Swamikal led Nair opposition to Brahmin dominance; V.T.Bhattatripad aimed to eradicate some of the 'evil' customs of his own Namboodiri caste; C. Krishnan's Kozhikode-based journal *Mitavadi* worked for the abolition of the caste system, and in particular, untouchability. Krishnan incidentally supported British rule because he believed, his great- granddaughter tells us, that political freedom without 'freedom from serfdom' was meaningless.[249] Many of the reform movements were based on caste. Gangadharan maintains that 'the communal factor is very much relevant in the present day politics of Kerala. The roots of this reactionary political consciousness could be traced back to the formation of the communal organisations at the turn of the century.'[250]

It was often cross-caste groups who fought against untouchability though. Mahatma Gandhi himself was one of the great campaigners against this evil and he named untouchables 'harijans' or children of God. The Indian Congress Party was a prime mover too. In Kerala, the movement concentrated first on the issue of public roads near temples that harijans were prohibited from using. A Congress Committee, including members of various castes was formed to fight for access for all to these roads. A satyagraha[vii] was started in March 1924 when negotiation was making no progress and achieved some success and by 1928 the government of Travancore was forced to issue a proclamation which opened all temple roads to everyone, irrespective of caste.

Next came the struggle to allow any Hindu to enter a temple, and in 1931, the Kerala State Conference of the Indian National Congress demanded that temples be open for all Hindu castes and communities. The Zamorin, trustee of the great temple of Guruvayur refused and the Guruvayur Satyagraha began. It was not immediately successful even though a referendum on the issue was held in Ponnani and 77% voted in favour of free entry. However, the awareness raised by the action at Guruvayur led in due course to the Temple Entry Proclamations by which all Hindus could enter temples in 1936 in Travancore, in 1947 in Malabar and in 1948 in Kochi.

[vii] Satyagraha means non-violent resistance, as advocated and practised by Gandhiji.

CHAPTER THIRTY-SIX

THE IYERS IN KERALA

'A Pattar who has heard of a feast and a pig that has heard of a chase run equally fast' Malayalam proverb

We left Manga's ancestors after they had crossed into Kerala by way of the Palakkad Gap, staying possibly in one of the agraharams of Kalpathy, and made their way west until they reached Trikkandiyur.

When the Iyers settled in their new homes in Kerala, they seem to have been involved in a variety of occupations, in addition to their work in religious affairs. They became for example administrators [from clerks to chief advisers], astrologers, cotton traders, manual workers, domestic servants, soldiers, moneylenders, and musicians. Logan tells of some extraordinary jobs they did 'in former times', when they were used as 'confidential messengers and spies'. A particularly unsavoury job was to 'prove' a Brahmin woman's adultery by naming the person or persons with whom she allegedly had a relationship. Logan says, 'This duty is invariably performed by a man of the Pattar caste. It is essential that the man who does it should be a Brahmin, and as no Namboodiri or Embrandiri would do it for love or money, a needy Pattar is found and paid handsomely for doing it. Directly he has performed the duty, he proceeds to the nearest piece of water, there to immerse his whole body and so wash away the sin he has contracted'.[251] I am afraid that neither the Pattar nor the Namboodiri who commissioned the lie comes well out of this.

K.P.P.Menon also has some things to say about our ancestors, which, taken at face value, seem a little disappointing: 'They do not generally build their houses in the country but manage to get a room in a Nair house and more often ally themselves ...with the female members of the Nair family, who, out of their superstitious reverence to their sacred order minister to them without stint. Thus they enjoy all the comforts of life till they are able to accumulate some wealth which being accomplished they coolly retire to their own country caring little for the offspring they may be leaving behind'. [252] We might fairly believe however that this is a misreading of the Marumakkattayam system, which we have already explained.

And Menon [not of course an Iyer himself] does go on to say that 'the Pattar is found in every walk of life and he makes his presence felt by his superior intelligence, application and industry.'

The original family house, beside the temple tank

Menon gives some information about the trading activities of the 'foreign Brahmins' too. Apparently the so-called Raja of Malabar exempted them from certain taxes and allowed them to take free meals at certain temples. We've done that: at Kallil. When we visited the temple a second time, an eating hall was being built, and we were offered free some tapioca and very hot chutney that nearly knocked out Raju and Manga! [The rest of us were humble enough to take the less spicy option] Presumably these privileges were to encourage the Iyers to stay in the country. They traded apparently not directly with the Europeans but brought the spices and other goods from the interior and sold them to the 'Moors, Jews and Canarese'[i] who had direct contact with the foreign merchants.

We don't have much information about what our family did for a living. Manga's maternal grandfather, she thinks, was a rent collector for the Zamorin. Her father of course was a healer, carried out certain religious rites, prepared and sold food at Temple festivals, and 'for his bread and butter' [not a very apt phrase I know!], cooked and served meals in the house for Brahmins and others who were working away from home. And his eldest son-in-law was

---

[i] Kannada speaking people originally from Karnataka

chef to the Rajah of Kochi. It is perhaps reasonable to conjecture then these occupations might have been followed by Manga's father's ancestors. It is certainly the case that pretty well all the existing family seems to have inherited my father-in-law's skill in cooking.

Of course our family in England, and many of the friends to whom we have introduced it, love Iyer cuisine. It is vegetarian and its recipes can easily be adjusted to suit vegans. It fuses traditional Tamil and Malayalee dishes to produce something better than either [in our opinion at least!]. It must have been hard at first for the Iyer cooks in Kerala, whether wives or professionals, because they couldn't get the ingredients they were used to, and it was this problem that created the dishes peculiar to the caste.

The *Keralaiyers* website offers the following as typical dishes of the Iyer immigrants. Sambar of course. Not many English people had heard of this dish fifty years ago when I first tasted it, but it is now a commonplace of the Indian restaurant menu. There is though sambar and sambar, and I have tasted some rather tame varieties in my time. The best is definitely the Kerala Iyer version, using a mixture of vegetables – pretty well whatever is available - and lots of coconut, as well as chillies and coriander, and of course tamarind. No one makes sambar like Manga – and I mean no one makes it as well as she does, certainly to my taste and plenty of others' too – and it seems to appeal to all our Indian visitors as much as it does to Europeans.

And of course its biggest fans are her daughters. And their friends. It's rare that the children return to their homes after paying us a visit without taking with them a plastic box full of the golden nectar, which they in turn shared with fellow students in the old days, or loved ones and neighbours now. Manga's secret is plenty of tamarind, and lemon juice too, so the dish is really sour; plenty of vegetables cut coarse, so that it's meaty, not a thin gruel; and the right amount of chillies, to make the stew spicy but not so hot that the taste is disguised. Wonderful. But it's no good asking for a recipe – Manga just puts into the mix 'a nice amount' of this and 'a few handfuls' of that, and cooks it 'until it's ready'. I ought to add that we all love Shanta's, Radhikar's and Geetha's sambars too and I have doubt whose cooking their husbands say is best!

After sambar comes aviyal. Mary Louise Skelton and G. Gopal Rao in *South Indian Cookery* (a recipe book much to be recommended, which I see cost us all of 7 rupees) describe aviyal [or avial] as the 'Malabar masterpiece.'[253] Again, a variety of vegetables are used depending on what's around at the time, and they're mixed with unripe mango, curds and coconut, and cooked in coconut oil. Malayalees wouldn't use fried mustard seed but Iyers would, and also perhaps tamarind.

I don't remember kalan but Manga says we have eaten it. It's called morkuzhambu in Tamil and is a thick and particularly sour buttermilk with chenai [a sort of cassava] or banana usually, and spiced with pepper or chilli. And of course it includes coconut, which is found in most preparations; and again Iyers would add crackled mustard seeds, but Malayalees wouldn't. Then there is malaguttal, like sambar without the sourness and good if your stomach needs a rest.

As far as dress and lifestyle is concerned, you'd be hard put to tell an Iyer from anyone else in Kerala now - in towns anyway. Most men wear either western dress or lungi and shirt; and the women, especially the younger ones, the ubiquitous salwar-kurta, whether married or not. But when the Iyers first moved into Kerala the dress code was strict. Very young children wore perhaps a cotton towel wrapped round their waist and reaching down to their ankles. As they grew up girls would wear a skirt and fitted blouse, and from about the age of about nine, a half sari, with the strip of cotton covering their chests. After marriage, they would only be seen in the full nine-yard sari that goes over the right shoulder and is pleated at the back. A bit cumbersome, it seems to me. These days the long sari will only be worn by old people or sometimes at weddings and other religious festivals. In days gone by, an Iyer woman could have been differentiated from a Namboodiri quite easily. According to the Namboodiri website, women of that caste were 'no sticklers for fashionable dress'. Manga says they used to wear white saris only, sometimes no blouse, and little in the way of jewellery. In particular they never wore a nose-rings or studs – a very important item to the women of the Iyer caste, who loved to wear as much gold as possible [and still do] – preferably the 22-carat variety; other castes in Kerala were satisfied with 18-carat gold. And Iyer women could be distinguished from those of other communities by the way in which the sari was tied, or indeed, whether a sari was worn at all. Christian women wore mundus of starched white cotton around their waists, sometimes tied in a very complex way, and those from lower castes a simple lungi. Often lower caste women left their breasts uncovered or bound a strip of cloth over their chests, or used a drape. Indeed some say that the choli or blouse was an invention of the British, who were perhaps embarrassed by seeing so many boobs as they took their daily walks!

Grown men wore a veshti [Tamil] or mundu [Malayalam] – a piece of unstitched cloth that may be as long as 7 yards and is wrapped round the waist. On important occasions, the border of this white cotton cloth might be coloured – gold [zari] or black and white. Another piece of cloth is sometimes draped round the shoulders – called an angovastram in Tamil. You can fold the veshti in half so it looks like a short skirt, but traditionally it isn't good to talk to women or one's 'betters' like that. Manga says that you would probably even today loosen the veshti so it would revert to its normal length if you were meeting a stranger. Many Iyers still wear this garment, or the shorter lungi, which I can vouch to be cool and comfortable, although I have suffered some embarrassing moments when the tuck has unravelled! But of course, many more wear western dress these days, even on ceremonial occasions. I do think that it's a bit of a shame for example when a bride wears a beautiful, colourful sari but the groom is dressed in slacks and a shirt.

What happened to our home and family in Kerala will help to illustrate how Kerala Iyers live and have lived. Our village is not I have to say an *agraharam*. In the old days many Iyer families lived in Trikkandiyur, but it was not a single street with a temple at each end, and did not have the characteristic rows of terraced houses. Instead most of the Brahmins' houses were built in the typical Kerala pattern – each in its own compound with plenty of trees, a well, and room for a cow. Manga remembers the kitchen in her old house.

'The kitchen was always very dark - it had only one window, overlooking the northern side. Eastern side there was no window; that's where there was a raised platform about two feet high made of laterite blocks, like the house itself. One end the platform was hollowed out to make a furnace; bit like an Aga cooker really except we didn't have an oven. There were two places on top of the platform where you could put your

pans. One was over the furnace itself, for proper cooking, and the other was alongside it for simmering.

The pots and pans [chetti] were mainly made of aluminium but we still used old copper ones too. If we used them for cooking, they had to be lined with aluminium or they would be poisonous, and a man skilled in doing this would visit the village once a year and spend a few days lining everyone's pans. For cooking sour things we didn't like to use metal at all and we had pots made of a sort of soft stone; I don't know what sort of stone it was. Poor people would use terracotta. Each pan would rest on three raised pieces of the laterite, sort of like a trivet. You fed the furnace with wood, coconut shells, cow dung cakes, things like that.

The kitchen stove in Trikkandiyur

We had a wooden cupboard that was black from the smoke, where you used to put sugar and things. Salt was kept in a jar on top of the cooker, and unripe mangoes for pickle in a big glazed pot with a lid. Amakutty-akka was very good - she used to keep the kitchen clean and the cloth used to be black like anything with smoke and soot. She used to wipe this cupboard nicely but still it used to be full of cockroaches each time you opened it. Those cockroaches get everywhere however much cleaning is done! There was a framework hanging from the ceiling where they put the wood to dry; otherwise in the rainy season it stayed wet and used to make the fire smoke horribly, and they all used to come out of the kitchen, tears streaming and red eyes. They used to have to fan the furnace to try and get it going then. It was hard work, cooking.

Next to the cupboard there was an iron post buried in the floor. That is where my Mum used to sit and churn the curds in the morning at 4.30 or 5 o'clock. She would use a churning stick called a mathu and a short length of rope. Another piece of rope went round the post to stabilise the mathu. At least I think that's how it worked. Mum would sit and say all the prayers while she worked. I used to wake up and go over and sleep on her lap as she churned, and towards the end she would get this lovely butter. She rolled it up and put it in the water and it would float; I used to be given a little bit to eat. It was nearly all for me anyway. Mum used to make into ghee and put it into my dinner because I used to be so frail and thin and always getting ill. So I had most of the buttermilk, which was delicious. It was from our own cow - we always kept a cow. Sometimes we had more than one cow; then the cowshed would be near the veranda. Otherwise it would be on the other side of the kitchen.

After making the buttermilk, Mum would go and have a bath and say prayers. The morning prayers are wonderful. When you looked outside at this time it was still dark and you used to see a star. I think it was one of the planets - Saturn or Jupiter - and it would shine like nobody's business. Mum would say 'There is Shukran Nashatran. Shukran comes in the story about Vamana and Mahabali. He was the Rishi who advised Mahabali not to trust Vamana. Vamana you know was the Lord Vishnu in disguise, and he was very angry with Shukran and put out one of his eyes. But later Vamana repented and gave a place to Shukran in the Heavens.' Later we would go to the temple. Outside the kitchen was the veranda. There was a flat stone there to grind rice for dosa and idli and also the ingredients for curry powder and things. I think the stone was made of granite. Every year or six months a man would come to make the stone's surface rough with a sort of nail so it would grind well. You had to work very hard. Our friend Mrs. Robinson in Newcastle gave me one of these grinding stones and also the black cylindrical stone you did the grinding with. She was a Burmese lady and had brought it from home. Now people use electric grinders.

My first memory is sitting with Mum when she was having her last period. You were not supposed to touch a woman having a period, but it was OK if you weren't wearing clothes, so I took all my clothes off and went to sit in her lap and she used to stroke my hair. I was very fair. All my sisters were quite dark and my Mum. Dad was quite fair though and my eldest brother too. But my sisters all used to tease me and call me 'vella kura', which means white cockroach, and say, 'You don't belong here. Mum bought you for a bowl of thavidu.' [That's when you pound the paddy: you get a reddish powder, which is full of vitamin B. You eat it with milk like beaten rice. It's good for you but people often don't like it very much.] 'That's why you are so fair' they would say, and I would cry and go to Mum and she would say 'don't worry - take no notice of them.' Poor Mum. We had a nice time though.'

These days our compound contains no less than four houses, one of them consisting of two dwellings, in two storeys, and none of them are of a typical Kerala style; even the old house has been re-built. When the second new house was planned, Manga and I were upset and cross. The first house, built by Raju had not seemed to intrude too much - any coconut palms affected were dug up and re-planted somewhere else in the garden, so the tree canopy was largely retained. But the building of the second house coincided with other developments on Narayanan's site next door and as a result a lot of trees were felled including the lovely dense mango where I'd seen a jungle owl. So it didn't feel as if we were in the country any longer. What was worse was that we had threatened that we wouldn't come to Trikkandiyur again if they did any more building! We were at least sure that there'd be no more developments. Any other house would have to be sited where the family ghost walked, and no one would agree to that. Well, we were wrong. A fourth house duly went up and then the original home was altered beyond recognition. By now Variyathmadam was barely recognisable as the place I had first visited, and of course totally unlike Manga's old home, so in a sense it didn't matter any more.

But of course there had always been changes. In Manga's early days, there was no veranda, the main door faced the gate, and the roof was thatched. The 'bathroom' was a shelter next to the well, made from palm fronds, and was re-built every year. There was no electricity or piped water, and no drainage. The loo was in a hut and of the dry-earth variety. Then as the years went by, a tiled roof arrived, the bathroom was moved next to the house with walls built of laterite, the entrance moved and a veranda added. Water and then electricity came. I expect if I'd been around, I'd have objected to every new development. 'Oh what a shame. The thatched roof was so romantic.' Actually I was there when the water supply arrived and helped to connect it up. And yes, part of me was thinking that things would never be the same again. [I did welcome western loos though]. Of course the point is that we are only there for a few weeks every few years. And the new houses represent retirement pensions not only for Manga's sisters and Ravi, but for Raju, Ramani and Mangalam too for they all share in the ownership of the land at Variyathmadam.[ii]

Manga continues.

'Life at home has changed so much and of course it's much more comfortable for everyone now. Even so, there's still a lot of work to be done in the kitchen. There are all new gadgets but no servants any more, so the chief cook - that is Shanta now - still has to start work at five in the morning.

I told you how we would all get ready to go to the temple in the morning. Apart from that Mum would churn the curds, and help with cooking, though my sisters would have done most of the work. Dad would do all the shopping – men usually do the shopping in India - and he'd sometimes help with chopping the vegetables too. When we used to raise money by having Brahmins come home to eat, Mum and Dad would both serve them. Mum didn't have much of a social life. She would only go out to visit friends if they were sick, but she would go to the gate and chat with people as they passed along the alleyway. In the afternoons she would read Holy books and might take a nap. Of course we had servants then so she wouldn't have so much to do.'

Our Kerala Christian friend Nelphy remembers that her mother's day would also start with prayers, but at home. This was a different generation, and there were no servants so her mother would then prepare breakfast and tiffin for people to take to school or work, and then do the sweeping. Though if there were any conservative older people staying she would have to sweep outside before they got up, as they would not approve of women working outside the house. After washing-up, her mother would start preparing lunch – a long job: she seemed to spend an awful long time cooking – and then serving, eating and clearing up the meal. In the afternoon she'd have a nap. She might then have to prepare more food for the evening meal and greet the workers with tea as

---

[ii] Manga voluntarily gave up her share when she went to work in England

they came home. After that, there would be prayers – at seven o'clock precisely. Nelphy's grandfather would just have to look at the clock to have the youngsters scuttling into position. Nelphy says he didn't insist on anything else – they could do what they liked, as long as they all came together at seven. If they failed to do this, he said, the family would fall apart. So life in a Christian family does not seem all that different from ours.

A typical day for a modern Iyer family was described for me in e-mails from Raju a couple of years ago. *'Why are we so busy? I don't know. And what are we doing all the time?'* A question not confined to Raju I have to say, or Iyers or Indians, but worldwide. *'We get very little time to do other things. We wake at 5 a.m. and Geetha takes bath while the milk boils, and then makes coffee. After that and the basic things, we start walking. Geetha will go to the temple while I do my usual walk, about 40 minutes every day. Back home and then a quick glance through the papers to settle the body before the bath. Then the news on TV together with breakfast, and it will be already at 7.45. Kitty will be awake around six, and will do her routine things.'* In my experience this includes her doing some schoolwork. *'After work, I'll pick up Kitty from school and be back home at 4.15. Meanwhile Geetha will have been out teaching her violin students, and at about six, I will drive into town to meet her bus and do a bit of shopping. Meanwhile, I'll prepare some of Kitty's favourite snacks for her, and she'll settle down to do homework. Then prepare and eat supper, watch the news and it will be time for bed. It's only when the clock's chimes start dragging and I have to wind it, that I know a week is past!'* Actually of course there are the weekends, and I know the family often makes trips to places of religious and historical interest, and spends a lot of time too socialising with friends and with Geetha's brothers who live nearby, or visiting Trikkandiyur. Geetha plays and teaches the violin, her sister-in-law Ambala sings professionally, and her sister Rema and Rema's husband Hari also sing beautifully. Rema and Hari spent Christmas with us once when Hari was on secondment to the London branch of the State Bank of India, and we stayed with them and their bright and intelligent children Shyam and Sandhya in their home in the former Asian Games complex in Chennai in the year that our sister-in-law Julie travelled with us.. It was then that we had our guided tour of the wondrous temples of Mahaballipuram and Kanchipuram.

CHAPTER THIRTY-SEVEN

EAST IS EAST

'East is East and West is West, and never the twain shall meet.' - Rudyard Kipling.

'At a time when respectable academics talk of a Clash of Civilisations, and when East and West, Islam and Christianity, appear to be engaged in another major confrontation, this unlikely group of expatriates [the 'White Mughals'] provides a timely reminder that it is indeed very possible – and has always been possible – to reconcile the two worlds.' - William Dalrymple, *White Mughals*

'*Love heeds not caste, nor sleep a broken bed.*' Hindu proverb

'A man should, whatever happens, keep to his own caste, race, and breed. Let the White go to the White and the Black to the Black' Rudyard Kipling, *Beyond the Pale, from Plain Tales from the Hills*

The quotes from Kipling might have been watchwords for his generation - the late Victorians and Edwardians - but the British in India in earlier times thought very differently. In *White Mughals,* William Dalrymple tells the story of Major James Achilles Fitzpatrick, who was British Resident at the court of the Nizam of Hyderabad from 1798 until his death in 1805, and his love affair with the beautiful Begum Khair un- Nissa. James and Khair un-Nissa were married in 1800 and had two surviving children, who moved to England after their father's death. James' daughter fell in love with Thomas Carlyle and his son had three children, but died age 27. Incidentally, James' grandma was 'a Creole lady from Georgia'. James' half-brother, Lt-Col William Fitzpatrick, had four daughters, one of whom married an MP, a second married a knight and a third became the grandmother of Lytton Strachey. William also lived with an Indian woman, Dhoolaury Bibi, both before and after his marriage, and had two Anglo-Indian children. Lots of happy mixing! James' mother was Katherine Munro who was the daughter of Dr Andrew Munro, the founder of Chennai Hospital, where Manga did her nursing training. It's fun to find connections like this! Another is that *White Mughals* was reviewed for the

Literary Review by Charles Allen, a contemporary of mine in V.S.O., though I never met him.

Victoria at the shrine dedicated to Krishna

James Kirkpatrick was apparently not unusual in marrying an Indian woman. Dalrymple writes: 'The deeper I went into my research, the more I became convinced that the picture of the British of the East India Company as a small alien minority locked away in their Presidency towns, forts and cantonments needed to be revised. The tone of this early period of British life in India seemed instead to be about intermixing and unplanned mingling of peoples and cultures and ideas.'[254] Many, probably a majority, of Englishmen coming out to India to work for the East India Company, took a *bibi,* an Indian companion or concubine. This is known because the wills of Englishmen who died in Bengal in the late eighteenth century have been preserved, and one third of them included bequests to Indian wives or concubines or their children. 'It may be safely assumed', says Dalrymple, 'that many others kept mistresses but did not wish to leave a formal legal record of the fact.' And the bequests were not trinkets. As an example, one of many, Dalrymple refers to the companion of a Major Thomas Naylor who was left the equivalent of a quarter of a million pounds plus a house, businesses and slaves.[255]

No one would pretend that young men from England took Indian mistresses for high-minded reasons connected with the promotion of integration and 'transculturation'. Since there were very few European women in India, if one wanted female companionship and sex, there was no alternative to miscegenation. However, the fact is that having a bibi did lead to an understanding and appreciation of local customs and beliefs. Richard Burton wrote that Englishmen learned 'not only Hindustani grammar, but the syntaxes of native Life' from the bibis. The process was two-way. Just as some men converted to Islam as a result of their liaisons, so some Indian women became Christian. And just as many British men stayed in India for the rest of their lives, many Indian women travelled back to England with their men, where they frequently fitted easily into European society, as indeed did many Indian men who made the same journey. I must mention the famous Dean Mahomet from Patna who came to England in the 1790s and integrated exceptionally well into English [and Irish] society. Among other exploits, he became the first Indian to open a curry restaurant in this country.

Sadly this period of healthy and natural intermingling came to an end and Dalrymple points out that for many years it was forgotten that it ever happened. The change in attitudes began in 1765 when the East India Company stopped simply trading in Bengal and started to govern the state. Then the Company changed its rules so that only Europeans could hold senior posts. And the British began to believe that they were ruling Indians for their own good. The change is exemplified by the difference between Warren Hastings, Governor General between 1773 and 1785, and his successor, Lord Cornwallis. Hastings was a lover of Indian culture, and appreciated the country's art, literature and philosophy. He founded the Asiatic Society, and wished India to be governed in accordance with its own legal codes. Cornwallis on the other hand considered all things Indian to be inferior and uncivilised. The country's only salvation was to be ruled on British lines, and for its ancient practices to be abolished. Of course, many administrators after Hastings continued to be lovers of India, but official attitudes had decidedly changed. Further European-style influences were exerted when in 1813 Christian missionaries were allowed to operate in the Company's territory.

Then came a development that totally altered the relationship between the Company's employees and the women of India. This was the arrival of steamships, which meant that people could travel much more safely between India and Britain. As a result, women began to join their husbands in India instead of waiting at home for their men's return, and others came to the sub-continent specifically to seek husbands. The latter were rather cruelly called the 'fishing fleets'. Of course soldiers and others continued to visit Indian prostitutes, but it was no longer acceptable to keep mistresses or marry Indian women. I can't believe this was a matter of choice, especially when one reads the following appreciation of 'Hindoo women' by Major-General Charles Stuart: 'The majority are comparatively small, yet there is much voluptuousness of appearance: a fullness that delights the eye; a firmness that enchants the senses; a sleekness and purity of skin; an expression of countenance, a grace and a modesty of demeanour, that renders them universally attractive...'[256]

And the gentleman [I guess it was a gentleman] who contributed the article on Dancing Girls to an 1871 Encyclopaedia seems to have been even more obsessed! -

> Some of these girls are very good-looking, handsome, with open countenances, large sparkling eyes, regular features and with elegant pleasing appearance. They are perfectly self-possessed in manner, verging on assurance, staring at one with their large, intelligent-looking eyes. Notwithstanding, they possess a vast deal of courtesy and polish, tempered with a languid grace and serene self- possession, whilst their manner is courteous and their bearing unembarrassed...Telugu girls are very handsome, with skin of a light pale colour, somewhat yellowish in tinge, with a softness of face and feature, gentleness of manner, with a peculiar grace and ease...a lady- like manner, modesty and gentleness, such beautiful, small hands and

> little fingers, the ankles so neatly turned as to merit the admiration of the sternest connoisseur...'[257][i]

I haven't found any information about Malayalee women forming liaisons with East India Company employees, though James Kirkpatrick had a companion prior to his meeting Khair un-Nissa, who was always referred to as 'the Dark Girl'; Dalrymple infers that she might have been Tamil, but she could equally well have come from Kerala. Neither is there any record of either Malayalee men or women [Krishna Menon apart, and that was not till the 1930s] making an important contribution to British society. No doubt there were Malayalees among the Ayahs [nursemaids] who had settled in England having accompanied the families who employed them back home and then been ditched when they were no longer required; and no doubt Malayalee seamen were among the lascars who jumped ship in British ports or who were abandoned here.

Lascars were ships' crew originally recruited in India. Malayalee Hindus were normally deck-hands, and Kochi Christians worked as cabin crew. And there was a sad advertisement in the London Gazette in 1772, offering a reward for the return of an escaped slave, 'a black, a native of Malabar, well-made, likely featured, with long hair'.[258]

When Manga and I married in 1967, interracial marriages were rare, but for the most part not frowned upon. Some of my relations of my parents' generation were concerned, mainly about the prospects of any potential off-spring I think, but none of Manga's seemed to be, although Manga says she'd have never married an Englishman if her parents were still alive. Raju once told me that when he was looking for a wife, some, but not many, families were put off by the fact that his aunt had married a foreigner. Geetha's father, though, very graciously welcomed us personally into his family. Now a recent

---

[i] I suppose I have to record an alternative viewpoint. Richard Purvis, a lieutenant in the service of the East India Company, when based in Mirzapur in 1810, received a letter from one of his colleagues asking whether he 'had met with any sympathising beauty of the monkey tribe, who enjoyed your attentions and won your affections by her playful leaps and fascinating grimaces' Gordon, Iain (2001) *Soldier of the Raj: the Life of Richard Purvis 1789-1868 Soldier, Sailor and Parson,* Barnsley: Leo Cooper. p.119

survey has revealed that 10% of Indian women in the UK are in a relationship with a white man. It will be good if this leads, and soon, to a better understanding between different ethnic groups, and an appreciation of the value and richness of the multi-cultural society in this country, which has recently, and to me inexplicably, come under attack.

With Manga at the Taj Mahal

CHAPTER THIRTY-EIGHT

THE BRITISH RAJ

'When the rock at Iringath becomes gold, half of it will be given to Devi'- Malayalam proverb

'The notion that the Pax Britannia brought peace and order for the first time to India is one of the most extraordinary of delusions' - Nehru.

'The tragedy of Bengal and the famines of Orissa, Malabar, and other places are the final judgement on British rule in India...' Nehru, *The Discovery of India*[259]

There were, and still are, differing views of the British occupation, both in this country and in India. Salman Rushdie sums up the arguments in an amusing and illuminating conversation in *The Moor's Last Sigh*. It is during the First World War when Francisco the spice trader decides that the British 'must go' for they are bleeding India dry of wealth, food, raw materials and manpower. His wife Epifania[i] is horrified and responds: '*What are we but Empire's children? British have given us everything isn't it. Civilisation, law, order, too much*'.[260]

As far as 'law and order' is concerned, much is written about the 'Pax Britannia', which allegedly reigned in India after 1820. Keay however maintains that 'in the experience of most Indians' it meant 'Tax Britannia', for the cost of British wars could not be met from the profits of trade, and so the people had to pay increasing amounts of taxes and duties. And there wasn't a lot of 'pax' anyway. [261] The 1820s saw the first Burmese War and the annexation of Assam; and the defeat of the Jats in the Agra area. In the 1830s, Coorg was taken from Mysore, and the hill tribes of Orissa were defeated.

---

[i] Epifania has an ally in the shape of the brilliant Bengali writer Nirad C.Chaudhuri; the first part of his biography is dedicated to 'the British Empire in India. All that was good and living within us was made, shaped and quickened by the same British rule'. From Chaudhuri, Nirad C, (1964) *Autobiography of an Unknown Indian,* Jaico Publishing House

In the 1840s came the disaster [for the British] of the first Afghan War, and the conquest of Sind. This conflict gave rise to the popular though erroneous story that when Sir Charles Napier conquered Sind he wired the single word 'peccavi' to HQ. Peccavi means 'I have sinned' in Latin. He did however say, 'We have no right to seize Sind', shortly before doing so. There is a similar story about the annexation of Oudh [Awadh] by Lord Dalhousie, Governor- General from 1848 to 1856. His telegraph allegedly read 'vovi' – I vowed = I've Oudh.

Later came the first and then the second Sikh Wars. In the course of the latter the British lost 3,000 men at the battle of Chillianwala, but later defeated the Sikhs at the battle of Gujarat. Further annexations followed. Peaceful the period was not.

The so-called Mutiny or Great Rebellion, better known from the Indian viewpoint as the First War of Independence started in 1857. William Dalrymple's great work *The Last Mughal* tells all you need to know about this sad, bitter and cruel conflict. The Rebellion started among the sepoys of the Bengal Army who had a number of grievances that damaged the trust between officers and men, which was an important factor in keeping the army together. The more perceptive members of the British administration had been aware for many years that the Indian army could be a threat to more than the Company's enemies. Jonah Blank quotes Colonel Sleeman, a Resident in Awadh, as saying in 1856, 'the annexation of Oudh… would inevitably lead to a mutiny of the sepoys'.[262] Mountstuart Elphinstone, a senior member of the Governor General's staff and a scholarly historian to boot, had described the army forty years before as 'a delicate and dangerous machine, which a little mismanagement may easily turn against us.'[263] And the mismanagement was in due course supplied. Every schoolboy knows for example about the introduction of new rifle cartridges that were greased with animal fat [pork or beef] and had to be bitten before loading; so both Hindus and Muslims were offended. There were other more important reasons of course - nationalistic and religious - but it doesn't seem as though the Mutiny was the result of any grand plan. The Great Rebellion was pretty well confined to the north, and the Sikhs supported the British, perhaps surprisingly as they had very recently been conquered, and this was probably decisive in the failure of the sepoys' cause.

I saw a television programme recently in a rather ill-conceived series called 'The Clash of Civilisations' which attempted to show that the mutineers were the forerunners of the Taliban: part of a current fashion that I have heard described as 'morally bankrupt', which blames Muslims or Islam for many of the ills of this world, and maintains that there are irreconcilable differences between our civilisations. But whatever its causes, the Rebellion absolutely changed the relationship between Britain and India. The British Crown took over the government of the country, Queen Victoria becoming the Queen, and in 1876, the Empress of India, and the Governor-General becoming the Viceroy. The Indian princes remained theoretically independent although very much under the thumb of the Raj. Before the Rebellion, there seems to have been quite a warm relationship between the British and those Indians who lived close by them, especially in the army. One example: General Tucker, speaking as late as 1857 'exhorted his audience [of army cadets] to treat their sepoys with kindness and respect, praised those of his generation who had loved and known their men.'[264] However this relationship changed for the most part to one of dislike and distrust after the Mutiny, which occurred later that year.

Other events apart from fighting did occur in this period of course. The rulers banned suttee - the [allegedly voluntary] burning of widows on their husbands' funeral pyres - and vowed to wipe out thugee, which was the ritual strangling of travellers by highway robbers called Thugs. Very right and proper too of course. I'd be venturing out of my depth if I were to introduce a discussion about the extent to which it is inappropriate to interfere with what seem to us to be objectively evil practices of other cultures. But I can of course understand John Keay's view that these reforms - introduced by Lord William Bentinck, Governor–General from 1828 to 1835 and often thought of as a liberal[ii] - were motivated mostly by a desire to 'stigmatize Hinduism', and therefore have perhaps a hollow ring. The westernisation of the legal system was another ostensibly justifiable reform. The trouble was British legal 'concepts and procedures were bewilderingly alien' for Indians.[265] Similarly, there were no doubt benefits to be garnered from the re-modelling of the education system on western lines. The problem was the arrogance, insensitivity and ignorance that accompanied

---

[ii] By Francis Watson, for one, in his *Concise History*

these reforms, well summed up by Macaulay's announcement that 'a single shelf of a good European library is worth the whole native literature of India and Arabia'. 'His eloquence derived from an ignorance of what he was denigrating' according to Watson.[266] Then came the Earl of Dalhousie's governor-generalship, between 1848 and 1856. He was very keen on westernisation and modernisation, and for example passed laws that gave ex-Hindu converts the right to inherit their father's lands, and Hindu widows the right to re-marry. He also developed lots of engineering schemes like railways and roads and the telegraph, so much so that 'on the new maps it looked as if India was about to be ensnared in a steel tangle of wires and railway tracks'.[267] But this promotion of all things European sowed 'among his seminal measures, the tares of revolt'.[268]

After the Rebellion, as far as social policy was concerned, Keay writes that this 'reforming zeal was repudiated' and 'the attempt to legislate away discriminatory traditions and eccentric practices was largely abandoned'. In the Army, the proportion of sepoys was reduced. And the British government took over the powers hitherto exercised by the East India Company. So the way in which India was ruled was transformed.

The Imperial concept was encouraged particularly by Lord Lytton, 'a Tory with Bohemian inclinations' who was the Viceroy from 1876 to 1880.[269] In 1877 he organised an 'Imperial Durbar', a lavish celebration of Queen Victoria's proclamation as Empress that most inappropriately took place at the same time as a major famine in the country, and I am indebted particularly to Mike Davis, David Arnold and David Hall-Matthews for this brief account.[270] The immediate cause of the famine was the failure of two consecutive monsoons as a result of an *El Nino* event. Monsoons do fail from time to time of course and the poor suffer, but most of them survive, often through help from neighbours, use of stored food from the previous year or by turning to alternative food sources. There was it seems a different picture in India in the 1870s. The pressure to grow cash crops, which had been started by the Portuguese, had continued under the British and it meant that there was little spare food, either to store or share with neighbours. And unfortunately for India, Lord Lytton was a believer in the then fashionable theory of 'Social Darwinism' invented by Charles Darwin's brother-in-law, and it is likely that this exacerbated the effects of the crop failures. According to the theory, just as the weakest and less well adapted animals had died out over the history of the world so would [and should] the weaker and less successful members of the human species. It would therefore be wrong, said Lord Lytton to help the starving peoples of south India, where the famine was at its worst. Not only that, but the distribution of free food would be 'an unconscionable interference with the free market'.[271] Eventually, Lytton was persuaded by members of his government who possessed a little more humanity than he apparently did, that to do nothing in these circumstances was unacceptable. So he did something: he ordered that those without any means of support must be put into labour camps, where they were forced into heavy manual labour in order to receive scraps of food. Those who could not work, like young children and the very old, were given no food at all. Furthermore, Lawrence James tells us, the 'work camps were often sited far from the areas of greatest scarcity'.[272] 'At the same time' writes Simon Schama, 'grain depots in Chennai and Mumbai were full of imported rice... The famished, as horrified journalists like William Digby [who published a two-volume history of the famine] testified, dropped dead in front of the fenced stockpiles'.[273]

Paddy fields in Kerala

Between 5 million and 8 million people died of starvation in India in the 1870s, and a total of 30 million in the second half of the nineteenth century. In 1876-8, 'between 3.5 and 4 million people perished in the Madras presidency alone' according to Lawrence James; and he adds that 'the actual totals were probably for higher, for uncounted thousands died unrecorded where they fell'.[274] And this was while food crops and other produce from the farms of India were being exported, mainly to Europe. Florence Nightingale wrote in 1877: 'The more one hears about this famine, the more one feels that such a hideous record of human suffering and destruction the world has never seen before'.[275] Whether the 'catastrophe could have been avoided by technology, planning and cash' is no doubt true – but what was primarily required was the will to act.[276]

This was not the first time that the British had presided over an epic disaster, and it would not be the last. One hundred years before, the harvest had again failed in consecutive years, in Bengal. Roy Moxham tells the story in *The Great Hedge of India*. 'There has never been a failure of crops all over India. Local shortages can always be rectified if there is money to buy in grain. However, following the looting of Bengal by the [East India] Company and its employees, money was very scarce. The company had no mercy; it took its dues in full. As people began to die, the amount of land revenue due from the survivors increased...Meanwhile the Company's employees and their agents cornered the rice market...'[277] Rice became thirty times more expensive than usual, and many peasants died of starvation. Others escaped into the jungle and became outlaws. Bengal was ruined and stayed that way for many years.

In the light of the way in which these and other disasters were handled, the way in which the country was stripped of its wealth, and the sundry massacres and executions that be-smirched the occupation, it comes as something of a surprise to read on the cover of Lawrence James' magnum opus, *Raj: the Making and Unmaking of British India*, that British rule was 'simultaneously an exercise in benign autocracy and an experiment in altruism'; and that the author concludes that 'for all their faults, and the worst were spasms of *impatience* and *high-handedness* [my italics], those who set about the remaking of India showed remarkable dedication to their ideals and the welfare of its peoples'. And even more disappointingly, James suggests that those who have a different viewpoint are merely following the dictates of fashion, or striving to be 'politically correct'. Indeed, he says 'the residual Marxism which still lurks on many university campuses' is also to blame.[278]

I hope I have shown that there were indeed many Britons who worked tirelessly for the welfare of the country; and many too admired and appreciated its peoples. To take two examples, both taken from William Digby's *India for the Indians.* The first is Sir Thomas Munro, 'incomparably the best governor Madras ever had' says Digby, who believed that '...if a good system of agriculture, if unrivalled manufactures...if the establishment of schools for reading and writing, if the general practice of kindness and hospitality...are amongst the points that denote a civilised people, then the Hindus are not inferior in civilisation to the people of Europe'.[279] The second is the *Spectator* magazine, which published an article 'recognising the new India which has sprung into existence under the fostering care of Lord Ripon' [Viceroy, 1880-4]. '...they devised the tank system of irrigation, not we; they built the Taj and the Temple of Sheringham, not we; and they and not we, founded Benares, Jeypore and Umritsar...'[280] There is Dr Cornish, Sanitary Commissioner of Madras 'whose good work' wrote Digby 'can never be over-praised';[281] and William Digby himself, about whom the *Deccan Herald* commented, 'he has the satisfaction of knowing that thousands and tens of thousands of lives have been saved by his instrumentality and through the determined action he took, in spite of the cold water thrown upon it in the highest quarters'. And finally there was what is usually described in these or similar terms: the army of young men fresh from their public schools and universities in Britain, who were sent to the farthest corners of the sub-continent, there to dispense justice, to the best of their ability, without fear or favour. But the fact remained that the government's apparent indifference to the suffering of the poor, concurrent with the greed of many of its officials and its colossal expenditure on 'wasteful extravaganzas' were evidently turning more and more Indians against colonial rule. [282]

But this is a story of Kerala, and Kerala seems to have survived the 1870 famine better than most of the south. Perhaps the people survived because they could catch fish from the sea and those rivers that had not completely dried up, and could turn to that important alternative crop – tapioca. In any event there is no record of a concentration camp in the state and no mention of particular horrors in any of the histories of Kerala that I have read.

CHAPTER THIRTY-NINE

ELSEWHERE: MUMBAI, THE CITY THAT NEVER SLEEPS

'The city hums with activity and…seems to be constantly on the move'
- Toby Sinclair, *Introduction to India*

Gateway to India, Mumbai

Mumbai is on course to be the biggest city in the world. It's also where Manga and I were first together in India, and it's where a large and important part of our family lives. This is the branch born of

Manga's eldest sister, officially named Lakshmi, whom the family called Rashakka. Rashakka's husband, Ramaswamy, was a cook – and a very special one, for he was chef to no less a person than the Raja of Kochi. He had been married before and had a son whom Manga calls Mani. Mani was only three when Rashakka was married and his father wasn't entirely sure how well his new wife would treat a stepson [one of his sisters stirred things up a bit too] so he used to take Mani with him to work. The story was that Mani took his daytime naps in the big cauldrons used to cook payasam! Mani never called Rashakka 'Mum' till he moved to Mumbai twenty years later. Manga says that her sister was overcome with emotion when she heard the lad say the magic word at last after she'd looked after him for all those long years. When Mani was settled in Mumbai – he'd obtained a good job with Standard Batteries there – he suggested that Rashakka's eldest son Raju might join him, because there were many more employment possibilities there than in Kochi. Then the second, third and in due course the fourth, sons joined him too for the same reason as soon as they left school.

By all accounts, the boys had a wonderful time together until Mani got married. His wife was a perfectly pleasant person, but seems to have been a little too careful with her money and expected the boys to pay all the bills. When they found she was squirrelling away a substantial sum, they upped and went, saying goodbye to Mani, and moving out to Vasai in the district of Thane, just outside the city, on the mainland. After the four boys, Rashakka finally had a daughter, named after our Manga, and when young Mangalam had passed her SSLC [Secondary School Leaving Certificate], she and her parents moved to Vasai too. Although Mangalam was the first surviving daughter, Rashakka's firstborn had been a girl too. Manga remembers Vijayalakshmi being born. She helped look after the baby for the fifty-six days that Rashakka stayed in her mother's home, according to the established custom. But within a month of Rashakka re-joining her husband, the little girl died. Young Manga was inconsolable when she heard the news, and at once developed fever, causing anxiety about her own survival.

The boys' house in Vasai was the one we stayed in when my mother visited India. By that time, most of the family had moved out. 'Bombay' Raju, as we always call him to differentiate him from my nephew in Kerala, was living in a very small house close by; it didn't seem anywhere near big enough for him, his wife and three young daughters. Chandran, the second son had a flat down the line. He had a white-collar job and at that time gave me at least the impression that he felt a bit superior: he did not deign to come to see us. Their third son Hari had joined the exodus to the Gulf, but his wife Kala had stayed behind and she was in the house with her mother-in-law. Ramani was still there too at that time with his wife. Mangalam had been married for several years and was the mother of two beautiful baby daughters. She was a teacher and lived in the city, again in a tiny but immaculate house.

Vasai in 1979

The house in Vasai was a decent size, without a water supply of course, but the well was just outside the back door. The well-water was sweet at that time but for some reason it became salty later and the water from a standpipe had to be used for drinking. Mangalam says they decided to make the well deeper, and drilled into the roots of a tree while doing so. It was the tree apparently that made the water bitter; Mangalam thinks it might have been a bhendi or Indian tulip tree. The standpipe was a good distance away, and you needed to queue – for a long time if there was a drought - and carry the heavy containers back on head or hip.

The main problem for all of us on that first visit though was the toilet facilities – an outside loo in a small wooden hut standing proudly in the middle of a large yard shared by pigs, chickens and goats, with an open drain proceeding from it. One's excrement was supposed to go into a bucket, the contents of which were collected by a 'scavenger' every other day. But there must have been overflows or near misses because I'm sure after I'd paid a visit I saw familiar-looking poo flowing down the drain and being enthusiastically investigated by the local porkers. One thing I have always wondered at. From their tiny houses, overcrowded, barely furnished and lacking the most basic facilities, the members of my new Indian family would emerge every morning, like butterflies from cocoons, immaculate, colourful and beautiful. My admiration knew no bounds.

Rashakka's family now live in luxury flats - still in the Vasai district with all mod cons, and drinking water delivered in large containers which connect to refrigerators to supply ice-cold water on tap!

The new apartments in Vasai, 2013

The flats are beautifully furnished and there is more living-space than in my house. It rather amused Rashmi therefore when her husband's application for a visa to spend a holiday in England was turned down. Apparently the British authorities thought that he was prepared to ditch a comfortable life in Mumbai, not to mention his wife and daughter, in order to become an illegal immigrant. I'm afraid our rulers are sadly out of touch. Given their apparent hostility to visitors from the sub-continent, it's not surprising that the most discerning students, doctors and nurses now choose to move to Canada, Australia or other parts of Europe, rather than this country, and it will not be long before our universities, hospitals and care homes will suffer as a result. And incidentally, that sort of attitude is unlikely to improve this country's trade record with India. At the moment, less than 1.5% of India's imports come from Britain.

But we should return to the early days of the family's history in Mumbai. In time, Ramani, the youngest son, followed Hari to the Gulf where he found a good job in Bahrain and earned enough money for his own needs and those of his extended family, and to help anyone else who was having problems. Manga, Juliema and I visited Ramani in Bahrain once. He was living in a house shared with five other ex-pats and was clearly looked upon as everyone's elder brother, dispensing advice, support and sympathy to all. Incidentally, the 'boys' were far from the stereotype of an under-class exploited by heartless Arab paymasters. One was a tailor who admittedly worked all hours but was pretty well his own boss; and another dealt with contracts for a big construction firm. Ramani was a driver, but on very good terms with the Arab owner of the business that employed him. He introduced his boss to us and even I was a little over-awed by this tall and elegant individual, with large brown liquid eyes and dressed in a dazzlingly white dishdashah. I looked round at Manga who'd always been a big fan of Omar Sharif. Both she and Juliema were pretty well literally entranced, looking up at the Sheikh with adoring expressions, quite speechless! But the point I am trying to make is that Ramani is subject to no one. He spoke freely in Arabic and English to his Sheikh, and later, on the street chatted to a ragged Pakistani ex-pat labourer in Urdu. His daughter Pooja incidentally is studying in Canada.

So that's a very brief account of our Mumbai family history. And in some senses it does mirror one aspect of Kerala and indeed Indian history as a whole. For Mumbai has for years been a magnet for people from all over eastern and southern India and as a result has grown into a monster city of at least 14 million – and that excludes the district of Thane where Vasai lies. The family all work and/or study in the city though – involving, to say the least, uncomfortable trips sometimes lasting for hours in Mumbai's famously overcrowded commuter trains: from which everyone nonetheless seems to spill out unruffled and in good humour. It's remarkable. I must tell one quick story. One day, when the children were quite young, we found ourselves on the commuter train at rush hour. We were so packed in that there seemed little possibility of us getting out at the right station – but when we arrived there, Manga looked after Victoria and I grabbed a twin's hand in each of mine and powered my way through to the exit. I made it, but looking down to check on Indi and Laksh, saw that I had brought with me two other passengers as well, firmly stuck one under each of my arms! Although they'd lost their train, far from being angry, both laughed good-naturedly as did the rest of the platform! But this journey from the city to Thane is not one we enjoy, especially if we're weighed down with all our luggage. Mangalam's daughter Rashmi tells me that now there are alternative road routes to Vasai. There are still long delays but, as she points out, at least one can be comfortable as one goes through the ordeal of rush hour. I'm afraid the rail journey is one reason why we have not visited Vasai as often as we would like to have done, for we always had a wonderful welcome and a good time there. It's not surprising that Mangalam and Ramani built houses in the peaceful haven of Variyathmadam in Trikkandiyur for their retirement! Although Rashmi says she now feels more at home in the city, and probably won't ever move permanently back to Kerala. Everyone from Mumbai loves to spend holidays back home though.

Rashmi and Pooja from Mumbai

Well, I've written a lot about the family and not much about the city. I guess that's because I have a lot of love for the former and not so much for the latter. The problem probably stems from my first experience of Mumbai, when I arrived late to meet Manga off the boat from England. That was not a good introduction to the city. On a later occasion poor Grandma was reduced to tears as she watched so many desperately poor families living out their lives in the rail-side shanty towns that characterised Mumbai. On that occasion we did enjoy our visit to a large emporium where we bought some interesting souvenirs and saw an almost life-size model of Tipu Sultan's tiger eating an English soldier with suitable sound effects; though even that day was marred by the apparent impossibility of changing travellers' cheques in one of the world's most important financial centres. We've never used travellers' cheques since.

We once stayed in the luxurious Taj Mahal Hotel! Uncharacteristically, we used top-class accommodation when we explored India by rail with Rosemary and Tony and family, a state of affairs born of Tony's enthusiasm for railways, his unfailing generosity, and his appreciation of the good things in life. After the long train journey from Mysore, we refreshed ourselves in palatial bathrooms and swam and lazed by the pool. Nearby, Manga and I rocked gently on the famous two-person swing. Then we all explored, found our way to the top of the hotel and climbed onto the roof to enjoy the views. Behind us, across Back Bay, rose Malabar Hill, where the city's rich have their houses and where the Parsis leave their dead on the Tower of Silence. Right in front of us was the Gateway to India, commissioned by the British to mark the visit to India of King George V, and beyond that massive edifice we could see the wooded Elephanta Island, home of Hindu and Buddhist temples, carved out of the basalt rock well over a thousand years ago. And then we dined beneath crystal chandeliers, outnumbered by our waiters, before making our way back to the railway station, to catch our train north to Rajasthan.

We've had fun in the city on other occasions too – eating in little cafés recommended by Mangalam [junior], buying bangles by the roadside and browsing the pavement bookstalls among the Victorian arcades in the streets near Flora Fountain, in the shadow of the Martyrs Memorial. The martyrs, incidentally, were not in this case fighting for freedom from the British, but fighting for a unified state of Maharastra.

I'm afraid there have been many martyrs in Mumbai since 1960. Sujita Patel and Alice Thorner have described the first of the communal riots that have since rocked Mumbai at regular intervals. They took place in December 1992 after the destruction of the Babri Mosque in Ayodhya by Hindu militants. '...the news travelled across India within minutes...In the Muslim-majority areas of Bombay, particularly the Mohammed Ali Road in south Bombay where one can buy anything from a safety pin to a refrigerator, the news came as a shock.

The swing in the Taj Hotel

The reaction was almost instantaneous. Hundreds of angry people, mostly young men, streamed onto the road to express their anger. The police, partly caught unawares and partly over-reacting, shot into the crowd. Later on the same night, a police constable was stabbed to death in an adjoining area.'[283] This led to counter-demonstrations, deaths, mainly of Muslims, and destruction of property including mosques. Then in January 1993, many people were killed, again mainly Muslims, after two Hindu dockworkers were murdered. Every time there is a new bombing we fear for our relations. In one case, the attack on a commuter train, Rashmi was in the one following, and Ramanan and Pooja were commuting that day too. And we also await with sadness, news of the seemingly inevitable reprisals against the innocent. The attack on the Taj Hotel in November 2009 was particularly high profile and shocking, I think because instead of the secretive bombs, this was an open attack by an armed group.

It is often said that the rioting and communal hatred and suspicion have been fomented by the Maharastran nationalist party, the Shiv Sena. Its founder Bal Thackeray was a Nazi sympathiser; perhaps that says enough in itself.

CHAPTER FORTY

KERALA FIGHTS FOR FREEDOM

'Will a man with a sore on his hip pass through a narrow style?' - Malayalam proverb

'When I despair, I remember that all through history the ways of truth and love have always won. There have been tyrants, and murderers, and for a time they can seem invincible, but in the end they always fall. Think of it – always' - Mahatma Gandhi.

'In any society the dominant groups are the ones with the most to hide about the way society works. Very often therefore truthful analyses are bound to have a critical ring, to seem like exposures rather than objective statements...for all students of human society, sympathy with the victims of historical processes and scepticism about the victors' claims provide essential safeguards against being taken in by the dominant mythology. A scholar who tries to be objective needs these feelings as part of his ordinary working equipment' - Barrington Moore [quoted by Robert Hardgrave]

'I object to violence because when it appears to do good, the good is only temporary; the evil it does is permanent' - Mahatma Gandhi

Very little mention is made of Kerala's part in the independence struggle in the popular histories and Gangadharan agrees that 'the role played by Bengal, Maharastra, the United Provinces, Gujarat etc. was more important and great' than that of Kerala[284]. However he goes on to say that Kerala's contribution is easy to under-estimate, for after all, the first popular revolts against the British in India took place in Wayanad – the Pazhassi and Kuruchia revolts described earlier - and there were constant small-scale actions by the Mappilas. It has to be admitted however that the issues involved were mainly local and/or communal in nature and there was certainly nothing on the scale of the Sepoy Mutiny. It was not until 1919 that the Indian National Congress, which had been founded in 1885, made any impact on the people of Kerala, even though a number of Malayalees were involved in the Congress in the early days, notably G.P.Pillai and Sir C.Sankaran Nair, President of the I.N.C. in 1897. None were active in Kerala though. Things began to move a little following a public meeting held in Kozhikode in 1916. The Collector ruled that all speeches at the meeting had to be made in English, and the outrage caused by this decision led many into the freedom movements. A branch of the Home Rule League was formed [with an Iyer as President: Manjeri Rama of that ilk]. Political Conferences in 1916 at Palakkad, chaired by Annie Besant, one of the founders of the Theosophical Society, and in 1917 at Kozhikode, under the chairmanship of another Iyer, C.P.Ramaswamy, passed resolutions requesting Home Rule and the release of political prisoners. But it was all very middle class and polite, and resolutions were also passed declaring loyalty to King George V.

Dissatisfaction with British rule increased after the end of the Great War, and in 1921, it exploded in the Great Malabar Rebellion. The world expert on this event is Robert Hardgrave and my account of what happened is based on his study entitled *The Mappila Rebellion 1921: Peasant revolt in Malabar.* Unless otherwise stated, any quotations are taken from this work.

The catalyst for the uprising was a rather odd occurrence – the rise of the Khilafat movement. This was all about the Sultan of Turkey who was also the Caliph - the religious leader - of Muslims in Turkey, Egypt, Central Asia and also India. Turkey fought on the losing side in World War One and as a result the Sultan was deprived of his temporal empire. Some Indian Muslims in particular regarded this as a British attack on their religion and so were motivated to revolt against their infidel ruler. Added to this was the bitterness felt by Kerala Muslims [the Mappilas] against their [mainly Namboodiri] landowners, who were supported by the British. And Gandhiji supported the Khilafat movement as a means of bringing more Muslims into the liberation struggle. The scene was set for what became known as the Mappila Revolt of 1921.

In the beginning the Mappilas were happy to follow the non-violent principles of Congress, but as the tenancy situation worsened, violence became more and more likely. Robert Hardgrave points out that both Travancore and Kochi had passed laws providing security of tenure for peasants, but Malabar hadn't. This was further grist to the mill of revolt. Those who wanted tenancy reform and campaigners for freedom from the British both looked for action from the Mappilas. This 'proved tragically successful...

egged on by the more fanatical of their leaders, the Moplah peasants transformed what had begun as a series of well-organised boycotts of evicting landowners into a large-scale spontaneous insurrection against all forms of authority...' It was 'pure mockery' wrote R.H.Hitchcock in his 1925 official account of the events, to dress the Mappilas 'in the garb of a soldier and yet tell him he should attain his aims by spinning'.[285] Impetus was provided by the arrest of a Muslim leader from Madras and members of the Malabar Congress when they attempted to defy a ban on Khilafat meetings. The *Madras Mail* judged that : '...the great bulk of the Moplahs are steeped in ignorance, and mischievous agitators, taking advantage of this fact, are playing upon their credulity and are trying to inflame them...' and fanned the flames of fear by recounting 'Moplah outrages of the past'... and warning that 'the danger of some sudden outbreak of fanaticism especially among the ignorant and backward Moplah inhabitants of Ernad and Walluvanad taluqs, is an ever-present cause of anxiety.'

And sure enough, the violence arrived, and in Ernad. In the village of Pukkottur, police had to disperse a crowd apparently preparing to attack the home of a Namboodiri landlord; and a few days later, a group of Hindus drinking at a toddy house was attacked: banning alcohol was one of the Khilafat aims. The authorities were becoming concerned and decided to arrest supposed ringleaders in their hometown of Tirurangadi [which is only about 20 km from Tirur]. They failed, but in the process, searched a mosque. What followed is described here by Mahmud Schamnad, the only Mappila in the Legislative Assembly in Delhi.

> ...news got abroad that their sacred mosque at Tirurangadi was besieged and going to be bombarded. All the people who heard this news hurried to the mosque from all the neighbouring villages, just to intercede and save the mosque. When the Collector heard that a crowd was arriving by the road...he went with an armed party, fired and dispersed them. In the meantime, the neighbours and friends of the arrested had gone to the kacheri [court] and requested the sahibs there to release their friends. They were told to sit down and wait for the Collector to come...The Collector's party came. Their arrival was a signal for opening fire on the mob, there waiting without any suspicion. When they saw they were being fired on from either side, they rushed forward and attacked the officers...' The official

> account was, as one might imagine, rather different, and the Collector wrote to Madras to say that, 'the attempt to make searches and arrests under legal warrants and in due conformity to the law has been the signal for an outbreak of fanaticism'...

Nine Mappilas and two British were killed. Military rule was imposed and there was open rebellion in the countryside. British rule was said to have ended and the Mappila leader in Tirurangadi announced that the British were finished, and he was now Raja of Malabar. Early reports indicated that both Hindus and Muslims were involved; indeed, it was reported that the leader of the Khilafat movement in Malabar was himself a Hindu. However, as time passed it was mostly Hindus who were being killed - in Ponnani, Walluvanad and Ernad taluks in particular. The *Madras Mail* again exerted its baleful influence. 'Every alleged murder, atrocity and forced conversion was reported in grisly detail, feeding the anxieties of the Hindu community.' And here is where...

History Gets Personal

The Hindu community in Tirur at this time included our family. Lakshmi and Parameswaran, my parents-in-law, who had been married for 15 years and had several young children, were of course Brahmins, but Iyers not Namboodiris, and certainly not landowners. They had a number of Muslim friends, and though they themselves had little money to spare, were always willing to help the poor Mappilas who lived in the village. They didn't read the *Madras Mail* but anyway would not have believed that the local Mappilas would hurt anyone. But they did know that two or three of their neighbours had decided that they urgently needed to see distant cousins who lived in Madras or was it Bangalore, and had left the village for an unspecified period. Then one morning in mid-August 1921, Lakshmi was about to take her two youngest children to school, and had just reached the garden gate when she heard rustling in the bushes. She spun round and caught sight of a figure partially hidden behind one of the coconut trees in the compound. She was beginning to feel a bit scared. The figure was now beckoning. She couldn't decide what to do. There was no sense in calling out. Both her neighbours had been among those who had decided that discretion was the better part of valour, and had temporarily moved away from the dangers of south Malabar. So there was no one nearby to hear her. The milk had been delivered, the bangle man was not expected till tomorrow and the fish seller wouldn't be around till evening. [She didn't buy fish of course, but always said hello when the meenviapary - fishmonger - passed by along the alleyway]. No visitors would come now – they would all be busy preparing lunch. There was no point in trying to run either: if the man or men wanted to they would catch up with her easily...

Lakshmi took a deep breath, gripped the hands of her children tightly, and drew herself up to her full height of 4 feet and 8 inches. '*What do you want*?' she called out. The response sounded nervous. '*Quiet, please*!' whispered the intruder. '*Come this way; I mean you no harm*'. Lakshmi had little choice but to obey. She took two paces forward and saw him – a Mappila certainly, wearing a length of cotton roughly wrapped around his head as a turban, a torn and dirty shirt, and a short lungi which might have been blue in better times. His eyes were wide and flicked from side to side. Far from being dangerous, he was obviously scared stiff. And now Lakshmi recognised him. It was Abdul, who worked as a porter at the railway station. '*I have to be quick,*' he said. '*And you have to promise you'll tell no-one you've seen me. Do you promise*?' Lakshmi nodded. '*Listen: there's going to be a raid. On the bank in the town. But then they're going to come down here to pull down the Temple. They're mad – they're after blood. You must hide: follow me – but be careful. You can stay at my house; you'll be safe there.*' With that he hurried off and Lakshmi followed, thoroughly scared now. She was at least pleased that her husband had gone to see a patient in Ponnani and would be staying the night. If he were here he'd try and defend his beloved temple and perhaps pay for it with his life...

In fact the raid does not seem to have been as murderous as Abdul had feared. A telegram from Madras to the Viceroy claimed that a 'mob' of 10,000 Mappilas had burned down the bank, but even the British did not claim there was loss of life – though they noted that several men including at least one European had been captured. And as for the invasion of the Trikkandiyur Temple, the *Madras Mail*, not known for its reticence, although speaking of 'unimaginable sacrilegious acts' could only illustrate them by adding: 'It is said that the Moplahs spat and left the Koran near the sanctum'.[286] Manga, although she recalls that some of the idols in the temple are chipped, doesn't remember any comment by friends or family about what the Muslims did. That could be a sensible decision to forget the past in the interests of living in peace in the present; or it could be that the atrocities were not as great as the British authorities and the *Madras Mail* had reported. It's certainly of interest to read what the leaders of the Hindus and Muslims said at the time. Gopalan Nair in his book *The Moplah Rebellion* wrote that the Hindus of Malabar were suffering terribly at the hands of 'the overzealous fanatical Mappilas. He wrote as much to Yakub Hassan, a member of the Madras legislature. Abdul Rahman of the Kerala Khilafat Committee also wrote to Hassan, but he was expressing concern about the plight of the Muslims: '...The military is said to fire Muslim houses and loot Muslim shops... Reports of very horrible atrocities which I won't mention for want of authenticity are reaching us. For god's sake, for the sake of these poor Muslims, try your best to stop the martial law regime...' So innocents on both sides seem to have suffered. Most people seem to think that Gopalan Nair exaggerated the number of attacks on Hindus and enforced conversions. Saumyendranath Tagore wrote [in *Peasants Revolt*] that The Arya Samaj, a militant Hindu organisation, took photographs of the few Hindus who were murdered and displayed them as 'the horror of Moplah atrocities' in order to stimulate communalism.[i]

Shortly after the raid on Tirur, British troops were reinforced and attacked Tirurangadi, which they believed was the centre of the uprising. The Mappilas were defeated and 24 killed and 38 surrendered. The numbers seem rather small if this really was an important battle. On this same day, the Governor of Madras informed the Viceroy that the 'rebels' controlled the 'whole interior' of South Malabar, apart from Palghat. So the next step was to move inland where there were an estimated ten thousand armed Mappilas, operating in a number of separate groups, the biggest of which was said to be three thousand strong. But the British applied the standard strategy of terrorising the villagers into

---

[i] The authors of The Proudest Day, describe the raid thus: 'a mob of 10,000 set fire to the police *station and courts and siezed all the arms and ammunition. They sacked Hindu homes, destroyed their temples and raped the Hindu women...' One might perhaps take this account more seriously if the authors hadn't described the perpetrators as 'a fanatical Muslim group known as Moplahs

withholding support from these groups, at the same time as offering the carrot of amnesty to anyone who surrendered. And although one would have thought that guerrilla warfare would have been extremely successful in the Malabar hills, the Mappilas held out for no more than a few months. The leaders surrendered or were captured and in due course, executed.

Hardgrave reports: 'in the course of the rebellion, official figures recorded that 2339 rebels had been killed, 1652 wounded and 5955 captured. An additional 39,348 surrendered during the later stages of the rebellion.' It sounds as though a few non-combatants were surrendering in the hope of reward, rather like the very old men in the Indira Gandhi era who volunteered for vasectomies to earn a free transistor radio. Also there was a very high percentage of dead to wounded, possibly because the wounded continued to fight. Government casualties were 43 killed [including 5 British officers] and 126 wounded. And that was the end of it.

There are two more issues to think about. The first is whether decisions by the British, especially the Governor of Madras, the future Lord Willingdon, exacerbated the situation. Hardgrave maintains that they did. Congress leaders, both Hindu and Muslim, did not want violence and 'offered their services to help the victims of the disturbances. Many were arrested for their efforts.' The secretary of the Ernad Congress Committee saved the lives of several Englishmen by persuading a group of Mappilas to release them, only to be rewarded with a twelve-year prison sentence for treason. The author of the *Kozhikode Gazetteer* argued that 'the Government's policy of arresting Congress leaders and preventing them from using their influence with the Mappilas on the side of moderation and non-violence only helped worsen the situation.' Yakub Hassan, member of the Legislature, when he received the letters from Muslim and Hindu leaders quoted above, tried to go to Ernad to see what he could do to reduce tensions. But Lord Willingdon refused to allow this and wrote: 'The blackguard Yakub Hassan sought an interview with me yesterday, asking me if he might have a free pass from Government to go into Malabar and try and pacify the people... It's an outrage that these ruffians, who have been continuously preaching against the 'satanic' government, and have set the heather on fire, should now come cringing to me asking to be allowed to help us put it out'. A martial law order was even made to prevent Gandhi himself coming to help. Arrogant, short sighted, misguided, plain foolish, perhaps. Willingdon had wanted totalitarian powers over the whole of Malabar, but fortunately his boss, the Viceroy in Delhi, would not agree. Willingdon seems to have hit the nail on the head when he replied: 'You may think me a brutal and militant person; you may feel we are not to be trusted with summary powers…'[ii]

The Army was as extreme as the civil authorities in Madras. General Burnett-Stuart, the commanding officer of the forces in the Madras Presidency, wrote: 'I cannot commit myself to any prophecy as to when the rebellion is likely to end. It may go on in some districts until every Moplah is either exterminated or arrested.'

The Tirur Wagon Tragedy hardly helped pacify the rebels. Hardgrave comments: 'That the British were engaged in a policy of virtual genocide seemed evident to many Indians when it became known that in the transfer of prisoners in a closed railway van, 70 died of asphyxiation.'

Manga's home town of Tirur is probably more widely known for this event than for anything else, yet no one has ever mentioned it to me, and I knew nothing about it till comparatively recently. What happened was almost certainly an accident, though in the words of Laurence James[287], comparing the incident with another tragic [though exaggerated] accident, the Black Hole of Calcutta, 'in neither case did the perpetrators seem particularly bothered by what happened'. Because of the very large number of arrests in the locality, there was a shortage of accommodation for prisoners in Malappuram. Some of the prisoners were therefore sent to Tirur but as there was no room in the jails there either, they had to be moved on again, this time to Bellary, which could be reached by rail. Hardgrave continues: 'A van was unloaded, cleaned out and disinfected. The prisoners - 97 Mappilas and 3 Hindus who were also implicated in the rebellion - were loaded in the van after being provided with food and water. The doors were shut and fastened, and the train left Tirur at 7.15 pm., November 19th. At 12.30 that night, the train arrived at Podanur, and the van doors were opened to give the men water.'

The report of the Committee appointed to enquire into the tragedy described what presented itself: '…the prisoners were

---

[ii] This did not stop Willingdon from being promoted to Viceroy himself in 1931.

found lying down in a state of collapse. Some of them were groaning and it was evident that a disaster had occurred.' Seventy prisoners died from asphyxiation and heat exhaustion. The Committee decided that what had happened was that the ventilators had been covered with fine-mesh gauze, which had been painted, and the paint and dust had blocked the airway and left the wagon 'practically airtight.' So nobody was blamed and the survivors and families of the dead were given a payment in compensation of just three rupees.

Causes of the Uprising

The British authorities hardly seem to have treated the Rebellion with sensitivity and diplomacy, and their arrogance almost certainly worsened the situation. But the leaders of the rebellion were not without fault either. Congress supported and encouraged the movement, in an attempt to show the British that they faced a united Hindu/Muslim front, but were unable to operate any sort of control, and might well have been unable to do so even had the British allowed them to try. And many of the Mappila leaders led their people on with unrealistic promises of a Muslim kingdom in Kerala. Or as Lord Willingdon put it in his usual thoughtful and constructive way: '[the Mappilas were] ignorant and misguided dupes of unscrupulous agitators'

Which leads us into the second debate: the extent to which the Rebellion was primarily a socio-economic, religious, or freedom movement. Hardgrave writes: 'The official government position on the causes of the disturbances was most succinctly expressed in the ruling of the Special Tribunal in the trial of Ali Musaliar:

> But it was not mere fanaticism, it was not agrarian troubles, it was not destitution that worked on the minds of Ali Musaliar and his followers. The evidence conclusively shows that it was the influence of the Khilafat and non-co-operation that drove them to their crime. It is this that distinguishes them from all previous outbreaks. Their intention was, absurd though it may seem, to subvert the British Government and to substitute a Khilafat government by force of arms.'

The *Madras Mail*, whose 'inflammatory diatribes...had done so much to arouse Hindu fears and hostility towards the Mappilas...' agreed with this view and described the sufferings of the agrarian poor as a 'myth'. And Annie Besant agreed too: P.K.K.Menon's *History of the Freedom Movement in Kerala* quotes her as saying that the 'heart- breaking wretchedness of the rebellion was due directly to the violent and unscrupulous attacks on the government made by the Non-Co-operators and the Khilafists...'

Ranged against these luminaries was first the 'Bengali Trotskyite' S.Tagore, for whom the revolt was part of the inevitability of history: the poor seeking to overthrow their masters. A more detailed explanation and 'the most sophisticated analysis of the rebellion yet published' according to Robert Hardgrave, was put forward by the famous Kerala communist E.M.S.Namboodiripad. He said that the simple agrarian explanation was unlikely because the uprising was confined to Muslims. The poverty and despair of the landless poor was certainly important but there were other factors: the Khilafat affair certainly was a catalyst and the 'higher sense of organisation' of the Muslims - it is a far more 'corporate' religion than Hinduism - meant the movement quickly took off. Newspaper reports and provocation by the Government then fanned the flames. Taking all views into account, it seems fair to say that as is often the case, there was no single reason for the revolt.

Hardgrave sums up the conclusion of the episode, thus: 'as the violence increased, polarising conflict between the two competing polities, more people were drawn into the struggle. Against the massive force of official violence, that which the Mappilas might offer in resistance proved feeble. Within six months, the rebellion was over.'

Civil Disobedience

Not surprisingly, little was heard from Kerala for some years after the crushing of the Mappilas. And the Khilafat movement failed elsewhere in India too. Developments such as those in Malabar - violence, communal conflict, absence of a clear objective – depressed Gandhi, now clearly the leader of the Congress party, and made him feel that Indians were perhaps not yet ready to rule themselves. He gave up the struggle and made no protest when he was arrested and sent to jail for 6 years. Muslims felt that Congress had let them down, and felt further betrayed when the Caliphate was abolished by the new secular leader of Turkey, Kemal Attaturk. So the 1920s saw a lull in 'rebellious' activity and a concentration on social reforms. But when the Simon Commission was formed in 1928, the nationalist movement began to fire up again, for the Commission, charged with designing the future of India, did not include even a token Indian member. Enraged, Congress demanded immediate Dominion status; then [courtesy of Jawaharlal Nehru] 'purna swaraj' – complete independence. And when Gandhiji was released from jail on health grounds, direct action began again.

And Kerala joined the party. A significant group of Malayalee activists joined in Gandhiji's Salt Satyagraha in 1930. This act of defiance arose from disgust at the imposition of a tax on salt, a necessity of life and as such a symbol of the Indian freedom-seekers. Salt was made illegally using sea-water at Payyanur and on Kozhikode beach and the leaders were arrested. Throughout the country it was estimated that 90,000 demonstrators were jailed. This was followed by a boycott of foreign goods as part of the Civil Disobedience movement, which continued until March 1931, when the campaign was called off by Gandhiji as part of an agreement with the viceroy: the Irwin Pact.

Peace did not last and in January 1932, Civil Disobedience was resumed. Courts, schools and colleges, foreign goods and liquor shops were boycotted, especially in north Malabar, and illegal public meetings were held in Kozhikode. But in India as a whole, the momentum was lost, and Congress were showing more interest in talks, joining the second session of the Round Table conference in London.

Fluctuations in policy there may have been at home, but Congress leaders were constant in being aware of the importance of influencing public opinion overseas, and to that end, they set up The India League, which became 'the voice of Congress in Britain.'[288] And the leader of the League was Mr. V.K.Krishna Menon, a very distinguished son of Kerala, so it is pertinent to tell his story in this chapter.

Vengalil Krishnan Krishna Menon was born in Panniyankara, Kozhikode, in May 1896 and rose to become one of the leading figures in the newly independent Indian Government in 1947. Krishna Menon's father was a lawyer and his mother a musician and his family was well off; indeed some say that it was one of the richest in Malabar. Menon's education began at the 'Calicut Native High School', and from there he went to the Madras Presidency College and in 1918, to the City's Law School. He did not follow in his father's footsteps however, for he met Annie Besant and joined her Home Rule Movement before completing his studies.

In 1924, Menon travelled to London simply to take a teaching qualification – but stayed for 23 years! While in England, he obtained a first-class B.Sc. degree, followed by an M.Sc. and an M.A.; and was called to the bar in 1934. He did not however make his name in the legal profession. Rozina Visram says KM did most of his studying in the evenings: in the daytime he was busy earning money by teaching, journalism and publishing [he was involved in the founding of Penguin and Pelican books] and above all by working for 'purna swaraj' – India's complete self-rule. This son of Malabar addressed meetings all over England, wrote many articles and booklets, enlisted support for independence from something like 100 MPs and acted as secretary to a group of Labour Members who visited India to write a report on the British Raj; sadly they found many instances of injustice and brutality. In addition Krishna Menon was elected as a Labour councillor in St Pancras, where he worked for the people and proved so popular that not only did his majority increase at each election[289], but he demonstrated by example that Indians were quite capable of government.

The Beginnings of Kerala Communism

Many Congress Workers in Kerala were interested in socialism, and were losing confidence in the mainstream Congress leadership, because it didn't seem to be consistent in its campaigns or policies. Nonetheless they wished to stay under the Congress umbrella, and so they formed the Kerala Congress Socialist Party in Kozhikode in 1934, leader P.Krishna Pillai. The same thing was happening in other parts of India too and in May 1934, at the conference of the All-India Congress Committee in Patna, at which the Kerala socialist representative was E.M.S. Namboodiripad [the renowned 'Ems', who became the first Chief Minister of Kerala in 1957], a national Congress Socialist Party was formed. Its leader was Jayaprakash Narayan and he visited Kerala later that year. [Much later 'JP' became a member of the Janata Party, the first non-Congress party to form a national government in India. When I was working in Bihar, he was a much-revered Gandhian and leader of the Sardovya movement, promoting land reform and the advance of untouchables and the importance of village life.]

Gangadharan says that the 'formation of the CSP provided a new enthusiasm in the national movement in Malabar. The Socialist Party... [had] an independent label in Malabar...[and] most of the socialist leaders in Kerala had a different political outlook from their national leaders.'[290] In fact, the ideology they preferred was that of the communists – but, since the Communist Party was banned in India, its adherents had to stay in the KCSP. They soon took control of the Kerala Congress Party, with EMS and C.K.Gopalan Nair as Joint Secretaries, and embarked on a policy of organising and mobilising under-privileged groups especially in Malabar. Woodcock maintains that the communists infiltrated into these groups.[291] Certainly they led and motivated them but no one else was prepared at this time to fight alongside the peasants, and the communist leaders were widely hailed as saviours. They helped the peasants fight against oppressive taxes and encouraged the formation of workers' organisations that sought to improve wages and working conditions, in the beedi, cotton, and railway industries. The All- Kerala Trades Union Congress met for the first time in Kozhikode in 1935; there were strikes and a Hunger March [Pattini Jatha] from Kannur to Chennai was organised.

India joined the Second World War in 1939, but this was the British Government's decision and no Indian leader was consulted. The Congress Party said they would nonetheless co-operate in the war effort, but only if Britain promised India independence when the war was over. Britain did not agree and the leftist Congress leadership in Kerala reacted by organising another round of civil disobedience. On Anti- Repression Day, 15 September, marches and meetings were held in north Malabar in defiance of government orders and indeed against the instructions of the national Congress leadership too. Police opened fire on the demonstrators and there were deaths on both sides. The results of these clashes were far-reaching. K.P.R.Gopalan was sentenced to death [he was later reprieved], but of more import, the national Congress Party dissolved the Kerala Committee, which 'put an end to the period of 'Congress communism' in Malabar'. Communists and Congress were now two quite separate parties, and their policies seemed diametrically opposed. While Congress under Gandhiji called for passive protest, the Communists in Malabar continued to take direct action and a number of clashes took place. Peasants marched against their landlords, a policeman was accidentally drowned, and 'terror was unleashed for many days as the police turned on the communists and peasant groups.'[292] Four activists were sentenced to death and hanged.

So when Congress called for action – the 'Quit India' movement of 1942 – and non co-operation with the war effort, one would have expected Malabar to be at the forefront. Far from it. Communist Russia had now joined the war on the side of the Allies. To the Kerala CPI, this was no longer then an Imperialists' war, but a people's struggle - and they called off action against the British! As Manga says, these Malayalees have minds of their own. There were of course still Congress supporters in Malabar and they conducted various acts of sabotage, including the destruction of a number of public buildings.

Incidentally, many British people are baffled by the failure of some Indians to support our side in the war. They argue that there is little doubt that the Japanese or Germans would continue to keep India under the colonial yoke and be much less sympathetic rulers than the British. Indeed one writer to a national newspaper went so far as to call Subhas Chandra Bose a 'turncoat' for forming the Indian National Army to fight on the side of the Japanese. What they don't seem to understand is that if one is suffering the deprivation and indignity of colonial rule one is hardly likely to try and weigh the scales between various possible oppressors. And remember Bose's Bengal was suffering an appalling famine at this time, and the British were doing nothing to help. Between two and four million of the poor in Bengal died from hunger and its associated diseases in 1943. And 'even if the lower figure is accepted, the famine still killed more Indians than did two world wars, the entire independence struggle, plus the communal holocaust that accompanied partition'.[293] To Nehru, this was 'the final judgement on British rule in India'.[294] No doubt the Bengali administrators and landowners were not blameless, but as Keay points out, 'the British governor of the province had ample powers for such a crisis and did nothing'[295] so Bose and his companions would have been unlikely to believe that their current masters were especially benevolent.

The year 1943 also saw a famine in Malabar. Like so much of the history of this faraway corner of India it has a very low profile, and is not mentioned even in Gangadharan's history. Manga's family remembers it as a time of food shortage rather than full-blown famine. It is likely of course that they did not feel the full effects of the shortages because, although they themselves were very poor, they did have friends who were landowners and would doubtless have helped them out. Also, my nephew Raju explains that famine seems to have been less of a problem in Kerala than elsewhere because of the availability of 'the humble tapioca'. This plant is easily grown in Kerala: 'just push the stem into the ground', says Raju, 'and the plant will sprout'. It's not a food that is much enjoyed in Kerala, but it is filling and so has been a life-saving fall-back throughout history. Raju explains *'some species need boiling and the water draining or they will taste bitter – can even be poisonous. They are very high in starch and I wonder if that's the reason for there being so many diabetics in Kerala. At one time only the lower castes would eat tapioca* [apart from our family, apparently - Manga says her father grew the vegetable for the pot] *and* [most] *Brahmins would avoid it unless there was nothing else. Now Geetha makes a dish out of it. She cuts the tapioca into small pieces, boils it with turmeric, drains and boils again with a little salt, and drains again. Then she adds whole chillies and shallots, and pounds the mixture gently. Next she grinds mustard seeds and curry leaves and adds the tapioca.'*

However, there does seem to have been famine in north Malabar on this occasion, especially in Kannur, where food shortages and an outbreak of cholera killed thousands of the poorest peasants.[296] Famine was certainly due to war conditions that reduced supply by hampering the internal distribution of food in India as well as cutting off the import of rice from Burma, which was occupied by the Japanese. There was also increased demand because of the greater number of overseas soldiers in the country. One such, Clive Branson, wrote a letter home while on leave in Bombay, on July 20, 1943. 'Malabar is a district where cholera is raging...in Thanur village 155 deaths occurred in one week; in Tirur Range 55 deaths in two days...' Branson went on to describe how local committees often led by communist party members or trade unionists were fighting the outbreaks while the Government stood by and did nothing.[297] In fact Malabar always existed on the edge of famine because of the use of agricultural land to grow cash crops, and of its consequent reliance on imports of food. In the country as a whole in the 1930s, 41% of Indians were regarded as poorly nourished and 20% as very badly nourished, according to figures from the 1933 report on public health prepared by Major General Sir John Megaw, the Director General of the Indian Medical Service. And yet Lord Linlithgow said he had left the country 'in pretty good shape' after his term in office as Viceroy (1936 - 1943). Wavell, his successor, was more realistic, acknowledging the famine in Bengal as 'one of the worst disasters which has befallen any people under British rule'.[298]

The Condition of the Princely States

We can get a glimpse of Travancore in the nineteen-thirties from *India of the Princes* written in 1939 by the traveller and adventurer, Rosita Forbes. At this time, Travancore's population was about 5 million, making it third biggest of the princely states of India after Hyderabad and Mysore. Miss Forbes tells us that about fifty per cent of men and fifteen per cent of women in Travancore were literate at that time, compared with national figures of fifteen per cent and only, believe it or not, three per cent. She goes on: 'There is a school for every two square miles. A hundred and twenty different newspapers and periodicals are printed in English and Malayalam, a fifth of the revenue is devoted to education...women play a prominent part in public life...'[299] The state then is progressive and modern, 'though without' says Forbes 'being pseudo-European'. As well as being an intrepid traveller, Forbes writes picturesquely, though some of her political opinions are somewhat controversial.[iii] This is how she describes the countryside near Trivandrum, the capital of Travancore state since 1745: 'Nowhere had I seen such a magnificently palmed landscape. However still the day, the long, curved fronds were stirred by a wind of their own and they covered hill and valley like a yellow-green smoke, for they had no particular form. Light as smoke

---

[iii] For example, she describes Tipu Sultan as 'half-lunatic' and has little time for the Mahatma.

they drifted over the horizon. All I could see were these billows and billows of palm trees with here and there a square pink house or a white one...'[300]

Rosita Forbes met their Highnesses, the Maharaja and his mother, who at this time was acting as Regent due to her son's youth. Being of the Nair caste, the Royal Family of course was a matriarchy.

> The succession to the throne and the big estates goes in the female line. So the heir to the present exceedingly intelligent and hard-working young Maharaja, after his brother, will not be any son of his own, but the infant boy born last year to his sister. The title of Maharani belongs not to the wife of the ruler, but to his mother, his aunt, or his elder sister. In effect, every male of the royal house has the right to reign, but none can transmit that right...[301]
>
> His Highness, very slender, with a face like an ivory miniature, wore one of those complicated turbans spreading into a fan over the left ear. His mother had draped many yards of fine white muslin in Grecian fashion so that it fell from shoulder to heel in lovely lines, showing only a scrap of tight, short-sleeved white bodice. Her head was bare, her very long black hair, steeped in oil, drawn back into an enormous loose knot on her shoulders. She wore no jewels. A power in the land and conscious of it, the Maharani, speaking, like her son, a much better English than mine, said: 'Naturally, the women in Travancore have a great deal of authority...[302]

The ruling family was also aware of at least some of the problems in the state. These arose partly from a well-educated population with few suitable employment opportunities. And the Maharaja and his Prime Minister were attempting to take action by financing industrialisation in the state.

But there had been unrest in Travancore for some time. It was our kinsfolk, the Tamil Brahmins who were involved in the first anti-government popular movement. But the movement was not pressing for freedom or democracy, and the Pattars were not the leaders. On the contrary, they were the cause of the unrest, for at the end of the nineteenth century they occupied the majority of senior Civil Service posts in the state. According to one Indian historian, the preference for Tamil Brahmins was not because they were better at the job, but because of 'their sycophancy, art of enticement and religious exhibitionism'![303] The Malayalees of course wanted these plum jobs for themselves. Ten thousand signatures [mostly of Nairs] were collected in support of the slogan 'Travancore for the Travancoreans!' and although little was achieved, it 'helped in the growth of political consciousness among the people of Travancore'. Other 'memorials' were presented to the Government containing the demands of different caste groups, and at the beginning of the last century criticism of the Diwan's [Prime Minister's] administration was contained in a new newspaper produced by Ramakrishna Pillai, the *Swadesabhimani*, which declared that government should reflect the will of the people. Although Pillai was deported, his ideas had taken root in the minds of the people, and a Congress Committee was formed in 1919. Among the small scale Gandhian acts of non-co-operation that were carried out was agitation against an increase in student tuition fees introduced by the Diwan.

The people of Travancore had had some experience of democracy since 1888, when the Maharaja introduced a small Legislative Council to advise the government; and a 'Popular Assembly' was elected in 1904. These bodies, which had little power, were consolidated into a single Council in 1921, with 28 elected and 22 nominated members. The 'Struggle for Responsible Government' as it was called, began in Trivandrum in 1929 when representatives from the princely states of Hyderabad, Pudukottai, Mysore, Kochi and Travancore met and demanded that the British enforce responsible government in the Native states. Some administrative reforms were granted in 1932, but the right to vote was restricted to landowners only, and as a result, the 'abstention' movement was started, and the elections were largely boycotted. At the next elections in 1937 the right to vote was extended but the demand of the Legislative Assembly for full responsible government was denied. This led to the formation of the Travancore State Congress - not part of the national party because it had been agreed that those in the native states should be responsible for their own destiny.

The State Congress was swiftly banned, but then legalised when the authorities were faced by a huge popular demonstration. Much of the anger of the people was directed against the Diwan, who happened to be an Iyer – Sir C.P.Ramaswami. He was prepared to start negotiations with Congress as long as it was agreed that he would remain in office. This caused a split among congress members, with the left demanding Ramaswamy's departure but the right agreeing to the compromise. The left subsequently withdrew from Congress and formed the Travancore Communist Party. The Communists quickly became influential especially among the poorer workers - the toddy-tappers, the coir workers, the fishing community and the agricultural labourers - all of whom had grievances against landlords, bosses and/or moneylenders. Soon there were clashes with those in power, culminating in a bloody battle near Alappuzha when 'the police and the army used machine guns to face the sickles and stones used by the workers'[304] and brutally crushed the uprising. Sir C.P.Ramaswami Iyer declared that Travancore would not become a part of India when the British left, but would remain an independent state. But the Diwan's declaration received little support [except from the Nizam of Hyderabad] and in due course following an attempted assassination of the Diwan, the Maharaja decided that Travancore would integrate into the Indian Union.

It does sound rather as though Sir C.P.Ramaswamy Iyer is not a relation of whom we should be especially proud! However there is another side to the story. Under C.P., the Temple Proclamation was made, under which all Hindus could enter temples in Travancore. This did not happen in the rest of Kerala until after the war. And C.P. introduced compulsory elementary education, founded the University of Travancore, provided free school meals, introduced a system of government loans to farmers, and invested in state factories. According to Woodcock, he 'turned Alwaye from a village in the middle of a laterite waste dotted with lantana thickets into a prospering industrial area'[305]. Among the industries founded by CP was FACT, the mostly very successful chemical factory at which my nephew Raju works. Raju says: *'Diwan Sir CP was a very good administrator except that he used his power to suppress the spread of communism in Kerala, like the Punnapra Vayalar mutiny etc. The Pallivassal hydroelectric power plant, FACT, the Indian aluminium company etc. are examples of his vision. To me he is very good, but to communists he is like Hitler.*' Sir CP believed that social and economic difficulties needed to be solved before 'political experiments' were tried, and was therefore disliked by Congress and by the Communists, who determined to stain his character. As usual, there is little that is black and white in history. And while we're on the subject, the Communist leaders have been themselves accused of cruelly and cold-bloodedly sending the workers of Alappuzha to their deaths at the battle of Pannapra, as a calculated political act. None of the Communist leaders were killed in this bloody affair, it might be noted.

In Kochi, the independence struggle was accompanied by rather less violence. But first let's have a glimpse of Kochi in the thirties, again courtesy of Rosita Forbes' deathless prose. 'Apart from the woodcutters, sawyers, carpenters, and other forest workers, Cochin is given up to fishermen...They drift out [to sea] on the land wind about six in the morning, when from windows opening on to the harbour, sails like petals of chrysanthemums and dahlias appear to be blown across the sky. With the sea breeze they return in mid-afternoon. Sometimes when it is calm, they remain out all night, and then the fishermen keep up their spirits by singing as they sit round their pans of charcoal under a screen of plaited palm leaves'.[306] Forbes described her encounter with an 'ancient' Namboodiri lady of Kochi. '... [she] exchanged her quaint umbrella for a fan made out of a palm leaf as soon as she entered the house and during all the time I was with her she never let me look her full in the face. Always the fan slid between us, hiding now her eyes, now her lips, now a fragment of the grey, seamed cheek. From her extended ears hung stud- shaped circles of gold, but these were her only jewels. Her fine grey hair that had once been blue-black, was uncovered and twisted into a knot low on the back of her neck. Yards and yards of white stuff were wound in complicated fashion about her still shapely person, under a little cotton jacket, also white and immaculately starched.' [307]

As far as politics is concerned, no Legislative Council was established in Kochi until 1925, but it did then have an elected majority straight away [there were only ten appointees out of a total of 45 members], and one of the members of the Council was a woman. Thottakkattu Madhuvianna was in fact the first woman ever to be elected to any legislature in India. The Council of course had no executive power, but was mostly successful because the Maharaja was a reasonable man and was prepared to listen to what the Council said. There were demonstrations against the Chief Minister's decision to privatise the electricity supply [in 1936] and this led to some government reforms two years later when 'Dyarchy' was introduced to Kochi: one Minister was to be responsible to the legislature rather than the government, a similar pattern to that adopted in British India in 1919. Further reforms were demanded by the Prajahmandalam Party, the Kochi Congress Party; arrests were made and the Party temporarily banned. In 1946, however, the number of responsible ministers was increased to six, and Kochi was well on the way to full democracy by the time that India achieved independence.

While these matters of high politics were being discussed and decided, while round table conferences conferred, protesters protested, marchers marched, the Mahatma made salt and fasted, the Pandit made speeches and was jailed, World War raged everywhere, famine raged in Bengal, civil war raged in Panjab; while all these great events were going on around her, Manga was born and began to grow up.

CHAPTER FORTY-ONE

MANGA'S MUM'S STORY

'Do not thatch your gatehouse till after you have thatched your dwelling.' Malayalam proverb

'When the first baby laughed for the first time, the laugh broke into a thousand pieces and they all went skipping about, and that was the beginning of fairies.' J.M.Barrie, *Peter Pan*

Painting of Manga's Mum and Dad

'Have you lost your senses or your count? Don't you realise this is your thirteenth pregnancy? '

Lakshmi bent her head down. She was very ashamed hearing this from her favourite sister-in-law. She knew Kamala meant well – and did not speak out of malice or wish to insult her. All the same she was hurt and didn't say anything.

'In your ripe old age going and doing a silly thing like this' Kamala went on. In fact she felt sorry for Lakshmi, who was full and more with the baby. Her legs and arms were swollen and with her pale puffy face she was looking rather pathetic.

'If it is a girl, call her Mangalam. You know what that means: the end – no more children. Already you have a job to feed and dress the others. And if it's a boy, call him Managaleswaran. That will be it.' She paused, but not for long. 'And where is your beloved husband? Has he already gone visiting his kept woman now you are no use to him?'

This was more than Lakshmi could bear. She began to sob, tears flowing down her face. Whatever else he might be, her husband was a loving and caring man. She knew this other woman, who also had a daughter by him. It was her birthday and Lakshmi had asked him to go and see her. She had made some nice sweetmeats for the child. Lakshmi hated others talking badly about her husband. They had been married when she was just 13 years old, and he had always been good to her. She thought about the early years of her marriage before the children started to arrive. They had been happy days and a smile crept over her face. Kamala was feeling rather ashamed of herself for making Lakshmi cry. She started to apologise then stopped when she saw Lakshmi smile.

'Oh, I see. You are dreaming about your beloved I believe. Anyway, I must go now. Take care of yourself. I will be offering special prayers to Iswara for you.'

Lakshmi sighed. For once, she was alone. Her two little girls aged 3 and 5 were out with their married elder sister who had come down from Vasai to give her mother some much needed rest. Her other daughter was 11 years old. Sometimes Lakshmi worried about her. She was not good at helping around the house and didn't take much care of her little sisters. She was spending a day at her friend's house but Lakshmi worried that she might get into mischief. She let her mind wander back to the day that she first saw her husband. That was the time that he came to the house with his parents to discuss the marriage proposal. Lakshmi lived then near a temple in Ponnani in a spacious house with her three brothers and a sister. She was the eldest, and the youngest, the baby of the family, was a boy of three. They had a moderate income, and were able to live comfortably most of the time. Lakshmi went to school till she was 11 years, then stayed at home to help her mother. As it was a custom of the caste, girls were given away in marriage from 10 years onwards. Lakshmi was a quiet loving girl. She took bath in the temple tank and prayed to Lord Shiva every morning to get a good husband and healthy children. The same prayer was offered in the evening also. 'That is what all girls do and hope for', her mother advised her.

When the would-be groom came from the village 40 miles away on the other side of the river Bharatha, some of his relations came with him. An auspicious day had been set for the visit by the astrologers. The rooms were cleaned especially thoroughly, and the front of the house was decorated with Kolam [rangoli], a pattern drawn on the floor with powdered lime. Special sweetmeats and savouries were prepared. Lakshmi had an oil bath in the morning. She put on her reasonably new and pretty sari, kunkum on her forehead and flowers on her long plaited hair. She had a silver chain and anklet & small ear drops. She looked pretty and dainty.

When the visitors arrived they were given water to wash their feet, hands and face and were ushered in to the inner room, which was fairly large, mostly used as a prayer room and a resting place in the afternoon. Puja room was in the corner, and various Gods' and Goddesses' pictures all decorated with paper garlands hung on the wall near the sanctuary. An oil lamp was lit and the agarbathis gave out perfumed smoke. The door of the room was slightly ajar so that the guests could see inside.

When they were all seated, her father asked Lakshmi to come and pay her respects to the guests. The would-be groom could see the girl before he agreed to marry her and also judge how well she would be able to run a home. Lakshmi had learned to do all the chores as well as cook a nice meal, though she was still learning the special culinary procedures. Lakshmi came in silently with bent head looking down, never even attempting to look at the visitors. She came in quietly and pranaamed to them all. Her heart was beating faster; face was blushed and drops of sweat gathered her forehead. She was in a way very excited about getting married and becoming an important mature person; at the same time the uncertainty about the future, what fate held for her, made her very nervous. Being only 13 and not knowing a lot about the life outside, her mind didn't stretch very far. For instance how old he was, what job did he do or has he any education. All these questions were asked and opinions and decisions were made by her parents and uncles. She had no say in anything.

However, when she had gone back to the inner room Lakshmi couldn't resist taking a peep at him through a window. She liked the man. He was ever so fair compared to her; she was on the darker side. His eyes were of paler colour almost like cats' eyes. He had his long dark hair in a knot at the back, and the front part shaved as the custom of the Brahmin. Single sandalwood paste mark went across his forehead. He looked very calm and composed. He didn't ask or say much, as the elders were engaged in the formalities. Lakshmi's father sang her praises in many words. What a helping hand she is, how much he will miss her and so on.

Lakshmi and her mother brought coffee and tiffins for them. They all ate and drank. Then the serious talk began about dowry, jewels and the wedding day and many more details that go with a marriage proposal...

Lakshmi woke from her reverie with a start. Her husband was coming up the path towards the house and she hadn't got his tea ready. Lakshmi struggled to get onto her feet and start work, but she needn't have worried. Parameswaran was not the sort of man who would get cross over a little thing like tea, especially when his wife was pregnant.

Parameswaran was a cook; as such his job was not a steady one, because he cooked for big feasts and accompanied a group of other cooks to big mansion houses and palaces for special events. They travelled far and wide. When cooking jobs were available there was enough money to keep the large family properly fed at least, but otherwise he needed to turn to other work to earn a living, and the budget became very tight indeed. He had inherited the gift of healing and although he could not charge for this work, his patients would express their gratitude to him by giving rice, cooking oil or maybe clothing. And he would sometimes be able to earn money by cooking for Brahmins who were living away from home, or he could sell food at festivals. Both Parameswaran and Lakshmi were of course pleased that they were going to have a baby, but there was no doubt that another mouth to feed was not going to make life easy.

Parameswaran smiled at Lakshmi, and said 'Ponnukutty, ni occaru nan chaya vekkaran' - 'Ponnukutty, you sit down; I can make the tea'. In many Iyer families, she would have gone to her parents house for the last few weeks of her pregnancy and for the birth of the child, but Lakshmi was happy to stay in her own home - her husband, her older daughters and her neighbours could give her all the support she needed and anyway, she was not very close to her mother.

Very soon, Lakshmi's pains began. She called to her eldest daughter to fetch the old midwife who lived near the temple. Paru was not a trained person but had delivered many of the babies in the village and had been present at the birth of the last four of Lakshmi's children. Most people trusted Paru more than the doctors in the local hospital. She came quickly, knowing that Lakshmi was experienced enough to know when the birth was imminent. Neighbours gathered – in the time- honoured way water was boiled and the cleanly-washed cloths prepared to wrap the baby were laid out.

Lakshmi asked her eldest daughter to take the little ones out into the garden to play. When her waters broke she realised that much of the bulk she had been carrying was fluid – this would be another small baby... she felt a rush of fear and love so intense it overcame her pain. Lakshmi mourned for all six of her children that had not survived; each had a place in her prayers, but now she thought of her first son. His birth had been so frightening – she was so young and the labour so long and in spite of having her family around her she had felt so alone. When he arrived she knew a miracle had occurred and at his death - tragically soon - she had felt, along with the grief, a sense of unworthiness as though she had been told to guard a precious jewel and had allowed it to be lost... She prayed for this coming child who was to be born on a beautiful spring day and who would probably be her last baby.

Soon the tiny form lay in her arms and her other children and all the neighbours gathered round. Her mother knew that Mangalam was special from that minute.

CHAPTER FORTY-TWO

TRIVANDRUM, EVERGREEN CITY OF INDIA

'The City's voice is soft, like Solitude.' P.B.Shelley, *Stanzas Written in Dejection, near Naples.*

One of the top ten cities of the world? I used to think so. It was a bit of a game at one time in my youth to produce lists of favourite cities, the winner being the person who could come up with the most pretentious compilation. You had to have visited the cities yourself of course. It was started by Ian Fleming's book about his favourite cities. I think Macao might have been his number one. Not many of us had been out of Western Europe at the time - it was the early sixties - so most lists were dominated by Paris, Hamburg, Venice, Stockholm, Amsterdam, Dublin, but there was a smattering of New Yorks [made possible because Icelandic Airways[i] ran a very cheap transatlantic crossing at that time], Istanbuls and Tangiers. A possible list for me might have been Tunis, Lisbon, Paris, Zadar, Venice, Fez, Canterbury, Vienna, Rome, Barcelona. In truth in one or two cases I hadn't done much more than arrive in the evening after a hard day's hitch-hiking, find the youth hostel, and leave the following morning, and the list is still less than exotic. So when I went to India, Calcutta, Jaipur and Delhi soon went to the top of the league. Trivandrum became number one because it was so different from the cities of north India as well as Europe. It's in a lovely setting, close to the glorious blue Arabian Sea and surrounded by rolling hills. The sun seemed to shine all the time, the city was full of tropical greenery, it was amazingly clean, and the people seemed to be perpetually smiling. And of course, when we first visited Trivandrum we were just married and in love with pretty well everything around us, as well as each other. From one point in the city one can see a church, which looks very English, though whitewashed; a stately mosque; and a temple in the modest Kerala fashion. We went to the zoo - now famous as it provided the

---

[i] It was an independent airline, aka Luftleioir, operating out of Iceland and not a member of IATA, and could therefore charge lower fares. It flew Canadair CL44-d's, turboprop aircraft based on the Britannia.

model for the zoo in the Booker prize winning novel *The Life of Pi* by Yann Martel - and to the excellent museum.

Kovalam beach, near Trivandrum

While Thiruvananthapuram is the official name of the city [it means 'City of the Lord Anantha'], most people outside Kerala, including other Indians, stick to Trivandrum, as it is rather easier to pronounce. Though if you split up the word into three parts – *Thiru \ vanantha \ puram* - it's not so bad. [The same can be said of many Malayalam words]. It is of course the capital of Kerala and its largest city – 957,000 in the city, but 1.68 million in the urban area. Many people have moved into Thiruvananthapuram from the surrounding countryside and the unemployment rate when I was there was impossibly high – about a third of would-be workers were without a job. Traditionally most jobs were in the coir and hand loom industries and in government, but now IT is a big employer and the University of Kerala along with several other prestigious higher education establishments and the Indian Space Research Organisation have their homes in Thiruvananthapuram. There are a growing number of small and medium-sized manufacturers, private and state-owned, such as Kerala Automobiles, a public sector company making three-wheeler cars, but there is much less large-scale industrialisation as there is in Kochi or Chennai. Tourism is important too but I have the feeling that it has not taken off to quite the extent that might have been expected. It wasn't long ago that Kerala was regarded as the real future growth area as far as mass tourism was concerned. But perhaps because Kerala is rather too far away from Europe, or because it's still quite a difficult place to get used to, or it's a bit too hot or humid, or it's a bit too foreign and isn't prepared to change for the sake of tourists, I don't know; but the tourist industry doesn't seem to have arrived in Kerala and specifically in Trivandrum in the way that it has in North India or Goa or Turkey. Instead there have been a lot of specialist tourists such as those seeking health cures. There are over fifty recognised Ayurveda centres in and around the city and also facilities for visitors interested in yoga and Indian dance.

All this has put a lot of pressure on transport in particular, and a light metro rail system and a big roads project are being planned. I hope the authorities do not follow the failed traffic management solutions of the west. One bright note: *India Today* reported on 22.2.13 that the city was the best in India for public transport and housing.

History

The story of Thiruvananthapuram goes back a long way. Some historians claim that her merchants traded with the west – specifically with King Solomon's ships – as long ago as the eleventh century BC, when Jewish writings refer to gold being brought to Jerusalem from Ophir. Logan says that it is 'hazardous' to guess where Ophir is – though he plumps for Beypore in Malabar – because so much research has been done without any definite conclusion. He quotes the eighteenth century writer Master Purchas: 'This Golden Country is like gold...hard to find, and much quarrelled, and needs a wise Myner to bring it out of the Labyrinths of darknesse...' But some firmly maintain nonetheless that Poova in Thiruvananthapuram is Ophir. Whether or not that is true, it would be surprising if the city was not involved in some sort of trade with the west from ancient times, even though it seems to have been a much less prominent port than Kollam or Kodungallor for example.[308]

The first known ruling dynasty of Thiruvananthapuram and its surrounding area were the Ay kings. It's not entirely clear when the Ays arrived or where they came from, but they are mentioned in the Sangam literature and most authorities say they were Dravidians. Their name comes from the old Tamil word 'aayan' meaning 'cowherd'. The scale of their kingdom is also a matter of conjecture, as is the extent to which they were independent from various overlords like the Cheras and Pandyas, but the *Gazette* believes they did at times exercise their independence.

It's worth mentioning a couple of Kings [or Chieftains as the *Gazette* calls them][309]. Ay Andiran is said to have been '*a lover of Tamil and of men of letters on whom he bestowed gifts abundantly*' and to have ruled a country that stretched as far north as Palghat; his successor was defeated by the Pandyas and the Ays were never so powerful again[310]. One of the Sangam poems describes the battle thus – '*Thou didst fly like the wind, spread fire around, Destroy the country of thy foes, Encamp at Alangaman scaring them, Cut down the chiefs and seize their drums*'.[311] And then there was Athiyan '*a magnanimous and brave chieftain*' who however presided over a further decline in Ay fortunes as the Pandyas continued to prosper[312]. After Athiyan, whom we think ruled in the third century AD, there is a dearth of information about the Ays; after their fall Thiruvananthapuram was occupied by the Venad rulers, the successors of the Kulashekhara king, Rama Varma, who retreated into the south following his defeat by the Cholas. The city did not in fact become important until the rule of Marthanda Varma some six hundred years later, when it was made capital of the state later known as Travancore. It became a centre for the arts and education and its development continued into the nineteenth century when the Observatory, General Hospital, Oriental Library and colleges for the study of Law, Sanskrit and Ayurvedic medicine were established. The city was never under British control, being the capital of an independent 'native state' which was ruled relatively progressively by its rajas. The journalist William Digby wrote in 1885 'There is no British district which for general prosperity can compare with the state of Travancore'[313].

On independence in 1947, Travancore, after some vacillation, chose to become part of India, and Thiruvananthapuram became capital of the combined state of Travancore-Kochi, and capital of the new state of Kerala when it was formed in 1956.

Thiruvananthapuram's Sri Padmanabhaswamy temple is very ancient, dating according to the Archaeological Survey from the ninth or tenth centuries. The Survey goes on to say however that during the sixteenth and seventeenth centuries, 'lofty enclosures and sculptured corridors' were added, hiding the main temple altogether. I haven't been into the temple [although these days, non-Hindus can pay a fee to gain entrance as long as they are wearing suitable clothing: I'm not sure that this concession to tourism is quite right] but I have of course seen the seven-tier gopuram. The first time Manga and I visited Trivandrum, we spotted some attractive woodcarvings for sale on one of the stalls lining the lane that led to the temple entrance. Sadly, no amount of bargaining could bring down the price enough for us to be able to buy one; but we did have an old camera and I couldn't find any film for it, so we did a swap for one of the statuettes. On another of the stalls a small boy was playing beautiful tunes on a miniature violin. We could afford one of these and while I waited outside the gates for Manga to complete a quick tour of the temple I tried to get the hang of playing my new bamboo and wire instrument – of course, with no success whatever! Manga returned and told me about the image of Vishnu in the main shrine. '*The god is lying down on a snake – a cobra – and its head with its hood is shading him. Brahma and Shiva are standing beside him. When Vishnu is in that position he's called Padmanabhaswamy.*' The statue is made from over one thousand pebbles from the River Gandaki in Nepal, and covered with gold leaf. When Tipu Sultan invaded Kerala, the monks had the statue painted in black so the invaders wouldn't know about the gold. They've very recently found billions of pounds worth of treasure hidden in the temple.

Maharaja Marthanda Varma made Sri Padmanabhaswamy the ruler of Travancore, with he himself a dasa or servant of the god. And the insignia of Lord Vishnu, which is a conch shell, became the emblem of Travancore state, and was stamped on its coins. Marthanda also named the summer palace after Vishnu, and there is a painting of the reclining figure of the god in the entrance hall. Padmanabhapuram Palace is a wonderful building made largely of wood and is filled with intricate carvings and murals. There are no fewer than 127 rooms in the palace, parts of which were built at various times between around 1600 and the rest in the middle of the eighteenth century, and it was the seat of the Raja of Travancore before Trivandrum became the capital. There is also a museum full of interesting exhibits, some of it rather gruesome like instruments of torture for example, much of it beautiful such as carvings in teak and jackfruit wood, and some, intriguing - Vattezhuttu script, related to Brahmi script which is said to have been used across the whole of India in ancient times. We visited the palace with Raju and Geetha in Juliema's year. There was a storm brewing and the beautiful lines of the wooden roofs looked particularly impressive against the brooding black skies.

CHAPTER FORTY-THREE

ELSEWHERE: THE STRUGGLE FOR INDEPENDENCE 1880-1947

'It is alarming and also nauseating to see Mr Gandhi, a seditious Middle Temple lawyer, now posing as a fakir of a type well known in the east, striding half-naked up the steps of the vice-regal palace, while he is still conducting and organising a defiant campaign of civil disobedience, to parley on equal terms with the representative of the King-Emperor.' Winston Churchill

'You should never have your best trousers on when you turn out to fight for freedom and for truth.' Henrik Ibsen, *An Enemy of the People,*

'It is better to die on your feet than live on your knees'. Dolores Ibarruri [La Pasionaria], Speech in Paris, 1936

The Indian National Congress, which did not surface in Kerala until after the First World War, was founded in 1885, and although it started with very modest aims, became in due course the driving force for India's freedom. Surprisingly perhaps, it owed its establishment to a large extent to the encouragement given by a group of British officials who believed in close contact with educated Indians, whatever might be the policy of the government of the day. One of them, Allan Hume, remained in India after his retirement from the Indian Civil Service, and was particularly influential. Congress was not interested in independence at this stage, but just in reforms, such as the opening up of the Civil Service to Indian applicants. The movement (it was not yet a party) was cautious in its approach to reform and the country's leaders paid it little attention.

The INC was not taken particularly seriously by successive viceroys. Lord Dufferin [1884-88] said that Congress represented 'a microscopic minority' of the country; Lord Curzon [1898–1905] predicted that it was 'tottering towards its fall'[314]. In fact it was from 1905 that Congress started thinking of independence. This was partly due to Curzon's decision to partition Bengal and the severe way in which protests were countered. Curzon is described by Watson as a 'sincere but outdated' imperialist; he had no idea that what he felt was a sensible move would have such consequences – but then he consulted no Indian about the matter. And the partition had another unexpected side effect – the birth of the Muslim League. The opposition to Curzon's decision had, Watson believes, 'a markedly Hindu ring' and Muslims felt that the majority community was taking over Congress and that they needed their own voice.[315] Thus began a process that ended in partition in 1947. The Aga Khan was a prime mover in the formation of the League, but Mohammed Ali Jinnah, who became the 'Father of Pakistan', was one of many Muslims who remained in Congress.

A number of incidents fuelled the struggle for India's independence. The disappointment of the Morley-Minto reforms, which introduced elected but powerless Legislative Councils in 1910; the lack of positive reaction to India's demonstration of loyalty and support for the crown during the First World War about which John Buchan, Empire-loving novelist, wrote 'It was the performance of India which took the world by surprise and thrilled every British heart'; the Khilafat Movement; and General Dyer's command to fire upon peaceful demonstrators in Jallianwala Bagh, Amritsar. 'In a few minutes of vindictive folly, the moral pretence for British rule had been riddled into transparency, and all hope of peaceful post-war collaboration blown away in the maelstrom of killing.'[316] The official death toll was 379 dead, but a British civil surgeon said that 1800 men, women and children were killed. Dyer was censured and sacked, but public opinion in Britain seemed to be on his side since a subscription for him raised £26,000. Many Tory MPs will certainly have contributed – they almost had his censure reversed in the House of Commons on a motion proposed by the Ulster Unionist Edward Carson. [Churchill though defended Dyer's censure]. Amazingly, Dyer still had his defenders in more recent times. One of the books I was recommended to read before being posted to India as a VSO was *The Men Who Ruled India*, whose author tried to make a case for Dyer's action being acceptable in that it discouraged any further rebellion and therefore in the end saved lives!

The period saw the rise of Mohandas Karamchand Gandhi and 'satyagraha' - passive resistance and 'holding on to truth'. Gandhi described the doctrine as leading one's opponent to recognise truth not by inflicting suffering on them, but on oneself. Also in the early twenties, Moti Lal Nehru, father of Jawaharlal abandoned his pro-British stance; Rabindranath Tagore returned his Nobel Prize; Rajendra Prasad [a future President of India] and Vallabhai Patel became followers of Gandhi. The twenties saw satyagraha, swadeshi boycotts ['buy Indian'], and hartals [strikes]. A day or two ago, I was flicking through an old encyclopaedia that we have at home. It must have been published around 1930 and I didn't expect it to say anything very critical of the British position at this period. But in fact it admitted that all had not been well as far as British rule was concerned since the end of the First World War 'Unfortunately many of the best and most experienced officers were serving outside India, the civil services were short-handed, and all were weary and in need of leave, so some things were done in a manner which seemed strange to many Indians…' The article added incidentally that Mahatma Gandhi's campaigns of satyagraha and swadeshi were merely expressions 'intended to cover racial bigotry'! – and so can hardly be described as pro-Indian.

Some limited progress was achieved: the Montague-Chelmsford reforms gave more power to elected councils in some areas of government such as education; improved opportunities were offered to Indians in the Civil Service; the Simon Commission recommended an extension of democratic government; and Dominion status was offered [and rejected as India now wanted purna swaraj – complete self-rule]. The thirties began with the Round Table conference [such anathema to Churchill!], the Salt Marches, and the Gandhi-Irwin pact of 1931. The Government of India Act of 1935 proposed a Federal system with regional autonomy but retention of British overall control. The 'Quit India' movement of 1942 led to the promise of virtual independence by the Cripps mission and in 1946 the Labour Prime Minister Clement Attlee declared that India would be free by 1948. Then came the long struggle between Nehru and Jinnah over the question of Pakistan and finally Independence at last on the 14th and 15th August 1947.

Let's take a break from politics and the great freedom struggle for a while and look instead at the games that people in Kerala play.

CHAPTER FORTY-FOUR

KERALA'S GAMES

'He brought an eye for all he saw; / He mixt in all our simple sports.' Alfred, Lord Tennyson, *In Memoriam*

'The costly game of cricket has not only become a fashion in our country but something over which we are spending crores of rupees only proves that the English are still dominating our mind and intellect. The cricket match that Pandit Nehru and other MPs played some years back was the very depth of this Anglicism. Why could they not play Kabaddi, our national game, which has been acclaimed by several countries as a great game.' M.S.Golwalker

Kabaddi **is** a great game. It costs nothing, can last for only a few minutes or as long as you want, needs no equipment, has easily-understood rules, and doesn't need a big playing area. The game can be played by men or women [but not really both at the same time], young or old, and it rewards strength, speed, agility, stamina and cunning. It's good to watch. It's indigenous to India. Kabaddi is never going to become a big international sport but it's fun and I hope it remains popular in Kerala rather than becoming a victim of increased sophistication.

But it is true that cricket is the number one sport in India and at the beginning of the 21st century at least, the only one in which she excels at world level. Kerala is not exactly a hotbed of the game. In fact it is one of only 2 or 3 states [the others being West Bengal and Goa] where football is as popular as cricket; once again, Kerala and Bengal differ from the rest of the country! Nonetheless people of all ages in Kerala crowd round their radios and televisions when a Test Match is being played, and even more so these days for a One Day International, and international cricketers are heroes, only film stars being the subject of equal worship. Pick-up games are played in the streets and fields, especially in Mumbai and other big cities, and our family often plays in the garden in Trikkandiyur, as well as in the dusty compound outside the old house in Vasai. Indi wrote in her 1979 diary: *'Some Indian boys were teaching me how to play cricket in India. It's the same as cricket in*

England. It was really nice. I didn't get many runs but my team won'!

Cricket in the garden. Apu batting with a palm frond; Ammu keeping wicket

As far as we know, the first cricket to be played in India was in 1721 in Gujarat. Ramachandra Guha in his excellent book[317] on the history of cricket in India quotes one of the British sailors playing in the match: 'When my boat was lying for a fortnight in one of the channels, though the country was inhabited by Culeys, we every day diverted ourselves with playing Cricket and Other Exercises, which they would come and be spectators...' 'Culeys' continued to be only spectators for many years. The Calcutta Cricket Club, the first such club outside the British Isles, founded in 1792, was very much for Europeans only. Occasionally an Indian would be recruited as a net bowler, and sometimes Indians were called upon to make up a team; Guha refers to a game played between The Salt and Akbari Department in rural Tamilnad and a visiting team of artillery officers. Only three Europeans worked for the Salt Dept. so they had to recruit, in the words of one of these officials, 'an octet of aborigines' to make up an eleven. Indians however were generally regarded as lacking 'those virtues which characterised the British and made them uniquely able to shine at cricket, such as patience, fortitude and self-denial; order, obedience and good humour, and an unruffled temper...and wits down to the fingers' ends'.[318]

For anyone interested in the early history of cricket in India, Guha's book is the one to read. He tells of the Parsis of Mumbai, the first community to take up cricket seriously - there were around thirty Parsi cricket clubs by the middle of the nineteenth century - and the spread of the game to the Hindus and Muslims at first in Mumbai and then across the country; of the first international matches, and of the first Indian cricket heroes – K.S.Ranjitsinhji of course, the Jam Sahib of Nawanagar, who in fact played nearly all his cricket for Sussex and England, and the now almost unknown 'untouchable' Palwankar Baloo, a left arm spinner who was hugely successful against European as well as Indian opposition. And Guha also debunks the myth that Lord Harris, Governor of Mumbai and sometime cricket captain of Kent and England was an important influence in the development of Indian cricket.

India played her first test match in 1932 and although the team always included a number of excellent players, for many years India lost most series embarrassingly easily. It was during this period that I watched my very first first-class cricket match - Kent v The Indians at Canterbury in 1952. The family was on holiday in Margate and all of us took the train and then the bus to the St Lawrence ground. As I remember it was packed – the match against the touring team was always a big event. I still have the scorecard for the day's play, completed in my childish hand, and not entirely accurately. Wisden indicates that Fagg and Phebey, the Kent openers, put on 127 for the first wicket but there followed a collapse to Sarwate and Phadkar and the county were all out for 217. Kent's two stars, Godfrey Evans and Colin Cowdrey both made ducks![319] On the second and third days, when we weren't there of course, Polly Umrigar hit a brilliant double century for India, Cowdrey, aged 19 years, scored his first century for Kent, and there was a thrilling finish as India just failed to score 51 to win in 20 minutes. The story of my life! India lost the test series 3-0 in 1952, being blown apart by the pace of the young Freddie Trueman, and there was little improvement in their results for most of the next two decades.

The arrival of the magicians of spin, Bedi, Chandrasekhar, Prasanna and Venkataraghavan heralded an improvement in the country's fortunes and it was in their era that I watched my only first- class match in India. Until very recently, it was almost impossible to get a ticket for a Test match in India; everybody wanted to be there. I was very fortunate to be given one for the Calcutta test against the popular West Indies side of 1966-7 and I watched the first day of the second test there on New Year's Eve. It wasn't a great day's cricket – only 212 runs were scored, for the wickets of Hunte, Bynoe, Butcher and Clive Lloyd. Kanhai crawled to 78 not out, and the Indian spinners were out of luck. I was looking forward to the second day when Sobers was due to come in. But in spite of the pedestrian batting, the crowd was enthralled. Every ball was cheered; every piece of action was greeted with a roar. It was like being at a 6-hour football match. But this game is notorious for another reason. I never got to see the second day because there was no second day's play. I went to a New Year's party with the friends I was staying with in Calcutta; they were doctors who used to work at Nether Edge Hospital in Sheffield with my mother. The party went on into the early hours and I was late getting up on New Year's Day. Fortunately; for when we listened to the radio just before I went off to Eden Gardens, it was announced that cricket had been abandoned because fans who had bought tickets but couldn't get a seat had burned down the stands!

All this of course has little to do with Kerala. Kozhikode finds a mention in some cricket histories only because Lord Harris went that way to play a match in Chennai, to try and pull the wool over the eyes of people who thought he should have been carrying out his duties as a Governor. But that's about it. The game made little impact in Malabar, and the rajas of Kochi and Travancore, unlike many of their colleagues further north, showed no interest in either playing or sponsorship.

During and immediately after the Independence struggle, many freedom fighters opposed cricket vehemently, because it was brought to India by the colonists – 'the game is meant for servile countries that have always been ruled by Britain' said the nationalist Mulayam Singh Yadav and many Indian communists considered cricket an elitist game. Even more so, politicians hated the Quadrangular Tournament between Hindus, Muslims, Europeans and The Rest as it fostered communalism. But even the 'cricket-baiters' exhibited some ambivalence. One Communist MP left a meeting at which he had been railing against the sport claiming that he needed a beedi to smoke but in fact to discover the latest Test Match score! So cricket flourished. Inter-communal games were the most popular tournament until a Regional competition, the Ranji Trophy, took over after the war. And with the new Trophy came the participation of Kerala. Travancore-Kochi played their first game in the South Zone of the competition in 1951, losing heavily to Mysore. The new state of Kerala played its first game 6 years later; they lost by an innings to Madras. In fact Kerala only won 34 of their first 242 games in the Ranji Trophy, their record against Madras/Tamilnad [won 1 lost 33], Mysore/Karnakata [won 2 lost 40] and Hyderabad [won 1 lost 35] being particularly one-sided.

Two international cricketers have emerged from Kerala this century. Their first test player was Tinu Yohannon who played 3 tests, the first in 2001 against England. He took only 5 wickets at over 50 apiece. The second is Shanta Sreesanth, another fast-ish bowler who made a big impression on world cricket, at least partly because he has a rather fiery temperament. He is inclined to leap about even more excitedly than most when he takes a wicket and is, according to some, an example of the new Kerala, with a 'functional' rather than idealistic ethos.[320]

And finally as far as cricket is concerned let's look at the participation of Iyers in the first- class game. Sadly, this section will not detain us for long. A trawl of the 'Cricinfo' website reveals just one single first-class cricketer in the family. His name is Sadashiv Iyer, born in Nagpur, Maharastra, in 1972, and he played for Vidharba in the Ranji Trophy between 1993 and 2005. But there are three Iyer umpires listed! Perhaps that is significant!

Back to Kabaddi. That is the north Indian name for the game that is known as Sathgudu in Kerala, and has different names throughout the subcontinent. The names derive from the word that a raider has to chant continuously as he advances into opposition territory – it ensures that he can only stay there for the duration of one breath. These days there is normally a time limit of 30 seconds, instead of the chant. While a player is in opposition territory, he tries to touch opponents to earn points for his team and then get back on to his own side of the court. The defenders try to avoid being touched and to hold the raider in their territory until the 30 seconds is up. And there it is. In the Sainik School Tilaiya Kabaddi was an important game, particularly welcome because it was the country lads - who often struggled academically because they didn't speak English very easily, and had often not had much opportunity to practice the more sophisticated games who were the best Kabaddi players. The smaller boys could swerve and wriggle to escape the clutches of the defenders; the bigger ones could barge through the defences. Great fun. There is some international interest in the game. It was played – by the four countries of the subcontinent plus China, Japan and Malaysia – in the 1990 Asian Games and subsequently; and there are regular tournaments in areas to which Indians have re-located, especially California. It has been on television here in Britain. But basically it's a village game, and an excellent one.[i]

Carromboard is another splendid game which I have always thought of as a purely of Indian origin. I had certainly never heard of it before playing with Keralite exiles in Mumbai on our first visit. That version of carrom [the game and not just the playing area is called carromboard in Kerala] was similar to snooker but played on a slippery wooden board with wooden discs instead of balls, propelled by one's fingers rather than cues. But there are apparently many other comparable games in the East and Middle East that may or may not have originated in India. It is even suggested that the game in England developed separately out of billiards and shuffleboard or shove ha'penny. One of the carroms websites has a well-expressed explanation of the spread of games. 'Games are part of a living culture...Like language, they are adopted from other countries, or brought in by travellers and adapted to suit. This is the nature of language, it is the nature of games, and it is the nature of human culture'[321]. Apu and his wife, friends from Mumbai, brought us a carrom board from India after our first visit. That was a heroic performance as the boards are big and heavy! I guess there couldn't have been that many of them in England at that time. In fact, the only other board we saw was, rather bizarrely, on the Isle of Skye in a toy museum. The curator didn't know anything about the game and asked us for the rules.

We had some good games with Apu and Devi, but haven't played that often since. We did have a great match in a coffee house in Bahrain. The venue was just like a pub: various bar games going on, relaxed atmosphere, slight suspicion of strangers, a preponderance of men [well, all men except for Manga and Juliema] but no alcohol

---

[i] For more information see www.kabaddi.org

of course. There were both Indians and Bahrainis in the bar, and we challenged a couple of Indians to a contest. Julie had never played before but with her first flick she sank a counter!

Manga remembers playing lots of games with her friends in the village. Hopscotch or pandi was a favourite – our children played it with the neighbours on their first visit, and said it had just the same rules as at home. Manga says there's also a slightly different version with a differently patterned 'court', where you have to kick the stones out of the square while hopping. She also enjoyed skipping games. If nobody had a rope, she and her friends would cut down some ivy and use that. Hide and seek, and juggling were other games played, mainly by girls, in the same way in Kerala as in England. As they grew older the girls in the village would play badminton, with a soft wool ball like a pompom rather than a shuttlecock, or, on the same court, throwball or ring tennis. 'Sitting down' games included palanguri. There are similar games played in other countries especially in Africa, although in India it's played only by Tamilians. The group of games is called the 'mancala' group. That was the name of the game first seen by Europeans, in Egypt in the nineteenth century. It involves picking counters from hollows in a wooden board and re-distributing them into other hollows. It's a game of skill and an experienced player will always beat a novice. Instead of using a wooden board, Manga and her friends made hollows in the sand, and for counters, took hard seeds called manjadikurru [which are black and red] or kunnikkuru [which are red] from climbing plants in the garden. There are some very interesting remarks on the game in Thomas Varghes's academic paper *On Globalisation and Ethnomathematics,* which is well worth a read. [322]

Thayam sounds very similar to ludo. Again, the 'board' was drawn on the ground [with a slate pencil]. Instead of a die, children throw 6 cowrie shells and the score is worked out by counting how many of the shells fall on their backs. The counters will be beads, seeds, attractive pieces of stone, broken bangles or something like that. 'Fivestones' is popular. The stones will be pebbles from the garden. They need to be round so it sometimes takes a long time to find the right ones.

My nephew Raju remembers three games he used to play as a child. One was 'tile-ball'. One individual or team builds a tower of tiles and defends it against an opponent or opponents who throw a ball in an attempt to knock it down. If they do so, they win if they can hit a defender with the ball before the tower is rebuilt. [Roof tiles are in plentiful supply in Kerala!]. 'Attakkalam' sounds a little like kabaddi, a little like sumo. Manga says it's related to kalaripayattu, the Keralan martial art. A circle is drawn in the dust and one boy stands inside it. The others try to wrestle him out. I guess the one who stays in the circle longest is the winner. The third is 'pattayam kuttiyum'. [Manga calls it chottayum kuttiyum]. This is almost identical to a game my father used to play in the English Midlands in the early years of last century, a sort of simplified knurr and spell, which is itself similar to 'bat and trap' for which there's still a pub league in Kent. A small piece of wood is flicked into the air by a longer piece of wood, which is then used to hit the smaller piece of wood for as great a distance as possible. If the stick is caught, the 'batsman' is out. If not, the small stick is thrown at the longer one by the fielding side, and if it hits it, then the batsman is out also. Runs are scored by measuring the distance the 'ball' was hit.

Balan used to play cards with great animation. Especially rummy, which is associated with the USA rather than India, though it might have originated in China. Manga remembers Balan, Ramani, Hari and others playing rummy all night the time she went back to India by herself. They were waiting to take her to the airport very early in the morning to catch the flight home, and couldn't bother to go to bed. On the long train journey from New Delhi to Tirur on our second visit, we played a game similar to Hearts endlessly with Raju, Prem and a group of soldiers on their way back from the fighting in Kashmir. The soldiers, especially a lad called Chandrasekhar, were very fond of the children. Like Hearts, you had to avoid winning a trick with the Queen of Spades in it; but instead of counting points, you collected the cards in the tricks you won, and the loser finished up with all the cards.

Manga says that some of the older people in the village were enthusiastic players of a forerunner of chess called chaturanga. I've never seen anyone play the game though, or come across the board or pieces. The first evidence for its existence seems to be the seventh century AD, whereas it is thought that Chinese chess or xuangqi dates from several centuries BC. I was introduced to xuangqi by my friend Mike McNaughton when he returned with his new wife Kok Heong from Malaysia. In his experience Chinese chess was played with much more abandon and enthusiasm than the western version, and it was considered bad form to think too much before a move. The same principle incidentally applies to palanguri in India. I used to play conventional chess regularly at the Sainik School with Sunil Mukherji, a fellow teacher, during the siesta; he always beat me in the first game and let me win the second, but eventually I improved enough to beat him properly now and again. Sunil-da was a good man. He was that rare specimen a Communist and an Anglophile, and a great friend to Manga and me. He left to become Head of a school in Santiniketan in Kolkata, and invited me to join the staff, but this was after we'd settled back here, had a mortgage and Victoria was getting old enough to start school, and I'm afraid I just wasn't brave enough to accept. Sunil-da made the arrangements for our wedding and his friend Santi-da acted as our host. We owe him a great deal.

But back to games and a final word. We had lots of fun playing a hilarious game of Uno at home in Trikkandiyur with about twenty of us, family and friends, sitting in a big circle on the floor. Perhaps that will become a favourite card game in Kerala!

CHAPTER FORTY-FIVE

AN IYER MARRIAGE

'Let's have a wedding!' Charles Dickens, *Great Expectations*

'I chose my wife, as she did her wedding gown, not for a fine glossy surface but such qualities as would wear well.' Oliver Goldsmith, *The Vicar of Wakefield*

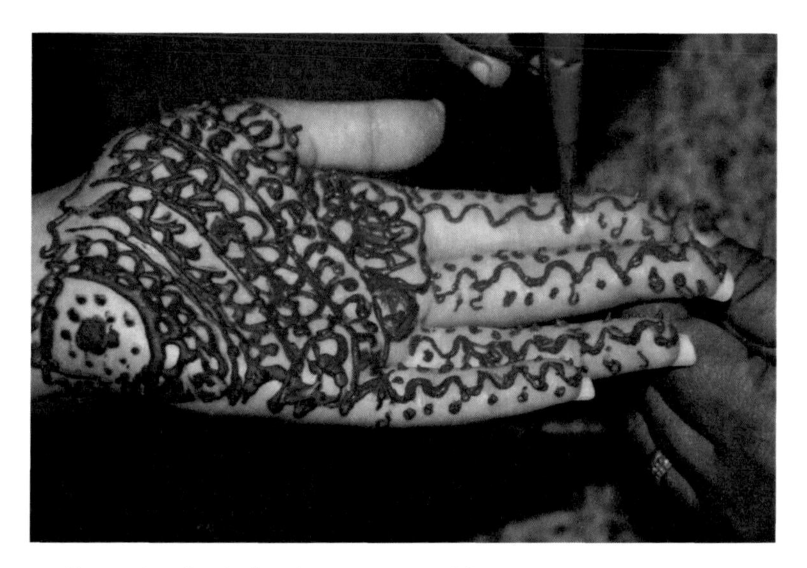

Decorations for the female guests at a wedding

No book about life in India can miss out a reference to weddings. In all religions and castes they are joyful and festive occasions, large numbers of guests normally attend, and far too much money is spent on them, sometimes leaving the brides' parents in debt for the rest of their lives. The majority of marriages are still arranged by the brides' and grooms' families even in middle-class circles, and the ceremonies themselves are replete with religious symbolism. And procedures differ according to caste, region and tradition.

Most of our Indian family have had arranged marriages, but there were exceptions, even before Manga married me. Manga's sister Rajam met her future husband Balan when he was boarding at the family house, and there have been several love marriages among the Mumbai members of the clan.

Our wedding was not at all typical, taking place as it did in a Registry Office [in the administrative district of Calcutta and the 24 Parganas] with a minimum of fuss. So we'll take as an example of an Indian wedding that between my nephew Raju and Geetha. This was an arranged marriage, and was the only one that Manga and I, Rosemary, and Victoria, Lakshmi, Indira all attended. So I asked Raju to send me an account of the celebration from his point of view. This is what Raju wrote.

'The proposal that Geetha and I should be married came as a result of an advertisement my family placed in the matrimonial column of various newspapers. Geetha's father replied and a close friend, Ganesh, recommended the proposal, as he had known the family very well for ages. He also recommended me to Geetha's family. Then after a number of telephone conversations we fixed a date to see Geetha at her maternal aunt's house in Aluva town. Geetha's dad was a little worried about the condition of their old house, because one proposal had been dropped simply because the house was not posh enough.

Mangalakka from Mumbai and chitti from Tirur [that's Rajam] *came with me to Aluva and so did my friend Anand and his wife. The family welcomed us grandly and soon Geetha appeared, beautifully dressed in a silk sari. We exchanged glances and for me it was love at first sight – I'm not sure whether Geetha felt the same! They gave us some time to talk together about our ideas and expectations and we got on well and decided to proceed with the proposal. Back in the main room, we gave our OK signal to Geetha's father and chitti, and we sat down to coffee and snacks: it is not done to have a full meal before the formal agreement is completed. Then, as is the usual practice, Geetha's father asked us about our demands regarding the dowry, wedding arrangements and so on. Chitti formally announced our policy: no dowry. Geetha's father was really pleased but he told us he was going to give Geetha various things to take with her and chitti said that if that was his wish, what he wanted to give Geetha could be given. The party concluded by fixing the marriage venue as Aluva; the date and time of the Muhurtham to be fixed later.*[The Muhurtham is the actual marriage ceremony, usually held on the morning of the second day. Its timing is crucial, and is decided by astrologers and priests]

Geetha's family was a little suspicious about the meeting though. Neither my father nor my mother nor my brother and sister were present, and that was very unusual. So a two-member spy team – Geetha's brother Kannan and her sister's husband Hari - was sent to gather information about my family in secret. They came to the village and watched and waited and asked questions but found nothing wrong and were impressed by the closeness of the joint family. Then without any notice they appeared on the doorstep of our old house, smartly dressed,and asked to see me. We were not at our best! Chitty and Mangalakka were lying on the floor wearing just a blouse and lungi – it was April and very hot – and reading magazines, and I was feeling hungry and eating a meal I'd made myself, so when Chitty called me I wandered in carrying a plate in my hands! I told Chitty and Mangalakka that it was Geetha's brother Kannan and at once they disappeared into thin air! Kannan introduced me to Hari and while we were talking, two very well dressed ladies appeared from nowhere: Chitty and Mangalakka, now in their best saris and with neatly brushed hair and jewellery! We took coffee and snacks and soon Balamama, Appa, Amma, Ravi, Manni, Appu and Ammu appeared, all in their best clothes and on their best behaviour, and after lots of introductions and friendly chatter, the 'spies' left with nothing bad to say about the boy or his family.

Meanwhile, back in Aluva, the entire family was waiting anxiously for the news. The 'spies' presented their report dramatically to heighten the suspense, then to the great relief of the father, announced that all was well. The family then decided that 6th June 1993 would be an auspicious day for the formal contract, Kalyana Nischayam [a sort of engagement ceremony].

The Bombay branch of the family arrived well in advance for the Nischayam: Periyamma, [Manga's eldest sister who was very frail], Swapna, Rashmi, Mangalakka. As Periyamma would not be coming for the marriage itself, we asked that Geetha should come; usually the bride is not present at this ceremony. The party from Aluva arrived at about 2pm on 6th June with containers filled with laddu, murukku, Mysore Pak and other goodies. The families sat opposite each other with me and Appa on one side and Geetha's father on the other side along with senior family members who would be witnesses. The priest chanted mantras and presented me with a thambalam [a silver sort of tray or container, traditionally handed to the groom by the bride's family during the Nischayam], *together with cloth, fruits, betel leaves and nuts. A token sum of money was passed to Appa by Geetha's father. In return we offered a sari for Geetha. Then all had coffee and a light meal: uppuma or idli, I'm not sure. The party returned to Aluva with agreement on a tentative date for the marriage – to be confirmed when the Banners had booked their air tickets, obtained visas, sought leave from work and so on.*

Soon travel arrangements from the UK had been sorted out, so we could finalise the wedding date: November 10th. Relations on both sides were informed so they could do the necessary things. Both sides had to get invitation cards printed. The card had to contain names of grandparents as well as parents and bride and groom, and of course the place, date and time of the Muhurtham, the most important of umpteen ceremonies, one when the Mangalyasutra or Thali [that's the wedding symbol worn on a chain round the bride's neck] is tied. Another task was to buy materials for the dhotis, shirts, saris etc. which were to be gifts to relations. Balamama, Manni [Ravi's wife Shanta] *and Radhika set off for Coimbatore to make the necessary purchases. A special silk sari was to be bought for the bride to wear on the eve of the wedding.*

A few days before the wedding at an auspicious time decided by the astrologers, a priest erected near the house a pole known as a Muhoortha Kal. This indicates that a happy event is about to happen there so anything bad should keep away. From now onwards the house will be full of relations, cooking, playing and merrymaking. The elders will sit seriously discussing strategy, and receiving guests. Those who wouldn't be able to attend the wedding, as it was to be conducted away from the village, will pay a visit and bless the bride and groom. At the bride's house they were also busy, making foodstuffs like ladoo, murukku, muthuswaram, Mysore Pak, athirasam, palkhoa, together known as seeru which would be placed at the venue and given to the groom's party. They also purchased dress materials, one outfit for the groom to wear on the evening before the wedding and a silk dhoti for the first night.. Experts were engaged to decorate the mandapam, where the wedding was to take place, with rice flour kolam. [These are the designs on the ground that you see at the front doors of houses, renewed daily.] Rooms were arranged for the groom's party to stay in; known as sambandhi. One or two people were entrusted with the duty of looking after the groom's party to make sure that they were always comfortable and had no difficulties in finding things they needed.

Here, at our end, one car took the elders, and the remaining members of the party started off in a bus to Aluva. The party reached Aluva around 4 pm. The car had arrived 30 minutes earlier and thinking that it would contain the groom the reception committee had sprung into action but retreated as soon as they realised that the groom was not in it! Finally the groom was given a kingly welcome with nadaswaram [music], *a bouquet and garlands, and was led to the dining hall for tea. We had coffee, jalebi, sevai, bhaji and chutney I think. From there we were led to the guest house to take a bath, refresh and dress. The reception team came and led us to the venue, the Aluva Municipal Town Hall, accompanied by nadaswaram. Nadaswaram consisted of a percussion drum played on one side with fingers with special caps at the tips and with a stick on the other side. Another man played a clarinet-like pipe and one more guy was there accompanying with a pair of small brass cymbals.*

I came in with my best man, Ramesh - as usual the next eligible bachelor in the family - along with my parents and elders, and we were led to the dais. I sat in a chair and Geetha's brother, Kichen, garlanded me, applied sandal paste to my forehead, and handed over a bouquet. Then with the accompaniment of nadaswaram he handed over a costume to be worn before Mappilai Azhaippu [the official welcoming of the groom]. *Next thing, along with friends and relatives I moved in to the dressing room. I got dressed with the help of a friend (Suresh) and a sister (Indi) - that's our Indira - and came out to sit again. After a few more ceremonies the groom's party, with me seated in an open car, left for Nagara- pradhakshinam* [a procession around the village]. *The purpose of this was to show the groom to elders and widows who are not able to attend the marriage. We then visited the temple.*

After the welcome, we were received at the entrance of the mandapam, handed a silver tray holding a coconut and again led to the stage. Now the formal engagement took place and after photo sessions and the handing over of gifts by those who could not come to the party the next day.

Next morning, the bride's people woke us with coffee and also oil, soap and toiletries for my use. After bath and dressing everyone went to the mandapam. I was dressed in the traditional soman, pancha gacham style [a dhoti tied in an old-fashioned way]. *The vritham* [blessing] *was conducted, and then Kappu Kettu* [the tying of a saffron thread around the groom's left wrist]. *After that, breakfast was served, with one sweet - halva or kesari - and idli, vadai, sambar, chutney and mulagaippodi with oil and then filter coffee. Next the kashiyathra was performed. The groom pretended in the traditional way that he was reluctant to marry and the bride's father had the task of persuading him to change his mind, following him to the gate and finally succeeding! On the return journey I sat in a cradle with a straw mat laid inside carried by uncles and friends. In olden times the marriages took place at an early age so that the couple would be children of low weight, which made things easier for the uncles.* [On this occasion, things were especially difficult, because one uncle was much taller than the others, and when he lifted the cradle onto his shoulder, it tipped violently and nearly deposited Raju on the floor! That uncle was me of course!]

Each side has its own priest - on left of picture

The bride was waiting and we were led towards a decorated swing. I held Geetha's hand in a particular way, with her fingers meeting together like a cone. We exchanged mattumalais [flower garlands] *with much fun and laughter and sat on the swing. The singers around began performing various keerthanams - special musical verses for the occasion - like seetha kalynana. Our feet were washed with milk and dried with the tip of the silk saris by the elder ladies. Then rice balls were thrown to ward off evil. The next step was the giving of the palum pazhavum* [banana and milk] *by the elder ladies to us both. All these activities were done by senior ladies only and being holy rites generally widows do not take part. Lastly we made a pradhakshinam* [circuit] *around the swing. We were then led to the mandapam and up to the dais. Actually, only then did the real marriage ceremony start. I was received by the father of the bride, who washed my feet with water. This was because I was supposed to be Vishnu. Then after certain manthras and ceremonies the bride was handed over to me through Kanyadhanam, offering of the virgin. This represented a transfer of gothram, the responsibility of care, from her father to her betrothed. This was done with the pouring of water through the hands of the bride, groom and her father. Then the koora pudavai, the long sari, was handed over to the bride and she went into the dressing room with her sister-in-law Ambika and came back dressed in the traditional way. Then the thali was tied with the blessing of the elders and the recital of prayers.*

After this the bride's toe rings were put on and more manthras were said. I held Geetha's right big toe and supported her while she made seven steps reciting traditional phrases. Next we made three pradhakshinams around the fire and on each circuit we stopped near the bottom half of the grinding stone and I held Geetha's foot over the stone. We then sat near the fire and both offered rice to the flames. Geetha's brother helped us fill our hands, which we held together to contain the rice. This was done three times too. Then more psalms were sung until it was time for the final item of any Iyer ritual. This was the Ashirvadham; a blessing both from the elders and the gods. We stood together with my wife on the right side following strict tradition. We had small dhotis spread over our hands to collect flowers and raw rice coloured with turmeric. This combination, called akshdhai was to represent prosperity. The priest chanted manthras and the elders in turn threw the yellow rice on to the dhoti. This was when Chittappa ate it! [Somebody gave me a handful of rice and if they told me what I was supposed to do with it, I didn't understand. Eating it seemed the natural thing to do! Nobody seemed to mind - they all had a good laugh - but I hope it didn't bring bad luck or anything]. *Finally the rice was collected up and we paid namaskarams* [respects] *to the elders and moved towards the cottage where I had been staying. Here we were received by my mother and aunts. Palum pazhavum was given and then everyone went back to the dining hall for sadhya - the feast - meeting and talking, music and merrymaking. Then the crowd dispersed to rest.*

Raju and Geetha's wedding: the seven steps

Later we were offered light snacks – bhaji or bonda with coffee – before we finally left for my home town with my new bride. As she was going to stay for the first time, her sister Rema with her husband and two young children accompanied Geetha. Our party was provided with enough food – puliogarai and lemon rice – to be eaten on arriving home as well as provisions and vegetables to be cooked for the following day. The entry into my house – Grihaprayrsham – happened at 5.30 in the evening and neighbours gathered round with good wishes.

The next part of the programme was Nilangu. We sat opposite one another on a straw mat spread over the floor. First a roasted papad was broken over Geetha's head then I combed her hair. A mirror was shown to her for self appraisal and then she repeated the same actions on me. After this a small coconut, de-husked and rather polished was placed between us. I used one palm to hold it while she tried to grab it using both hands. This happened to the accompaniment of cheering from the surrounding friends and relatives, to encourage both of us. The coconut was then rolled slowly to and fro between us like a ball and now the nightingales of the group started up. They performed special songs for this occasion known as Nilangu songs.'

On the following day, a reception was held in the garden to honour all those guests who had not been able to attend the wedding ceremony. It was certainly a grand party. One of Raju's friends had stayed behind when we went to Aluva to supervise the construction of a complicated series of canvas covers between the trees and the walls of the houses transforming the whole garden into a giant marquee; and everyone had spent the day before the reception helping with cooking and decorating. I think the whole village attended the party! One of my abiding memories is of Victoria and Lakshmi sitting for most of a very hot day near the gate welcoming guests as they arrived – popping up from their seats with a bright smile as each new person was introduced, and after they had passed along, subsiding sleepily back into their chairs.]

My sister Rosemary greatly enjoyed the wedding; she wrote that it was 'a wonderful occasion'. Rosemary had promised Raju during an earlier visit that she would come and see him get married and she followed the process carefully. In her diary she mused about the 'clinical' sounding nature of arranged marriages – advertisements [these were not at that time a commonplace in western courtship], matching of horoscopes, skin colour, caste and educational requirements and so on – and about their outcome, concluding that, from her experience at least, the system seemed to be as successful as any other, however alien it might seem to us. She remembers receiving a letter in the spring telling us that a match had been made and that the wedding was to take place towards the end of the year; then came a photograph of '*a proud man, his beautiful demure fiancée* [Geetha], *and Lakshmi, Raju's Periyamma or senior Auntie, sitting in front of them on the familiar rattan chair. Everyone' she added 'is obviously delighted, though Periyamma is wearing a rather stern photograph face*!' November came and we set off for Kerala in good time so as we could join in the preparations for the ceremonies. Rosemary remembers being '*absorbed into the life of the family in a way that had not been possible*' on her earlier visit, and she chose her sleeping place in a quiet corner of the living room with a mat and pillow. The latter was covered with a pillow case made from an old sun-dress that Rosemary had passed on to Manga many years before - an example of the 'waste not want not' philosophy prevalent in our family, and indeed most of the rest of India at that time. Rosemary had also taken a cassette recorder with her and she *'left it on to catch the flavour of everyone chatting in the kitchen, the sound of the monsoon rain on the verandah and crows on Tirur Station'.*

Laughter at the wedding. It's not all serious!

During the few days before the celebrations began, the house was full of relations and other visitors. Always keen to remember who was who and how they were related, Rosemary drew up a family tree, and learned to introduce herself she says, as *'the sister of the husband of the groom's mother's youngest sister'*! Raju helped her with the family tree and also *'went through the marriage ceremony in detail explaining the significance of all the rituals.'* And *'Meals were an enormous undertaking; we all joined in the preparation.'* We also took a trip to Periyar Lake, Indi having arranged a meeting with a Professor with whom there was a possibility of doing some research connected with her Ph.D. He was working with with Project Tiger, which made it all rather exciting, but nothing came of the proposal in the end. Rosemary recalls our first meeting with Geetha and her family en route to the hills. *'We called at Geetha's family house and had a wonderful welcome, snacks and drinks and laughter. Geetha played the violin for us and her brothers and sister-in-law, Amba, came in and impressed us by being instantly friendly and unfazed by this sudden increase in family members from another continent.'* Periyar was not a great success. Vijaya, Lakshmi and Rashmi from Mumbai found it a bit chilly in the evenings, we got up too late to join an early boat trip and as a result saw very little wildlife, and poor Vijaya was very travel sick. Everyone was cheerful though and we played singing games in our overloaded Trekker.

And so to the wedding ceremony. This is Rosemary's account of what happened.

'The day before the wedding saw us travelling through the rain in an old fashioned charabanc bumping in and out of pot holes on the way to Aluva. When we arrived at Geetha's home, the courtyard beautifully decorated with rice water pictures and garlands, the excitement was palpable. We were given snacks and then found our sleeping places in the hostel, had delicious cold showers and changed into our finery for the engagement party. This took place at the Town Hall, where the stage was decorated with balloons and coloured lights; we were lead there accompanied by a percussion band. Raju was welcomed into the family and then went in procession round the village and to the temple.

The night was short as there was a large amount of ritual to go through before the auspicious time for the Muhurtham was reached. We were woken before dawn with coffee and I was helped into my elegant sari. Unfortunately I did it less than justice; I think my stride was too long and posture ungainly. During the day my confidence improved however. After breakfast we went outside for two of the traditional rituals which are light hearted and allow everyone to join in and admire the handsome couple. First was 'going to Benares'. This is when the groom pretends to have doubts and sets off for the gate – the bride's father has the job of persuading him to return with cajoling and little gifts. Of course he succeeded and soon Raju came back carried precariously in a woven cradle. He joined Geetha on a swing draped in flowers and we all encouraged them to enjoy the moment. Then the senior ladies – including me – were given the task of offering holy blessings. We all then paraded around the swing three times and on into the Hall. This was large and filled with trestle tables and chairs, the musicians were on a raised dais to one side and the important ceremonies were to take place on the stage, were we, as honoured family members were to sit. And now the important part of the marriage service began. I tried to take in all the intricacies; several pictures come into my mind – the moving moment when the bride's father hands over responsibility for his daughter to her new husband and water is poured through their outstretched fingers ['Who gives this woman?']. The tying of the gold thali around the bride's neck came next and is equivalent to the exchanging of rings. I see Geetha returning to the stage with Amba who had helped her into a traditional nine metre sari of a gorgeous deep red; her delicate little figure almost swamped. I remember that oil and turmeric, sandal wood paste and coconuts featured in the rituals, and of course we joined in the throwing and, in some cases eating, of the yellow rice. I remember being impressed by the classical wedding music being played by a small group with I think a sitar, a flute and a pair of tablas. When gifts of money were offered we were able to add novelty by presenting notes in pounds sterling.

We were clearly of interest to the wider audience who were probably not previously aware of our existence in the family. It was a sobering experience to be even a minor celebrity. Some of the elders asked us for our views on the ceremony and of course we were effusive in our admiration. Some of our questioners though evidently thought we should be more critical. But what could we say? We were simply totally fascinated by the whole experience.

We wandered outside to look at the river and came across the cooks in a court yard, hard at work chopping herbs with murderous looking knives and stirring huge cauldrons of vegetable and lentil curry. Steaming vats of aromatic rice and muslin-covered bowls of yoghurt were ready to serve and the aroma was mouth watering. We took our seats in the Hall and were given banana leaves as plates and small stainless steel beakers of water to wash them with; we ate with the fingers of our right hands. It was a full traditional feast with all the elements presented in delicate heaps around the circumference of the leaf and was delicious and satisfying, including my favourite, payasam.

The journey home was somewhat difficult as we seem to have gathered many more passengers and piles of wedding gifts including bulky bedding and large cooking pans. We were pleased to be back at home where we soon forgot that we were tired and over wrought in the excitement of the post wedding fun and singing. These activities date from times when the couple were strangers to one another and the playing of simple games gave them a chance to relax.

There was much bawdy jollity and gentle teasing as they were lead to the bedroom, which was decorated with balloons and flower petals. Outside, Raju's bachelor friends let off fire crackers.

I remember we slept mat to mat on the living room floor and Geetha made tea for us all in the morning. We then had to prepare for the party which was held for local people who had not been able to attend the ceremonies in Aluva. Our family helped to greet the guests and offer snacks, drinks and paan in the garden. It was lush from the rains but warm and sunny. I enjoyed watching Rema deal with her tiny baby and also meeting relatives from Manga's brothers' families.

Unfortunately, we had booked our return tickets without realising it would be Diwali. It would have been wonderful to have been able to stay, but we did see the decorations and little lamps in the windows of the houses'.

CHAPTER FORTY-SIX

NURSING: MANGA'S MEMORIES

'*Would you catch a leech and put it abed?*' Malayalam proverb

Manga left school at the age of fifteen and went to work in the Panchayat Board as a clerk. The Panchayat is the smallest unit of local government in India and developed from the ancient practice of five [panch] elders being elected at a village meeting to run local affairs. So working for the Board was a very honourable profession and could well have led to a respectable career in local government. But sitting typing, filing, organising meetings and writing letters did not satisfy Manga. She had heard that other girls were applying for nursing training, and thought that would be much more to her taste. But there were problems, and the main one was that Brahmins did not do nursing. Even touching people from lower castes was frowned upon, and to touch them in the intimate way inevitably involved in nursing was completely unacceptable. And nursing would mean going away from home to train and having opportunities to get up to all sorts of mischief. Finally, nurses were to be seen talking to doctors, usually male at that time: no decent girl would be so friendly with any man to whom she was not related.

So Manga was a bit worried about asking her parents if they would allow her to embark on this dodgy profession, and knew she would have to approach them with care. But in the end they didn't need too much persuading. Manga, being the youngest and weakest often got her own way, and Manga thinks that her mum might have felt she'd make a good nurse because she was so kind to animals. As for her dad, well, he'd got Manga's older sisters married, so even if there was a whiff of scandal it would not affect their prospects. And to be honest, the money would come in handy.

Manga takes up the story.

'I had to go to Calicut for an interview. I had the right qualifications because I'd done well at school and passed the SSLC. But I was a bit scared about the interview, which was going to be in English because the training would all take place in the English language. I could

speak English quite nicely and got good marks for grammar and writing but I didn't really know how to hold a conversation. We'd just learned everything by rote. Some of the girls found out that the most important question was 'Why do you want to take up nursing?' And the right answer was 'To help the Humanity [sic]'. So we all by-hearted this though we had no idea what it meant! Anyway, I passed the interview - I expect they were short of candidates - and the next step was to get ready for the trip to Madras. That was where we'd do our training. We had to go with three uniforms. So our friend who used to eat with us and who worked in Madras – so they thought he might know something I suppose – and my brother, arranged for a tailor to come and make the uniforms. But none of them had a clue. I ended up with clothes like a dancing girl's: much too short. And the hat looked very strange too. But when I got to Madras all the girls had different uniforms and mine wasn't too bad. And the wrap-round apron covered my knees, so that was OK.

Manga in Delhi

We started with six months preliminary training. We studied nine subjects I think – anatomy, physiology, surgery, you know all those things. In English of course. I passed the exams with good marks and so I went onto the wards. Would you believe there were seventy patients on each of those wards. The whole hospital was run by a matron and assistant matron. There were three or four staffs [fully trained staff nurses] and a sister was in charge of the ward, but the students did nearly all the work. I said we had seventy patients – sometimes there were a hundred – but there were only 50 beds. The other patients slept on the floor between the beds or down the middle of the ward. There were two day shifts and apart from me there was one helper on the ward and sometimes a staff or the sister would come in and work with us. We had medicine to give every four hours and temperatures to be taken and in between that we had to make all the beds in a proper way so they all lined up.

We didn't do night duty till our second year. During the night I was the only nurse there. I had to take temperatures four-hourly, give medicines four-hourly, and towards the morning take gastric juices to check ulcers. We only had a half hour break, or was it an hour, I'm forgetting. I think it must have been an hour because we went for dinner and then had a short sleep lying on hard tables till someone rang a bell. We had to write reports, three or four lines on every patient and read them to Sister when she came in the morning, and go round the ward with her and show each patient. We got into trouble if we did anything wrong. In between all this we had to change the labels on medicine bottles if they were bit dirty. We only had one and a half days off every month, and even then we had to go to matron's office to ask. And we didn't always get permission – if any of our patients had bedsores, matron might say no. And it was difficult to stop bedsores, especially on typhoid cases – the poor people were very thin and got sores easily. Training lasted three and a half years, including midwifery.

Our patients had all sorts of infections, gas gangrene, often high fever. For that we wrapped them in cold sheets and put ice bags on their heads. I've got lots of stories about nursing but I think that's enough for now. Oh, I did nurse Rajiv Gandhi, Indira's eldest son, and a future Prime Minister. Well he was on my ward for one day to be exact! He came in for an appendix operation I think. He was such a nice boy and I was so sad years later when he was assassinated.'

I asked Manga's friend Hyma, now in Canada, if she could remember anything they got up to when they were training together. She said that once a group of nurses had gone out to see a movie in the evening and on their way back to the Nurses' Home, some boys started following them. Manga stopped, turned round and scolded them: '*You have sisters at home, don't you? What would you think if someone was following them like this*?' The boys lowered their heads and slunk off muttering apologetically! And another time, some nurses and doctors went to Varanasi for a pilgrimage. Unfortunately one of the doctors fell into the river and there was panic until Manga found some rope, threw it to him and pulled him to safety!

CHAPTER FORTY-SEVEN

INDEPENDENCE

'Long years ago, we made a tryst with destiny, and now the time comes when we shall redeem our pledge, not wholly or in full measure, but very substantially. At the stroke of the midnight hour, when the world sleeps, India will awake to life and freedom. A moment comes, which comes but rarely in history, when we step from the old to the new, when an age ends, and when the soul of a nation, long suppressed, finds utterance. It is fitting that at this solemn moment we take the pledge of dedication to the service of India and her people and to the still larger cause of humanity.

At the dawn of history India started on her unending quest, and trackless centuries are filled with her striving and the grandeur of her success and her failures. Through good and ill fortune alike she has never lost sight of that quest or forgotten the ideals that gave her strength. We end today a period of ill fortune and India discovers herself again. The achievement we celebrate today is but a step, an opening of opportunity, to the greater triumphs and achievements that await us. Are we brave enough and wise enough to grasp this opportunity and accept the challenge of the future?... To the nations and peoples of the world we send greetings and pledge ourselves to co-operate with them in furthering peace, freedom and democracy.

And to India, our much-loved motherland, the ancient, the eternal and the ever-new, we pay our reverent homage and we bind ourselves afresh to her service. Jai Hind!' Pandit Nehru, first Prime Minister of India, 15 August 1947

'While our achievement [independence] is in no small measure due to our sufferings and sacrifices, it is also the result of world forces and events; and last but not least, it is the consummation and fulfilment of the historic traditions and democratic ideals of the British race.' Dr Rajendra Prasad, first President of the Indian Republic

'The weak can never forgive. Forgiveness is the attribute of the strong.' Mahatma Gandhi

Schoolchildren celebrating.

On the fifteenth of August 1947, India became independent. There were of course huge celebrations in Delhi – people of all religions crowded joyfully onto the streets. But three days later the joyful atmosphere was shattered. The Boundary Commission announced which parts of the Panjab were to be in India and which in Pakistan. There followed a mass migration into and out of India, accompanied by the most appalling riots and widespread killing; all sides were implicated, including the British who had failed to make any provision for the protection of the millions of refugees. John Keay wrote, 'East to west and west to east, perhaps ten million fled for their lives in the greatest exodus in recorded history...Two hundred thousand at least, possibly as many as a million, were massacred between August and October in the Panjab partition and associated riots. But as with the [Bengal] famine...the names of the victims went unrecorded, their numbers uncounted. Unprepared and overwhelmed, neither of the new nations could do more than feed the living. Meanwhile, Mountbatten, 'determined to keep clear of the whole business', as he put it, had washed his hands of the

Panjab and headed for the hills.[i] The history-makers looked the other way.'[323]

Nehru duly took up the reins of government and led the world's largest democracy until his death in 1964. His governments followed a socialist programme at home, and a policy of peaceful co-existence and non-interference abroad, and India was a founder-member of the Non-Aligned Movement. One of Nehru's closest friends and allies was a Kerala politician whom we have already met – V.K.Krishna Menon. KM was High Commissioner in London for 5 years and was then appointed as Ambassador to the UN where his intelligence, sometimes sarcastic wit, and fluency impressed a wider world. It is apparent that as a public speaker he was intense and passionate. Rosina Visram quotes one listener as saying 'you could almost hear the pounding of his heart'.[324] He is most famous for a record-breaking eight hour speech in the Security Council when he defended his country's position on Kashmir. Manga had direct experience of his prolixity. Once Krishna Menon came to visit her school. The occasion must have been something to do with Thanchat, or the Tirur Wagon tragedy – perhaps the 25th Anniversary of the latter, but Manga does not remember. What she does remember is that she, as the school's best singer, was to lead the singing of the National Anthem at the conclusion of KM's address. Problem was, the address went on rather, and the young audience was beginning to flag. Fortunately the great man needed to take a drink during his peroration, and an alert aide seized her opportunity, called Manga forward to start the singing, and KM was uncharacteristically cut off in full flow!

But in the UN Krishna Menon was a shrewd operator who was never forgiven by the American government for successfully articulating India's policy of non-alignment. For his part, KM did not like America's aggressive anti-Communism. An example of their many clashes is quoted by Rozina Visram: when the Americans provided the Pakistani military dictatorship with arms while refusing to help the democratic Indians, they gave as their excuse, 'We wish to help Pakistan defend herself against Russia.' KM responded, 'I never heard before that American guns can only fire in one direction' – for in fact, the weapons were only ever used

---

[i] A defence of Mountbatten is set out in Alex von Tunzelmann's *Indian Summer: the Secret History of the End of an Empire,* pp 252-7

against India. KM came to grief as a result of the Sino-Indian War of 1962, when as Minister of Defence he was blamed for India's rapid defeat.

Meanwhile in Kerala, people seem to have been barely conscious of independence - Manga remembers little in the way of celebration - or of the national and international policies overseen by Nehru and the likes of Krishna Menon. The fact is, says Manga, what was happening nearly two thousand miles away in New Delhi was of little interest to the vast majority of the inhabitants of Kerala. It had ever been the case. Empires and Emperors based in the north had come and gone for centuries, but the life of the Kerala peasant had changed little. Most of their concerns were local – could they get their hands on enough rice, what was the price of salt, would their landlord increase their rents, was it safe to speak their minds, did they have any protection against the arrogance of the rich or higher castes? It seemed to make little difference who was in power in the north. The Empires generally supported the landowners and the wealthy, relying on them to collect taxes and maintain order; all rulers tried to maximise profits by growing cash crops instead of rice; and few were prepared to interfere with the caste system or encourage a politically active working class. If progress were to be made, it would depend on who was in charge locally.

For the people of Malabar, local government meant rule from Chennai. And whether the rulers were British or Indian, and whether the system was democratic or autocratic, rule from Chennai was bad news. Five hundred miles away, in an area where a different language was spoken, which had different customs and different priorities, a Chennai government was unlikely to have at the forefront of its collective mind the best interests of a small coastal strip on the far side of a dividing mountain range, containing a relatively small number of voters. So their struggle was for a government for Kerala.

Kerala Becomes a State

A single state for Malayalam-speaking peoples had first become an aim of the independence movement in 1928, when the Princely States Peoples' Conference and the All Kerala Tenants' Conference demanded 'Aikya Keralam' – a unified Kerala state. This followed the decision of the INC, at its Nagpur conference in 1920, to organise its state committees on linguistic lines. The Aikya Kerala movement was subsequently supported by the socialists, the trade unionists, and students. However on independence, progress was a little slow. Travancore and Kochi joined together to become a single state ['Tiru- Kochi'] of the Indian Union in 1948, but Malabar remained for the time being as part of Tamilnad.

It took many committees and commissions, resolutions and memoranda, and even a self-immolation [in Andhra], before the States Re-Organisation Act was passed in 1956 and on November 1st, the state of Kerala came into being. The boundaries of the new state were drawn on strictly linguistic grounds, and as a result, some land was lost [in the far south, including Kanniya Kumari and Nagercoil, which were Tamil speaking areas and joined Tamilnad] and some gained [Kasaragod in the north].

The first elections to Kerala's Legislative Assembly took place in February 1957. Travancore had already held, in February 1948, the first ever elections under universal adult suffrage in India, when Congress had won 97 out of 120 seats and the Communists had polled only 10 per cent of the total vote. There were splits in the Congress party however and after less than a year the government fell, taking with it much of the party's prestige. There had been two more ministries in Travancore and a total of three in Kochi before amalgamation, and another five in the 7- year life of Travancore – Kochi! They were usually coalitions led by Congress.

It seemed therefore that Kerala was ripe for a change in 1957, and indeed a change there was. The result of the poll was as follows: Communist Party [CPI] – 63 seats; CPI-backed independents – 5; Congress – 43; Muslim League - 8; others – 10. So for the first time in the history of the world a significant Communist Government was freely elected, and Kerala was barely born before it hit the headlines.[ii] To many historians [including Keay] Kerala wasn't the sort of society one associates with communism – it was largely rural with very little industry and no mines for

---

[ii] The miniature Italian Principality of San Marino chose a communist government in the early fifties. The far left won an election in Guyana in 1953, but under the guise of the Peoples Progressive Party, and they did not in any case go on to form a government, as the colonial power, Britain, annulled the election.

example, and there was a strong Christian element. But the Communist Party in Kerala had been the only one which had given support to the rural poor, having fought for the rights of tenants over unscrupulous landlords, and having stood up for the lower castes in the most rigid caste system in India. In addition, the electorate was a well-educated one who could appreciate the attraction of communist theory. Furthermore the great national Congress leaders carried relatively little weight in far-away Kerala, and the local party was largely ineffectual, and led, like the socialists, by Christians and Nairs. So it was not perhaps so surprising that communism would thrive; though when the new government led by E.M.S.Namboodiripad gained power, it was not to survive long.

The Kerala Government's priorities were to attack private ownership in education and agriculture, but these aims were vigorously opposed by the church and the landlords in particular. A 'freedom movement' [Vimochana Samaram] was formed and law and order was threatened to such an extent that Nehru recommended President's rule'; and on 31 July 1959, the government was dismissed. There was talk of CP assassination squads, and the 'trigger happy' Malabar Special Police. And the landowners and higher castes certainly did suffer. It is easy for us to characterise these members of society as the 'baddies' who had been living in luxury on the backs of the hard labour of the poor and downtrodden, and maybe that scenario was in many cases accurate. One can have little sympathy for the Brahmin landowners who had to give up many of their paddy fields to hitherto landless labourers whom they had for the most part ruthlessly exploited. But it is of interest to listen to what one of Manga's friends has to say. He was an Iyer whose family, relatively unusually, owned a substantial number of rice fields outside the village, and whilst ready to accept my assertion that the re- distribution was a good thing in principle, he was quick to point out that this policy had led to a substantial reduction in the quantity of rice grown. '*The new owners have built houses on my father's land and used the residue for inefficient subsistence agriculture*,' he told me. '*Malabar was already short of rice and now it is more so. Prices are going up and who suffers? Why, the poor. They might have been landless before but they could always afford to buy rice, and we would always help them through the bad times. Now we can't, the new rich won't and the government says it will, but is too corrupt or disorganised to do it properly*.' And it is sure that Manga's family, Brahmins and enjoying some respect for that reason, were anything but exploiters of the poor. They themselves quite often did not know where the next meal was coming from, and as we have seen had to beg for money to pay for their daughters' dowries.

The Constitution, a very Centre-biased one, allows the President of the Republic to dismiss state governments. Nehru used the device ten times [most often in Kerala!], mostly where multi-party coalitions were unable to operate; his daughter suspended state governments seventy times!

Manga was a young girl at this time, and her ideas were of course shaped by the views of her family's friends, mostly better-off and higher caste people, but she remembers the birth of Kerala as a time of disruption and dislocation. The collapse of the old order in her experience meant lawlessness as the Communists released people from jails: not only political prisoners which would have been right, she says, but also violent criminals to lead the alleged murder squads. And it meant that some people whose families had for many centuries undertaken tasks essential for the community, ceased to carry out these duties overnight as they awaited their share of the riches hitherto, they believed, enjoyed by the 'higher' castes. Whatever might be said, and rightly, about the inequities of the caste system, it had held society together and an abrupt change did not necessarily lead to the greatest happiness of the greatest number. Others in Kerala would have had a different story to tell, but at the next election the Communists were defeated, even though they polled more votes in this election than the previous one, losing only because the opposition parties organised themselves better than before. It was also said, according to my nephew, that the CIA spent 300 crore rupees on toppling the Communists [one crore is 10 million].

This was just the prelude to a disjointed decade of Kerala politics: there were to be four further governments before the end of the sixties, including a second Namboodiri ministry, which this time lasted for only eighteen months. There was another period of president's rule – for nearly three years after the anti-communist coalition broke up. And further confusion arose when the Communists split into Marxist [CPM] and non-Marxist parties in 1964. In March 1965, the Communists returned to power. The Marxists won 40 seats to 36 for Congress and governed with support from the Socialists. It is curious to note that the Marxist [pro-Chinese] Party took power just as China was invading India in the north east. The Prime Minister at the time, Lal Bahadur Shastri, remarked that this was '*a symptom of a peculiarly Malayalee detachment from national concerns.*'

Achutha Menon then led a Communist ministry that lasted from 1970 to 1977, but when it fell, there were four more governments [two Congress, one CPI and one Muslim League] in the two and a half years before the end of the decade. In more recent years the pendulum has swung between coalitions led by the Indian National Congress - the United Democratic Front, and the CPI [M] - the Left Democratic Front. Marxist or not in principle, the Communist Party in Kerala is no longer a revolutionary outfit, though, if my experience is typical anyway. I chatted to a group of young businessmen in Tirur on a recent visit, asking them how they were going to vote in a forthcoming election. '*Oh CPM of course*' they responded. '*But I thought Communists were against private enterprise*' I said. '*Not here*' was the answer. '*They give us more encouragement than Congress. And they're not so keen on lining their own pockets*!' I suppose one shouldn't be surprised: the same seems things seem to be happening in modern China.

Woodcock, and others, would say that Kerala's political volatility reflects the character of Malayalees. 'One quality which the Malayalees lack completely is reticence ...[and] it is no exaggeration to say that there are as many shades of opinion as there are literate inhabitants. 'We are like grains of sand: separate and ever shifting' said one Malayalee to me'. Woodcock also highlights the differences between people from the north and south of Kerala. The people of Kochi and Travancore regarded the northerners as being disruptive and backward, as they had not benefited from the 'kind of high culture fostered by the native princes, who were devoted patrons of the arts and learning.'[325] K.P.Kesava Menon counters by saying that 'the disruptive elements were to be found not in the north but in the south ... the people of Malabar [are] law-abiding and peaceful by nature, while the people of Kochi-Travancore are turbulent and given to mob action; [the northerners – Malabarese are] honest and straightforward and heirs to the best traditions of Britain, while the southern Malayalees are devious and subtle, marred by the servile habits that stem from feudal rule and the tradition of patronage'.[326] And while we are making generalisations, there is the famous one that Indians [not especially Keralites] are always eager to please and for example will supposedly tell you that the nearest post office is just round the corner when it is two miles away to keep you happy at least for the moment. My story comes from Maharastra in fact, the town of Vasai, where half of our family live. I had just bought a refreshing drink of sugar cane juice from a small establishment in a back street, and the owner told Manga that I was the first Englishman ever to come into his shop. I was rather pleased and so at the next shop we visited – it sold fresh milk if I remember rightly – I asked the shopkeeper if I was the first English to make a purchase there. He hesitated. '*Why yes sir. You are the first... today*'

In spite of Kerala's political problems, the state made astoundingly rapid social progress. In some ways a backward state before the war, at least as far as its caste structure was concerned, by 1990 Kerala became famous for offering its people a better quality of life than anywhere else in India or almost any other low-income state. The *New Internationalist* magazine listed the following as factors leading it to that conclusion:

-Over 90 per cent of families owned the land on which their houses stood

-Land ownership was limited to 8 hectares per family

-The literacy rate [91%] was higher than any 'third world' country

-30% of state spending was on education.

-Life expectancy was 70 years, hardly less than the USA, compared with 55 in the India as a whole.

-The infant mortality rate was 20 per thousand; USA 10 per thou., India 93 per thou.

-99% of villages have a fair-price shop within 2 kilometres

-94% of primary age girls and 99% of primary age boys were in school

-The fertility rate was a little over 2, USA just under 2, India 4+ [by 2012 it had dropped to 2.5].

Our family can certainly relate to this area of progress: Manga's Mum had 7 surviving children, but the average size of her children's families was just over three, and that of her grandchildren only 1.5, exactly.

-Women accounted for 28% of government employees and 36% of employees in 'organised economic entities'

-The 'Physical Quality of Life 'index was 68, compared with 98 for Sweden and 44 for India as a whole.

On the other hand, the indicators of the health of the economy placed Kerala way towards the bottom of the league table. Gross National Product per capita was only $250; that of the USA was $22,000 and India's was $350. Unemployment was the highest in India but consumption was relatively high because of remittances from Malayalees working in the Gulf States, which amounted to as much as 25% of the GNP. Unfortunately Kerala families have not used this windfall in a way that is conducive to development. Instead of going into business ventures, most of the money has been spent on land [for houses], on building houses, on cars or on gold. So a house in the village which we might have bought for a few hundred pounds [if we had had such a sum] in the early sixties, and for not much more in the seventies, was worth many thousands of pounds in the eighties after the Gulf boom and considerably more than that today.

Of course, the Gulf was not the only place where expatriate Malayalees are to be found. The proliferation of well educated young people and the shortage of suitable work for them has long been a feature of life in Kerala and for many decades there has been an exodus to other parts of India or abroad. Shashi Tharoor comments: 'Keralites never suffered from inhibitions about travel: an old joke suggests that so many Keralite typists flocked to stenographic work in Mumbai, Kolkata and Delhi that 'Remington' became the name of a new Malyali sub-caste!'[327]

We'll take as an example of the Kerala Diaspora, the case of young Variyathmadam Parameswaran Mangalam.

The Kerala Diaspora

Manga wanted to be a nurse from an early age and left home and Malabar at the age of seventeen years when she went to Chennai for nursing training. It wouldn't be fair perhaps to say she was part of the diaspora at this stage, though. For one thing, there was no suitable training school in Malabar, and for another Malabar was part of the Madras Presidency at that time anyway. But when Manga qualified as a nurse [incidentally having been awarded a medal, which she still has, for being the top trainee in surgery in the whole of the Presidency][iii] she did join the ranks of the well-educated and professionally-trained Keralites who found work outside the state. At first this was at the famous Safdarjung Hospital, in New Delhi. Manga explains why she sought work there.

'Oh lots of reasons. I don't know really. We were quite adventurous. And for a Brahmin, nursing wasn't a good job. You had to touch people of low caste. A lot of our friends didn't like that, and so there weren't many Brahmin nurses. Also nurses had a bad reputation in those days. We had to talk a lot to male patients of course and naturally were friendly with the doctors. People thought we must misbehave with them. So it wouldn't have been easy to work near home. When I was training in Madras a friend from the village who used to eat at our home and who then got work in Madras kept an eye on me. He was very good - made sure I had plenty to eat for one thing, but he would also see that I behaved myself: he'd have told my Dad if I didn't and I would have had to go home. Once I had my photo taken and it was such a nice picture that the photographer displayed it in his shop window. This chap said that was very bad and told the man to take it down. But one of the main reasons for going to Delhi was that there were very few jobs in Kerala. I was just one of lots of nurses from the south. My best friends were Stella from Mangalore and Hyma from Palakkad; most of the girls came from Kerala. We would catch the train to go home and count the hours before we would see our Mums, and tick off the stations. I would get so excited. We only came home once a year - nurses were given one free ticket a year - unless someone died or there was a wedding or something.

Dad would be waiting at the station. Mum used to say he got there hours before the train was due, he was so impatient to see me and didn't want to be late. Mum would be waiting at the end of the passageway that went past our front gate. She'd be certain to have my favourite food cooked for me. I always brought saris for Mum and my sisters, and something small for Dad. Mum would cry so much, and even more when I left to go back to Delhi. I only had a small stipend they called it - 67 rupees a month, and out of that we had to pay for our food 17 rupees and Rs.4 for the dhobi. That left me 46 rupees for everything else - that's about £3, or 75p a week. We had an occasional treat - tea at

---

[iii] A region substantially bigger than the whole of the United Kingdom

Gaylords perhaps or a trip to a historical site; and I would save up for a sari or a pair of shoes, or for presents for the family, like talcum powder or oranges and apples - things like that which weren't available in Tirur in those days. But most of the money I sent home - about 20 rupees a month. That was important for Mum because Dad was never sure how much he would earn. He would get money from cooking for Brahmins, usually people who were working away from their homes, and often they would have a lodger or two. Dad would sell sweets and things at festivals and people would give him rice if he did a healing or performed a religious rite.

After Mum and Dad died I went to England. It was a big step but not so unusual. A lot of Kerala nurses went abroad. They would often say that they would come back home when they'd got experience in foreign hospitals, but mostly they didn't. Hyma went to Canada and is still there, married to a man originally from Pakistan. Stella Gomes did come home though, after she had spent many years in New Zealand. Christopher met her in Delhi when he was first in India. But for most people, they got used to life away from India. It wasn't just more money. I think it was the freedom. Of course I married an Englishman and we were always going to live in England. I wouldn't want to go back now. I feel I'm more English than Indian in some ways. Just little things. The English are much kinder to animals, they keep nice gardens, there is less gossip. Life is more comfortable too even though we don't have servants and the weather can be so bad.'

The Kerala Model

The phenomenon of favourable social conditions but a backward economy was known in some quarters as the Kerala Model, and it largely continued till the end of the twentieth century. Life expectancy was up to 73 [India as a whole 64, US 77]; birth rate down to 14 per thousand women [India 25, US 16], and infant mortality down to 10 per thousand births [India 70, US 7]. All Kerala's 1500 villages were connected to roads and there were almost twice as many miles of roads per inhabitant as the rest of India. The gender ratio was 1058 females per 1000 males; in India the figure was 933. This is no fluke of nature, but another indicator of the better social conditions in Kerala - the fact is that in the rest of India the figures are distorted by selective abortion or even infanticide. Not surprisingly, Kerala was the top state in India in the Human Development Index, and an American anthropologist, Bill McKibben has written: 'Though Kerala is mostly a land of paddy covered plains, statistically Kerala stands out as the Mount Everest of social development; truly, there's no place like it.'[328]

Ravi and family

Economic change arrived with the new millennium. In spite of Kerala's obsession with gold, which ties up millions of pounds of capital in non-productive savings such as jewellery, large quantities of which are seemingly an essential feature of weddings in particular, the state's economy seems to be on the mend. Professional people are now likely to be better off staying in Kerala rather than moving abroad – an accountant who could earn 8000 rupees a month in 2002 could command five times that amount 4 years later. In the same period, unemployment is falling and Kerala is even attracting workers from other states. There's been a big increase in public service employees and in private companies too as well as a rush to site IT companies in a state where there are a lot of well-educated workers. So far, Kerala's enviable and widely envied way of life is not being seriously threatened, although it is now not uncommon in my experience for Keralites to say that 'strong' government and economic progress are more important than tolerance and equality. In this connection, it's worth remembering that the enormous improvement in the lives of our family in both Kerala and Mumbai has been achieved under a democratic and pluralistic system.

Manga and I have now been married for more than 50 years and during that time we have seen many changes in the family home, in the village and in the State itself. I believe that these changes have been weathered successfully and joyfully, but there will be many more challenges over the next few years. For Kerala this means increased social and physical mobility, loosening of family ties, pollution, consumerism, increased inter-communal tension, traffic congestion, to name but a few. Let's hope that the people of Kerala will learn from the mistakes of the West and tackle these obstacles to health and happiness in a positive way. If they do, God's Own Country, which my family and I have loved and admired for so many years, will remain a homeland to be proud of.

THE END

My Incredible Sister-in-law

Her name -it means a final blessing - Mangalam.
She was the thirteenth baby; precious benjamin,
adored and treasured as a child who soon may die,
as others, with her sickly pallor, went before.
The fortune teller wouldn't write a horoscope,
because he saw no future in her stars.

And yet this fragile seedling put down roots so deep
in Kerala, among the palms and paddy fields,
that she confounded dire predictions; grew up strong,
intelligent, a maverick, adventurous.
Perhaps the fortune teller saw experience
beyond his comprehension and declined to speak.

The family, though well respected in the town,
was poor; she often barely had enough to eat,
no toys, new clothes or books but went to school and learned
by rote the Vedas and the sacred texts, she spoke
with fluency three languages, she visited
the temple every day, and celebrated feasts.

She chose to nurse; vocation unbecoming to
a high caste Hindu girl. Her father was a healer
and cooked at Brahmin feasts; she watched, acquired his skills.
Espoused her mother's kindness, generosity
but not the wonted calm acceptance of her fate.
The xylem in her soul too firm, resolve too taut.

She came to Sheffield, met my mother working on
the wards, became a daughter to the family.
She joined my brother in Bihar, a wretched place
of drought and famine. There they fell in love and wed,
came back to Kent to raise their girls as tolerant
and independent folk; their mother's special wish.

She learned to cook a Sunday roast, and recognize
a great tit's call, helped every week with the Mums and Tots.
She climbed Blencathra, swam a mile for charity,
developed fingers green as frozen peas, and shared
her famous sambar, tasty cherry plum preserve
with many friends, but couldn't learn to ride a bike...

She ran an orthopaedic clinic, studied English
Literature, became a conservationist,
a connoisseur of wine, supported those without
a voice, embraced Buddhism, chanted every day.
A life quite unexpected when the thirteenth babe
was born; of course it made the fortune teller blanch.

Rosemary Birmingham

DATES OF VISITS TO INDIA

AUGUST 1966 to May 1968: My first visit, with VSO. I flew BOAC to Calcutta via Karachi, and lived and worked in Bihar

MARCH 1967: Manga returned to India on the S.S.Orsova via Suez. She lived and worked in Bihar. On November 14 1967, we married in Calcutta. We returned to England in May 1968

CHRISTMAS 1976: Manga flew to Mumbai and also visited Tirur.

CHRISTMAS 1979: Grandma's visit with Manga and me, Victoria, Indira and Lakshmi. We flew Air India to Mumbai and stayed in Mumbai and Tirur. We visited Vasai, Madurai, Periyar, Mysore, Kanyakumari.

CHRISTMAS 1983: Rika's visit, with her then husband Frank, and Manga, me, Victoria, Indira and Lakshmi. Rika flew by Lufthansa to Kochi and stayed in Tirur and New Delhi. We visited Kochi, Kodaikanal, Tirichendur, Agra, Delhi.

APRIL 1987: Manga attended Radhikar and Gopal's wedding in Tirur.

APRIL 1991: Rosemary and Tony's visit, with Manga and me, Victoria, Indira, Lakshmi and their friend Lucy, Antonia, and Sebastian. We flew BA to Chennai and visited Madurai, Periyar, Tirur, Mysore, Mumbai, Rajasthan, Agra, Delhi.

NOVEMBER 1993: Manga and I, Rosemary, Victoria, Indira, and Lakshmi attended Geetha and Raju's wedding. We flew Gulf Air to Mumbai and Indian Airways to Kozhikode, and visited Aluva, Periyar.

FEBRUARY 1995: Manga and I, Indira and Lakshmi flew Kuwait Airlines to Kozhikode and stayed in Tirur.

OCTOBER 1999: Indira's visit, to learn to speak Malayalam. She stayed in Mumbai and Tirur and visited Ernakulam, Kovalam.

NOVEMBER 1999: Victoria and David's visit. They stayed in Mumbai, Tirur and Coimbatore

MARCH 2002: Julie's visit with Manga and me. We flew to Chennai by Gulf Air and stayed there and at Bangalore, Tirur and

Ernakulam. Visited Mamallapuram, Kanchipuram, Mysore, Kochi, Alappuzha - The Backwaters, Thettakad, Kallil

Julie's visit in 2002

MAY 2005 Indira, Lakshmi and Julie attended Rashmi and Krishnan's wedding. They flew Emirates Airways to Mumbai. Visited Ellora and Ajanta.

AUGUST 2008 Manga and I, Indira and Lakshmi flew by Qatar Airways to Kochi. We stayed in Tirur, Coimbatore and Ernakulam and visited Bekal, the Silent Valley, Munnur, Alappuzha -The Backwaters.

NOVEMBER 2009: Manga and I, Indira and Lakshmi flew by Etihad to Kochi. We stayed in Tirur, Coimbatore and Ernakulam. Visited Beypore, Nalambur, Palakkad, Dhyanalinga & Perur Temples, Kochi, Thettakad, Kallil.

NOVEMBER 2011: Manga and I, Indira and Lakshmi flew by Kuwait Airways and visited Tirur.

MAY 2013: Julie and Rosemary attended Divya and Ritesh's wedding in Mumbai, flying by Jet Air.

JAN 2018: Indi, Lakshmi, Julie, Rosemary, David and Victoria with Thomas, Zoe, Ronan and Rebecca attended Pooja's wedding in Kerala and Vasai. Victoria's family travelled half way round the world from San Francisco.

REFERENCE LIST

[1] Saul, David, (2003) *The Indian Mutiny 1857*, London: Penguin, p.367

[2] Nair, Anita, ed. (2002) *Where the Rain is Born – Writings about Kerala*, New Delhi: Penguin India, p.ix

[3] Mir Abdul Lateef Shushtari, *Kitab Tuhfat al'Alam*, quoted in: Dalrymple, William (2002) *White Mughals*, London: HarperCollins, p. 170

[4] Sanghamitra Mazumdar (2008) 'Where are you going this winter? Jhumri Telaiya?' *Indian Express*. 21st June.

[5] Anon (2005) 'A Rags to Riches to Rags Story', *Deccan Herald,* 5th December. http://www.archive.deccanherald.com

[6] Gangadharan, T.K. (n.d) *Kerala History*, Calicut: University of Calicut, p.30

[7] Logan, William (1995) *Malabar* [generally known as The Malabar Manual] 1887, vol.1, New Delhi: Asian Educational Service, p.222

[8] Gangadharan, *op cit*, p.30

[9] Gangadharan, *op cit*, p.97

[10] Nair, A.K.K.Ramachandran, (1986) *Kerala State Gazetteer Vol.2, Part 1*, Trivandrum: Kerala Gazetteer, p.194

[11] Roberts, Alice (2010) *The Incredible Human Journey*, London: BBC, p.77

[12] Wood, Michael (2008) *The Story of India*, London: BBC, p.13

[13] Wells, Spencer (2006) *Deep Ancestry: Inside the Genographic Project*, Washington D.C: National Geographic, p.67

[14] Anon (2007) 'Archaeologists solid behind Edakkal Cave' *The Hindu*, 28th October [updated 29th April 2011] http://www.archive.deccanherald.com

[15] Nair, *Gazeteer vol 2, part 1*, op cit, p.3

[16] Keay, John (2000) *India: A History*. London: HarperCollins, p.15-16

[17] Wood, Michael (2005) *In Search of the First Civilisations*, London: Random House, p.54-5

[18] *Ibid*, p.56

[19] The Wikipedia article on the Indus Valley Civilization refers to a number of experts supporting this thesis including Giosan, L.; et al. (2012). 'Fluvial landscapes of the Harappan Civilization'. *Proceedings of the National Academy of Sciences of the United States of America*, 109 (26): E1688–E1694. doi:10.1073/pnas.1112743109

[20] Thapar, Romila (2003) *The Penguin History of Early India*, London: Penguin, p.15

[21] Kennedy, Kenneth (1995) 'Have Aryans been identified in the Prehistoric skeletal record for South Asia'. In: Erdosy, George (ed) *Aryans of Ancient South Asia: Language , Material Culture and Ethnicity*, Berlin; New York: de Gruyter, p 60

[22] Fagan, Brian, (2005) *The Long Summer: How Climate Changed Civilization*. London: Granta Books, p.173

[23] Wood, Michael (2008) *The Story of India*, London:BBC, p.39 IBID

[24] Hastings, Warren (1784) *Letter to Charles Wilkins*, quoted in Keay, John (2001) *India Discovered*, London: HarperCollins, p.25.

[25] Olivelle, Patrick (1998) *The Early Upanishads*, Oxford: OUP, p.xxii

[26] Sen, K.M., (1961) *Hinduism*, London: Penguin, p.73-4

[27] *ibid*, p.18

[28] Blank, Jonah (1992) *Arrow of the Blue-Skinned God: Retracing the Ramayana Through India*. Boston: Houghton Mifflin, p.6

[29] Nair, A.K.K.Ramachandran (1986) *The Kerala State Gazetteer Vol 1*, Trivandrum: Kerala Gazetter, p 276-7

[30] For much of the information in this chapter, see Sarkar, H., (1992) *Monuments of Kerala*, 3rd ed. New Delhi: Archaeological Survey of India

[31] Mulk Raj, Anand, ed. (1983) *Splendours of Kerala*, reprint, Bombay: Marg Publications, p.10

[32] Sarkar, *op cit*, p.43

[33] Keay (2000), *op cit*, p.xvii

[34] Majumdar, R.C *et al* (1950) *The history and culture of the Indian people vol 1*, Bombay: Bharatha Vidya Bhavan, p.47, quoted in Keay (2000), *op cit,* p.xvii

[35] Logan vol 1, *op cit,* p.vii

[36] Keay (2000), *op cit,* p.xvii

[37] Megasthenes, *Indica* quoted in Logan vol 1, *op cit,* p.246-247

[38] Logan vol 1, *op cit,* p.248

[39]Logan vol 1, *op cit.* p.245-246

[40] *Periplus Maris Erithraei*, quoted in Logan vol 1, *op cit,* p .32

[41] Pliny (23-79 A.D.) *Naturalis Historia*, quoted in Logan vol 1,*op cit,* p. 249-50

[42] *Petronius* (c27-66 A.D.) quoted in Logan vol 1, *op cit,* p.249

[43] Epic poem from the Sangam era quoted in Kulke, Herman and Rothermund, Deitmar (1991) *History of India,* New Delhi: Rupa & co., p.107

[44] Sharma, H.K., Tripathi, B.M. and Pelto, P.J., (2010) 'The evolution of alcohol use in India', *Aids and Behavior,* 14(Suppl 1), pp.8-17.

[45] Logan vol.1, *op cit,* p.68

[46] Prakash V, Bishwakarma MC, Chaudhary A, Cuthbert R, Dave R, Kulkarni M, et al. (2012) 'The Population Decline of Gyps Vultures in India and Nepal Has Slowed since Veterinary Use of Diclofenac was Banned'. *PLoS ONE* 7(11): e49118. doi:10.1371/journal.pone.0049118

[47] Forster, E.M., (1996) *Abinger Harvest and England's Pleasant Land,* London: Andre Deutsch, p.310

[48] Barbosa, Duarte (2001) *A Description of the Coasts of East Africa and Malabar in the beginning of the Sixteenth Century* [Translated by Henry E.J.Stanley. Boston: Adamant Media Corporation, p.73

[49] Ayyar, P.V.Jagadisa (1998) *South Indian Customs*, New Delhi: Rupa & Co, p.162

[50] *Ibid*, p.163 [both quotes]

[51] Govind, Biju (2004) 'Fresh hope for betel growers', *The Hindu* [online], 10th February, www.hindu.com

[52] Alinga, Shafiq (2016) 'Row with Pakistan hurts betel leaves exports from Kerala', *India Express,* 2nd December.

[53] Logan, William (1995) *Malabar 1887, vol.2,* New Delhi: Asian Educational Service, p.ccccii

[54] Joseph, George (2000) *The Crest of the Peacock,* New Jersey: Princeton University Press, p.440-1 [discussing the work of Ramasubramanian et al (1994) 'Heliocentric model of planetary motion in Kerala school of Indian astronomy.' *Current Science* 66(10) pp 784- 90]

[55] Logan, vol. 2, *op cit*, p.ccccv

[56] Logan, vol.1, *op cit,* p.77

[57] Logan vol.2, *op cit,* p.ccccv

[58] *Ibid,* p.ccccvii (Appendix XXI)

[59] Logan, vol.1 *op cit,* p.339

[60] *Ibid*, p.410

[61] White, T.H., (1941) *The Sword in the Stone*, London: Collins, p.170

[62] Anon., (1967) 'Two Starvation Deaths Alleged', *The Indian Nation*, 25th March.

[63] Anon. (1967) 'Furious Gale and Hail Lashes Hazaribagh', *The Indian Nation*, 29th March

[64] Anon. (1967) 'Grim Battle Against Hunger', *The Indian Nation*, 2nd April

[65] Thakur, Janardan (1967) 'Story of a Dying Village', *The Indian Nation*, 6th May

[66] Menon, A. Sreedhara (2008) *The Legacy of Kerala*, Kottayam: DC Books, p.70

[67] *Atharva Veda* 1.22, quoted in Embree, Ainslie T. *et al,* (eds.) (2014) *Sources of Indian Tradition Vol. 1,* 2nd ed. rev., New Delhi: Penguin India, p.22

[68] Casson, Lionel, trans. (1989) *The Periplus of the Erythraean Sea: Text with Introduction Translation and Commentary*, New Jersey:

Princeton University Press, p.87

[69] Wood, Michael (2002) *The Smile of Murugan - a South Indian Journey*, London: John Murry, p.110

[70] *Cosmas Indicopleustes*, fl. 6th cent, translated by McCrindle, J.W. (1897) *The Christian topography of Cosmas, an Egyptian monk*, Book 3, London: Haykult Society, pp.91 – 128, available at: https://archive.org/details/christiantopogr00cosmgoog

[71] Dalrymple, William (2000) 'The incredible journey' *Guardian*, 15th April.

[72] Stanley, H.E.J (1869) *The Three Voyages of Vasco da Gama, and his Viceroyalty: From the Lendas da India of Gaspar Correa* (16th century), London : The Hakluyt Society, p.145

[73] Sangam poem 'Malaipadukadam' [c.100 BCE – 100 ACE], quoted in Nair, *Gazeteer* vol.2, part 1, *op cit*, pp.38-39

[74] Sangam poem 'Akananuru', quoted in Nair, *Gazeteer* vol.2, part 1, *op cit*, p.45

[75] Unless otherwise stated, information on the Cheras comes from Nair, *Gazeteer* vol.2, part 1, op cit., pp.63-72

[76] Sesha Aiyer, K.G. (1937) *Cera Kings of the Sangam Period*, London: Luzac & Co., p.16

[77] Nair, Gazeteer vol.2, part 1, op cit., p.70

[78] Untitled Poem by Kappiyat Kappiyanar, stanza 31, quoted in Nair, vol.2, part 1, *op cit.*, p.71

[79] Avvaiar, (n.d) 'Purananuru', quoted in Nair, vol.2, part 1, *op cit.*, p. 76 [footnote]

[80] Nair, *Gazeteer* vol.2, part 1, op cit., p.110-11

[81] Menon, 'Kozhikode', *Kozhikode Gazetteer*, p.107

[82] This and subsequent quotes from Logan, vol.1, *op cit*, p.6

[83] Dubey, Manjulika and Grewal, Bikram, eds. (1990) *Insight Guides, South India*. New York: APA Publications

[84] Logan, vol.1, *op cit.*, p.8

[85] *Ibid.*, p.412

[86] *Ibid.*, p.413

[87] *Ibid.*, p.414

[88] *Ibid.*, p.438

[89] *Ibid.*, p.438

[90] *Ibid.*, p.9

[91] *Ibid.*, p.13

[92] Nair, *Gazeteer* vol.1, op cit., p.292

[93] Data taken from Nair, *ibid,* pp.303-14

[94] Dallapiccola, A.L. (2006) *Indian Love Poetry*, London: The British Museum Press pp 14-38.

[95] Tharoor, Shashi (2003) *Kerala, God's Own Country*, New Delhi: Books Today, p.20

[96] Kasturi, Prema and Suresh, S. (2009) 'Across Space and Time' *The Hindu Sunday Magazine*, 29th March.

[97] Sinha, Kounneya (2011) 'Snake bites kill 46K in India yearly' *The Times of India*, 6th December

[98] Ali, Salim (1964) *The Book of Indian Birds,* 7th ed rev. Bombay: Bombay Natural History Society, p.18

[99] Ibid, p.51

[100] Ibid, p.24

[101] P.V.Jagadisa Ayyar (1998) *South Indian Customs*, Calcutta: Rupa & Co., p.108

[102] Logan vol 1 *op.cit.*, p.vi

[103] Nair, Kerala State Gazetteer Vol.2, Part 1, op.cit., p.147

[104] Thapar, Romila (1966) *A History of India*, Vol.1, London: Pelican, p.39

[105] Shah, Pravin (n.d.) *Jain Philosophy: The Art of Living*. http://www.jainbelief.com/intro_jainism.htm

[106] Kipling, Rudyard (2015) *The Jungle Book*, p78-92. CreateSpace Independent Publishing Platform. First published 1894, Macmillan.

[107] Nair, *Gazetteer* Vol.2, Part 1, op.cit., p.169

[108] *Ibid.*, p.170

[109] *Ibid.*, p.174 (footnote 13)

[110] *The Mahavamsa* [The Great Chronicle of the Kings of Sri Lanka, written 5th AD], quoted in Nair, op.cit., p.177

[111] Zarrilli, Phillip B. (1998) *When the Body Becomes All Eyes: Paradigms, Discourses and Practices of Power in Kalarippayattu, a South Indian Martial Art*, Oxford: Oxford University Press, p.96.

[112] Nair, *Gazetteer* Vol.2, Part 1, op.cit., p.197

[113] Sen, *op.cit.*, p.28

[114] Logan vol 1, *op.cit.*, p.190

[115] DuBois, Abbe J.A. (1985) *Hindu Manner, Customs and Ceremonies*, 3rd ed., trans and edited by Henry K.Beauchamp, C.L.E., New Delhi: Asian Educational Services New Delhi, p.407. First published 1906, by Clarendon Press, Oxford.

[116] Sen, *op.cit..*, p.66.

[117] Thapar (1966) *op.cit.*, p.165

[118] DuBois, *op.cit.*, p.407

[119] Sen, *op.cit.*, p.78

[120] Sen, *op.cit.*, p.91, footnote

[121] Sen, *op.cit.*, p.91

[122] Gangadharan, *op.cit.*, p.128

[123] Logan vol 1, *op.cit.*, p.153

[124] Woodcock, George (1967) *Kerala: a Portrait of the Malabar Coast*, London: Faber & Faber, p.30

[125] Gough, Kathleen, (1954) *The Traditional Kinship System of the Nayars of Malabar*. Harvard University, p.161

[126] Tharoor, *op.cit.*, p.4

[127] Mustoe, Anne (2002) *Two wheels in the dust: from Kathmandu to Kandy*, London: Virgin Books, p.247

[128] Gangadharan, *op.cit..* pp.216-218

[129] Logan vol. 1, *op.cit.*, p.91

[130] *Ibid*, pp.96-101

[131] *Ibid*, p.102

[132] K. V. Soundara Rajan, N. G. Unnithan (1974) *Temple architecture in Kerala,* New Delhi: Government of India, p.21

[133] Roy, Arundhati (2002) *God of small things.* New Delhi: Penguin books India, p.127

[134] Nair, *Gazetteer*, vol 2 part 1, op.cit., p 273

[135] DuBois, *op.cit.*, p.586

[136] Dalrymple, William (2006) 'In the lap of the gods' *The Guardian* 9th December

[137] Sarkar, *op.cit.*, p.65

[138] Woodcock, *op.cit.*, p.115

[139] Narasim-Miyengar, V.N (1981) *Mysore Census report,* quoted in Dubois, Abbe J.A. *op.cit.*, p.xxxvii-xxviii

[140] Catholic Encyclopedia (2012) *Diocese of Cochin* [online] Available at www.newadvent.org/cathen/04076a.htm

[141] Other sources include: Buchanan, Dr C. (1812) *Christian researches*, London, p.159 to 165 and Deleon, Charles (2017) *Relation de l'inquisition de Goa*, Reink Books, chapter XXIV. Reprinted from the 1687 edition.

[142] Yeates, Thomas (1818) *Indian Church history, or An account of the first planting of the gospel, in Syria, Mesopotamia, and India*, London: A.Maxwell, p.163

[143] Dellon, Charles (1687) The Inquisition of Goa, quoted in Priolkar, A.K (1961), *Goa Inquisition*, p. 224 and 225. From https://jewsofgoa.com/blog/page/2

[144] Catholic Encyclopedia (2012) *Diocese of Cochin* [online] Available at www.newadvent.org/cathen/04076a.htm

[145] Verse quoted in Woodcock, *op.cit.*, p.125

[146] 'Tofutal Mujahadeen' quoted by Woodcock, op.cit., p.127

[147] *Kerala and her Jews*, [pamphlet bought from the Kochi synagogue] compiled from a paper read by Mr. S.S.Koder before the Kerala History Association in 1965; his article in the Souvenir printed on the

occasion of the inauguration of the Nehru Memorial Town Hall, Mattancherriin 1968; and Fiona Hallegua's thesis *The Jewish Community of Cochin – its Twilight Years* for her Master's degree in sociology, 1984.

[148] *Ibid*, p.1

[149] Pereltsvaig, Asya (2010) 'On the Cochin Jews and Judaeo-Malayalam', *Languages of the World* [Blog], Available at: www.languagesoftheworld.info

[150] Information for this section taken from Keay (2000), *op.cit.,* p. 183-5

[151] Al-Biladduri, *Book of the Conquests of Lands,* quoted in Keay (2000), op.cit..,p.184

[152] Ibid., p.185

[153] Ibid., p.185

[154] Rev. Samuel Lee, B.D. (1829) *The Travels of Ibn Batuta etc.* London, Oriental Translation Committee, as cited in Logan vol 1, *op.cit.,* p.287

[155] Keay (2000), *op.cit.*, p.276-7

[156] Polo, Marco (1968) *The Travels of Marco Polo,* [trans and introduced by Ronald Latham], London: The Folio Society, p 245

[157]Nikitin, Athanasius (n.d) 'Travels of Athanasius Nikitin', quoted in Major, R.H., ed. (1857) *India in the Fifteenth Century*, London: Hakluyt Society, p.8

[158] 'Narrative of the Journey of Abd-er-Razzaq' quoted in Major *ibid* p. 31

[159] Keay (2000), *op.cit.,* p.278

[160] Ibid., p.278

[161] Logan vol 1, *op.cit.*, p.189-9

[162] Keay (2000), *op.cit.*, p.215

[163] Ibid, p.215

[164] Watson, Francis (1974) *A Concise History of India,* London: Thames and Hudson, p.85

[165] Anon (n.d) 'Sculpture', *Indian Mirror*, available at: http://www.indianmirror.com/arts/arts2.html

[166] Istakhri [a tenth century Islamic traveller], quoted by Nair, *Gazeteer vol.2, part 1, op.cit.,* p.209

[167] *Keralolpatti*, quoted in Logan, vol.1, *op.cit.*, p.277

[168] Asher, A, trans. & ed. (1840) *The Itinerary of Rabbi Benjamin,* Volume 1, London & Berlin: Asher & Co, p.139.

[169] Asher, *op.cit.*, p.138

[170] Polo, Marco, Ibid, p.289

[171] Lee, Rev. Samuel (ed.& transl) (2003), *The Travels of Ibn Battuta.* New York: Dover Publications. p.72

[172] Polo, Marco, *op.cit.*. References are as follows: Suttee p.225; Cow worship p.225, Cow dung p.225, Use of right hand p.226, Astrology p. 228, Diamonds p.232

[173] WebIndia123 (2017) 'Dutch (Mattancherry) Palace', *WebIndia123 - Tourism.* Available from:

http://tourism.webindia123.com/tourism/monuments/palaces/dutchpalace/

[174] Ibid

[175] Logan vol.1, *op.cit,* p.78

[176] Ravenstein, E.G. (trans.) (2010) *Journal of the first Voyage of Vasco da Gama 1497-9* , Cambridge: CUP, p.52

[177] Ibid, pp.52-53

[178] Ibid, p.46

[179] Logan vol.1, *op.cit.,* p.296 (footnote)

[180] Calamosto, *The Voyage of Cabral and Other Documents*, quoted in Day, Francis (1863) *Land of the Perumauls, or Cochin: its past and its present*, Madras: Gantz Brothers, p.79

[181] Logan vol.1, *op.cit.,* p.302

[182] Hartig, Otto (2017) 'Vasco da Gama', *Catholic Encyclopedia.* Available online at: http://www.catholicity.com/encyclopedia/g/gama,vasco_da.html

[183] Logan, vol.1 *op.cit.*, p.307

[184] Correa, Gaspar (1869) *The Three Voyages of Vasco da Gama and his Viceroyalty.* London: Hakluyt Society, p.331

[185] Keay, John (2006) *The Spice Route,* London: John Murray, p.177

[186]Kurup, K.K.N. and Matthew, K.M. (2000) *Native resistance against the Portuguese: the saga of Kundalini Marakkar*, Calicult: Calicut University

[187] Woodcock, *op.cit.*, p.157

[188] Foster, William (ed.), (1999) *Early Travels in India 1583-1619,* reprint, Delhi: Low Price Publications [First published in 1929 by Humphrey Milford, London: OUP], p.44

[189] Watson, *op.cit.*, p.108

[190]Keralaiyers.com (n.d) 'History' and 'Migration' *Keralaiyers.com* [blog], www.keralaiyers.com/

[191] Von Tunzelmann, Alex (2007) *The Indian Summer: the secret history of the End of an Empire,* London: Simon & Schuster, p.11

[192] His adventures are told in Foster, William *op. cit.*, pp. 1-47

[193] Ibid. *p.45*

[194] Logan vol 1, *op. cit,* p.335

[195] Ibid, p.340

[196] Kulke and Rothermund, *op. cit.*, p.217-9

[197] Ibid, p.220

[198] Logan vol.1, *op cit.,* p.341

[199] Keay, John (1993) *The Honourable Company: A History of the English East India Company*, London: HarperCollins, p.252

[200] Logan vol.1, *op. cit.,* p.338

[201] Ibid, p.338-9

[202]Logan, W. (ed) (1879) *Collection of Treaties, Engagements and other Papers of Importance relating to British Affairs in Malabar*, Calicut: Madras Civil Service

[203] Quoted in Logan, Ibid, p.2

[204]Quoted in Logan vol 1, *op. cit.,* p.340

[205] Gangadharan, *op. cit.,* p.206

[206] Keay (2000), *op. cit.,* p.395

[207] Moon, Penderel. (Sir) (1989) *The British Conquest and Dominion of India,* London: Duckworth, p.203 [pub posthumously]

[208] *Napoleon's letter is quoted in Dalrymple, William, (2013) Return of a King: The Battle for Afghanistan,* London: Bloomsbury, p.6

[209]Keay (2000) *op. cit.,* p.401

[210] Gangadharan, *op. cit.,* p.212-16

[211] Keay (2000) *op. cit..,* p.398-9

[212] Goel, Sita Ram (1993) *Tipu Sultan: Hero or Villain: An Anthology* [online] Voice of India, New Delhi, available from http://voiceofdharma.org/books/tipu/ch09.htm

[213]*Thanchath Ezhuthachan,* Thanchan Memorial Research Centre [pamphlet]

[214] Burnell, Arthur Coke (1874) Elements of South Indian Palaeography from the Fourth to the Seventeenth Century A.D., London: Trubner & Co., p 35

[215]Ellis, F.W., *Indian Antiquary* [dissertation on Malayalam] quoted in Logan vol. 1, *op. cit.*, p.92

[216]Farris Michael (2007) *From Tyndale to Madison,* Nashville: B&H Books, p.37

[217]Logan vol.1, *op. cit.,* p.93

[218] Ibid, 38-58

[219] Patnaik, Naveen (1994) *The Garden of Life: Introduction to the Healing Plants of India.* Aquarian Press. p.28

[220] Food and Agriculture Organisation of the United Nations, (2013) *Crops,* www.fao.org/faostat/en/#data/QC

[221] Cowen, D.V. (1952) *Flowering Trees and Shrubs in India,* Bombay: Thacker & Co Ltd, p.39

[222] Logan vol.1, *op. cit.*, p.38

[223] Ibid, p.39

[224] Ibid, p.40

[225] Ibid, p.41

[226] Britannica (2006) 'Teak Tree', *Britannica Concise Encyclopedia*, Chicago: Encyclopedia Britannica Inc, Available from: https://www.britannica.com/plant/teak

[227] Logan vol 2,*op. cit.,* pp. ccclxvii

[228] Ibid, ccclxvii

[229] Ibid, ccclxxii

[230] Morton, Julia F. (2013) *Fruits of Warm Climates*, Miami: Echo Points Books and Media

[231] Wikipedia article references the following: Leone, A.,Spada, A., Battezzati, A., Schiraldi, A., Aristil, J., Bertoli, S. (2015) 'Cultivation, Genetic, Ethnopharmacology, Phytochemistry and Pharmacology of Moringa oleifera Leaves: an Overview' *International Journal of Molecular Science.* 16 [6]: 12791-835. AND National Research Council (2006) 'Moringa'. *Lost Crops of Africa: Vol II: Vegetables.* New York: National Academies Press.

[232] Chaloner, Lt Col G.T., (1944) *Some Jungle trees and their Uses*, British Southern Army. Taken from the foreword. Recently republished by lulu.com and available on Amazon!

[233] Ibid, p.5

[234] Woodcock, *op. cit..*, p.183

[235] Logan vol.1, *op. cit.*, p.473

[236]Quoted in Logan, Ibid, p.481-2

[237] Ibid, p.549

[238] Gangadharan, *op. cit.,* p.238

[239] Logan vol.1, *op. cit.,* p.552

[240] Ibid, p.561

[241] Ibid, p.576

[242]Quoted in the *Malabar Manual vol 1*, Ibid, p.594

[243] Woodcock, *op. cit.*, p.190

[244] Logan, vol 1, *op. cit.*, p.149

[245] Ibid, p.150

[246] Ibid, p.152

[247] Gangadharan, *op. cit.*, p.266

[248] Ibid, p.269

[249] Bedi, Savita (2005) '1867-1938 Kerala's Leading Social Reformer', *Mitavadi C. Krishnan*, October 30th, available from: http://mithavadi-ckrishnan.blogspot.co.uk

[250] Gangadharan, *op. cit.*, p.274

[251] Logan vol.1, *op. cit.*, p.125

[252] Menon, K.P.P. (1966) *History of Kerala*, New Delhi: Asian Educational Services [originally published in 1924 by Cochin Govt. Press, Enarkulum]

[253] Skelton, Mary Louise and Rao, G.Gopal (1975) *South Indian Cookery*, New Delhi: Orient Paperbacks, p 43

[254] Dalrymple, W. (2002) *White Mughals*, London: Penguin, p.lx

[255] Ibid, p.34

[256] Ibid, p.44

[257] Balfour, Edward, ed., deputy General Secretary of Hospitals, Madras (1871) *The Cyclopedia of India and South Asia, commercial, industrial and scientific, mineral, animal and vegetable kingdoms, useful arts and manufactures vol.2*, Madras: Scottish & Adelphi Press, p.17

[258] Visram, R. (1986) Ayahs, Lascars and Princes: Indians in Britain 1700-1947, London: Pluto, p.14.

[259] Nehru, J (1981) *The Discovery of India*, New Delhi: JN Memorial Fund, p.499. Originally published in 1946 by the Signet Press, Calcutta.

[260] Rushdie, Salman (1996) *The Moor's Last Sigh*, London: Vintage, p. 18

[261] Keay 2000, *op. cit.*, p.414

[262] Blank, J. (1992) *Arrow of the Blue-Skinned God*, Boston: Houghton Mifflin

[263] Cotton, S. (1911) *Mountstuart Elphinstone and the Making of South- Western India*, Oxford: Clarendon Press, p.186 https://archive.org/stream/mountstuartelphi00cott/mountstuartelphi00cott_djvu.txt

[264] James, Lawrence (1997) *Raj, the Making and Unmaking of British India*, London: Little, Brown and Co., p.278

[265] Watson, F., *op. cit.*, p.139

[266] Ibid, p.136

[267] Keay 2000, *op. cit.*, p.432

[268] Watson, *op. cit.*, p.139

[269] James, *op. cit.*. p.316

[270] Davis, Mike (2001) *Late Victorian Holocausts: El Niño famines and the making of the third world*, London : Verso; Arnold, David (1994) 'The discovery of malnutrition and diet in colonial India', *Indian economic and social history review*, March 1st, ,New Delhi, Sage; Hall-Matthews, David (2008) 'Inaccurate Conceptions: disputed measures of nutritional needs and famine deaths in colonial India', *Modern Asian studies*, 42.

[271] Schama,S., (2002) *A History of Britain, Volume 3, The Fate of Empire*, London: BBC Worldwide, p.360

[272] James, *op. cit.*, p.304

[273] Shama, *op. cit.*, p.361

[274] James, *op. cit.*, p.304

[275] Florence Nightingale quoted by Schama, *op. cit.*, *p*.361

[276] James, *op. cit.*, p.304

[277] Moxham, Roy, (2002) *The Great Hedge of India*. London: Constable, p. 42

[278] James, L., *op. cit.*, p.304

[279] Digby, William, (1885) *India for the Indians - and for England*. London: Talbot Brothers of London, E.C., p.11

[280] Ibid, quoted from *The Spectator*, Jan10 1885 on pp xxii to xxiii of the preface

[281] Ibid, p.28

[282] Keay 2000, *op. cit.,* p.454.

[283] Patel and Thorner *Bombay, Metaphor for Modern India,* New Delhi: OUP India, p.276

[284] Gangadharan, *op. cit.,* p.288

[285] Hitchcock, R.H., (1925) *A History of the Malabar Rebellion, 1921.* Usha (Malabar)

[286] Read, Anthony and Fisher, David (1997) *The Proudest Day – India's Long Road to Independence*, London: Jonathan Cape, p.192

[287] James, *op. cit.,* p.32

[288] Visram,R. *op. cit..,* p.307

[289] Keay 2000, *op. cit.*, p.504.

[290] Visram, *op. cit..* p.165

[291] Woodcock, *op. cit.*, p.243

[292] Gangadharan, *op. cit..* p.302

[293] Keay 2000, *op. cit..* p.504

[294] Nehru, *op. cit.* p. 499

[295] Keay 2000, *op. cit.,* p.504

[296] Dreze and Sen (1997) *Indian Development, selected regional perspectives*, New Delhi: OUP

[297] Branson, Clive (1945) *British Soldier in India: The Letters of Clive Branson*, International Publishers, New York, p.80

[298] Keay 2000, *op.cit.,* p.504

[299] Forbes, Rosita (1939) *India of the Princes*, London: The Book Club, p.208-9

[300] Ibid, p.211

[301] Ibid, p.205

[302] Ibid, p.213

[303] SadaShivan, S.N., (2000) *A Social history of India.* Bombay: APH India, p.484

[304] Gangadharan, *op. cit.,* p.316

[305] Woodcock, *op. cit.,* p.237

[306] Forbes, *op. cit.,* p.185-6

[307] Forbes, *op. cit.,* p.121

[308] Logan vol.1, *op. cit.,* p.245

[309] Ramahandran, A.K.K., (1986) *Kerala State Gazetteer* vol 2 part 1. Govt of Kerala, p.45

[310] Ibid, p.50

[311] Ibid, p.52 (footnote). The lines are taken from the poem 'Akananuru' part of the Sangam literature.

[312] Ibid, p.52

[313] Digby, *op cit,* p.39

[314] Keay 2000, *op. cit.,* p.476

[315] Watson, *op. cit.,* p.150

[316] Keay 2000, *op. cit.,* p.476

[317] Guha, R., (2003) *A Corner of a Foreign Field: The Indian History of a British Sport*, London: Pan MacMillan, p.3

[318] Pycraft, James (1851) *The Cricket Field* included in Arlott, John,ed. (1948) *From Hambledon to Lord's: The Classics of Cricket*, London: Christopher Johnson, p. 62

[319] Preston, Norman (1953) *Wisden Cricketers Almanack*, Sporting Handbooks.

[320]Nair, Anil (2006) 'Livewire from laidbackwaters' *Cricinfo.* Sadly Sreesanth has recently been banned for involvement in betting scams. Available at: http://www.espncricinfo.com/magazine/content/story/273399.html

[321] Anon, (n.d) *The Game of Carrom.* Available at: www.carrom.co.uk

[322] Varghese, Tomas and McCusker, Daniel P. (2006) 'On Globalization and Ethnomathematics,' *Canadian and International Education / Education canadienne et international,*

Vol. 35: Iss. 1, Article 2. Available at: http://ir.lib.uwo.ca/cie-eci/vol35/iss1/2

[323] Keay (2000) *op. cit.*

[324] Visram, *op. cit.,* p.162

[325] Woodcock *op. cit.*, p.27

[326] K. P. P. Menon, quoted in Woodcock, *op. cit.*, p.28

[327] Tharoor *op. cit.*, p.24

[328] McKibben, Bill (1999) 'About Kerala' *National Geographic*, October, as quoted in [the Kerala government's tourism publication] Anilkumar,

A.P. (2015) 'The Promised Land', *Kerala Calling*, vol.36, no.2, p.12. Available from: https://www.kerala.gov.in/web/guest/archive-publications/